Norman Foster
Team 4 and Foster Associates
Buildings and Projects
1964-1973

About this book

Even when this series of volumes was first planned, in February 1987, it was clear that Norman Foster found the prospect of this first volume the most intriguing. At that meeting — which involved Norman Foster, designer Otl Aicher, the writer Chris Abel and myself — we outlined four volumes. This has now grown to five, though as Foster Associates continues to expand and develop, further volumes will undoubtedly be added.

At that first meeting, when our ideas were still forming, we realised the production of four volumes simultaneously would prove too difficult. We decided to concentrate on the middle two first — covering all Foster Associates' major built projects — and, two and a half years later, these were published to considerable critical acclaim. As these volumes reached the bookshops, during August 1989, research work for volumes 1 and 4 began, and by December sketch layouts for both volumes were complete.

As Norman Foster predicted, it was the first volume that generated the most excitement, and both Otl and I have been infected by his enthusiasm. For Norman, it has been an opportunity to rediscover earlier ideals, a chance to reassess, with the benefit of hindsight, the real successes of these first projects. For myself, it became a way of understanding the full significance of his work. It is work of astonishing integrity and intensity, and the opportunity to explore it through the production of this book has proved both illuminating and enjoyable.

As with the earlier two volumes, this book is the result of the efforts of a great many people. Many members of Team 4 and Foster Associates, their consultants and clients, past and present, have again given generously of their time and advice. Richard Rogers, Tony Hunt and John Walker, all who worked closely with Norman Foster on projects included in this volume, kindly prepared their own personal recollections. Alastair Best and Francis Duffy have produced two excellent essays and, as before, Otl Aicher has amazed us all with his unique ability to distil an overwhelming amount of visual information into layouts of elegance and clarity.

My thanks to them and all the other contributors, with special thanks to Martin Pawley for his considerable efforts 'behind the scenes' and his ever-useful advice.

Ian Lambot, Hong Kong, September 1990

Volume 1
Norman Foster
Team 4 and Foster Associates
Buildings and Projects
1964-1973
Watermark 1991

Volume 2
Norman Foster
Foster Associates
Buildings and Projects
1971-1978
Watermark 1989

Volume 3
Norman Foster
Foster Associates
Buildings and Projects
1978-1985
Watermark 1989

Volume 4
Norman Foster
Foster Associates
Buildings and Projects
1983-1990
Watermark 1992

Volume 5
Norman Foster
Foster Associates
Buildings and Projects
1985-1991
Watermark 1993

Volume 1
1964-1973

Norman Foster
Team 4 and Foster Associates

Buildings and Projects

with contributions by

Richard Rogers
Alastair Best
Brian Hatton
John Walker
David Jenkins
Norman Foster
Rowan Moore
Ben Johnson
Graham Vickers
Francis Duffy
Reyner Banham
Louis Hellman
Tony Hunt
and
Martin Pawley

edited by
Ian Lambot

Watermark

I would like to remember the many colleagues, past as well as present, both inside and outside Foster Associates, of diverse skills and trades, whose generosity and dedication have made possible all the projects in these volumes.

Norman Foster, Grasse, August 1990

Designed by Otl Aicher

First published in Great Britain in 1991
by Watermark Publications (UK) Ltd

Typeset in Rotis 45 by Centra Graphics Ltd, London
Colour separation by Evergreen Colour Separation (Scanning) Company Ltd, Hong Kong
Printed by Everbest Printing Company Ltd, Hong Kong

British Library Cataloguing Data
Norman Foster: Buildings and Projects
   Vol.1 1964-1973
    1. Architectural design. Foster, Norman
    I. Lambot, Ian
    720. 92

ISBN 1 873200 01 3

Contents

During the time this book was in final production I visited the Cistercian Abbey of Fontenay in Burgundy. Founded by St Bernard in 1118 — when he was only 28 — it became the model from which all the abbeys of the Order, that spread far and wide across Europe during the twelfth century, were reproduced.

It was like rediscovering the roots of architecture. How do you describe such buildings? Do you talk about the intellectual rigour which permeates the spaces and their external expression, the integrity of materials and structure, the poetry of light, their sheer emotional impact? The quotation opposite, by their 'architect', says it all so eloquently, and like the architecture, sparsely. A simple summary of volume to which 'depth', the spiritual dimension, has been added.

Norman Foster, Wiltshire, September 1990

"What is God? God is length, width, height, and depth."

St Bernard de Fontaine (1090–1153)

There was a long-standing tradition at Manchester University of preparing measured drawings of Georgian buildings during the summer vacations. Every year Norman Foster challenged the system by rejecting the preferred Classical designs in favour of windmills, barns and on one occasion — as the ultimate affront — a very exuberant Victorian pub. This is one of a series of survey sketches of a Welsh barn at Cochwillan, Llanllechid, drawn in July 1959.

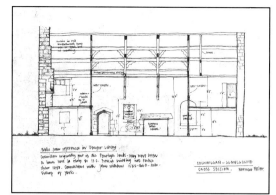

The Cochwillan barn has an illustrious past and can be dated back, with some certainty, to the mid-1400s when it was the great hall of a fortified house.

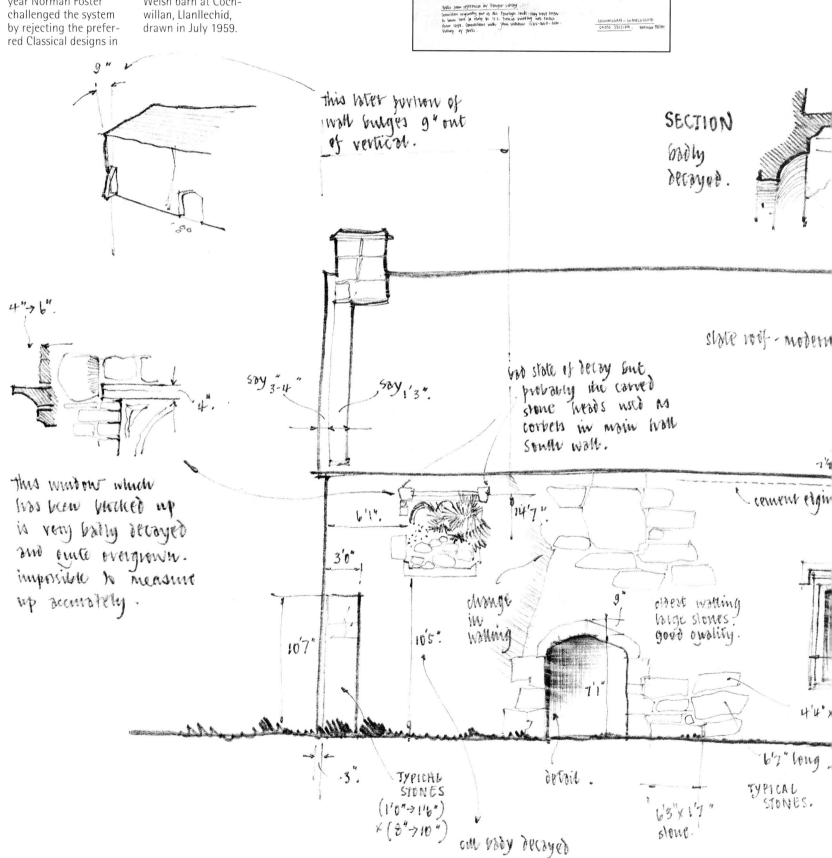

9"

this later portion of wall bulges 9" out of vertical.

SECTION
badly decayed.

4"→6".

say 3-4"

say 1'3".

bad state of decay but probably the carved stone heads used as corbels in main hall south wall.

slate roof - modern

this window which has been blocked up is very badly decayed and quite overgrown. impossible to measure up accurately.

cement etching

6'1½"

14'7"

3'0"

change in walling

9"

oldest walling large stones. good quality.

10'7"

10'5"

7'1"

4'4"

.3"

TYPICAL STONES
(1'0"→1'6")
× (8"→10")

detail.

6'3"×1'7" stone.

6'5" long

TYPICAL STONES.

all very decayed

"It wasn't that I rejected the Georgian tradition — I enjoyed it immensely — but the obsession with drawing up, year after year, decorative details, almost by rote, seemed questionable at best."

Norman Foster, *Norman Foster Sketch*, Birkhäuser 1991

The plan of the Cochwillan barn, indicating the positions of wooden screens, obvious remnants from the building's earlier history. Following the guidelines that all survey notes be clear enough for someone else to draw up, all of Foster's sketches are richly annotated.

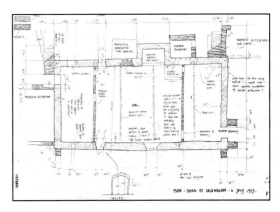

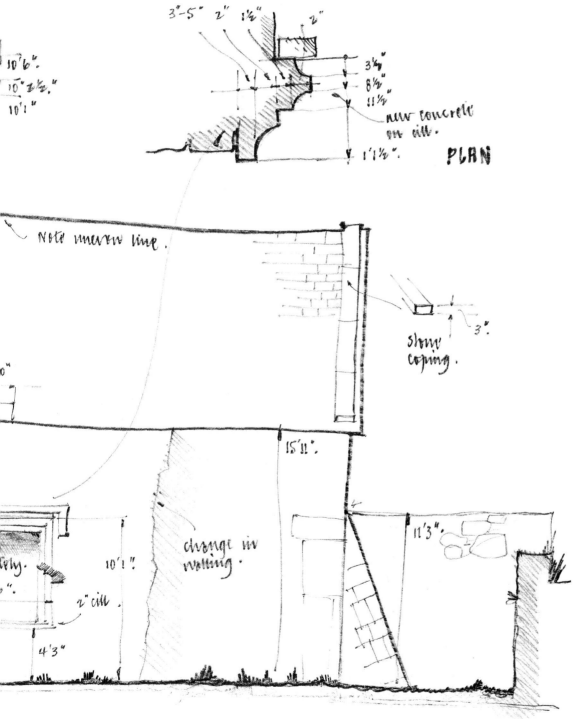

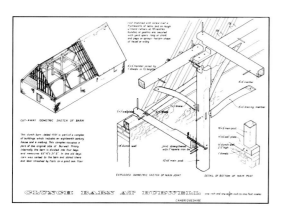

Another barn, this is an eighteenth-century, timber-framed 'clunch' structure with a thatched roof. Each year the best measured drawings were put forward for awards, so from an early stage Foster became aware of the power of clear, concise presentation.

In the same summer that he sketched the Cochwillan barn, Foster spent several days at Rufford Hall in Cheshire, an elaborate, sixteenth-century timber-framed manor house. Elevations and sections were drawn, but it was the construction of the oak-pegged timber roof that captured Foster's imagination. A series of some 30 sketches were drawn, some concentrating on the major joints and assemblies, others exploring the simplest elements and the most ingenious traditional connections.

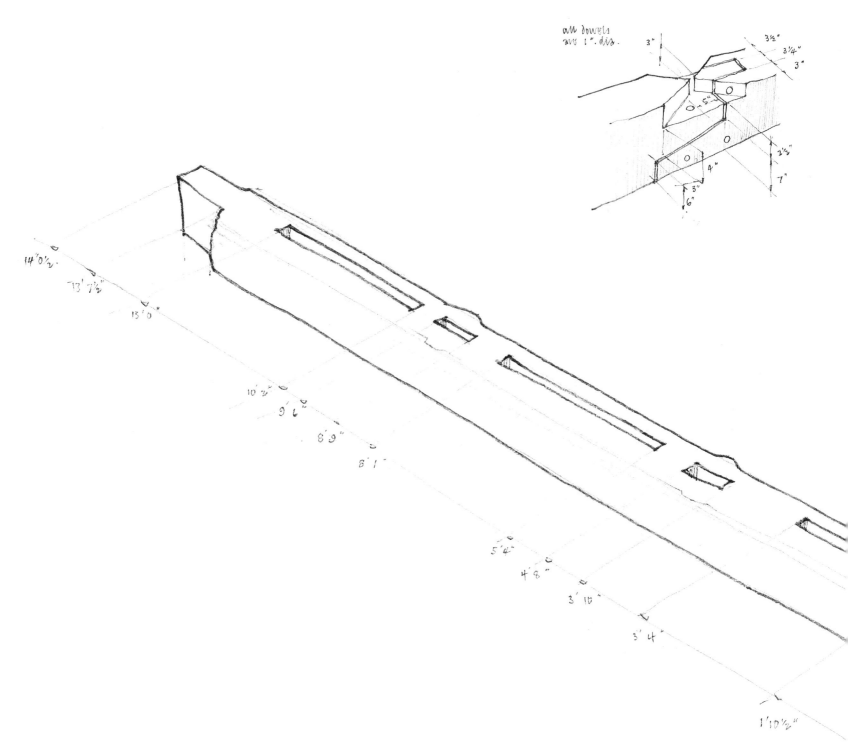

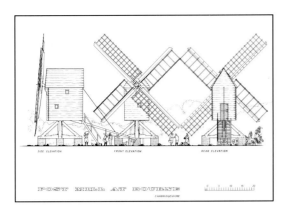

Foster's drawings of the post mill at Bourne, Cambridgeshire – drawn in August 1958 – were some of his most successful measured drawings, winning an RIBA award and a prize of £100, a considerable sum for a student at that time.

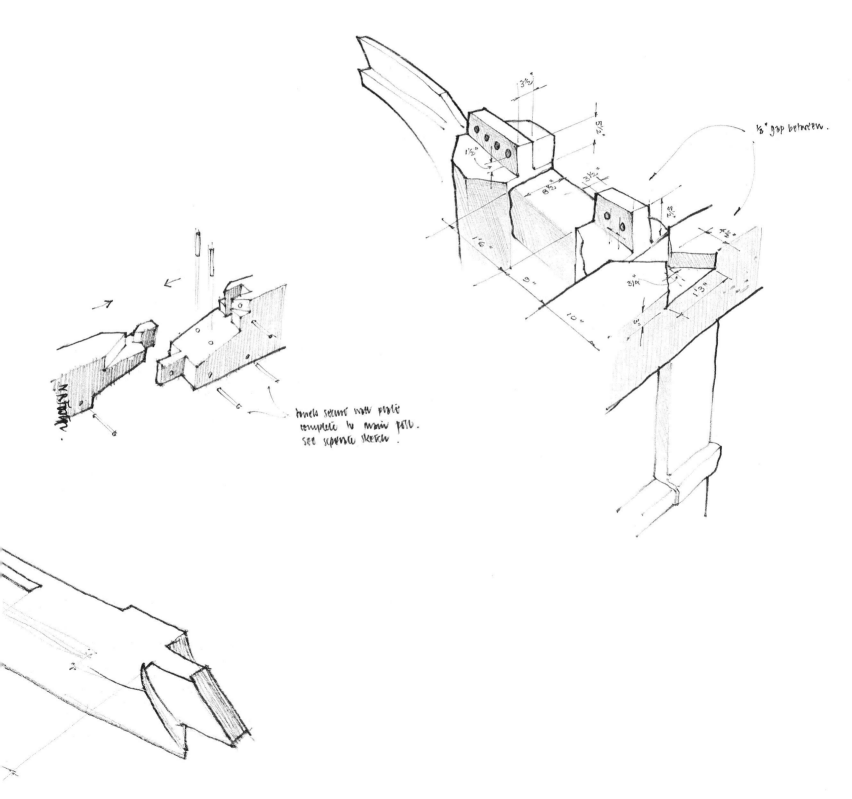

Team 4
by Richard Rogers

One of the most internationally famous of British architects, Richard Rogers studied at the Architectural Association and Yale University, and was in practice with Norman Foster under the name Team 4 from 1963 to 1967. In partnership with Renzo Piano he won the 1971 international competition to design the Centre Pompidou in Paris which was completed in 1977.

In the following year he formed Richard Rogers & Partners which won the competition to design the new Lloyd's building in the City of London. Today, the Richard Rogers Partnership (as it is now known) works on a broad international base with projects in the USA, Japan and Europe, including the new Court of Human Rights in Strasbourg.

Norman and I met in 1961 at a reception of British students who had been awarded scholarships to American universities: he had a Harkness, the best. We were going to Yale to study with Paul Rudolph, although we both wondered whether we should have not applied to Penn University where Louis Kahn taught.

There were some 13 master-class students working on the top floor in Louis Kahn's beautiful Yale Art Museum. Rudolph expected full commitment, 24 hours a day, with surprise tutorials at 2am. Those who collapsed at their drawing-boards didn't make it. Fortunately, there was a couch on which we took turns to sleep. The four English students didn't take kindly to being 'taught'; being somewhat older we questioned, talked, objected and tried to avoid drawing. One day a plaque appeared over the English group's work tables "start drawing"; to which we answered with "start thinking". We certainly learned to work extremely hard and to use our eyes, not an English tradition.

Philip Johnson and Jim Stirling were among our critics. The historian, Vincent Scully, was at his peak; his lectures were great theatre and attended by hundreds of students from all the faculties. He stressed the difference between Europe and the States, opening our eyes to America, to Richardson, Sullivan, Kahn and especially Frank Lloyd Wright. Norman, Su Rogers, who was taking a Masters in City Planning, and Carl Abbott, a classmate, and I set out in Carl's VW Beetle to see every Frank Lloyd Wright building in Illinois and Wisconsin. They made a deep impression on all of us.

For the second semester, Serge Chermayeff was the visiting professor. He was as academic and European as Rudolph was visual and American. Instead of designing beautiful buildings, we researched the concept of the city in terms of the hierarchy between the private and the public realm. We believed everything he said. His concise intellectual framework is still with us.

The two star pupils were Eldred Evans, urbane and mysterious, with cool, beautifully controlled, unfinished, geometric drawings, and Norman, who had left school at 16, gone into the Air Force and worked his way through Manchester University and eventually to a Henry Fellowship to Yale. A brilliant, versatile and concise thinker. Norman and I immediately became great friends. We discussed and argued about everything. Our backgrounds were very different. His was industrial Manchester while I was Italian; he was as brilliant a draughtsman as I was a poor one. Norman, a natural leader, would have succeeded in any profession. These were wonderful heady days. I especially remember Norman's stunning office design, a series of strongly articulated towers marching round the corner, where office space was supported by a structural service core with great splayed feet; and a design for the Yale science campus which, to the horror of Paul Rudolph, we did together. These two projects, partially based on Kahn's concept of served and servant spaces inspired much of my later work, as well as some of Norman's, such as the Hongkong Bank, a truly seminal building.

Before leaving Yale, Norman, Su and I designed a small Wright-influenced house for old friends of mine, Michael and Pat Branch in Kent. Never built, it was conceived in Naum Gabo's house where Su and I lived to the music of Ella Fitzgerald and Elvis Presley. This was the beginning of our partnership. America enthralled us, its scale, energy, optimism and openness. We travelled by thumb, by car and by Greyhound bus; voraciously absorbing the culture, both of the massive open spaces and the tall, taut, energetic cities. Norman, Su and I ended up working in San Francisco: Norman for Anshen & Allen and others on a new campus for UCLA, Su for the US government and I for SOM. Su and I returned to Britain, drawn by the opportunity to build a house for Su's parents in Cornwall and by the prospect of the Branch house. A few months later Norman joined us and the Cheesman sisters to form Team 4.

I had met the sisters Georgie and Wendy Cheesman at art school in Epsom in 1953. Wendy was still at the local convent. I have never met anyone who could laugh as Wendy did, or was so gentle. The sisters were brilliantly inquisitive, fiercely intellectual, bohemian, battling to break away from a very dominant, successful and conservative Lloyd's broker father who had no time for the arts. Georgie, Wendy and I became inseparable and decided to try to become architects: 10 years later we set up office together. Norman had never met them before returning to England and was more than a little surprised at their eccentricity. Wendy rented an Edwardian two-roomed flat in Belsize Park. She slept and lived in one room and the other was our office. From the beginning we went from crisis to crisis. Within a few months, the only registered architect, Georgie, had resigned. She could see there was little room for a wonderfully strong and intelligent loner. This left Norman, Wendy, Su and me and a letter heading that read Team 4 Architects. There followed a series of hilarious episodes with the four of us trying to persuade some friendly architect to lend us their name, while at the same time staving off the Architects' Registration Council and the Royal Institute of British Architects, and all the time trying to get through our professional practice examinations.

None of us appreciated the difficulties of running a practice without experience. I remember episodes such as crying under a tree on Hampstead Heath and thinking, I will never be an architect; a client asking me what I thought his damp-proof membrane was made of and finding it was the Daily Mail painted black; unplanned-for springs of water bursting into beautifully conceived living rooms; and our precious unopened drawings being used by contractors to wrap up their fish and chips.

We searched for a magician, an experienced assistant who knew the answer to everything from plumbing to construction and law, but to no avail. During those early years some brilliant young assistants joined us; Frank Peacock, who was a traditional carpenter and a beautiful draughtsman before becoming an architect. He was also a wonderful craftsman, whose building knowledge helped us through those terrible early days. John Young, who was in love with technology, design and construction, and Laurie Abbott too, joined us as third-year students. Laurie used to file down even the finest nibs to get a more incisive line. An

enthusiastic racing car designer and driver, he brought a fresh approach to architecture and technology. On the backs of these three our practice was built.

We worked 15 hours a day, seven days a week. No one invited us to dinner as we would invariably fall asleep during the first course. It took the team three years to build the Brumwells' Creek Vean house, the first house to win an RIBA Award. This slowness of production, when related to the national housing shortage, stimulated us to reconsider our architectural direction.

Looking back, the 50 or so different designs we prepared for the house under the kind eye of the Brumwells, gave us the opportunity to work through a wide range of approaches and ideas. The Jaffé house in Radlett sowed the seeds of the future, more geometrically ordered projects. In-between, we designed what in conceptual terms was probably the most important project of our Team 4 period, a large planning scheme on some 300 acres at Coulsdon, Surrey for Wates Homes, including detail drawings for one section of about 120 houses. The scheme incorporated many of Chermayeff's theories on privacy and community and the definition and separation of public and private realms.

While on the West Coast, both Norman and I had been excited by the Californian Case Study Houses of Eames, Schindler, Soriano, Ellwood and Neutra, and a little later with the School Construction Systems Development programme of Ezra Ehrenkrantz. The use of standard lightweight industrial components and flexible plans in these projects led to an approach which broke away from the classicism of Mies van der Rohe, and the organic naturalism of Frank Lloyd Wright, both then major influences. In 1965, Jim Stirling recommended us to Peter Parker to build a 30 000 sq ft factory in Swindon in 10 months for Reliance Controls at a cost of £4 per sq ft. Reliance Controls gave us the opportunity to change the direction of our work.

By now Wendy and Norman were married. Their once clearly defined edges had become blurred. Wendy, the wonderful, sensitive bohemian and Norman, the natural leader had become an interdependent team. Their first two

children, Ti and Cal, and ours, Ben and Zad, were playing around the office. There was practically no work. Norman and I worked on every project as a team, each idea was forged out of heated discussions and tested out on rolls of yellow tracing paper.

After some five years of an intensive and stimulating relationship, where everything under the sun was argued about, Norman, Wendy and Su and I were beginning to grow apart. The divorce was difficult, jealousy tore us apart and it was not until Renzo Piano and I were building the Centre Pompidou five years later that the four of us became friends again.

Norman was as enthusiastic about Centre Pompidou as I was about his Willis Faber & Dumas and Sainsbury Centre buildings. His support gave me great strength and once more our meetings and discussions took on an excitement lost for a decade. Wendy, Norman, Ruth and I even talked seriously of linking up again when Centre Pompidou was finished.

Though the partnership never materialised, Norman, Wendy, Ruth and I became very close. We both adopted boys, Jay and Bo from Arizona. Ruthie's Restaurant became a base for planning the future and employed our elder sons. Tragically Wendy died in 1989.

University Projects
Manchester
England

Yale
USA

For his final year thesis at Manchester, Foster designed a new museum for the Faculty of Anthropology at Cambridge University. The proposed building's centrepiece was a three-storey glass-walled gallery to house the largest items in the collection.

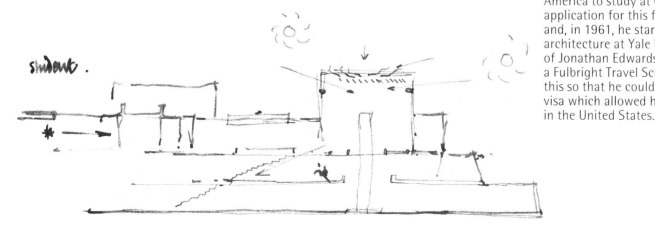

Norman Foster's background was working class Manchester. He left school at 16 to join the City Treasurer's department in Manchester Town Hall, followed, at 18, by two years of National Service in the Royal Air Force as a radar technician. He had always been interested in architecture and on his return to Manchester resolved to find a job in a design related field. By trading on his past administrative experience, he secured a position as assistant to the contracts manager of a local firm of architects. This brought him into contact with architects and students, making him aware of the potential to study and qualify as an architect. In his spare time he prepared drawings for interviews with architectural schools. When these were shown to the principal of the practice he was moved immediately from contracts administration to the drawing board.

In 1956, at the age of 21, he started full-time studies in the School of Architecture of Manchester University. Because he had no higher education the local education authority would not provide a grant, so he paid his way through university by a mixture of part-time and holiday work: jobs ranged from freelancing as an architectural perspectivist to 'bouncing' in a local cinema and working as a labourer in an industrial cold store. Over the five-year period of the course, he was also awarded many national and local scholarships, which enabled him to travel extensively in Europe and Scandinavia. After graduating with the Diploma in Architecture and a qualification in city planning he decided to travel and study in the United States. The Henry Fellowship enables a small number of British students to study at Yale and Harvard and their opposite numbers from America to study at Oxford and Cambridge. His application for this fellowship was successful and, in 1961, he started the Master's course in architecture at Yale University as a guest fellow of Jonathan Edwards College. He also received a Fulbright Travel Scholarship, but declined this so that he could travel on an immigrant visa which allowed him the flexibility to work in the United States.

Norman Foster presents his final project at Yale, in fact a group scheme undertaken by five students for which Foster was elected spokesman.

Norman Foster's first project at Yale was for an American high school. Paul Rudolph, renowned at Yale for his 'no-holds-barred' approach to crits, was impressed with the scheme, praising Foster for "thinking like an architect — even if his trees looked like cauli-flowers".

The cut-away section was a favourite drawing of Paul Rudolph's which he used often to explain his own projects. Foster explored the technique in this project for a private house. For Foster, the scheme was not a success but, as a means to understanding the integration and assembly of components, he was later to make this type of drawing very much his own.

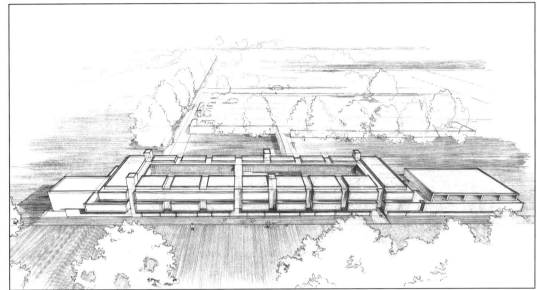

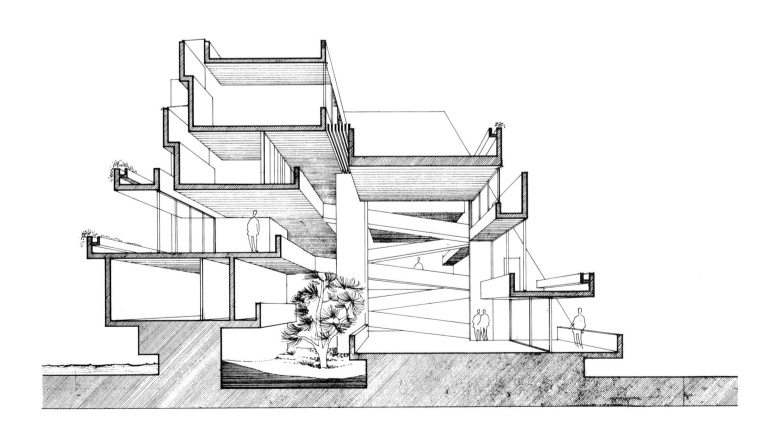

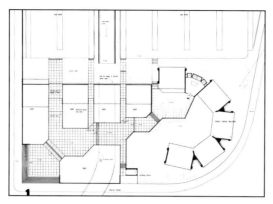

This scheme of linked office towers was an early lesson in integrating a large building into a tight city-centre site. The plan responded to the curve of the site, while also creating a series of protected plazas that linked the new offices to an existing shopping mall.

There was a tradition at Yale for first year students of the architecture school to help Master's graduates on selected projects. A young Japanese student worked with Foster to produce this immaculate white card model of the office towers.

The Master's course, with its studios open 24 hours a day, was a liberating experience after the constraints of living at home and studying at Manchester. The school was in transition between the outgoing head Paul Rudolph and Serge Chermayeff who was taking over. It was an unusual combination of influences: Rudolph would call snap juries at unpredictable times, often at the last minute before a hand-in and always with an emphasis on the drawn image; while Chermayeff would question motives at the most philosophical level. A parallel and important voice was Vincent Scully whose lectures on the history of architecture were followed avidly by the Master's class. While Rudolph would base school projects on real-life client briefs from his office, Chermayeff was at that time immersed in planning studies which provoked the book *Community and Privacy* with Christopher Alexander. In that

Considered by Foster the best of his Yale projects, the office tower juxtaposed the reduction in structure, as it ascended the building, against the contrasting stepping-down, from above, of the service ducts which were fed by roof-top plant. A mixture of smaller professional suites, at the lower levels, and larger corporate offices was included, inviting a broader spectrum of potential users.

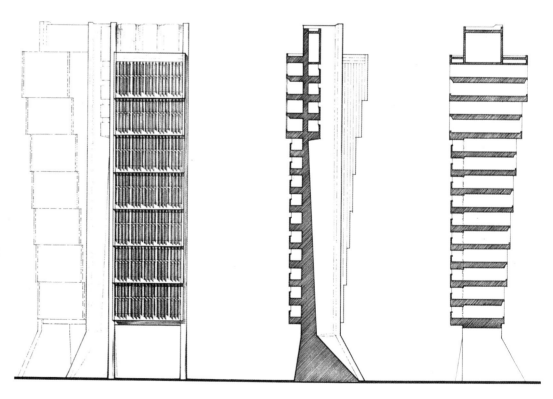

The scheme for a new city. Foster had been making models of his designs ever since his early years at Manchester, but few matched the precision of the model for this project.

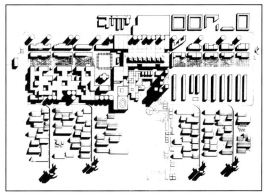

The final 'group' project at Yale was a scheme for a new city, directly inspired by Chermayeff's theories on community and privacy. A rich variety of drawings and models was prepared which even incorporated Foster's earlier office tower project.

Influenced by Louis Kahn's definition of 'served' and 'servant' spaces, Foster's office towers incorporate free-spanning office floors sandwiched between edge service zones, a model which was to inform his later headquarters for the Hongkong Bank.

sense, the course was an unusual combination of theory and North American practice.

Richard Rogers had embarked on the same course and there was an immediate rapport between the two students, which resulted in their eventually working together on student projects and collaborating on a house project which Richard had promised for a landscape architect friend in England. Inspired by Vincent Scully's historical insights they also travelled extensively to explore the work of Frank Lloyd Wright, Mies van der Rohe, Louis Kahn and the Chicago School. It was an influential period in which they absorbed both the architecture and the culture of American cities, their indigenous buildings, and the hardware of space and travel.

Serge Chermayeff invited Foster to work with him at Yale on the continuation of his theoretical studies but, after graduating with a Master's degree in architecture, he decided to work as a city planner heading out an urban renewal project in Massachusetts. He later moved to San Francisco as an architect/planner for a new campus for UCLA at Santa Cruz, with a group of West Coast architects who had won the project in a limited competition. In the autumn of 1963 he returned to the United Kingdom to join Richard Rogers and two architect sisters, Wendy and Georgie Cheesman, and together they established Team 4.

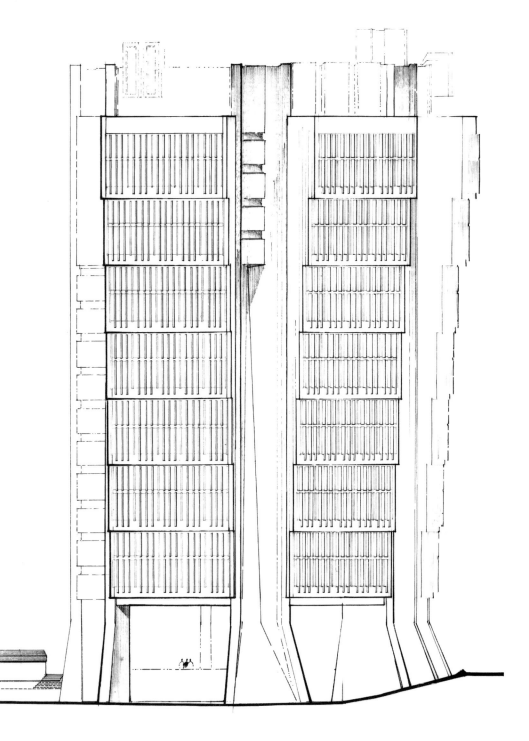

Introduction
by Alastair Best

Alastair Best is a writer and lecturer. Between 1987 and 1990 he was the editor of *Designers' Journal*; and from 1983 to 1987 he edited and published *Designer*, the magazine of the Chartered Society of Designers. He was closely involved with the work of Foster Associates in the 1970s and wrote catalogues for several exhibitions of their work as well as the book *Foster Associates: Six Projects*. Alastair Best has written extensively on architecture and design for *The Architectural Review, Design, Blueprint, The Economist, The Spectator* and *Harper's and Queen*.

When I look to the early years of Foster Associates, the recurring image is of a group, seated at a table and engaged in intense, almost conspiratorial discussion. I am thinking of the celebrated Tim Street-Porter photograph, taken during the course of a session with the late Buckminster Fuller. Among those clustered round the table are Norman himself, Michael Hopkins, Anthony Hunt, James Meller, John Walker and one or two others I cannot now identify. All are leaning forward intently to hear what the sage is saying. Again, I remember entering a Pizza Express in the Fulham Road and coming across almost the whole office seated at a large circular table. They were conducting an earnest post-mortem on a pitch they'd just made to Chelsea Football Club — in those days top of the First Division and planning to build a new stand.

It was, of course, fashionable in the 1960s to talk about the design team, but I find it difficult in those early years to detach Foster from his associates, or, for that matter, from the professional consultants, like the engineer, Anthony Hunt, or the quantity surveyor, John Walker, with whom he liked to surround himself. Partly, of course, this was pure window-dressing: clients like to see a multidisciplinary array of skills. Partly, perhaps, it was the result of Foster's extremely thorough, even cautious, approach to architecture. The process that he calls "exploring the client's range of options" is an exact description of the painstaking, sometimes almost diffident, way in which he feels towards a solution. Nobody who has seen the design exercises that went into the proposed radio centre for the BBC could ever believe that Norman Foster produces buildings like rabbits out of hats, and the brilliance of the Fred Olsen schemes in this volume is rooted in some very unflashy strategic research. Foster proceeds by marshalling all the arguments and taking all the best available advice. Only when he is convinced that his own position is unassailable will he make a move; and when he does he is unstoppable.

It was the same with his own entry into the architectural profession: oblique, and diffident at first; but once the fuse had been lit — explosive.

Norman Foster was born on 1 June 1935 in Levenshulme, a suburb of Manchester, and was brought up in an atmosphere of thrift and self-help. He attended the local high school and did well — passing seven out of nine O-levels, including art. Given his social milieu, a career in one of the professions seemed out of the question, yet even as a schoolboy he was exceptionally well-informed about architecture. One of his earliest possessions was a history of architecture written by Frederick Gibberd, and while still a teenager he had immersed himself in two key influences: Frank Lloyd Wright and Le Corbusier. Wright he imbibed via Henry-Russell Hitchcock's *In The Nature Of Materials*, especially the science fiction images of shimmering glass in the Johnson Wax building, whereas what impressed him most about *Vers Une Architecture* were the startling juxtapositions of past and present it contained — for example, a cornice detail from the Parthenon on the same double-page spread as the cockpit of a Caproni flying boat.

He had also begun to respond to architecture at first hand. His first job in the Treasurer's department of Manchester Town Hall exposed him to that remarkable building from the inside. And what impressed him, he told the RIBA in his Gold Medal address of 1983, were "not only the internal spaces and the presence on Albert Square, but also the details: the handrails and the light fittings, even the glass-sided cisterns in the toilets". Other buildings in central Manchester also left their mark: the delicate tracery of the Barton and Lancaster arcades, and, perhaps most of all, the Daily Express building in Great Ancoats Street — with its whizzing curves and dark reflective bands of glass an obvious blood ancestor of Willis Faber & Dumas in Ipswich.

It's difficult to say exactly when Foster came to terms with the fact that a career in architecture was inevitable. While working in the Treasurer's department he had started to test the temperature of the water; he had met a Mr Cobb whose twin sons were both studying architecture at Manchester University and by the time he joined the RAF for his National Service the idea was beginning to take hold. At least he knew that he had to escape from the Town Hall; and the RAF, where he trained as an electronics engineer, gave him the opportunity

"Seated at a table and engaged in almost conspiratorial discussion." Tim Street-Porter's celebrated photograph of James Meller, Norman Foster, John Walker, Tony Hunt and Michael Hopkins in a meeting with Buckminster Fuller.

Le Corbusier's *Vers une Architecture* and Henry-Russell Hitchcock on Frank Lloyd Wright were two early influences on Norman Foster before he had decided to be an architect.

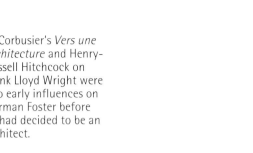

Manchester is home to some of the grandest Victorian buildings but it was their details that impressed the young Norman Foster most: the "handrails and light fittings, even the glass sided cisterns" of Waterhouse's Town Hall (left) and the delicate tracery of Barton Arcade (right).

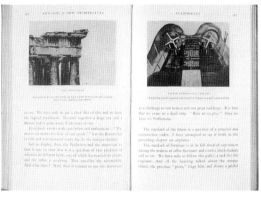

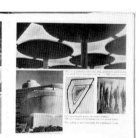

Ellis & Clarke's Daily Express building in Fleet Street, sister to their virtually identical building in Manchester and "an obvious blood ancestor of Willis Faber & Dumas in Ipswich".

to acquire another skill. He worked in a turf covered hangar — another portent? — that was high on camouflage and low on natural light, but, as he told the RIBA: "there was a certain futility to our struggles: the radar systems, which we repaired, were designed for propeller driven bombers; their response was too slow for the new generation of jets and by the time the navigator had established a fix, the aircraft had already travelled a long way to somewhere else."

When his 18 months were up, Foster took on a number of short-term jobs. He wanted to postpone the day when he would have to return to the Town Hall. He sold furniture, and at one point considered a career in furniture design. Paradoxically, it was his skill in book-keeping, acquired as a part-time student while working at Manchester Town Hall, that gave him an oblique entry into architecture, for he got a job as assistant in the contracts department of John Beardshaw & Partners, a large commercial practice installed in a Georgian house near the University. Here, for the first time, he started mixing with architects, or embryonic architects, and he discovered to his surprise that he was rather better informed than some of them. A chance conversation with an apprentice student, on a year out from Manchester School of Art, ran as follows: Foster, "What do you think of Frank Lloyd Wright's work?" Student, "Frank Lloyd Wright? I don't think there's anyone of that name on the course."

Foster has always been a compulsive sketcher and when he produced a portfolio of drawings for inspection by his boss he was promptly plucked out of the contracts department and transferred to the drawing office. Meanwhile he had discovered that he could obtain a grant to study architecture at the School of Art but not at the University — and the University ran a better course. So in true American style, he worked his way through college, performing an often bizarre range of jobs from night-club bouncing to selling ice cream. He was also drawing perspectives for building hoardings and amassing all the available prizes and scholarships at the University. Many of the prizes were for foreign travel, and he managed to see a great deal of Europe in

five years. He did the usual tour (town-planning studies of the Campo at Siena) and went to Denmark to look at the housing of Utzon and Jacobsen. The Manchester school placed a strong emphasis on history and drawing, both traditions stemming from Professor R. A. Cordingly, editor of the seventeenth edition of Banister Fletcher, but there was very little in the way of verbal communication or debate. In many ways Foster was out on a limb, and it was only when he won a Henry Fellowship to study for a Master's degree at Yale that his period of isolation came to an end.

There was nothing haphazard about his choice of American university. As at Manchester, Foster had done his homework and come to the conclusion that the faculty at Yale was better than Harvard or any of the other East Coast universities. Indeed, for someone with his background and particular temperament Yale was the perfect finishing school. The course was run, on rigid teutonic lines, by Paul Rudolph. There were marks every week and a strict regime of projects. All assignments were run against the stopwatch — a vital early lesson in the importance of time as an ingredient of design. Foster thrived in this atmosphere of regulated hard work, more so than fellow student Richard Rogers, with whom, nevertheless, he discovered an almost immediate rapport. Rogers, two years older than Foster but on the same course at Yale, came from a cosmopolitan background very different from the Manchester of Foster's youth. Coming to Yale from the AA school, with its traditions of iconoclasm and free-wheeling debate, he was horrified at the workload and unimpressed by the intellectual values.

These values were mainly established by Rudolph himself, who took the uncharitable view that if there were no drawings there was nothing much to discuss. But there were other influences: Vincent Scully, the resident architectural historian, opened Foster's eyes to the work of Wright, the Chicago School and Louis Kahn; and Serge Chermayeff, who was formulating theories of how it was possible to combine a basic human need for privacy with the

The imagery of man-made America, from Airstream caravans to the hardware of space travel continue to exert a powerful fascination for Norman Foster, a lasting influence of his student days there in the early 1960s. This is his own photograph of Cape Kennedy in 1962.

Team 4 Architects. Even at their height the office never exceeded eight full-time staff, all working from Wendy Foster's flat in Belsize Park.

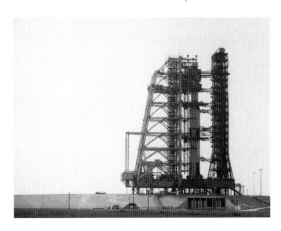
Craig Ellwood's Rosen House of 1962. During his time in America, Foster was to assimilate much of the ideology behind such buildings.

Rogers and Foster toured America after Yale and visited nearly three-quarters of Frank Lloyd Wright's buildings along the way, including the 'baroque' late work such as the Guggenheim Museum.

necessities of community living, invited Foster to help him with his thesis — eventually co-authored with Christopher Alexander as the influential book, *Community and Privacy*.

But more than Yale, more than these mentors, it was America itself that made the most powerful impression. The Britain that Foster and Rogers had left behind was still drab and relatively impoverished; the architectural profession still dominated by such essentially herbivorous characters as Sir Basil Spence or Sir Hugh Casson — for whom Foster had worked during his year out in 1959. The imagery of man-made America, its motorway architecture, its Airstream caravans and all the hardware of space travel exerted — and continues to exert — a powerful fascination. Then there was the architecture. Between them, Foster and Rogers must have visited about 80 per cent of Frank Lloyd Wright's buildings, and Foster, perhaps surprisingly, found them all enjoyable and instructive, even the baroque late works such as the Guggenheim Museum or the Marin County Civic Centre. His own personal tour took him across the southern states and up through California to San Francisco. On the way, he had seen the Eames house at Pacific Palisades and the Case Study houses of Craig Ellwood. Surprisingly, he did not visit the SCSD (School Construction Systems Development) mock-up on the campus of Stanford University.

It is tempting, with hindsight, to suppose that the Californian steel systems architecture made the greatest impact, since its influence was to resurface so decisively in the Newport School scheme and Reliance Controls; but it would probably be more accurate to say that, at that time, they were just some of many powerful impressions, docketed and filed away for retrieval later on. At all events, Foster's own architectural preoccupations were then well removed from the kind of problem-solving work of the Californian schools programme. While at Yale he had brought his town-planning qualifications into play (he had already taken Part One of the Town Planning Institute's exam) by working on urban renewal projects, and in San Francisco he had worked in the offices of Carl Warnecke and Anshen & Allen,

neither of whom — though respectable — were at the cutting edge of the Californian design scene. There was little to suggest future developments.

Back in London, in 1963, Foster and Rogers set up shop as Team 4 in the front section of Wendy Cheesman's flat in Hampstead Hill Gardens. From their first Yale encounters — they had collaborated on a stepped-section spine scheme for the Yale campus — they discovered they spoke the same language, even if at times it was only a shared language of grunts and signs. The term Team 4, however, was a misnomer. Wendy and Georgie Cheesman were the two other members of the quartet, but Georgie, who had just married the hop broker and furniture designer David Wolton, departed to practise in her own right. Foster himself, meanwhile, began to live with, and subsequently married, Wendy.

Those who worked at Team 4 in the early 1960s — usually the most talented students plucked from the AA school, the Bartlett or the Regent Street Polytechnic — remember a stylish atmosphere of creative tension, underpinned by good living. Furniture, walls and floor — as in a Dick Lester film — were white. Sir Herbert Read's daughter Sophie, complete with Afghan hound, manned the reception, Su Rogers did the accounts and Norman and Richard, seated on either side of a large table, scribbled, or squabbled, over endless rolls of buff paper. The quality of coffee, then as now, was exceptional. From the first, Foster and Rogers seem to have known instinctively how to be different and appealing. The very name, Team 4, struck precisely the right note, midway between the world of pop and serious architecture. There were echoes of groups such as the Beatles (who cut their first LP in 1963) and in architecture of Atelier 5, whose Siedlung Halen housing scheme, on a well forested hillside outside Berne, was the sought-for antidote to the English picturesque versions of Le Corbusier on the LCC's Roehampton Estate or Sir Basil Spence's University of Sussex campus.

They were both fortunate and unfortunate in their early clients. In Marcus Brumwell, Rogers' father-in-law, they found a cultivated and indulgent patron who presented them with two commissions, one on either side of a small wooded creek that flows into the Fal estuary in

Built for Su Roger's parents, Marcus and Rene Brumwell, the Creek Vean house in Cornwall was the outcome of three years' work for cultivated and sympathetic clients. In 1969 it became the first house to win an RIBA Award.

As with the Villa Savoye, the aesthetic pleasure of the Retreat is generated by the juxtaposition of man-made object and natural setting.

Atelier 5's 1961 Siedlung Halen housing scheme near Berne. Not just their architecture was to prove a formative influence on the Team 4 office.

Cornwall. The first and chief of these was for the conversion of a Victorian house on a steeply sloping site at Pill Creek; the other, facing it across the water, was for a small retreat which Brumwell could camp in while building work was in progress. The Retreat, with a commanding view over the Fal estuary, is in the form of a cockpit, or sunken gazebo, buried between the pine trees. It is a light, elegant industrial object — Brumwell had suggested something resembling the draught shield on the side of a car — and it sits uncompromisingly in its natural setting. As such it recalls later Foster works in sensitive landscapes, especially the proposed office complex for Fred Olsen in the ecologically sensitive pine forests outside Oslo. As with Le Corbusier's Villa Savoye, the aesthetic pleasure is generated by the tension between the untouched natural setting and the man-made object in its midst.

The house was another matter. The original scheme to convert was abandoned and it was decided to demolish and start again. Creek Vean took three years to complete and won an RIBA Award in 1969. I visited it this summer for the first time. The house is still lived in quite happily by Brumwell's widow Rene, and I was touched to note that the storage jars and coffee percolator are still arranged on the freestanding stainless-steel worktop in exactly the same configuration in which they appear in the early photographs. The house itself is clearly influenced by Wright, both in its internal planning — with a sequence of bedrooms arranged off a top-lit gallery — and in the way it snuggles into the protective hillside. The planted roof, and the steep flight of steps — overgrown with grasses and valerian, and fanning out between the sleeping and the living area — have helped to soften the rather stark elevations in handcut concrete blocks; but perhaps the only indication of future developments in Foster's work are the large areas of glazing in the kitchen and living room, held in their slim metal frames with neoprene gaskets.

Before the completion of Creek Vean, Team 4 had wrestled with other less rewarding housing schemes and less accommodating

clients. Murray Mews, a development of three houses for three different, but highly demanding clients, was plagued by water penetration, shoddy finishes, incomplete junctions — in fact all the vices of traditional, on-site building methods. Bryan Appleyard, in his excellent biography of Richard Rogers (Faber & Faber, 1986) describes the scene: "From the beginning water penetrated the houses seemingly at will and the sunken living room of the central house — number 17 — remained entirely flooded for long periods of the building process provoking lugubrious and embittered jokes about indoor swimming pools. A cast-iron chimney stack descended from a ceiling to miss the centre of a fireplace by nine inches and one increasingly horrified client revealed ... that what he had taken to be a damp proof course was, in fact, newspaper painted black. The worst moment came when the same client, who unfortunately knew something about building, stood with Rogers by the house's main drain which ran along the ceiling of the garage, told the contractor to flush the toilet and was instantly inundated with water from a junction that nobody had bothered to complete. Such problems generated new problems: they lengthened the building period to the point where the clients' changing requirements became significant elements in the design process."

It was becoming clear that Team 4's obsessive preoccupation with exploring every option and every option of every detail would only be supported by the most interested and patient clients. Mark Sutcliffe, who worked in the office in 1963, remembers making up 14 different models of a fireplace during the course of a conversion of a house in Sussex for Wendy's mother, but in most cases there was no time for lingering over the alternatives in quite such a leisurely way. Foster and Rogers both knew that they had to devise built forms and evolve design methods that would not only accommodate the clients' changing needs but which would also buy design time. This led to flexible plan forms and structures composed as far as possible from standard components. By removing fabrication from the site to the factory it was possible to control standards of

In its ability to assemble off-the-peg industrial components in new and unexpected ways, it is the Eames House (incredibly of 1949) that has proved the most enduring influence of Foster's time in America. Like Reliance it even has expressed cross-bracing.

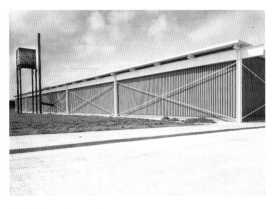

At Reliance Controls the influence of Craig Ellwood is clear, but his finite precision is rejected in favour of a more indeterminate flexibility.

Team 4's last building, a small office for Fletcher & Stewart in Derby, was an unhappy project for a difficult client.

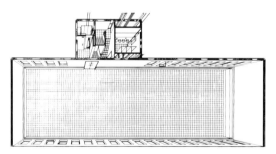

workmanship in a way that was not possible in conventional building with its procession of semi-skilled labourers and wet trades. All this led back to the Californian buildings of Eames, Craig Ellwood and Ezra Ehrenkrantz's SCSD with their stress on flexible space and factory-made components based on performance specifications.

Team 4's last big job, Reliance Controls at Swindon, marks a great turning point in the careers of Rogers and Foster. Reliance may owe something to the Smithsons' influential Hunstanton School of 1954 (the water tower at Swindon is a direct quote), but in most crucial respects it is closer to its Californian models. The low slim profile recalls the work of Craig Ellwood and the cross-bracing — carried round all sides outside the ribbed metal cladding — recalls the cross-bracing on the Eames house at Pacific Palisades. In strict structural terms, the cross-bracing was only required on the two long elevations, but then it was entirely superfluous on the Eames house. Foster produced most of the drawings himself (with assistance from Mark Sutcliffe) and in many ways Reliance Controls seems to have more Foster in it than Rogers. The absence of colour, the suppression of services, the expressed but not over expressed structure all recur in Foster Associates' subsequent work.

It was for Reliance too that Foster perfected a method of presentation which was to become standard at Foster Associates: the elevation, with all structural members in deep shadow; the structural options; the kit-of-parts drawing showing how each component fitted together; and most characteristically, the exploded section with, in the case of Reliance, service runs buried in the floor slab, but for many later projects wriggling out of the ceiling void. The theory and practice were Californian inspired, but refined by Team 4 into a taut, razor-sharp architecture quite distinct from the Californian originals. And although Reliance is designed to accommodate growth and change — the projecting 'I' beams emphasise this fact — Reliance still gives the impression of a building complete in itself, with a lingering monumentality which betrays a European rather than an American ancestry.

Reliance Controls is also a typical early Foster project in being an elegant building stranded in an inelegant industrial estate.

SAPA, Modern Art Glass, even the Olsen and IBM projects are not in surroundings normally associated with 'architecture'. As Ian Nairn pointed out, when writing in *The Sunday Times* on Reliance: "Reliance Controls would make a better village building than most new housing estates. The site, long and narrow, is just the kind of left-over land — an orchard or paddock maybe — which turns up so often in villages. The factory makes tiny electronic components, which are used in objects as different as heart pacing machines and servo-mechanisms for aircraft controls. So the operation is completely clean inside and out. In a sense Reliance's elegance is wasted on the Greenbridge estate in Swindon, and it wouldn't shame places as traditionally beautiful as Burford or Bourton-on-the-Water."

Reliance won the first Financial Times Award for Industrial Architecture in 1967, but, like many highly regarded buildings, it did not lead to any further commissions for its architects. Work began to dry up; and, as so often happens when two powerful personalities are left with too much time on their hands, the partnership began to show signs of strain. It was a frustrating period. In Britain a big building boom was under way. Housing, new university buildings, shopping centres, motorway service stations were all being designed and built while Rogers and Foster waited on the sidelines. The partnership was already dissolving when they embarked on their last project together, the first phase of an office building in Derby. The clients were Fletcher & Stewart, a subsidiary of Booker Brothers, who manufactured sugar crushing equipment. They were clearly not best pleased at having a pair of architects foisted on them by the parent company and were in no mood to be co-operative. But the building was completed; it had a simple rectangular plan, with the core pulled out and attached to one of the long sides. It was an unremarkable, but honourable scheme which had fallen victim to professional tensions and difficult clients.

When Team 4 was disbanded in 1967, Norman and Wendy continued to practise at Hampstead Hill Gardens as Foster Associates. At this stage the office included Mickey Kuch and

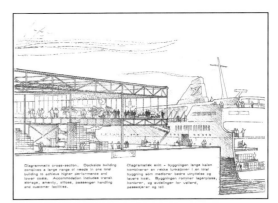

The success of the amenity centre was based on a thorough analysis and understanding of Fred Olsen's operations and working techniques reduced down to the simplest possible diagram. The section of the final building was a direct reflection of the ships it served.

The Newport School competition entry, a flexible deep-plan space under a highly serviced 'umbrella' roof, set the agenda for a whole succession of projects.

The theories that underline the Newport entry were first given practical form at the amenity centre for Fred Olsen at Millwall Dock.

Alan Stanton, as well as Martin Francis, an ex-furniture student from the Central School. The main project on the drawing-board was an entry to a competition to design a new comprehensive school for Newport County Borough Council. It was a period when the term architecture was seldom used, certainly not in connection with education. Cedric Price had recently guest-edited an influential issue of *Architectural Design* on learning, and it was generally conceded that the educational process could — and perhaps should — be conducted in supermarkets, caravans and indeed all forms of flexible shed. Foster's Newport School entry narrowly missed winning the competition, but it gave him the opportunity to work up a British version of the SCSD system. The proposal, perhaps a little too relentless for the assessors, showed a constant-height roof 'umbrella' combining structure and environmental control, floating above a variety of teaching and administrative spaces, some of them dug into the site. The scheme posited an optimistic view of British comprehensive education as a place of endless experiment, backed up by a wide array of advanced technical aids. Newport, though never built, represented a tremendous conceptual advance over the essentially hand-crafted Reliance scheme and it sowed the seeds for a whole string of industrial buildings that were to follow.

The amenities building for Fred Olsen at Millwall Dock is the key building of the early period of Foster's career, as it set the agenda for a whole succession of buildings — mostly for industrial or commercial clients — and gave the practice for the first time opportunities for self-promotion which Foster himself was not slow to exploit. The job came to Foster Associates by the back door, as it were. The father of a year-out student from Manchester University, Barry Copeland, then working in the office was an Olsen manager. He suggested Foster Associates might be interested in looking into the problem of siting a small amenity building, then little more than a canteen, behind the two transit sheds that the Port of London Authority were building at Millwall Dock.

By the standards of Port of London employers at the time, Olsen had an enlightened attitude to his workforce. The dockers had been 'decasualised' in advance of the Devlin Report

recommendations which abolished the labour free-for-all in the London Docks. That meant that everyone was on the pay roll, and Olsen had recently negotiated an agreement on shift work with the Transport and General Workers' Union. So he had a stable, flexible workforce, and the management were keen to match the agreement by providing them with good amenities. Then, as is the way with Foster projects, the brief began to change. Prompted, as he has since explained, by Foster's "ability to ask the right questions", Olsen expanded the brief to include office space and a passenger terminal, both of which had to be meshed in with the Port of London's transit sheds.

The Olsen project was a classic Foster *tour de force*. Proceeding from a simple but restricted brief to design a small amenities building on a remote part of the site, he began to question the fundamentals of the company's entire mode of operations. This resulted in a master plan for the site which demonstrated quite conclusively that instead of being abolished to the hinterland, the amenities and management should be combined in a single building at dockside, right at the centre of operations. It is highly probable that Foster had himself decided at an early stage that the logical site for the building was the firebreak slot between the two transit sheds, but it is characteristic of him that he should have cleared all the other options out of the way before he knew he could proceed with complete conviction.

The original intention was to combine the operations and amenity building with the terminal in a single building. The generator for this design was the procedure for loading and unloading ships. The three most modern ships in the Olsen fleet were loaded and unloaded from the side; a low silhouette truck, working inside the hold, transferred pallets through the side ports to stacker trucks on the wharf. Passengers were confined to the upper levels of the ship and it was realised that bringing them ashore at ground level could seriously impede cargo handling at the dockside. So it was decided to layer the new building to correspond to the ship's section. The passenger terminal, baggage handling and administration would be

The simplest diagram: raised above the activity of the working dock, Fred Olsen passengers passed quickly and safely through the new terminal at the same level as the passenger decks of the ships.

Moving ahead: the 1970 commissions for Computer Technology and IBM allowed Foster Associates to move to new offices, one floor of a building in Covent Garden shared with engineer Tony Hunt.

planned at an upper level, with the dockers' amenity centre on the ground. In the end the passenger terminal was inserted into a low cost, elevated tube, the steel legs of which were set in reinforced-concrete pads to protect them from dockside traffic, and the passengers were transferred from ship to terminal on modified Heathrow baggage-handling conveyors. The main building took a year to design and build. It had — before being taken over by the London Docklands Development Corporation, and eventually demolished — open-plan offices on the first floor, with a canteen, changing rooms and rest areas for the dockers at ground level. Both floors enjoyed spectacular views of the dockside, exactly as Foster had intended. What he also knew, was that the ships and cranes mirrored in the amenity centre's grey-tinted glazing would turn out to be a colour photographer's dream.

The Fred Olsen project was a prime example of Foster's wit, his daring, his originality and his unmatchable eye for the main chance. It was this building which so impressed the Sainsburys and persuaded them to give him the job (originally) of designing the shell of a small museum to house their collection at the University of East Anglia. And it established Foster Associates, who had then moved to offices in Bedford Street, in a still vegetable-strewn Covent Garden, as a leading practice in the new architecture of the late 1960s.

What exactly did this new architecture consist of? In many ways it was rooted in old values. One of the most attractive tenets of the Modern Movement — largely ignored by its detractors — was a genuine democracy of design. Both Rogers and Foster, partly as a result of their American experience, were committed to an architecture that improved the lot of the working man. Reliance Controls and Olsen were both, in that sense, manifestos. The manifesto being that humdrum buildings on unpromising sites could be transformed at high speed and lowish cost. The techniques used were state-of-the-art technology, a commitment to abolish wet trades from the construction site, and an uncanny ability to fathom the nature of client organisations. Whatever his other virtues or defects, it seems to me that in his understanding of the corporate animal, and his unswerving commitment to the architecture of the

bottom line, Norman Foster in the late 1960s was operating in a different league from the rest of his British contemporaries.

At the same time as the Olsen programme was making history, Foster Associates were tackling another industrial brief, this time on the Hemel Hempstead trading estate. Their clients, Computer Technology, had leased a three acre site, in one corner of which stood an old canning factory of the traditional depressing and obsolescent kind: a brick shed with offices clipped on to the front. Here indeed was a perfect match of architect and client. Like Foster himself, the computer men, led by the charismatic figure of Iann Barron, were keen to dismantle the false divisions between management and labour that were implied by sheds and offices, and they had established everyone on the same 37-hour week with payment by cheque and no overtime. So there was no quarrel with a conversion which proposed a single volume with one entrance and flexible divisions, and proposed turning the old office box into a common room for everybody, with 'easy' chairs created by the simple expedient of lopping off part of the back legs of conventional Hille plastic seating. A wall to wall carpet of non-woven natural fibre, developed in America by Union Carbide, was laid throughout the computer assembly area, and transformed the working methods of the assembly workers, who had previously flicked their solder carelessly on to the floor. Now they began to work with almost clinical neatness and precision. Foster himself had noted the same shift in attitudes at the Olsen Amenity Centre.

"Perhaps one of the most satisfying aspects of the Olsen project was to see the transformation of life style that followed from it. A workforce, supposedly notorious for its vandalistic habits, was apparently transformed to the point of being so possessive about its new building that it would not allow visiting truck drivers to use it because of their bad habits." This was not a plea for architectural determinism. "I am not suggesting", Foster goes on, "that this apparent miracle in industrial relations, characterised by a virtual absence of unofficial strikes during the

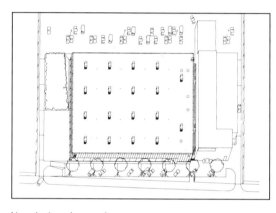

New industries, such as Computer Technology, allowed the false divisions between management and labour to be dismantled.

Carpeting the assembly areas at Computer Technology transformed working practices, the once careless flicking of solder on to the floor being replaced by an almost clinical neatness.

The air structure for Computer Technology — 8000 square feet of temporary office space provided in eight weeks including ordering and fitting out — is the most ephemeral of Foster's designs and fully displays his ability to extract 'more with less'.

working life of the building, was due to the architecture in isolation: rather it was the integration of a progressive management philosophy and a belief in the value of good communications between people."

Computer Technology were expanding so quickly that they were rapidly running out of space in their existing building, but plans to construct a new building alongside were crucially delayed by red tape. The problem — precisely the kind that inspired Foster to his most brilliantly unconventional solutions — was to provide 8000 sq ft of temporary office accommodation in eight weeks, including ordering and fitting out. All conventional forms of temporary building were investigated and, as later at IBM, found wanting. The quickest, cheapest and, notably, by far the most elegant option was an air tent. There was great interest in air structures among the architectural avant garde in the late '60s. They had been used for a wide range of purposes, from military stores to golf driving ranges, but never before for offices. There were some doubts about their thermal and acoustic performance. And there was the small matter of convincing the local authority that it was safe to put office workers into a structure which could swiftly deflate and engulf them all. The last of these problems was neatly resolved with typical Foster panache: a row of angled booms, running along each of the long sides of the tent would have held the deflating fabric clear of the escape routes, but they also carried fluorescent lighting tubes and bounced ambient lighting off the white pvc fabric of the tent. In much the same way, the roof deck at Reliance had been designed to act as a lighting reflector for the fluorescent tubes housed within the corrugations. In both cases the elegance of the solution was a form of thrift: the manner in which Foster was able to extract 'more with less'.

After the air tent, the new building that represented phase three of Computer Technology's expansion programme may seem something of an anticlimax, but it is significant in Foster's development for continuing the single-storey deep-plan philosophy that first made its appearance in the Newport School competition designs. The roof acted as a service umbrella and the external cladding panels, later to be refined in the Sainsbury Centre, were a sandwich of aluminium and polyurethane, adapted from materials used for refrigerated containers.

The principal deep-plan office building of Foster's early period — and his most admired building — was the pilot head office designed for IBM at Cosham on the outskirts of Portsmouth. The term 'pilot head office' was a typical piece of Foster hyperbole, but it sounded better than temporary office which was all the scheme was originally intended to be. To understand the scope of Foster's achievement at Cosham, it is important to grasp the fact the IBM had been intending to install their 750 workers and their computers in Portakabins or site huts. There was no call for architecture; what was required was a simple, practical solution to tide the company over until such time as it was ready to build a permanent head office on land reclaimed from Portsmouth harbour. The challenge to Foster, and Michael Hopkins who was the associate in charge of the project, was to demonstrate that it was possible to install something more elegant than a site hut within the allotted time of 18 months. The research carried out for the Newport School competition suggested that it was, and that a single-storey glazed pavilion with all the services carried in the roof trusses, would be preferable to Portakabins, with their land-consuming internal courtyards, or to any form of two-storey building which would have necessitated costly piling foundations on a site with poor load-bearing capacity.

As usual, all the options were explored and set out in an immaculate, yellow-covered final concept report. This demonstrated how the single-storey envelope would preserve views, retain trees, provide ample space for car parking and still allow for expansion. A single-storey, air-conditioned envelope with no courtyards or light-wells is more extreme than anything proposed in the Newport project or the Californian schools programme — since both envisaged some form of top-lighting to relieve the artificially lit, deep-plan space. Some desks were as much as 42 m from a window and the cavernous nature of the heart of the interior

An ephemeral building of a more permanent nature was the all-glass platform theatre proposed to 'float' over the river Thames off London's South Bank. It was one of several single-drawing projects undertaken by the office that never went further.

Given a budget and programme that assumed a Portakabin solution, Foster Associates designed for IBM at Cosham a 'temporary' building that has now been successfully in use for 20 years.

Daylight came flooding back into Foster's work at Willis Faber & Dumas, and since then — it was designed in 1972 — it has never been absent. This is the atrium of the new ITN headquarters in London, due for completion in 1990.

Unlike Bean Hill, the industrial aesthetic proved quite acceptable at the Spastic Society's special care unit in Hackney. Its kit-of-parts approach and flexible plan set a standard for the design of schools for handicapped children for years to come.

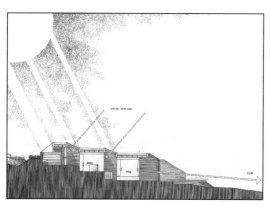

Top-lighting, a major feature of many of Foster's earliest projects such as Skybreak House, is curiously absent from the most notable of his deep-plan 'umbrella' structures.

The Bean Hill housing scheme, a superb flexible plan in an aesthetic that has never found favour with its residents.

was exacerbated by IBM's insistence on installing floor-to-ceiling height cellular offices for senior personnel.

The floor plate was a 10 880 sq m rectangle with two off-centre service cores separated from the bulk of the office space by a circulation mall running the full 140 m length of the building, and the office space itself was separated into bays by the cellular offices. Except for the computer room, with its raised floor, all services were contained in the roof space and carried down structural columns to rectangular 'dice boxes' for local distribution. IBM has several times availed itself of the flexibility thus offered: the staff restaurant has been moved and the computer room altered and expanded twice. In 1985, the building, which had already well exceeded its expected life span, was repainted and recarpeted and a massive amount of extra cabling inserted in the ceiling void. Against a five-fold increase in computers the number of people working at Cosham has actually fallen from 750 to 600. If the building is beginning to seem a little dated, that is because the computer industry has changed. In 1971 the staff was 70 per cent clerical and 30 per cent executive. But since then that ratio has probably been reversed. As Richard Watts, IBM's head of architecture put it: "Our surveys have shown that the calibre of staff we employ today don't like deep office space: they prefer shallower wings where they can be nearer to windows ... the only real obsolescence in this building, and it is not an architectural obsolescence, relates to that process of evolution."

Top-lighting at IBM would have made a big difference to the quality of its office space. In many ways, it's odd that it was not tried. The Newport School proposed a sound-insulated ceiling of Georgian wired glass, and much earlier schemes, such as Creek Vean and in particular the remarkable Skybreak house depend very heavily on top-lighting. This must have been a concern even when Foster was a student. His thesis scheme at Manchester, despite having a Beaux Arts plan, introduced quite large glass bubbles over libraries and museums and his proposal for the Sidgwick Avenue arts complex at Cambridge, drawn when working at

Casson Conder & Partners, envisaged a sort of glazed fly tower, with sunlight diffused and filtered through baffles. It's interesting that when Foster Associates moved to their new deep-plan offices in Fitzroy Street, many of the most important meetings would take place under the only skylight in the space.

But with or without top-lighting the deep-plan serviced shed, with fixed cores but undifferentiated floor space, was the building type for which Foster Associates were known in the late '60s and early '70s, and its appeal extended well beyond the kind of client who might normally be interested in commissioning sheds. For the Bean Hill housing scheme at Milton Keynes a timber-framed housing system was somewhat perversely combined with corrugated industrial metal siding. As Foster has since noted, wood may have been not only more logical but also more acceptable to the type of resident who wishes his home to contain as few reminders as possible of his place of work. Early versions of the Bean Hill scheme were admirably planned and would, if built, have mitigated the impact of the cladding, but the housing never seems to have found favour with the residents. Interestingly, subsequent phases, built in brick to an identical plan, have proved entirely acceptable.

There was another test for the industrial aesthetic applied to a domestic scale when the Spastics Society commissioned a prototype special care unit, for the London Borough of Hackney, for handicapped children suffering from a broad range of mental and physical disabilities. Until the Education (Handicapped Children Act) of 1971 brought them under the umbrella of the Department of Education and Science, such children were looked after either at home, or in a hospital or, if they were lucky, in junior training centres run by the local authority. The special care unit that Foster Associates designed in Hackney was therefore intended as a prototype school: a cheap, portable kit-of-parts that could be bolted on to existing property, set up alongside special schools or, like the Palmerston School in Liverpool, form a one-off building in its own right. Ever since Lubetkin and Tecton's Finsbury Health Centre, there has been an honourable link between modern architecture and care. The special care unit at Hackney, like Finsbury, was an attempt

The scope of Foster Associates' work in the early years is probably best illustrated by their planning studies carried out for Fred Olsen on the island of Gomera, an extremely sensitive proposal promoting traditional building techniques and appropriate technology.

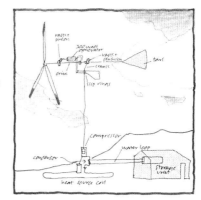

Ever since Tecton's Finsbury Health Centre of 1939, there has been an honourable link between modern architecture and the welfare state.

In 1973, with their proposals for the Orange Hand shops, Foster Associates introduced the kit-of-parts concept to High Street retailing.

to bring rational principles and modern construction techniques to bear on the problem. Essentially it was the shed solution in microcosm: a large core contained lavatories and bathing facilities for often severely incontinent children, with lots of flexible space divided by full-height sliding screens leading out on to a hard play area. I greatly admired this modest little building, especially the courage with which it tackled head-on one of the main problems of spasticity – incontinence – and made it the focus of the scheme. The Palmerston special school, in a tough, vandal-prone area of Liverpool extended these ideas into a larger building, with top-lighting and a less severe roof line based on lightweight steel portals linked together into five bays.

Even more short-lived were the experimental Orange Hand shops launched by the Burton Group. This was another application of the kit-of-parts approach to retailing. The idea, basically sound, was that the retailer could move from one rented shell to another, without leaving behind him expensive fixtures and fittings. Again, as at Bean Hill, it was probably the physical expression of the concept and not the concept itself which prevented wide acceptability. Its use of flexible hanging and display systems, many of them culled from industrial catalogues, introduced the notion of High-Tech at least five years before the High Street was ready for it. Since the retail boom of the 1980s, profit margins have been so high that retailers have been able to indulge in frivolous and wasteful refits more or less to their hearts' content. The lessons of the Orange Hand shops have been largely ignored.

Not many architectural practices can claim to have covered such a wide span of work in their first five years' existence as Foster Associates, but then not many practices have ever exhibited quite the same insatiable desire to design and build. Looking through this book one is immediately struck by the range of projects that Foster Associates were prepared to take on. While the core of the practice was centred on industrial or commercial buildings, there are also forays into town planning (St Helier harbour, Jersey), private and public housing, shops and showrooms, and special schools. Most surprising of all perhaps, were

the planning studies carried out for Fred Olsen on the island of Gomera, then the only island in the Canaries group still unravaged by tourism. This extremely sensitive little document questioned such *idées fixes* as the construction of an airport and ring roads, and proposed a revival of vernacular building techniques and alternative energy sources. If only it had been put into effect.

This is a young man's work, full of freshness, vitality and optimism. Norman once said of Buckminster Fuller: "The thing about Bucky is that he makes you believe anything is possible". The same could be said, in those exhilarating early years, of Norman himself.

1963-1964 Early Projects

Below: the Henrion studio extension seen from the garden. The steeply pitched glass ridge directed light down on to a fixed work desk running the width of the building.

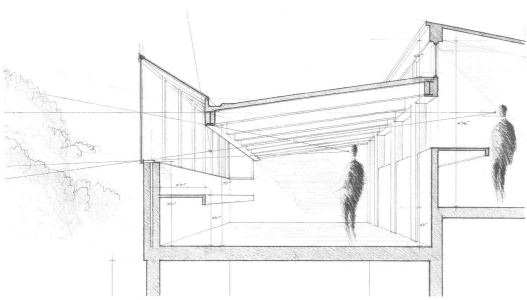

As Norman Foster's sketch demonstrates, the simple device of stepping down the Henrion studio extension, when combined with high-level clerestory windows, allowed both the new and existing studios to enjoy plenty of daylight and views of the garden.

One of Team 4's earliest commissions came from the graphic designer Henrion: a design studio built as an annexe behind his Georgian terraced house needed to be enlarged. The studio looked northwards over a garden from an upper floor. Instead of continuing the existing floor level, Team 4 proposed that the new extension be lowered to create a stepped section that included a built-in desk and window for each floor.

At the upper level, the window was split into a clerestory, which admitted north light into the depth of the older studio, and a lower opening looking out from the new extension across the built-in desk. An unbroken view to the garden was thus possible at both levels, despite the deep section of the rear studio. At the lower level, the window was a full double height, rising from a sill just below eye level to offer a raised 45 degree view of the sky to the designer seated at the desk. This openness to the sky was amplified by glazing the adjoining roof along its re-entrant pitch. The entire range of glazing, adapted from an industrially available system, presented the profile of a 'light-cage' or crystalline prism along the rim of the annexe, the angles of this prism seeming to follow and represent the sight-lines of a viewer within, thus lending an animated and expressive aspect to the building.

The Henrion studio, modest though it was, experimented with a number of themes that would run through many of the projects

undertaken by Team 4 over the next few years. Chief among these were: the separation of outlook and illuminant functions, in glazing, by the use of skylights and clerestories to bring light into deep sections; an orientation of outlook towards the best views; and the ranging of section by terrace and mezzanine-like elements, as if in a domestic theatre with the window as proscenium giving an outlook on the world. Internally this overview-format was often repeated so that, for instance, a kitchen work-range would look out over a social or play area. There was also a commitment to varying and variable degrees of open plan, sometimes involving movable partitions to enable a flexible facility for various occasions.

The influence of Serge Chermayeff, who had tutored Norman Foster and Richard Rogers at Yale, is clearly apparent in the planning of these early houses. Entrance from the public

domain was most often made through what might be termed the back elevation, presented as a closed defensive aspect in contrast to a very open outlook on the private side of the house. Lateral aspects were left blank, implying party-walls to a possible repetition of the unit as a typological element in a row, sometimes in contour-following echelon rather than strict alignment. Such typological extrapolations were proposed, with modifications, from the individual houses at Creek Vean and Radlett, while the houses in Murray Mews were expressly repetitive in implication.

One unbuilt model for this form of domestic planning was a project proposed for Camden Mews in London. Here, a pair of studio houses — consciously influenced by the work of

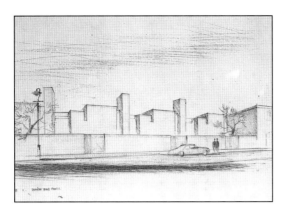

Norman Foster's sketch of the proposed four courtyard houses at Camden Mews with their repeated roofline profile and 6-metre set-back from the high site-boundary wall.

The planning of the Camden Mews houses made ingenious use of spiralling floor levels around a central stair-case to maximise the small internal volume.

Kahn and Rudolph — was to be sited in the back gardens of some Victorian villas, with a small, high-walled courtyard between each new house and the mews. The side of the houses facing the villas was to be a blank wall, so, in principle, they could have been built back-to-back on the old north of England pattern. Compensation for this confinement was provided by the great openness of each house to its courtyard and of its rooms to each other. This was effected not by sliding doors, as would be used at the later Skybreak house, but by wide centre-pivoted panels, which could turn like revolving doors to make living room, playroom and courtyard into a continuity.

The kitchen was raised a few steps in order to survey this space across its worktop. The living room itself was to be double height with open stairs leading up to a suspended mezzanine — a studio with top-light and steps up to a roof terrace. On the ground floor, a bathroom and lavatory were enclosed in an island block that stood between the playroom and children's bedroom — a space that was open to allow variable partition. Above, a door from the stairs led to an upper bathroom and a main bedroom that could open, by another revolving

wall, to the void above the living room. This ingenious *Raumplan* was compact, yet still provided 1350 square feet of covered, under-floor heated space.

Camden Mews was never built but its design marked the first of a remarkable sequence of works and projects that spanned a range of locations, from urban extension and infill, through to suburban addition, green-belt edge, rural village and isolated rural sites. The material and constructional means, however, were to remain broadly the same throughout: a jobbing-builder industrial stock of brick, concrete blocks, steel joists and plate glass. These materials were deployed with and in their own character, to a general rather than local tradition. Similarly, a common set of spatial and formal prototypes informed the whole sequence. Local idioms and clients' idiosyncrasies were transformed into prototypical formats. Each building, however, adapted these common conditions to create intensely specific solutions of great individual character.

Brian Hatton

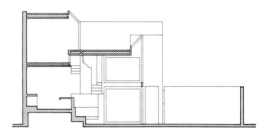

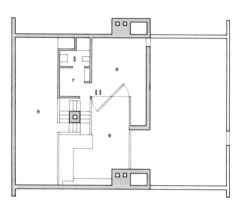

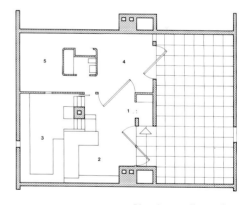

Pivoting wall panels allowed the small house unparalleled flexibility.
1 entrance
2 living room
3 kitchen
4 playroom
5 child's bedroom
6 master bedroom
7 bathroom
8 studio gallery
9 void

An early Norman Foster sketch of an alternative courtyard house with a raised kitchen and dining area. Its clear opening to the courtyard foreshadows the glass cladding achievements of a decade later.

The Retreat
Pill Creek
Cornwall

A balsa-wood model of the Retreat, the material enhancing its resemblance to a model aeroplane project. Part of the timber glazing frame slid sideways for access.

The Retreat at Feock was not the first major work designed by Team 4, but it merits priority by virtue of its radical singularity of purpose and clarity of solution. In certain respects it has proved the most advanced of the early projects; notably in respect of technical devices like the gaskets that sealed its windows, and in the sense that it prefigured the severe distinction in later works — like the Sainsbury Centre and Frankfurt National Athletics Stadium — between heavily-embedded groundworks and diaphanous, lightweight superstructures.

Like the house at Creek Vean, it was commissioned by Marcus Brumwell and his wife Rene. Sailing was for them an intrinsic part of life in Cornwall: at the waterfront at Creek Vean was a boathouse from which they could sail down Pill Creek into the broad ria of the Fal estuary. A mile or so down the creek, on the opposite bank, lies the wooded promontory of Feock. From here a wide prospect of the branching estuary opens, while a gentle water margin enables boats to be brought in to shore. The Brumwells and their family were fond of taking picnics at this place, and kept a hut for that purpose there, but following the designing of Creek Vean, they asked Norman Foster and Richard Rogers to create a special building for the site. It was to be an all-weather gazebo, with electricity for a hot-ring and piped water to a sink; otherwise as simple as possible. It was called the Retreat.

The architects adapted the splayed, trapezoid shape that had planned Creek Vean, but

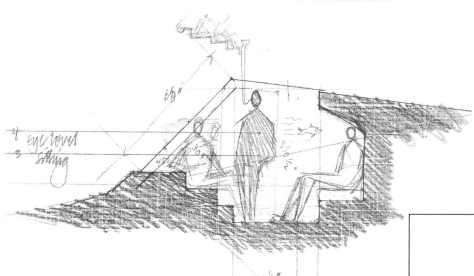

An early sketch section through the Retreat. The floor, worktop and seats were cast *in situ* in concrete, with storage units, a vestigial kitchen and a simple glazing frame in the shape of an aircraft cockpit added later.

An all-weather gazebo with modest facilities for tea and warmth, the Retreat, though tiny, was an unorthodox design. It was also the first Team 4 building to enjoy the services of structural engineer Tony Hunt.

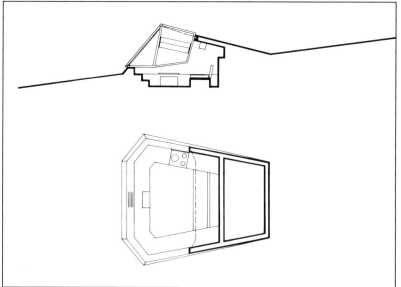

The view of the Fal estuary from the Retreat. The diminutive structure was used for family picnics, reading and watching regattas on the river.

Overleaf: the Retreat in its woodland setting on the crest of the Feock promontory overlooking the river Fal in Cornwall. Almost totally hidden by trees and undergrowth, only glass reflections betray its presence.

The wooden glazing frame required careful geometry in its joinery to ensure the complex polyhedron form was entirely sealed, but it has proved remarkably resilient. The only concession to ventilation was a pair of glass louvres set into the right-hand window to control condensation in poor weather.

now let it generate both plan and section to make a complex crystalline polyhedron with triangular, rectangular and trapezoid facets. Fanning outward from a notional source within the earth, the gazebo breaks surface from the slope of the bank towards the sea like the cockpit of a plane or boat.

The main structure is a concrete shell, set into the earth like a basin at the entrance to a cave with a trapezoid canopy at its portal. Into this shell, as if it were a monocoque, are set the bases of the seats, sink and cooker. The stainless-steel sink is covered by a teak lid, hinged on brass, while the drawers beneath the stove are also of stainless steel. Entrance is through a sliding panel in the windows, whose wooden frames required some careful geometry in their joinery. The panes themselves are set in butyl putty and pointed with Thioflex mastic.

For about £500, 100 square feet of well-serviced shelter was thus provided, a bridgehead to life on the water established, and the sward of a pine wood left intact. Nevertheless, this definitely non-primitive hut may be said to fulfil within Norman Foster's practice the same primordial archetype as the Abbé Laugier's mythological edifice: an idyllic cell, come down from Eden to make a prototype for paradise.

Brian Hatton

The interior of the Retreat seen through the sliding entrance door. In addition to a small electric cooker there was a stainless-steel sink (connected to piped water) and a supply of chairs and cushions.

Norman Foster's sketch stresses the Retreat's minimal structure and maximum transparency, a characteristic he was later to design into much larger and more complex buildings.

1964-1966 **Creek Vean House**
Pill Creek
Cornwall

The house at Creek Vean seen from across Pill Creek which leads into the Fal estuary. The boathouse below it was built for an earlier bungalow that was demolished to make way for the Team 4 project.

The house at Creek Vean is far more complex than the Retreat, but it is as connected to the road and village as the cell is to sea and sky, and is as embedded in artistic culture as the bunker is in its wooded bank. The project began as a proposed extension to a house already on the site and, at first, stacked up three floors behind a raking window wall not unlike the profile of the Feock cockpit or the later terrace side at Skybreak. When it was instead decided to clear the site, a linear plan emerged, stretching 150ft along a steep bank that falls from some trees at a turn in the lane above to the boathouse and creek at its foot.

The linear plan implied extensibility, in accordance with the Brumwells' brief, but it also accommodated another singular requirement, namely a gallery for the display of a collection of modern art: the Brumwells' other passion, along with sailing. Other requirements were for a degree of flexibility and openness for entertainment, provision of a study and self-contained guest flat and, of course, orientation to the light and views, west across the creek and southwards down the Fal estuary. It was also felt that a direct route from the top lane down to the boathouse should be retained.

The way that this was done was to articulate the house by a dramatic *coup* that transformed it from a solitaire to a small yet vivid rehearsal in urbanism — the art of relating two or more buildings to each other and to a common setting. The new plan arranged the house on a natural terrace immediately beneath the man-made terrace of the lane. Along this lower terrace an 18ft high blank wall was run, shielding the house from the lane and creating a kind of dry moat. Main entry to the house was then made by a bridge across this gap to a door at roof level to the left, but the path to the water continued straight down a flight of steps, broadening as it descended between the two wings of the house to form virtually a miniature open-air theatre.

This staircase, with its grassed terraces like that at Aalto's Säynätsalo town hall, in fact forms part of the roof, for the two wings are connected beneath its upper flight. Several commentators have described the house as organised by this crossing of two 'axes' — one

over and down the bank, the other under and along the contour. Yet axes is hardly an accurate description of the actual experience there, because whereas one axis designates an exterior wedge of space, the other refers to an interior route which is repeatedly impinged by encounters with oblique openings and planes at the insistence of the light and view to one side.

The true organiser is not a dogmatic imposition of the axes, but a formalised staging of prospects and sightlines. The 'open-air theatre' of the stairway is one such, but the whole of the south wing sets up a proscenium to nature by its broad-span canopy and giant glazed wall which, like the lowerable panorama wall of Mies van der Rohe's Tugendhat house, can slide back to open the kitchen-dining room to the garden. Above the kitchen, slung on a single concrete tray like the balcony or circle in a theatre, is a bridging mezzanine that functions as sitting room and library, with even better views down the creek than the dining room or 'stalls' below.

Yet it is from the kitchen bench — a long, cantilevered concrete and stainless-steel worktop — that a sovereign view of the interior as a whole is gained. For at that point a sightline follows along the top-lit gallery to a glass door and little terrace at the end of the north wing of the house. It is a view that Vermeer or Velázquez would have relished — a succession of light and dark cullises in perspective, corresponding to the discrete yet continuous phasing of access, reserve, and privacy in the house.

On the long 'back' wall of the gallery are hung paintings and drawings by Ben Nicholson, Barbara Hepworth, Patrick Heron and others from the English Modern Movement. Along the other are ranged the study, bedroom and guest flat. These are shaped, like the south wing, as trapezia, fanning outwards to the creek, over which their windows look. Yet they do not configure, as does the south wing, a 'proscenium to nature'. Rather the opposite: for the screen which divides them from the long corridor slides back, so that the theatre is reversed: the proscenium opens to the picture gallery from the three separate rooms, rather in the way that in Melnikov's Rusakov Club a single stage plays to three fanning, cantilevered auditoria. This indoor proscenium looks to art, not nature, as the setting for conviviality, relaxation and culture.

"The building attempts to fit more snugly into its waterfront surroundings by generating a garden on the roof. As this starts to become overgrown, the house will recede into its creek-side Cornish setting."

Norman Foster, Arthur Batchelor lecture at UEA, February 1978

An early sketch looking across the living/dining area and out to sea from beneath the sloping glass wall of the Creek Vean house in its earliest form.

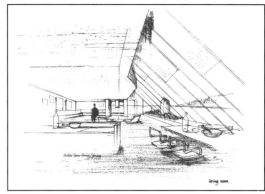

A Norman Foster sketch of the first version of the Creek Vean house looking down Pill Creek towards the estuary. The periodic emergence and disappearance of the final design from its surrounding vegetation was already hinted at here. Though not apparent from this drawing, as it has been purposefully omitted, this first scheme was an extension (or separate annexe) to an existing bungalow.

A section through the first version of Creek Vean house and an elevation of the existing boathouse drawn by Norman Foster. The huge cascading glass roof overlooking the water was later much reduced to survive only in the narrow rooflight over the interior gallery. The plunging buttress walls to the creek disappeared altogether.

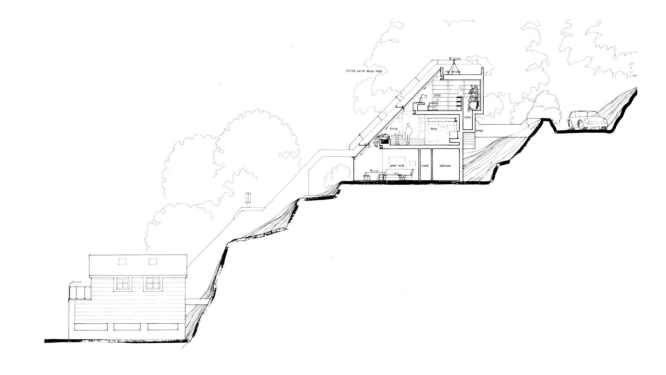

The fair-faced concrete block finish of the house is surprisingly striking in its setting. From across the creek the rectangular wall between the gallery and the road, and the higher living room convey no hint of the complex angles hidden in the plan.

"There is a distinctly mysterious aspect to the house as it emerges from the cliff in sections defined solely by the particular condition of the vegetation at the time. There is thus an indeterminacy about the appearance which contrasts with the finality of the blank wall on the road side. For the planting is not disciplined but rough, forcing its way through the steps and right up against the house."

Bryan Appleyard, *Richard Rogers*, Faber & Faber 1986

"The problems of quality control on straightforward exposed blockwork seemed almost insuperable; I suppose it was a house that was built several times before it was left alone."

Norman Foster, lecture at Hong Kong University, February 1980

Looking past the west wall of the gallery wing in the direction of the planted steps that lead down to the creek. Roof-top planting, on the right, covers the gallery roof; the glass entrance door is on the left.

A late innovation, but the most significant external feature of Creek Vean, is the planting on the roof of the bedrooms in the gallery wing. The rooflights shown here light and ventilate the internal bathrooms, while the slanted glazing to the right top-lights the back wall of the gallery.

The small sun terrace outside the dining room and kitchen of the main wing. The mezzanine floor of the living room studio above is set back from the flush glass walls, which have storey-height sliding glass panels at both levels.

The famous planted steps leading down towards the boathouse at Creek Vean. The irregular geometry of the plan means that the apparent curvature of the steps and the right angle formed by the corner of the gallery wing are both optical illusions.

A view into the living room of the earliest house scheme. Norman Foster's sketch shows planting on the roof for the first time.

The success of the early annexe design convinced the Brumwells that the existing bungalow was better demolished, and the whole site developed. A revised and enlarged scheme appeared, stretching along the site but maintaining the sloping glass walls of the earlier design.

The three 'theatres' — one outdoor, one indoor, and one threshold-athwart — configure the salient social spaces at Creek Vean, but they by no means exhaust its intricacies. There are, for instance, three entrances. The house is approached from a sunken garage along a path to the terrace at the end of the gallery, while, at the south end, steps lead down from the lane to a service door which connects to the kitchen through a parallelogram-shaped laundry.

There are, in fact, very few right-angles anywhere in the plan, but at the point where the two wings join, the geometries (which offered some challenges to the builders!) become particularly involved. The south wing lavatory, for instance, is a windowless rhomboid. Such torsions may remind one of Frank Lloyd Wright's elaborate compositions, and indeed there are many 'organic' dispositions at Creek Vean. Yet, as with talk of axes, it may be misleading to 'over-Wright' the plan, which eludes a rigorously geometric definition. Wright's 1950 Usonian Palmer house, for instance, conforms a flowing plan to a controlling grid of equilateral triangular modules. For all its intimate relation to site, its genetic principle stems from commitment to an idea of 'composition' which is hard to discern in the essentially more picturesque, even theatrical, Creek Vean.

The two trapezia that form the north and south wings do not stem from the same apex; rather the south wing takes its virtual fulcrum from a point 4/7 along the side of the major triangle implied in the north wing's splay. The location of that point appears to be determined by an extrapolation of the lateral wall of the south wing, into which the service door lets. This lateral wall is parallel to both the long back wall and the front wall of the north wing, just as the window wall of the south wing is parallel to the wall at the end of the north wing. The perimeter of the building, therefore, might be said to be described within a parallelogram. But this conceptual figure does not control the alignment of the room divisions within the north wing or the steps to the garden between the two wings. These are determined by a major triangle and minor, subtending triangle respectively.

In sum, therefore, we may speak of three dominant geometric figures that organise the plan: one conceptual, one perceptual in its

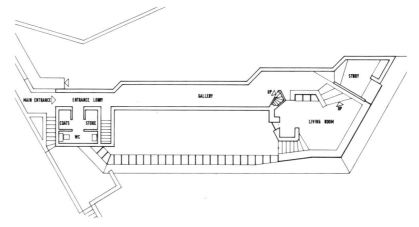

Upper gallery level plan of the house in its early form. An irregular plan with stair access at each end was proposed, the main entrance bridge on the left being diverted to a lower terrace and the boathouse steps.

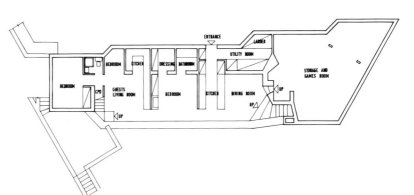

The lower floor plan of the early design bears similarities to the final scheme in its distribution of rooms, though the irregularly shaped storage and games room was to be put to much better use in the completed building.

motive, and another which mediates or partakes in both. The concept is a parallelogram: an autonomous figure that rationalises the site, but without reference to views. The mediator, orientated externally by the parallelogram, internally by the viewlines of the site, is a triangle from whose apex radiate the alignments of the rooms within the north wing. The third, and most perceptually orientated element, is the minor triangle from whose apex radiates the smaller south wing.

Yet these abstract considerations barely intrude upon one's experience in the house, which is encountered as a sequence of scenes and vantages rather than a manifest rationale. On entering the main door, for instance, a double vantage is immediately presented to the visitor, who can, as he hangs up his coat, view both the kitchen-dining room below and the lounge-mezzanine a few steps above. Will he be received below or above? The answer is there, for he can see and hear his hosts at either level as clearly as if they were on a stage and he in the stalls (if he glances across the gap to the mezzanine) or the circle (if he glances down through the gap to the kitchen). In fact, this 'little theatre' replicates the proscenium structure of the mezzanine and kitchen themselves, but now with those spaces playing the stage, not the auditoria.

If the visitor goes down to the kitchen, he descends through what is, in effect, a triangular helix to find himself at the focal point of both the trapezium-shaped kitchen and the picture gallery with its glass door and terrace at the far end. If, however, the visitor proceeds from the entrance to the mezzanine, he will turn and ascend three steps as if on to a bridge, so that, although the living room is open to view, it is reserved by a threshold of space as effective as that of a wall. To be sure, this reserve is 'embanked' by a long balcony wall, ranged with sculptures and fronted with bookshelves and seating facing out to the view.

In fact, a third, still higher, view is to be had by ascending a steep ladder-stair from the mezzanine to the roof. These steps, like the flooring throughout the house, are made of blue Welsh slate, and contrast with the honey-coloured concrete blocks of the walls. They make a precipitous cascade, but like a rock formation in a Mackintosh watercolour, their almost mannerist elegance fashions a functional structure. In fact, this corner of the

Under extensive vegetation, a section through the top-lit gallery wing of the house as built with, behind, the access bridge leading to the main entrance – not clearly shown here – in the elevation of the main 'living' wing.

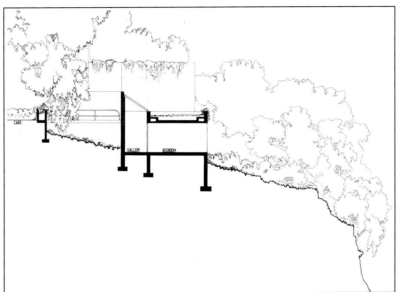

Creek Vean house in its final form, now dramatically split by a central access route into two wings.
1 main entrance
2 entrance gallery
3 cathedral steps
4 studio living room
5 kitchen/dining room
6 laundry
7 store
8 study
9 bedroom
10 dressing room
11 guest suite
12 gallery
13 garden terrace

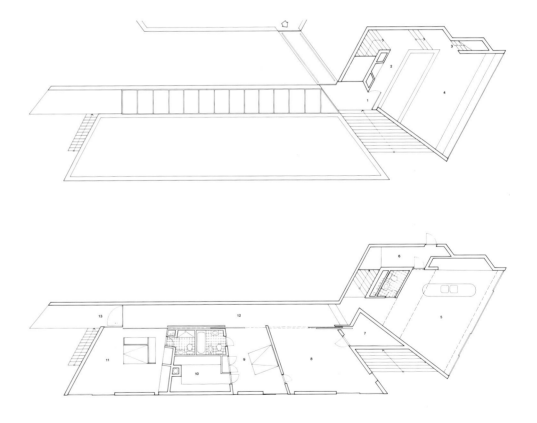

The gallery wall projects out beyond the house, sheltering the line of the top-lit gallery until it becomes a path that divides and leads off in two directions, one passing down the side of the house towards the creek, the other leading to a garage some distance from the house.

"In our opinion this small building is a work of outstanding quality. The architects have achieved an imaginative and highly original building without resorting to clichés or gimmickry. The design is carried through with commendable consistency using a self-imposed discipline in the choice of colours and materials. The general impression is that every arrangement in this design is an essential and significant part of the concept as a whole."

Extract from the jurors' report for the RIBA Award, 1969

house does seem its most restless, perhaps least resolved aspect, and the top-lit staircase culminates in a door that breaks the roof-line in a late-Corbusian gesture, like the bell tower at La Tourette. From across the creek, however, the house's extension along the brow and its raised, turned and gazing south wing bring to mind a prismatic version of the carved, reclining nudes developed from Mayan figures by Henry Moore.

From the roof terrace, another inspiration becomes apparent in the planted canopy that covers the north wing: Siedlung Halen, the famous terraced estate near Berne by Atelier 5. Here, three ranks of adjoining houses overlap down a south-facing slope in a compact range of terraces on a grid of stepped alleys and interstitial driveways. Creek Vean, in contrast, is but a villa, yet the logic of its stairway-and-gallery plan, and its balcony staging of horizontal planes condenses the collective idiom of Siedlung Halen to a highly-tuned individual variant. A year or two later Team 4 were to propose their own bolder version of the Atelier 5 scheme in a project for waterfront housing across the estuary from Creek Vean.

The gallery from inside looking towards the garden door and terrace. With its inclined roof-lighting and glass end wall, its fair-faced blockwork and slate flooring, it reads as a slot between two buildings as well as the communicating passage for a number of rooms that fan out from it like an auditorium.

The studio living room spans the main wing of the house leaving slots on either side to create one space with the kitchen/dining areas below. Set into a side wall, cathedral stairs lead up to the roof.

Looking down from the upper living room level towards the glass entrance door and, beyond, the external steps that divide the two parts of the house. Slate floors throughout unify the convoluted plan.

The view from the entrance door (left). The kitchen below is visible through a generous slot between the entrance gallery and living room a few steps above. Stairs from the left of the gallery lead down to the kitchen and a small corridor that leads through to the top-lit picture gallery (right), with its sliding doors on one side opening to reveal the master bedroom.

Seated in the dining room, Marcus and Rene Brumwell (and guest) enjoy the view out to the wooded slope and creek below.

The waterfront housing project never proceeded, and today another house, by John Miller and Su Rogers, stands on that site. It is occupied by the family and friends during holidays and often at weekends, so that life at Creek Vean is often carried on by boat between the two homes. As Deyan Sudjic remarked in the television programme *Building Sights,* "breakfast might be taken in one house and tea in another".

For Rene Brumwell the house is inseparable from the sea: "... one would sit upstairs; the windows above open with a winch on the wall there. Upstairs you get more view, you see the boats going past on the Fal, racing. That's when you are indoors, but quite often you are outdoors — in the boats!" In the winter, however, the mezzanine lounge is also the warmest place in the south wing, for the house is heated by warm air ducted through the ceiling.

Rene Brumwell recalls the change when they moved in from the old house across the creek: "it was so easy to run, so well thought out. We took to it very well, very easily. This room (the kitchen-dining room) is beautiful to sit in and have your meals. Even as I cook I can enjoy the view. One important thing is you don't feel shut in, and getting older, you don't feel, 'Oh, I must get out, up', because you can actually get exercise in the house, too. Children enjoy running up and down the gallery. Delivery boys who come to the front door, they look at it and say 'This is a marvellous place!' They really like it, and I don't think it's put on. And what have we

As befits a home for a couple who loved sailing, every room in the house enjoys spectacular views of the creek below; the kitchen looks out over Pill Creek, while the studio living room above looks down the estuary and out to sea.

The interior of the dining room at Creek Vean with sliding glass doors giving on to the terrace. The slot above communicates with the first floor living area. The control cords for the manual roller-blinds used to close off the large windows at night are clearly visible.

Site plan of Creek Vean. The house sits along a natural terrace in an otherwise steeply sloping site, the walls of its two wings sharply angled to make the most of the views. The entrance bridge spans across from the access road, the path created continuing over the house as a flight of steps spilling down to the waterfront and boathouse.

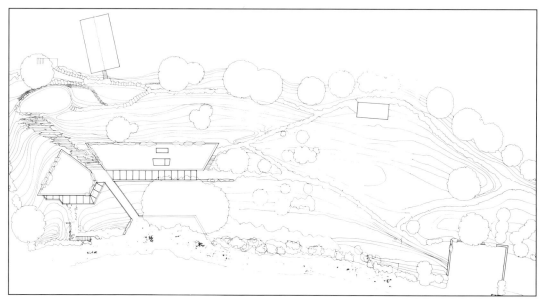

The two-storey living and dining room wing seen from further along the hillside is partially obscured by trees. The double-height glazed wall passes in front of the upper floor, as in so many later Norman Foster buildings.

The complex arrangement of glazing provides top-light to the stairs beneath, which lead from the entrance gallery down to the kitchen, or up to the roof. All are lit at night by external spotlights. In the foreground is the entrance footbridge.

spent on decoration? Local people are always doing up their places. We haven't spent a penny on decoration." For the bare block walls are still as crisp as on their day of completion.

Perret, who declared that his Naval Ministry contained "not an ounce of plaster", would concur. Le Corbusier also, whose *The Decorative Arts Today* declared: "If decorative art has no reason to exist, tools, on the other hand, do exist, and there exists also architecture and the work of art". The house is indeed decorated by the vitality it facilitates; its ornaments are the indices of an integral style of life. Oven, fridge and cupboards are built into the backdrop of the kitchen workbench, with books on sailing ranged across the facing wall. Upstairs, a collection of classic art books of the 1940s and '50s line the mezzanine shelf, many of their subjects represented among the paintings and sculptures throughout the house, many of their authors, such as Adrian Stokes who lived for some years in Cornwall, among the Brumwells' circle. In the history of English Modernism, Cornwall occupies a special place and, in Cornwall, Creek Vean sums up the feeling of a generation for that same place. Like Jim Ede's house at Kettle's Yard in Cambridge, Creek Vean convenes a vivid museum of the modern in the setting of a private home. Better than Kettle's Yard, though, is that the house is itself the main thing, and, of course, is still lived in.

Adrian Stokes, I believe, never visited Creek Vean, but the house shares much of his sensibility. It can be sensed in a passage from 'Inside Out; an Essay in the Psychology and Aesthetic Appeal of Space' in which Stokes describes his encounter at Rapallo with the Mediterranean: "I had the sensation that the air was touching things; that the space between things touched them, belonged in common, that space itself was utterly revealed. There was a heatness in the light. Nothing hid or was hidden. We are looking on Nature, but at the same time we look on a clearer distribution of forces within ourselves, a clearer interaction, one more Homeric, more in style and therefore more disinterested than is the case. Would that inner conflict were thus windswept, that visitation of the deeper caverns of the mind were subject to such causes as those that govern tides."

Brian Hatton

Waterfront Housing
Feock
Cornwall

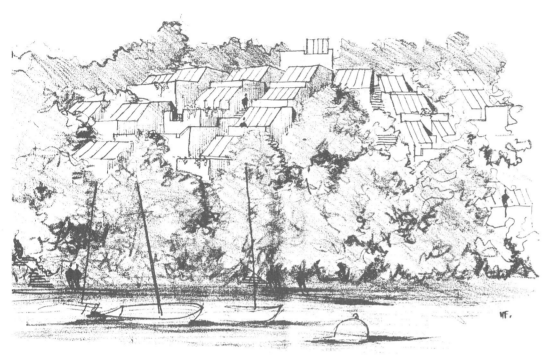

Norman Foster's sketch
of the first version of
the waterfront housing
scheme includes the
prominent sloped glaz-
ing of the early designs
for the house at Creek
Vean.

A consequence of the Brumwells' move into
the Creek Vean house was that the site of their
earlier home could now be reconsidered for
new use.

Marcus Brumwell was quick to agree with
the architects' view that the piecemeal development of isolated bungalows was spoiling the
Cornish coastline, whereas a traditional pattern
of compact settlement fitted its intricate creeks
far better. On the other hand, terraced cottages
presented car-parking problems and occluded
views to the sea. However, the steep slope to
the water at Feock offered a natural theatre for
a tiered arrangement of overlapping terraces of
a kind implicit in the sections of the Henrion
studio and Creek Vean house.

Brumwell commissioned from Team 4 a
plan for 19 houses on the 1.21 hectare site,
grouped in the earliest scheme as a staggered
echelon facing the creek. The echelon appeared
as a natural consequence of turning each
house obliquely to the line of contours in order
to face down the creek to the Fal estuary. But,
interspersed with clumped trees so as not to
obstruct any view, it also set out a broken and
picturesque rhythm that 'architected' the intrinsic shape of the creek. At each end, garages
were clustered, and there was a plan for a community hall by the central heating plant at the
village end of the site. A stone footpath was to
run along the frontage, stepping down to the
water at certain points; while the road, as at
Creek Vean, ran along the top behind a long
shielding wall.

As at Siedlung Halen, the terrace was cut
at intervals by steps between houses, which
comprised two to four bedrooms in several
variants within a standard type. Party-walls of
concrete blocks framed three-level dwellings,
consisting of reinforced-concrete shelves
descending in terraced courtyards looking out
to the sea. The uppermost rooms were for
kitchen, dining and living.

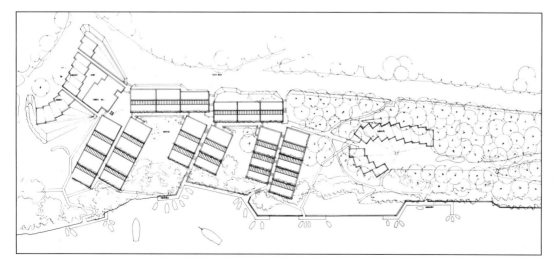

In the first site layout,
small groups of terraced
houses step down the
hillside, connected by a
central path that runs
between garage courts
at each end of the site.

"As a proposal for a wooded site overlooking a Cornish creek, the scheme represents an attempt to avoid the frequently encountered insensitivity of coastline development. The houses are clustered between existing groups of trees and are 'dug into' the site, resulting in a staggered section. Each house looks beyond its own private court over the pedestrian footpath below and diagonally out to the view and the sun."

Extract from the assessors' report for the Architectural Design Project Award, 1964

Norman Foster's section of the revised scheme clearly shows the influence of the Atelier 5 housing at Siedlung Halen, though the large under-footpath service and drainage duct was an innovative feature ahead of its time.

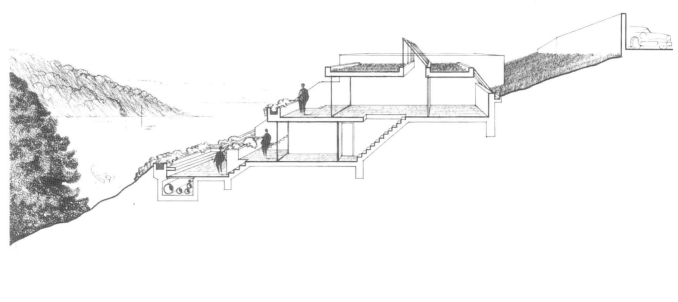

A part-section and elevation drawn by Norman Foster to illustrate how the integrated structure of the vertically terraced houses achieved Team 4's aim of adapting a modern idiom to traditional Cornish village densities. The single-outlook, stepped houses had no side windows but opened to the south-west to spectacular views of the creek and estuary.

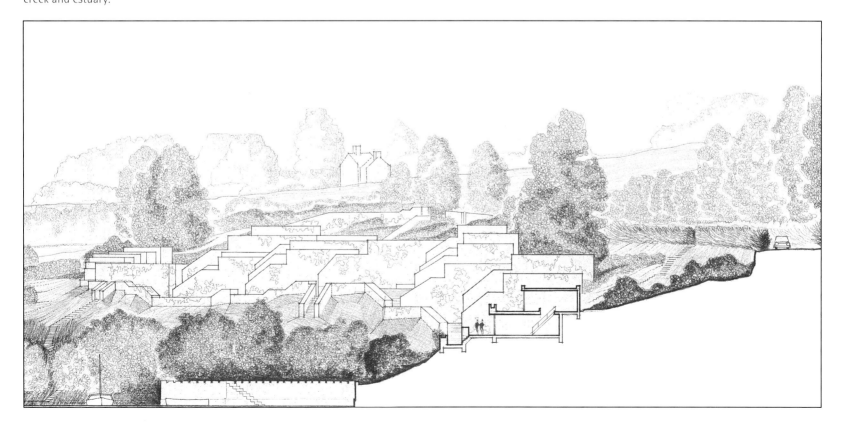

Taken from an early planning report, this sketch plan shows the village of Feock to the north of Pill Creek, surrounded by sporadic development. The waterfront housing site is directly south of the village on the north bank of Pill Creek, giving oblique views of the Fal estuary to the west.

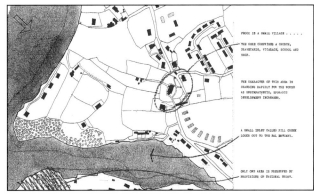

"Feock is a small village. The core comprises a church, graveyard, vicarage, school and shop. The character of this area is changing rapidly for the worse as unsympathetic, sporadic development increases. The village has little contact with the water although from surrounding areas there are fine views out to the Fal estuary. But despite this heritage more and more individual houses, each with their own acreage, accumulate."

Part of Team 4's written evidence to the local authority planning committee, 1965

As part of Team 4's early research for the waterfront housing project, Norman Foster spent a week at Feock sketching the village and surrounding area, and making notes on the problems the area had inherited due to earlier unsympathetic development. The sketch above shows how the main village is actually well separated from the Fal estuary by the rising land, though enjoying fine views, while the view on the left looks across Pill Creek to the site of the Creek Vean house, showing the original bungalow and waterside boathouse.

In his study of the area Foster was impressed by the quality of the older traditional buildings, noting they were "absolutely right in their setting by being clustered economically, complementing the landscape and leaving large areas undisturbed and rural". Team 4's waterfront housing tried to apply the lessons of the traditional cluster, accepting the inevitable growth but protecting as much of the countryside as possible. As Foster noted, it was the countryside and unspoilt views that made the area so popular.

In the revised scheme, a single footpath ran along the site giving access to the individual houses above, stepping up the hill.

As at Creek Vean, in the final scheme a pitched skylight and planted roof were anticipated above — the early version showed a range of sloping glass walls, later made vertical — and a Siedlung Halen-type interstitial alley between parallel ranks along the site, with car ports now at the top of each terrace instead of clustered garages at the ends.

The aim was to re-create, at a collective scale, the individual experience of Creek Vean. Numerous drawings by Norman Foster attest to a recurrent idyll in these projects. A table is sketched in the foreground, set with fruit bowl, glasses and wine. The 'palm' of the table is the first in a layering of planes looking out through a transparent glass wall to the stage of a patio and beyond to the sea. Le Corbusier, in his drawings for houses at Rio de Janeiro, depicted a similar scene, commenting, "the house is installed before its site".

The format of a still life as foreground, looking through shifting planes to a coastal prospect, had been a prime motif in the Cornish paintings of Ben Nicholson, who painted 'Pill Creek By Moonlight' at Feock in 1929. Writing in 1941, Nicholson said of 'Au Chat Botte', a still life framed in a window: "These three planes and all their subsidiary planes were interchangeable, so that you could not tell which was real and which unreal, what was reflected and what unreflected, and this created, as I see now, some kind of space or an imaginative world in which one could live".

Sadly, after lengthy discussions, the scheme was eventually rejected by the local planners. Despite the garage arrangements and innovations proposed for its septic system, objections about traffic and sewerage (along with prejudices) quashed the project.

Brian Hatton

As this model photograph of the final scheme demonstrates, the revised orientation of the housing blocks to achieve a uniform outlook, though settling unobtrusively into the hillside, required an extensive retaining wall on the steep slope to maintain good pedestrian access across the site.

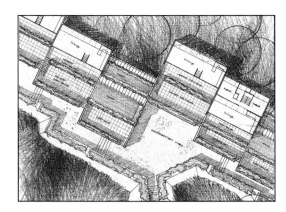

By subtle variation and responding to the contours of the site, the two-storey houses could be arranged to avoid overlooking a neighbour's terrace.

"The landscaping consists of large-scale tree massing, strongly mounded pathways and grassed roofs. The resulting section clearly defines public and private areas, car and pedestrian segregation, and movement through the site."

Foster Associates, RIBA Publications 1979

The sections and plans of the houses were arranged to give good views and daylighting to both floors. Several variations were designed — one with a double-height living room — the different configurations responding to the changing slope to allow an economical use of cut and fill excavation to minimise site work. Where necessary, tall party-walls ensured privacy. The influence of Atelier 5 remains clear but with a greater reliance on top-lighting for some rooms.

In its final form the site plan was tightly integrated, with a uniform orientation of the houses and separate garage courts at each end of the site. Extensive lower level groundworks include waterfront provision for boat access.

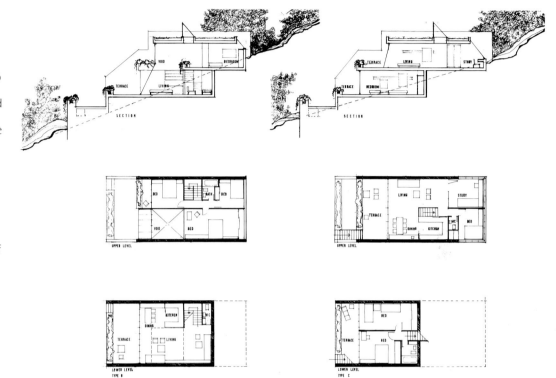

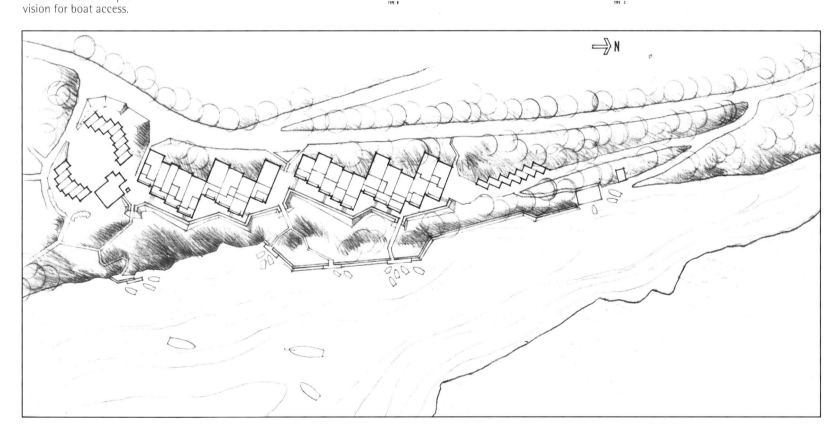

51

Murray Mews
Camden
London

Norman Foster's sketch
section of one of the
Murray Mews houses,
very much in the form
it was built.

In one sketch of the
mews, Norman Foster
suggested glazing in the
sides of the two-storey
blocks, an idea that was
later discarded.

"Overall, Murray Mews amounted to a competent synthesis of a large number of ideas about housing which were in the air at the time, and this quality means that the homes are still visited today by students of the use of small urban sites. The occupants have grown so accustomed to this that they start unrolling the original plans the moment the doorbell rings unexpectedly."

Bryan Appleyard, *Richard Rogers*, Faber & Faber 1986

The three mews houses soon after completion showing the inscrutable appearance gained by placing the courtyards at the rear instead of the front, as was proposed at Camden Mews. The dramatic interiors can hardly be imagined from what is visible in the mews itself.

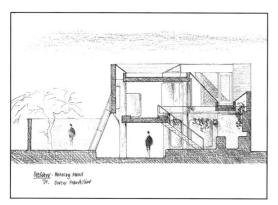

Despite their uniform appearance the design of each house was carefully tailored to its client and went through many variations. In this early design for the house of Dr Owen Franklin sloping glazing and an inverted 'V' glass roof are proposed.

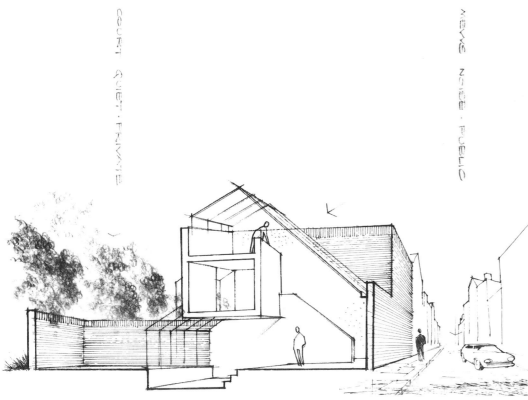

COURT · QUIET · PRIVATE

MEWS · NOISE · PUBLIC

Norman Foster's sectional perspective of the Murray Mews 'system': through visibility at ground level from front to back; double-height living room; and a second-floor gallery reached only beneath the peak of the patent industrial aluminium glazing.

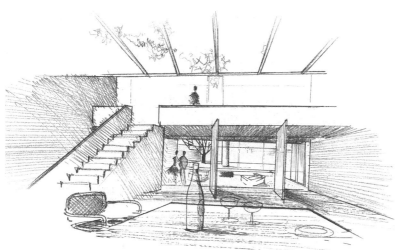

Taking up an idea introduced at Camden Mews, Norman Foster proposed in one sketch the use of pivoting wall panels between the kitchen and living room.

In its final form the typical sloping glass roof at Murray Mews resembled those proposed but never employed for the early Creek Vean and waterfront housing projects in Cornwall.

Team 4's earliest scheme for terraced houses, Camden Mews, did not transpire, but in nearby Murray Mews a row of three houses was built. Here, however, the site was confined, and local circumstance determined that only two of the three conformed to Team 4's ideas; moreover, one of these was modified to fulfil the wishes of one of the two clients.

In Murray Mews the site disposition was reversed: the houses now directly adjoin the street along the building line of the adjacent converted stables, while the courtyards are placed on the side that faces and adjoins the back gardens of the former villas. Although the street wall is now pierced by both house and garage doors, it is kept otherwise just as blank as those facing the villas in the Camden Mews design. From the upper bedrooms, slit windows look out at right-angles to the mews facade, while the ground floor is illuminated by a sloping top-light invisible from the pavement. The aspect is severe and private, not to say, solipsistic: minimal solids and voids in ABABA rank.

The street door opens straight into the kitchen which is raised, as at Skybreak, a few steps to look over a worktop and built-in concrete table to the living room and a glazed wall with the courtyard beyond. The glass wall of the living room, like that of the kitchen-dining room at Creek Vean, is placed a yard or so forward of where the ceiling ends, so that more day-lit space is created. Standing in the kitchen, one is aware of bright top-lighting, then of a band of dimmer, intimate space in the living room, and then again of a band of brighter space along the window wall.

At an angle parallel to the sloping, glazed roof in the double-height kitchen, an open staircase runs up to the bathroom and bedrooms, with a few more steps leading up to a

In these early elevations only the two right-hand houses conform to the final design. The small front doors open directly into the kitchen/dining areas, the larger doors into garages. The rear elevation includes glass walls to the courtyards with first floor 'bays', much as built.

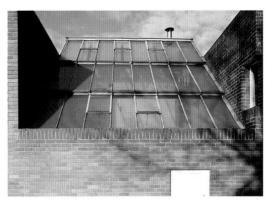

The industrial aluminium patent glazing used at Murray Mews was as successful as the neoprene sealant at Creek Vean. These early successes with advanced materials encouraged Foster in later years.

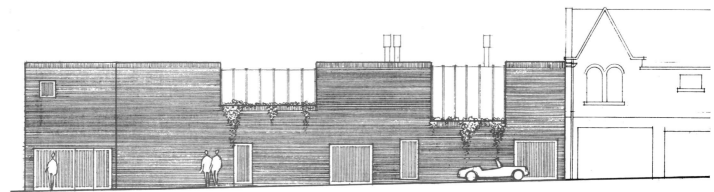

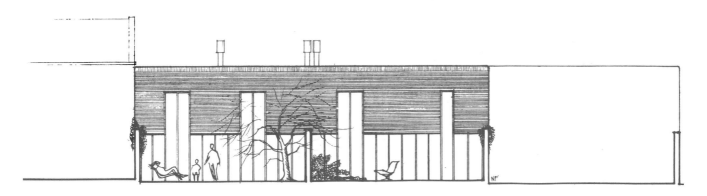

This typical section shows the high glazing ridge as built, as well as the stair arrangement to first floor and gallery. The sunken living room gave courtyard views to the kitchen behind, in an echo of the Henrion studio.

long top-lit picture gallery. From the balcony wall of this space one can look down into the kitchen as if from a minstrel gallery.

Courtyard, living room, kitchen and glazed 'attic' are thus related in a continuous spatial liaison; only the bedrooms and bathroom in the U-shaped middle level of the house are enclosed and separate. It is as if the mediaeval English 'Great Hall' has become miniaturised and centred around the kitchen.

Brian Hatton

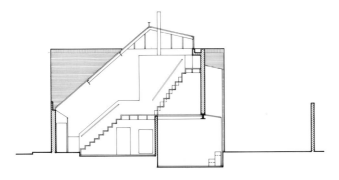

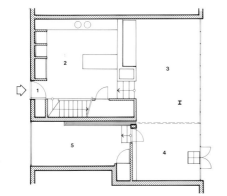

The ground-floor plan of the house could hardly be simpler.
1 entrance lobby
2 kitchen/dining room
3 living room
4 study
5 garage

An interior view looking across the full width of the sunken living room into the study. The raised kitchen/dining area is on the right behind the permanent seating built into the balustrade wall.

The kitchen/dining room with its built-in concrete table and steps down to the sunken living room. The main stairs lead up to three bedrooms at first-floor, the upper cathedral steps giving access to the gallery at the top of the house.

Looking through the glass screen wall to the courtyard formed from what was formerly a part of the garden of the house in the distance. The cut-outs in the ceiling are top-lit, the section of continuous soffit defining the floor of the bedroom's bay window above.

The rear of the house at night. The ability to open up, with glazing, the full width of the ground floor to the protected courtyard brought an air of spaciousness to an otherwise small and compact house. At first floor, 'bay windows' define the two rear bedrooms, the third being at the front of the house over the garage.

Foster Associates, RIBA Publications 1979

"The internal planning of each house responded to the particular needs of the occupants, a doctor with a strong interest in art, a husband and wife who were both barristers, and a skilled trade craftsman. The introduction of top-light and a concern for individual privacy were the major elements of the design."

A view along the dining table, over the worktop balustrade with its built-in planter, towards the sunken living room of one of the Murray Mews houses. The quarry tile finish was carried through from the inner front wall across all the concrete surfaces of the kitchen, including the balustrade/planter and table.

Looking down from the second floor studio gallery up under the ridge of the patent glazing roof. The tile finish to the front wall ground floor cupboard and appliance housings was angled up to meet the foot of the glass roof.

The Early Years
by John Walker

John Walker is a quantity surveyor now based in Vancouver where he is senior principal of Hanscomb Canada. He joined Hanscomb in 1961, two years after graduating from London's Northern Polytechnic. With them he was to act as quantity surveyor on all of Team 4's projects and, later, many of the early projects of both Foster Associates and Richard Rogers & Partners. He emigrated to Canada in 1967, but after one year returned to work in London. He moved to North America permanently in 1976 to work in Chicago and Ottawa before finally settling in Vancouver in 1979.

Writing about someone you knew well and worked with at length, who has since achieved fame, is an interesting task. Particularly if, as I did, you moved half-a-world away just at the onset of his success. I have watched with interest from afar as the ever-widening circles of reputation have finally reached my new home. Now, on the west coast of Canada, I bask in reflected glory because I once worked closely with Norman Foster, whose name today is a household word. At least, that is, among the architects, bankers and Hong Kong emigrés with which Vancouver abounds.

Almost all of the projects in this book were engineered by Tony Hunt and had the Hanscomb Partnership (or, more specifically, myself) as quantity surveyor. Many of them also had mechanical installations designed by Loren Butt.

This group came together in the Team 4 and early Foster Associates days by a process of trial and error. We were none of us, the first members of our particular specialities to work with Norman, but each of us happened into the group in his turn and, for a decade or so, we stuck together.

That we did so resulted from a number of factors. We were roughly similar in age. We were at a similar stage in our careers. Each had a greater than average interest in disciplines other than his own.

Architects who believed that buildings could be economical, as well as elegant, were not unique but, at that time, they were unusual. So too, were engineers who believed that stable, inelegant structures represented a different, but no less important, kind of structural failure. For my part, a real interest in both architecture and engineering meant suggestions for savings were much more likely to be accepted by other members of the team.

All of which, taken together, made it exciting, challenging and fun to be part of the group. Few things stimulate humans more strongly than pride in being a member of a winning team and there was, in this group, a strong sense from the beginning of being involved in something new and vital in the world of the built environment. As a result, work no longer seemed entirely like work and sessions which continued late into the night competed readily with rival attractions such as the pub, the cinema or even, sometimes, the family.

Strong reinforcement of this *esprit de corps* came in the form of architectural rewards. It was not unique to produce buildings which were completed on time and within their clients' budgets, although a depressingly large number of projects failed in this. It was, if not unique, then very nearly so, to achieve these ends while winning praise from the buildings' occupants and awards for the excellence of their architecture.

Perhaps not surprisingly, it is for me the combination of excellence and economy which gives the great sense of pride in looking back at these projects. Even with unlimited resources it is easy to produce garbage. To produce cheap garbage is even easier. But to have been part of the team which achieved this level of excellence at these all-time low prices is something really worth remembering.

The close working relationship which evolved between Norman, Tony Hunt, Loren Butt and me was an example of teamwork at its best. As a group we had a strongly questioning attitude. Respect for one another's abilities grew as time went by, but it was respect which was earned by a willingness to accept that any opinion would probably be challenged and must be successfully defended.

While each was a specialist, he had also a reasonable working knowledge of all the other disciplines. No one felt inhibited about challenging an expert's preconception and often those challenges caused the expert to re-examine his own point of view. The result was seldom that he agreed completely with the challenger but often that an entirely novel concept emerged. Most of the innovative thinking which is evident in the designs of that period emerged as a result of this 'brainstorming' approach.

But in the early 1960s success was far from assured. Norman, then a part of Team 4, was faced with the new architect's old problem — until you have done it, no one will trust you to do it. Catch 22, so you have to cheat a little. On a certain day a potential client arrived at Team 4's office and was sufficiently impressed to award a commission. He did not know that the 'draughtsmen' he saw included a number of friends (myself among them), and that the sound of typing from the adjoining room was

Hilary, my wife, pretending to be a specifications department. He certainly didn't know that under the conference table was a bed, hastily boxed in and covered with white plastic the previous weekend. Note the vague date. He probably still doesn't know.

Even then the key to success was there, however. First and foremost, determination: Norman absolutely refused to be satisfied with anything less than the best. Not necessarily the most expensive, for those early buildings were built within rigorous cost limits. But the best solution that could possibly be found given the resources available. Best because nothing was accepted without being challenged and challenged and challenged again. Talented designers, yes, but that alone would not have been enough. It was the determination to keep trying long after others would have said 'good enough' that proved decisive.

Of course, this did have its negative side. A certain bricklayer's labourer, who had distributed about a thousand bricks in neat, orderly piles ready to be laid, was not pleased when a better, cheaper brick was found. He wheeled them back up the hill to the road. He replaced them with neat, orderly piles of the new bricks. Alas, it was not the end. An even better, cheaper brick appeared. The labourer paused to speak with me as he struggled up the hill. "If that .... architect changes his .... mind one more .... time, I'm going to stick these .... bricks up his .... *sideways*."

Perhaps the most memorable building from the early years was Reliance Controls. Winner of the first ever Financial Times Award for Industrial Architecture, it was a first in many other ways as well. The structure was clean, simple and elegant. It was also repetitive, lean and very carefully engineered to cover the space at the most economical possible cost. The cladding spanned clear from the structure above to the slab beneath, an unusually economical arrangement. Drains were carefully grouped in certain predetermined areas so that, everywhere else, the simple floor slabs could be laid quickly and on undisturbed ground. The entire rear elevation was clad in a low-cost glazing system, the metal support bars carefully positioned so that the balance between their cost and that of the sheets of glass was optimised to an overall minimum.

There is no doubt that Norman's later buildings are more spectacular but the spare economy of Reliance still compares favourably with the best of them.

In 1967 I spent a year in Canada. I returned to discover that, alas, Norman and Richard had agreed to part company and Team 4 was no more. Foster Associates, consisting only of Norman and Wendy was one of the two spin-offs. It had but one commission: the conversion of an old house into three or four apartments. Not an exciting architectural opportunity but, when it was complete, a project marked with special attention to detail and determination to 'do it better', which was to continue to distinguish Norman's later work.

Norman's response to difficulties stands him apart from the common herd. For example, when it proved impossible to find the kind of curtain wall he wanted for the Olsen building at Millwall Dock in England, he jumped on a plane to America. While most of us would have been bogged down with doubt about whether the client would pay for such a trip, Norman simply went. To him, it did not matter whether he was reimbursed. He went and got what he needed, then argued later. To this day, I do not know whether the expenses were recovered. I do know, however, that photographs of that wall, or the reflections on it, were priceless to the practice. The same wall was used on IBM Cosham, with similar results. The commissions which resulted from the success of those buildings alone paid for innumerable trips.

He also has excellent instincts for discovering what will be acceptable to a particular client, and the necessary powers of persuasion to make his intuitive judgment come true. The idea of housing Computer Technology in an air tent while building a new facility for them was not, as I recall, Norman's. But, without his instinct that *this* client would accept such a concept or his persuasiveness in selling the idea, I doubt that it would ever have happened. The ability to recognise that an idea's time has come is perhaps more important in the innovative process than the spark which produces the concept in the first place.

IBM Cosham is an object lesson in the art of 'more for less'. The basic building is very cheap. A simple short-span shed with a flat, low-cost roof and packaged, roof-mounted, air-conditioning units was the cheapest possible way of protecting its occupants from the

elements. Adding high-quality carpet and lighting made it feel luxurious. The deep-plan concept made the unusually beautiful curtain wall affordable. The money saved by floating a flat slab over a rubbish dump with no pad foundations but a lightly loaded raft was spent on these 'where it shows' items and the result was a resounding success in commercial as well as architectural terms.

No cranes were used. The structure was light enough to erect using rubber-tyred fork-lift trucks. No digging. The flat ground slab had some extra mesh reinforcement under the columns and the short-span structure imposed such light loads that even the poor bearing capacity of the old rubbish dump proved adequate to its task.

Grouping the lavatories and other services requiring below-slab drainage, and collecting rainwater by horizontal pipework in the roof space with strictly limited drops to floor level, made it possible to lay many thousands of square feet of floor slab quickly, economically and without interruption.

Many of these design concepts came about as a direct result of the desire to achieve more for less cost and some were my ideas. But whatever contribution I made to the success of Foster Associates was amply repaid. Partly directly by fees, of course, and partly by pride in the results. But also in less direct ways.

Norman and Wendy were exceptionally generous by nature. For several months, when penniless and first married, Hilary and I sat in style on two of their Eames chairs. When, slightly less penniless but still decidedly hard up, we arrived back in England after our first stay in Canada, we bombed around London, free of charge, for several months in the Fosters' Land Rover.

Alas, Wendy is gone and her infectious laugh is heard no more. Without her, Norman has said, he would have been nothing. Personally, I doubt that. Without in any way undervaluing her contribution, I believe that Norman would have succeeded. But it matters not. What is important is that he continues as she would have wished. And succeeds.

Wates Housing
Coulsdon
Surrey

Wates Built Homes Ltd, a housing development and contracting company, had secured an option on 69 acres of suburban backland for housing development at Coulsdon in Surrey, 35 minutes by train from the centre of London. The site was well covered with trees, bounded by existing paths and divided by a steep bank, with a maximum drop of nearly 12 feet, running north-south across its centre. These were topographical challenges that ruled out conventional off-the-peg developer's housing.

Wates had their own architects' department but decided that in this instance they needed innovative architectural advice. Ken Bland, the company's chief architect, interviewed a number of firms of which Team 4 were by far the youngest and the least experienced. As a result of the interview, however, Richard Rogers, and Wendy and Norman Foster were granted an audience with Ken Bland and Neil Wates who asked their advice on how Wates should tackle the Coulsdon site.

Norman Foster recalls: "We suggested there and then that they should seek out Atelier 5 in Switzerland and see their Siedlung Halen housing near Berne. This caused an exchange of surprised looks — they had planned to do that anyway". The outcome was that Team 4 were engaged as architectural consultants, to produce an overall feasibility study for the whole site, suitable for outline planning submission, together with detailed proposals for a small pilot scheme. A landscape architect and, interestingly, a sociologist were also appointed, and Atelier 5 were asked to advise on the pilot scheme. Like the Siedlung Halen scheme, which was completed in 1961, Team 4's pilot studies proposed a high-density solution with the houses arranged in terraces on either side of a central hard-landscaped parking court. And like their earlier waterfront housing in Cornwall, the houses were 'dug-in' to the sloping site, with cars and pedestrians segregated so that the paths on the estate could be kept free of wheeled traffic.

For the overall masterplan, the existing landscape features were, as far as possible, preserved or manipulated to achieve a strikingly well-ordered site layout. A densely wooded strip running along the centre of the site was

Norman Foster's own sketches illustrate the textural qualities planned for the Coulsdon scheme. At the meeting point of two brick-faced terraces, a ramp leads up, separating pedestrians from the vehicle access to covered parking below. This segregation was maintained along the paved pedestrian walkways that give access to each house's private courtyard entrance, where children might play.

"The Team 4 scheme
pays unusually close at-
tention to the disposi-
tion of families and their
vehicles on a residential
site with the result that
their design suggests
what is really a new
architectural form for
a housing estate."

Architectural Design
Project Award, 1965

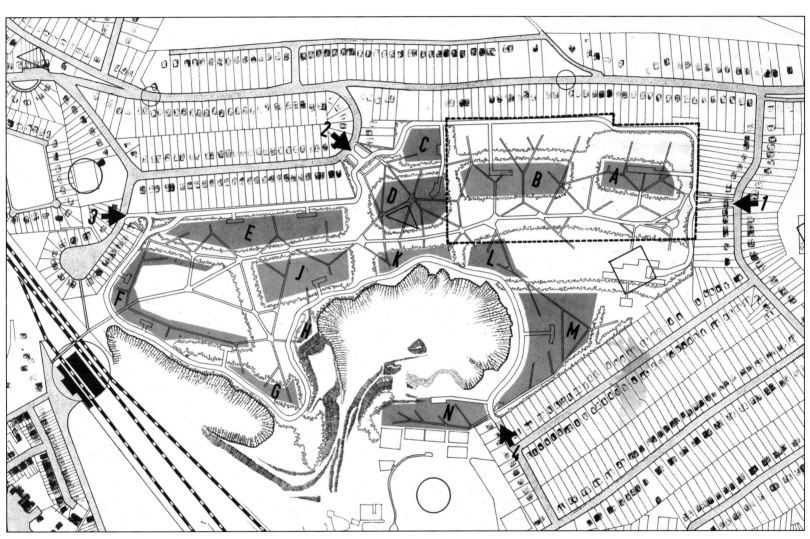

The Wates master plan of the Coulsdon development, with the Team 4 study area at top right enclosed by a dotted line. Throughout the site the existing landscape features were to have been retained. The densely wooded strip running across the middle of the plan was to have been developed as a pedestrian spine crisscrossed with diagonal footpaths leading to the housing terraces. As can be seen, vehicle circulation was to be confined to a perimeter road accessed at the arrowed and numbered points shown on the plan. Access to the covered parking courts at the very centre of each pair of terraces was to be by small feeder roads with vehicle speeds kept low by the use of cattle grids.

retained and developed as a pedestrian spine with a network of paths running through it, shorter spurs leading off this to each of the, more or less, self-contained housing areas. Interconnecting open spaces accommodated children's play areas and allowed a richer variety of walks through the trees together with more direct routes to the local railway station, bus-stops, schools and shops.

Vehicles were confined to a road running around the edge of the site with smaller feeder roads giving off at strategic points into the centre of the housing clusters. The four major entry points into the site were conceived as 'locks' where cars would be slowed down by cattle grids to 5 mph and then allowed to pick

up speed on the peripheral road to about 25 mph. Frequent bends in this road were intended to discourage drivers from speeding.

In conceptual terms, this organisation can be seen as analogous to Louis Kahn's 1956-1962 plan for the centre of Philadelphia, where traffic-carrying streets were thought of as 'rivers' or 'canals' and parking areas became 'harbours' or 'docks'. Other routes were freed of cars and given over to pedestrians, the two

"The scheme attempts to
take advantage of the
sense of community in-
herent in high densities,
whilst giving at the
same time good privacy
and pleasant outlooks
for the individual
houses."

Foster Associates, RIBA
Publications 1979

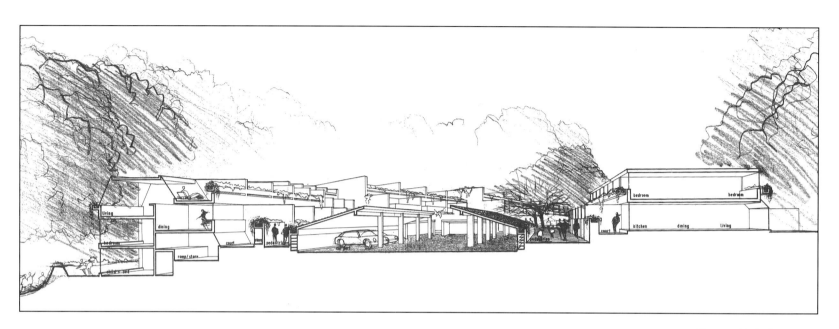

Norman Foster's per-
spective section shows
double terraces stepping
down the site, separated
by a central covered
parking area. A sketch
of the pedestrian walk-
way between the upper
housing block and
garages appears on the
previous page.

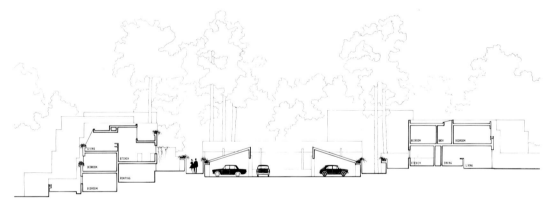

Different solutions had
to be found to accom-
modate the compound
fall across the site
which, from north to
south, reached a max-
imum of 3.5 metres.
Certain house designs
incorporated stepped
sections that would
benefit directly from the
slope.

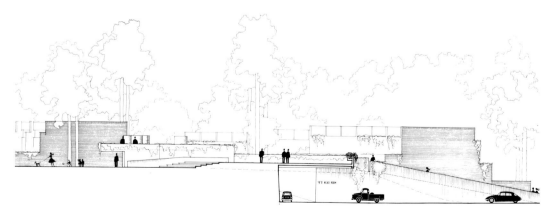

Where the fall was suffi-
cient, cuts were made so
that vehicular access
could be kept at a lower
level, thereby creating a
safer and more pleasant
environment for the
pedestrians above.

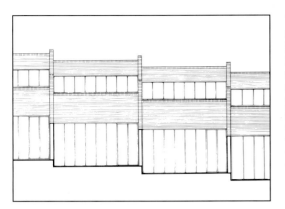

Typical elevations for the two-storey Wates houses. As later at Radlett, narrow frontages with cross-wall construction would have permitted large glazed areas. The separation of vehicular accommodation freed up the entire facade and diminished the problem of gradient.

Norman Foster's sketch of the interior of the ground floor of an upper terrace level house at Coulsdon, with its private walled garden beyond the living area.

types of movement being separated from one another not for speed of travel but for order and convenience.

Forming the vehicular route from the peripheral road to the parking area for the first two housing clusters involved excavating a cutting into the land bank, above which was a pedestrian viewing platform reached by a ramp. After this initial level separation, the segregation of cars and pedestrian routes was maintained horizontally by screened alleyways. This arrangement allowed cars to feed into the heart of the scheme and be parked close to each front door, while making convenient use of the 70-foot statutory open space required between facing terraces. The terrace layout was deliberately open-ended so that it could be easily extended or built incrementally.

Wates' original intention was to begin development by building the pilot scheme on an approximately nine-acre plot that incorporated two clearings in the south-east corner of the site. Altogether, 10 such clearings existed, each defined by surrounding woodland. The initial phase was to have comprised 131 houses with one garage or parking space per house, together with additional visitors' parking and a communal clubhouse which was to be run by a residents' association.

There were two main house types, the first of two storeys and three bedrooms, the second of three storeys and three to four bedrooms. Both were traditionally constructed with flat roofs and aimed at middle-income families. The two-storey house was conventionally planned with living accommodation on the ground floor and bedrooms above. The living rooms opened on to a private garden with the woodland beyond. The kitchens overlooked a paved entrance court and the vehicle parking area.

The three-storey house stepped in section following the natural bank, with a split-level living space at the top. This gave on to a private terrace, allowing residents to feel close to the trees on the wooded side. As in the smaller house, the kitchen looked down into the entrance courtyard. The dining area was located in the double-height zone generated between the kitchen and the sitting room, which was situated on the half level above it.

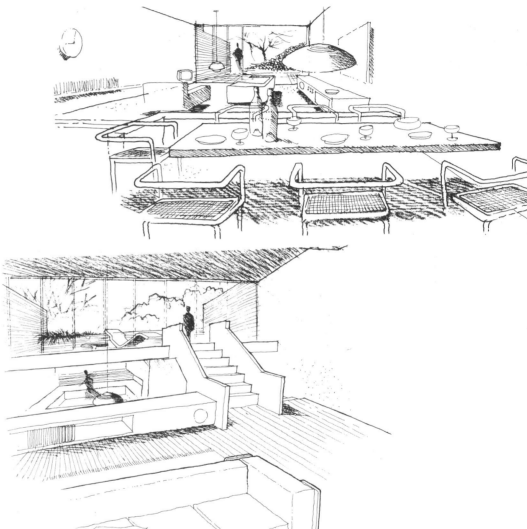

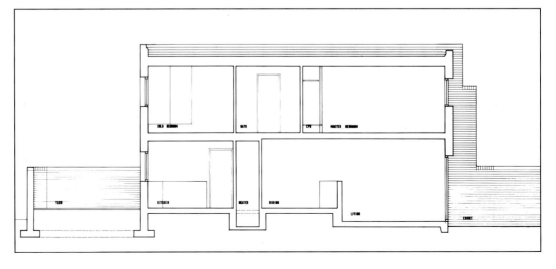

In its final form, the pilot scheme accommodated 130 houses. The terraces would not have been extendable as access roads were intended to cut through north and south creating a self-contained area.

The pilot scheme was to have been built on a 9-acre plot consisting of two large clearings. The optimum use of these clearings, together with the retention of as many trees as possible, led to the general arrangement of four east-west facing terraces as shown in this site model.

The site model for the pilot scheme looking south along the line of terraces. The three-storey houses lower down the slope to the right would have enjoyed excellent views together with privacy. The higher two-storey houses to the left of the picture would have been isolated from existing housing by trees.

Spatially the upper floors of these houses had much of the free-flowing quality of Skybreak house, an impression that comes across clearly in Norman Foster's perspective sketches. And, as again at Skybreak house, the influence of Chermayeff's planning theories is apparent, with a clear hierarchy of spaces leading from the public to private realms.

Below the living space, the bedroom floors again worked on the half level, with the children's bedrooms occupying the lowest level, giving them direct access into the back garden on one side and the entrance courtyard on the other. Organising the house into parent and child domains allowed for mutual privacy and a degree of independence, including the possibility of converting the lower floor into a separate flat for teenagers or an elderly relative.

The elevational treatment of the terraces reinforced the conceptual progression from communal 'hard' areas, via private entrance courts to the houses and out on to the 'soft' gardens facing the woodland. On the hard side the windows were treated as holes punched in the red brick walls, reflecting a defensible, mews-like urban character; while on the garden side the glazing stretched in horizontal bands from party-wall to party-wall, opening up the living spaces to sunlight and views.

Wates were granted outline planning permission in April 1965 but decided not to proceed with the Team 4 scheme. Norman Foster feels that Wates "were not really the right client", noting that "traditional housing developer values prevailed, with the respectable minimum of safe experiment". There was also some behind-the-scenes resistance to the Team 4 proposals from Wates' in-house architects, despite Ken Bland's early involvement and approval. In the end, the result was not so much losing a job — as Foster has since explained, "there was never really one there to lose".

David Jenkins

"The design is based on a clear progression from public and communal 'hard' areas, through private access courts to the houses, and on to gardens facing the woodlands. The house types respond to this concept in having small windows to the urban elevations and full glazing to the gardens. The scheme takes advantage of a sense of community whilst giving at the same time good privacy and pleasant outlooks for the individual houses."

Extract from the assessors' report for the Architectural Design Project Award, 1965

An early presentation drawing of the pilot scheme with the same central vehicle access arrangement as the Foster sketch on page 70, together with an increased number of setbacks in the rows of houses and a more pronounced angling of the terraces themselves.

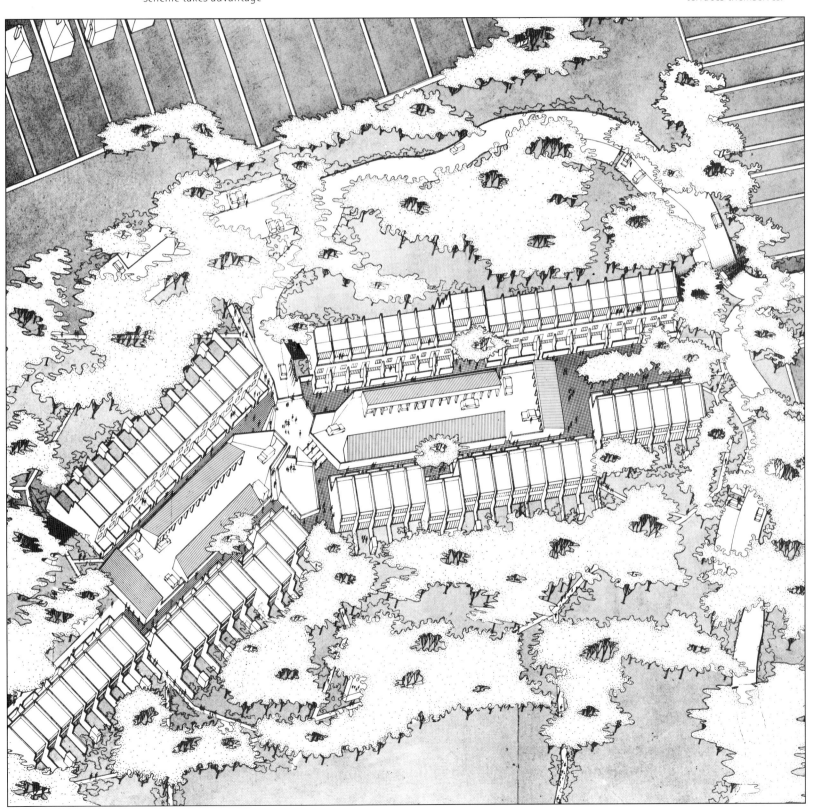

1965-1966 Skybreak House
Radlett
Hertfordshire

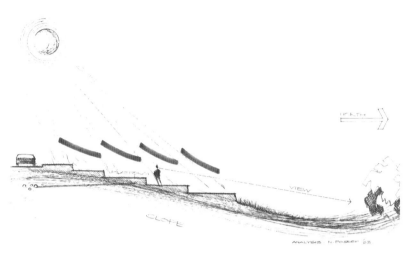

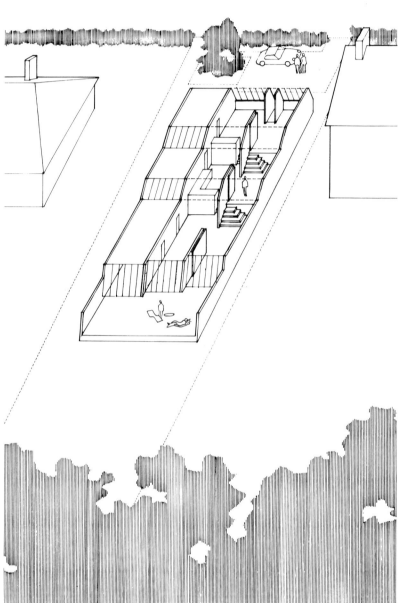

Norman Foster's own sketch analysis of the design of Skybreak house. Sunlight from the south is 'captured' by rooflights in an echelon roof, the house otherwise exploiting the Green Belt view to the north. Even in diagrammatic form the possibilities for terraced housing (later taken up in the high-density housing project) can be clearly seen.

The type of stepped house envisaged for the Cornish waterfront housing project was developed individually in the Skybreak house at Radlett, although on a gentler slope that allowed all of its rooms to be disposed as open-plan stages on terraces within a single continuous space. That each level in the house could thus be top-lit by skylights doubtless gave rise to its name.

Skybreak was simpler in format than Creek Vean, for its site offered none of the vantages and views that so invited articulation and drama from its designers. Instead, the location was a gentle, north-facing slope on to a dry, shallow dell at the edge of an incipient suburb. A straggle of detached houses had begun along the road, to which Team 4 reacted much as they did at Feock, with a study for an extension of the Skybreak unit into a continuous range of terraced houses, an idea later developed more fully in the high-density housing project.

Skybreak exploits the elementary ranging of the house between two parallel walls which could easily become party-dividers between adjoining neighbours. But while the low, single-storey profile and sloping, glazed end-walls might be considered unusual in its suburban setting, the real innovations at Skybreak are found on the inside. Here is a conception of living based not only on an open plan but also on a level of flexibility that facilitates change.

This axonometric drawing by Norman Foster illustrates the dauntingly suburban surroundings. The three levels of the stepped, slope-hugging section of the house are divided into three parallel planning zones, each defined by structural brick walls but with different degrees of internal openness.

The lowest level of the living room, at the foot of the long, stepped 'domestic' zone of the house that terminates in the sloping glass north wall. To the right a sliding door is open to reveal the children's playroom.

The inclined timber-framed glass walls that form the north elevation of Skybreak house. The three planning zones are defined by the staggered planes of glazing. Sliding doors permit entry and exit from the central zone.

With its piano placed in front of the north-facing window, the three stepped levels of the domestic zone take on the role of tiers in a theatre. Minimal balustrades ensure a clear view the full length of the house.

With its flat roof and single level stepping down the hill, Skybreak house presents an astonishingly low profile quite at variance with the suburban surroundings. In this early design tall triangular rooflights were proposed.

Skybreak gave rise to radical experiments and, as Richard Rogers indicates in his introductory essay in this volume, initiated thoughts on interior space that would be explored with increasing rigour in his own and Norman Foster's later work.

The Jaffés, who commissioned the house, had asked for a place that could be adapted to a variety of uses, for both family and social occasions, and which could be extended easily as required. Additionally, an arrangement was envisaged whereby the kitchen could overlook a play area. With regard to the best use of site and sunlight, a solution consistent with Team 4's work elsewhere clearly suggested itself: the separation of illuminant and outlook functions in the disposition of windows that had first appeared at the Henrion studio. An early sketch by Norman Foster shows how a section of stepped terraces was conceived with a view north to the field, while sunlight fell from above and behind through breaks in an echelon roof. Such a drawing makes no definite indications as to planning, but it does imply certain possibilities. One is of great length and extensibility — indeed, the echelon skylight roof is an industrial form developed for assembly shops and production lines. Another possibility would be of rooms without lateral windows, a form characteristic of museums and art galleries. Skybreak transferred the form, however, to that of a home.

An initial division by two parallel walls running the length of the space was made the tool for this transference, creating three linear

A model of Skybreak house showing the triangular rooflight system applied differentially across the three planning zones. The vertical glass elements were intended to reflect light passing through the angled panes down into the interior.

Norman Foster's drawing of the configuration of the brick side walls at Skybreak house. Built at the same time as Murray Mews, these two projects, in fact, mark the last designs by Foster that incorporated brickwork. With the abandonment of the triangular rooflights the design was not changed; instead, the rooflights were angled north following the slope of the roof over the stepped sections of the plan.

Unprepossessing in appearance, the entrance at the highest point of the site consists of a vertical front door recessed into a sloping timber glazing frame above a dwarf brick wall.

The plan of the house is an application of Chermayeff's theories in their simplest form, the three linear zones moving from a 'public' domestic area, through a 'semi-private' family zone, to the total privacy of the bedrooms. Different areas are defined solely by the stepped section.

1 entrance lobby
2 study
3 dining room
4 living room
5 conservatory
6 kitchen
7 playroom
8 guest suite
9 utility room
10 main bedrooms
11 children's bedrooms
12 terrace

zones on plan. The eastern side, or zone, is devoted to a series of closed rooms for sleeping, washing and utility. The west side is one continuous open space, a domestic concourse in three terraced stages. Two flights of three spreading steps each connect the stages. The upper two stages are square and the lowest, leading through sliding windows to patio and garden, a double square. These were designated for study, dining and living respectively. At the far end of the lowest stage, a piano was placed before the window, so that the upper two terraces, with their balcony rails, were put in the role of the tiers in a theatre. In a house designed expressly with the aim of entertaining guests, this is a role they must have often assumed, at least informally.

This facility for social occasion does not end there, for the wall which divides this continuous space from the house's central area can be opened by three sliding doors, connecting the study to a conservatory, dining room to a kitchen, and the living room to a playroom. This middle channel also descends by steps, but it is neither as open as the living room areas nor as closed as the bedroom side. The kitchen worktop is placed like a console to overview the play area, while built-in oven and fridge, as at Creek Vean, are placed behind.

A low wall separates the kitchen from the conservatory behind, but again this can be reached by three narrow steps. With access in four directions to playroom, dining room, conservatory and the outside, through a utility

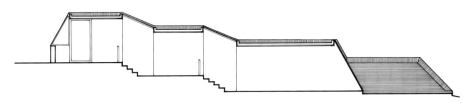

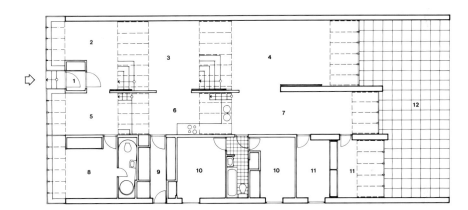

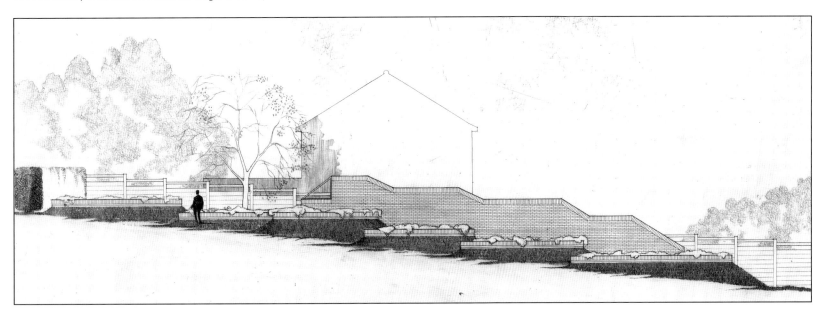

"It is an aesthetic experience to progress down through the main space of this house from platform to platform, through alternating areas of brightness, from the top glazing, and shade, always with the view to the green countryside opening up as one approaches the lowest level."

Richard Einzig, *Classic Modern Houses in Europe,* Architectural Press 1981

Looking up into the kitchen from the playroom in the central 'family' zone of the house. The narrow steps are repeated leading up from the kitchen to a small conservatory at the top of the house. To the right of the dividing wall are broader steps connecting the different levels of the domestic zone.

room, and with oblique views to study and living rooms, the kitchen is not just the physical centre of the house but, again as at Creek Vean, its master (or mistress) vantage-point.

At Skybreak the bedroom walls are nonstructural to allow for change, and indeed the whole house presents implications of thorough flexibility that were subsequently explored by both Norman Foster and Richard Rogers; implications that would lead rapidly away from wetbuild methods and heavy structures towards prefabrication, light metal frames and panels, and transferred technologies. Interesting and noteworthy here is that such innovations were prompted less in the pursuit of maximised production of unit modules, than by a desire to refine and tune up the quality and controllability of individual environments.

That controllability is indeed remarkable in a building that, contrary to appearances, is really quite small. As the Jaffé family grew, however, the possibility for extension was not taken up. Instead they decided to move and, for a while, Norman Foster seriously contemplated moving there with his own young family.

A view from the highest level of Skybreak house down through the open-plan domestic zone, with its white painted walls and successive wooden floors, to the sloping glass wall giving on to the tiled terrace and the garden beyond.

"Skybreak achieved a rather non-architectural fame in that its interior was used for some of the scenes of 'ultra-violence' in the film *A Clockwork Orange*. But Stanley Kubrick, the director, was not interested in the outside so he cheated by implying that the house had a different traditional exterior."

Bryan Appleyard, *Richard Rogers,* Faber & Faber 1986

The quantity and quality of top-light present at Skybreak confirm that the projecting skylights of the early scheme might have been less essential to the concept than they first appeared. Though the strips of rooflight are relatively small, the house is suffused with light.

A view from the lowest living room level, with the piano now moved away from the window. The timber double-sided steps connect the three areas of the domestic zone allowing the occupants to negotiate the 1-metre height difference between levels comfortably.

Painted tubular-steel handrails at the edges of the two upper levels in the domestic areas enhance the resemblance of the space to an auditorium, and lead the eye to the lowest level.

For both Foster and Rogers, Skybreak is a favourite of the early projects and can now be seen as a major turning point. Together with Murray Mews (being built at the same time) it was the last of the domestic projects. Unlike Creek Vean with its multiple views, Skybreak enjoyed only one major external aspect. Rogers and Foster therefore looked inward and created their own self-contained environment of changing spaces and views. The lessons were learnt and were to serve both architects well as together and, later, separately they pursued the development of ever larger and more complex deep-section buildings.

Brian Hatton

Forest Road Annexe
East Horsley
Surrey

One of the more unusual projects Team 4 designed and built was an annexe to the house of Wendy Foster's mother at Forest Road in East Horsley, Surrey. The plan is formed of five interlocking rectangles in echelon, containing a single apartment and, separate at the far end, a garage.

Here the aspect of a serial minimalism, at least in the most publicised view of the scheme, is striking enough to prompt the question of influence. In the same year, 1966, Don Judd and Robert Smithson were exhibiting staggered arrays of prismatic blank volumes. Smithson would go on, in his essay 'Entropy and the New Monuments' to describe such echelons of low-order structures ("the much-derided glass boxes of Park Avenue") in terms of timelessness and infinitude, as specimens of a pervasive industrial sublime. Certainly, that one published image of the project, devoid as it is of window or door, defeats any sense of measure. Only the texture of the bricks evident in the walls indicates the scale.

In fact, the annexe is a modest suburban extension. The main house was altered to open up its plan and perimeter by glazed walls, but rather than extending its older fabric, with attendant problems of compatibility, a radical alternative was proposed in the form of a new free-standing building. The blank walls are those which face the house (like the blank walls which were to face the earlier Victorian villas at Camden Mews), but the walls facing outwards are pierced at the corners of each step in

A view of the interior of the small apartment in the Forest Road annexe, looking from the kitchen/dining area, to the living room with its glazed doors, to the terrace and garden beyond. Apart from the enigmatic corner window the interior gives no hint of the strangeness of the view from outside.

The relationship of the main house and the separate annexe 'extension' at Forest Road showing the surprising size of the annexe in relation to the more compact main dwelling. The slope of the monopitch can be followed in the diminishing height of the new building's walls.

The project also included a major remodelling of the existing house which, unlike the closed nature of the annexe, included the opening up of much of the ground floor and the addition of an extensive glazed conservatory wrapping round three sides of the building.

the echelon by windows which look out upon trees while respecting neighbouring privacy sightlines.

Contrary to the impression given by the 'minimalist' photograph, the roof is not flat but a continuous monopitch, echoing, in a certain view, the roof-pitch of the main house. In this way the annexe both continues and rejects the 'context' of the older house, and the gap between the old and new buildings is sensitised by virtue of asserting a clean break, in much the way that Modernist painting and sculpture since Cézanne has dealt in reversing the notion of *gestalt*, affording voids as much stress as solids and replacing composition by a configuration of tensions.

For those familiar only with the stereotype of a 'High-Tech' Norman Foster (or Richard Rogers), the variety of qualities and concerns in these early works may come as a surprise. A range of lyric figures is to be found at work here which, if at times since appears repressed in favour of that rigorous concentration required to reach precision and refinement, in fact continues to inform and organise a concept of design far broader than the purely 'technical'. Moreover, we may find in these early works a genetic resource to be returned to, as well as the promise of reanimations yet to come.

Brian Hatton

The best known view of Forest Road taken from the lawn at the back of the main house. Its forced perspective is enhanced by the decreasing height of the windowless brick parapet walls in response to the roof slope behind them.

The plan of the main house and annexe illustrates the divorced relationship between the annexe garage, which serves the house, and the rest of the building which is effectively a self-contained flat with its own small terrace garden.

Previous page: A single structural bay of the electronics factory for Reliance Controls. The elegant simplicity of the design and its immaculate detailing belie the fact that this was Team 4's (and engineer Tony Hunt's) first steel-structured building.

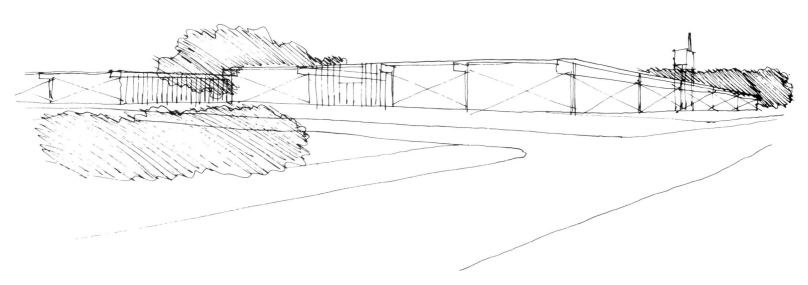

As Norman Foster's drawings indicate, the original design proposed a series of pavilions, linked by plant rooms positioned over a continuous underfloor service duct. Despite the building's success only the 3200 sq m first phase was built.

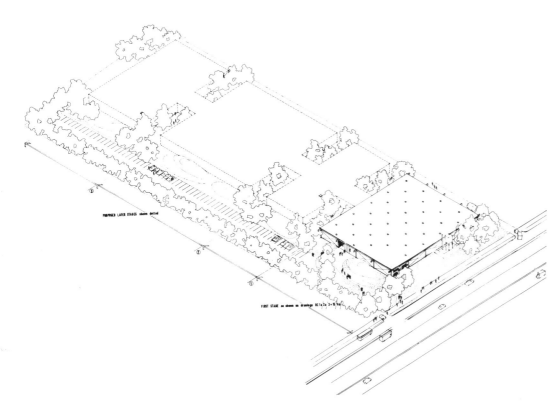

In Norman Foster's development as an architect, Reliance Controls occupies a pivotal position. It was the first industrial project for both Team 4 and engineer Tony Hunt, who had long worked closely together, and also their biggest project to date. At the same time it allowed Foster and Hunt to establish a working method that would develop significantly, involving them in the detailing of the project to an extent which later schemes would elaborate on in ever-more complex ways. A true notion of teamwork was established. It was also to be Team 4's last major building before the practice split up.

In its appearance and its philosophy, Reliance Controls made a decisive break with Team 4's preceding designs, and set out most, if not all, of the themes that have since dominated Norman Foster's work. To Richard Rogers, Reliance was a matter of "shaking off Yale" — and with it the massy, sculptural east coast approach of Rudolph and Chermayeff — and taking on board the lighter influences he and Foster had experienced on the other coast of America: most notably the Eames, Craig Ellwood and Case Study houses, and Ezra Ehrenkrantz's SCSD schools.

For Norman Foster, whose philosophy is developed more in the act of making, the reasons are subtly different. Foster recalls that it was the economic realities of the project — the need for speed and flexibility — that forced the change of building methods, and only as the scheme developed were the full benefits of these appreciated and taken up with enthusiasm. Which ever line is taken, it is clear that before Reliance the work of Rogers and Foster had been characterised by individual houses painstakingly put together 'brick on brick': after Reliance the emphasis shifted to industrial and commercial buildings and fast, mechanised construction. Before, it was a case of fighting the limitations of modern craftsmanship; after, it was getting the best out of modern technology.

Reliance Controls was the first built example of a diagram that recurs again and again in Norman Foster's work, the lightweight shed enclosing a simple space which rests on a well-serviced ground slab. The new terminal at Stansted and the Sainsbury Centre are among the most obvious later examples. Foster himself likes to emphasise the integration of structure and services, "the synergetic relationship between the different parts", for example in the way fluorescent lighting was run within the troughs of the corrugated decking, so that reflectors were unnecessary. It was a simple idea proposed for its economy, but the end result appears unified and effortless. Again, practical realities generated a way of thinking that, only with time, developed into a solid philosophy. Just as importantly, Reliance was also the first manifestation of the ideals of industrial democracy that Foster was to develop with the later projects for Fred Olsen and at Willis Faber & Dumas.

Reliance Controls was absolutely anti-hierarchical, with no differentiation between facilities for management and workforce, whether architectural, structural, or decorative. As at Willis Faber & Dumas, but a decade earlier, everything was to be shared equally by all employees. Instead of a management building standing separately in front of an

The front elevation of Reliance Controls. Of extreme simplicity it consisted of five 12-metre painted steelwork bays with diagonal steel bracing, and a sculptural steel water tower and flue intended as a homage to the Smithsons' Hunstanton School.

The building's main entrance took up one full bay of the west elevation, clearly identified by its full-height glazing. With its plastic-coated corrugated steel cladding and white-painted stanchions, beams and cross-bracing, the building was otherwise astonishingly discreet, even anonymous. Initially, there was not even a sign.

industrial shed, there was a uniform structural grid, subdivided by glass partitions into its separate functions and arranged in such a way that both offices and assembly areas were visible from the reception space. Through planning and construction a single workforce, company and building identity was achieved.

The motivation behind this identity was architectural and spatial as well as social, and worked itself out through all aspects of the building. It was a building that was determined not to have a front or a back, or even a front door where you would expect it to be, for its most prominent elevational features were a water tower and a boiler flue. The structure was expressed both inside and out, and the same corrugated sheeting was used for both walls and ceilings, so that there was minimal differentiation (at least in the surfaces) between interior and exterior. Reliance Controls

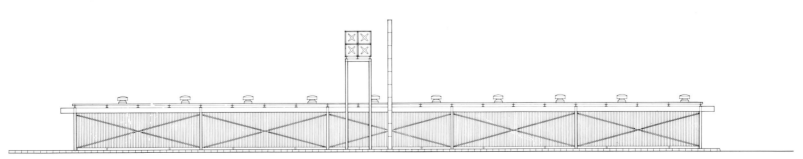

Hidden from the main road, the building's entire north elevation was glazed, full-height glass panels being supported in a minimal frame. Complementary interior glazed partitions allowed daylight to penetrate deep into the workspace. This view, at night, looks into the staff canteen.

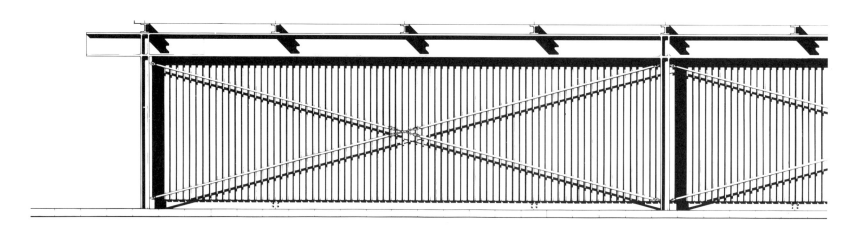

The elegance and simplicity of the elevational treatment is evident in this extended drawing. To the left what appears to be the long projecting end of the heavy steel eaves beam is actually half of one of the prefabricated cross-heads which, together with their stanchions, were erected at the first stage of construction. The beams linking these cross-heads were then lifted and site-welded into position.

was a thorough realisation of the unprejudiced, open-ended space that the modern production line tends to create.

Like earlier modern architects, Team 4 were inspired by the imagery of mass production, but they were more willing to pursue the consequences perhaps because, unlike Mies van der Rohe, they were applying industrial techniques to the construction of a factory. The production line implies incompleteness and infinite extension, while early Modernism tended to be final, conclusive and highly composed. Reliance Controls, which *Casabella* described as "assembly without composition", makes a virtue of this incompleteness.

This incompleteness was intentional, as was the externally placed structure, as the building had to be designed to be linearly extended at will. The first phase constituted only a prototype or principle for what was intended to be a far larger building. The 'schematic plan' that accompanied phase one shows the structural bay repeating itself *ad infinitum* along a central service spine, interspersed by occasional courtyards to introduce light and air. All that was necessary to enlarge

the building was the construction of the new extension alongside the old, removing the separating glass partition at the last possible moment. The interior could be rearranged over a weekend. The building's projecting steel beams and the glass fourth wall of phase one only emphasised this potential for change.

Where a Mies building forbids extension or alteration, Reliance Controls courted it. It also differed from the designs of Mies van der Rohe in allowing its structural parts to develop their own exposed personality and scale, rather than imposing one. Combined with a minimalist desire to make the building of as few separate parts as possible, this attitude produced the familiar and recurring image of the building: an expanse of grass and an expanse of sky mediated by I-section stanchions, a heavy eaves beam, smaller joists, and slender diagonal cross-bracing. In-between are profiled steel cladding panels, used far more ambitiously than their manufacturer originally intended.

The interior of the factory, soon after completion and before it was occupied, looking north through a movable glazed partition to the fully glazed north wall beyond.

Bottom: A detailed drawing by Norman Foster of the courtyard system proposed for the northward extension of the building shown in the sketch on page 86.

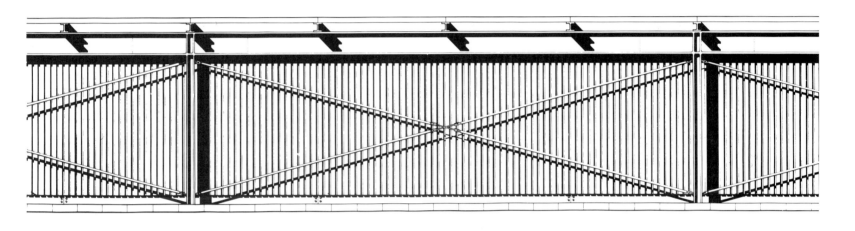

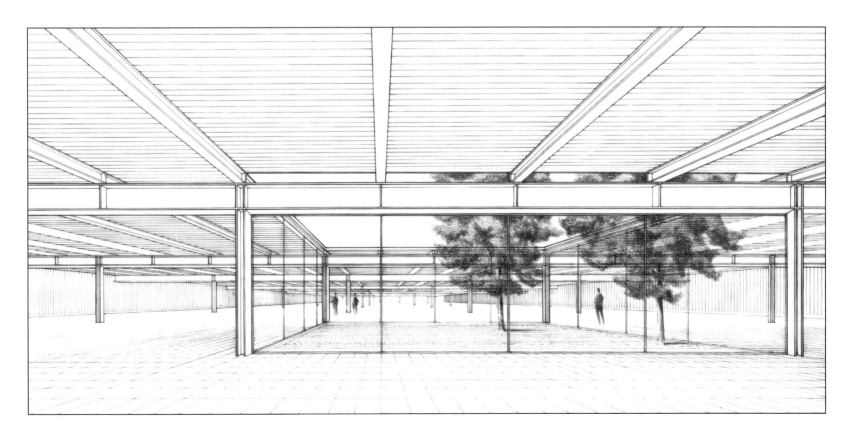

79

The view out from the staff canteen, looking through the full-height glazing of the building's north elevation. Against Norman Foster's wishes the glass was later replaced with solid corrugated panels, much to the detriment of the central working areas.

The entrance lobby was separated from the building's main production area by a simple glass partition. True to Team 4's spirit of equality both management and workforce used the same entrance; identical doors in the lobby, to left and right, gave access to offices and factory respectively.

The main production area spanned the centre of the building and, without rooflights, relied extensively on artificial light. Any sense of enclosure, however, was mitigated by the extensive use of full-height glass partitions and external glazing.

"... on entering it the visitor is immediately aware, even if he has not noticed from the outside (for it is consistent both externally and internally) that he is in a distinguished building. Its uncompromising simplicity and unity of general conception and detailed design create an atmosphere that is not only pervasive but notably comfortable to be in. It is refreshing to find something so beautifully direct that it looks like a lost vernacular."

Extract from the jury's report for the first Financial Times Industrial Architecture Award of 1967.

As with many of Norman Foster's later projects the internal colour scheme is muted, dominated by the white-painted structure and roof panels, and a neutral grey flooring. Accents of colour are provided solely by small signs, various pieces of equipment and the users themselves.

As with the exterior of the building, the internal finishes were reduced to the fewest co-ordinated elements, elegantly detailed and constructed to standards far higher than might be expected in a low-cost factory unit. An integrated design approach — involving the architect, structural and service engineers — allowed considerable savings to be made, best demonstrated by the fluorescent lighting which used the recesses of the roof decking as a reflector; the secondary beams were spaced to allow standard tubes to fit exactly.

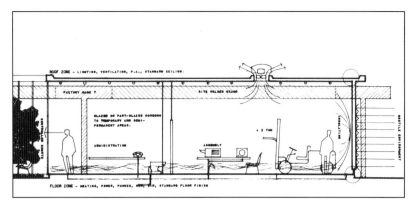

In this diagram, Norman Foster proposed containment of fumes, noise and vibration in the production areas of the building by means of insulated wall panels, head-height screens and powerful roof extract fans.

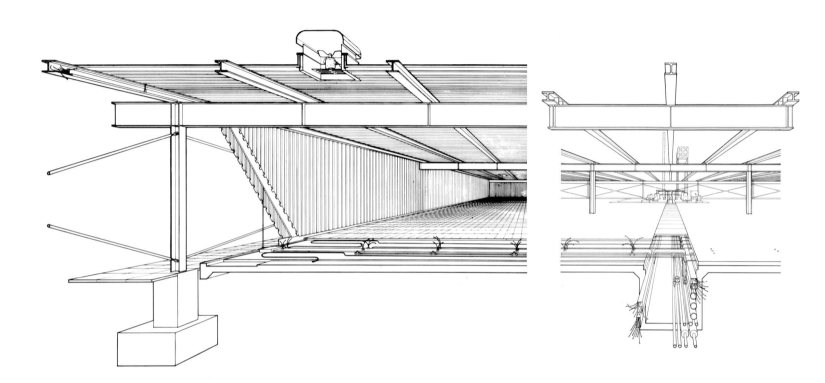

This cut-away sectional perspective looking north up the building's central axis shows all the principal features of its ingenious construction. The main support stanchions stand on short-piled foundations with the power-floated site slab indented along the axis line to provide a deep underfloor service duct. The sandwich cladding panels of the external wall consist of an outer plastic-coated, corrugated steel skin and an inner zinc-coated corrugated skin riveted to enclosed horizontal steel 'Z' sections at 600 mm centres. The internal skin is formed in the same painted, zinc-coated corrugated steel as the exposed roof decking. Because of the double profiling of the wall sandwich panels, and the vertical orientation of both sets of corrugations, the walls span 4 metres vertically from wall plate to eaves beam without intermediate support.

Water pipes from the oil-fired heating system were buried in the concrete ground slab in loops extending out laterally from the central service duct.

The central underfloor service duct carried electrical and telephone wiring, water, gas and heating pipes, and compressed air runs. Nearly 2 metres deep, it permitted running maintenance tasks to be carried out without disturbance to the factory floor.

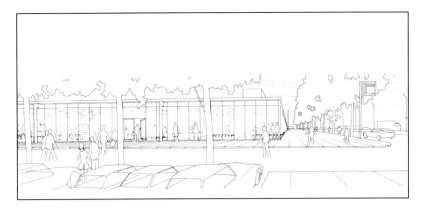

In one early sketch Norman Foster explored the possibility of floor-to-ceiling perimeter glazing similar to that first used at IBM Cosham four years later.

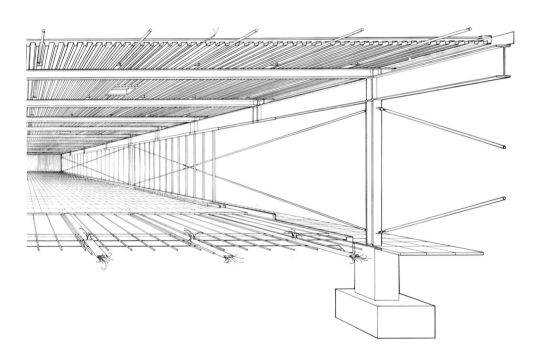

As a companion to the drawings opposite, this north-south section shows the glazed north wall of the building with diagonal bracing seen through the glass. As with the solid panels, the glazing spans unsupported from ground slab to eaves beam. The underfloor heating pipes and the corrugated roof decking are also visible. Like the sandwich wall panels, the profiled, riveted roof decking proved strong enough, when securely fixed to the secondary beams, to act as a stiff diaphragm. Carrying fibreboard insulation, roofing felt and independent fan mountings above, the decking spans 3 metres without intermediate rafters.

It was this simplicity and directness, focused by a stringent budget and a tight programme, that led the jury of the first Financial Times Award for Industrial Architecture to describe the construction of Reliance as a "lost vernacular". However, it was not a vernacular specific to any one place, least of all Swindon, but universal, specific only to a time and a way of making. It differed from previous vernaculars in that it was brought about by the intense inventiveness of and collaboration between architect, structural and mechanical engineers. It was also far from unreflective. Certain details were self-conscious, occasionally expressionist, as in the projecting beam ends which have something of the primitivising quality of an Anthony Caro sculpture.

Reliance Controls created space that was universal and open, held together by a consistency of making and of thought, and rooted in a sophisticated primitivism: a demountable, extensible, primitive hut, but enjoying the advantages of the latest technologies. These ambitions are the precise opposite of those that Post-Modernism was to develop but, given the type and setting of Reliance Controls, are entirely reasonable.

The type is one that is now commonplace, but was then relatively new: a factory for precision electronics in an out-of-town estate or park, a building on a site without history for an activity where history is only an encumbrance. Accordingly, the clients were pleased to be given a building that proclaimed its newness, and broke away from the limiting industrial practices of the past, as well as being on budget and ahead of schedule. Significantly, other companies exploring similar philosophies at the time included Texas Instruments and Hewlett Packard, both American and both concerned with electronics. Certainly Team 4's principals' transatlantic training and outlook can only have been to their advantage in convincing the client of the correctness of their approach.

Reliance Controls valued both the egalitarian social and spatial philosophy, and the quality of thought that permeated the building, down to the purpose-designed furniture, the clean graphics, the consistent white-grey-black aesthetic and the neat black-painted

A detail of the projecting cross-head above one of the corner stanchions. This detail could have been used structurally if it had been possible to extend the building in an east-west direction, but the limitations of the site suggest it was largely an aesthetic feature.

"We all worked non-stop 16 hours a day, six days a week. The client nearly had a nervous breakdown, the contractor almost went bankrupt, but Reliance was a breakthrough. We had found our style."

Richard Rogers, *The Sunday Times*, 27 February 1983

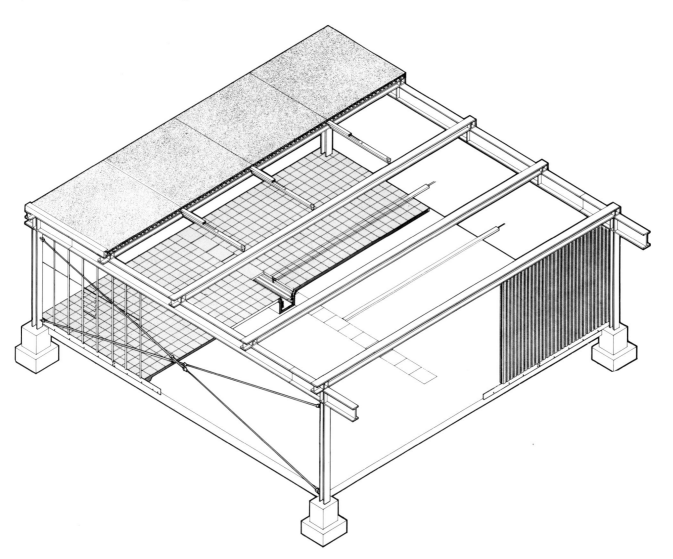

A cut-away axonometric drawing of the welded structural roof framing at Reliance Controls. The main steelwork rests on vertical stanchions at 12-metre centres with the eaves beam crossheads shown here projecting out to the right. Forming a portal structure, these frames then support secondary beams that cut the decking span down to 3 metres. Smaller steel rafters support the fluorescent light tubes and cross these secondaries to form a 3 metre square roofing grid that is finished with insulation and built-up felt. A pvc tile finish completes the concrete floor slab.

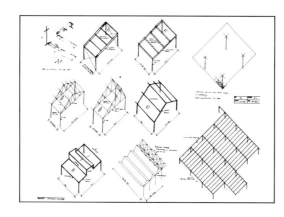

The clarity of the structure meant that many of engineer Tony Hunt's construction drawings could be released as hand-drawn sketches. At left, comparative structural systems for cost analysis; at right, the roof edge condition as built.

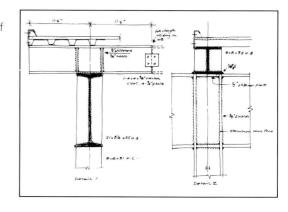

A corner cross-head during construction. The cross-head and its stanchion were fabricated off-site and arrived ready for erection as a complete welded unit. Primary and secondary beams were temporarily bolted until they too were welded into place.

Intending to prepare proper working drawings, Norman Foster sketched out on a large scale all the major joints and connections found at the edge of the building, thereby collating all the specialist information from consultants, suppliers and subcontractors. The drawing worked so well that final working details proved unnecessary and, together with the structural and mechanical engineers' drawings, a series of these 'sketches' formed the basic shop drawings from which Reliance Controls was built.

brick wall that kept the clutter of bicycles and refuse out of sight. According to the managing director, Peter Paul-Huhne, more closely involved in the commissioning and construction than anyone else at Reliance, "people appreciated that a lot of thought and care had gone into it". It was easier for the building's occupiers to work with care and precision in a space that manifested the same qualities.

From the beginning Reliance Controls had sought innovative architecture, approaching first James Stirling who, in turn, had given them a list of bright young practices, including both Ahrends Burton & Koralek and Team 4. What they eventually got was not just design, but a whole approach to industrial relations and the organisation of the workplace.

Reliance Controls was composed of a set of ideas that are hard to draw or photograph, but it has generated some memorable and direct images — it was very successful at a simple visual level. It had an analytical, diagrammatic and anti-aesthetic quality, which was none the less mediated by the desire to be, in Norman Foster's words, "cool, calm and unadorned". He sums up the now sadly demolished building as "an elegant pavilion that made a statement about the nature of work and social equality; efficient with a degree of joy". It embodied an idea that has since become common among more enlightened clients, that a forward-looking, well-run company should find an architecture to match; but it was more than a high-quality exercise in image or corporate identity.

The great strength of Reliance Controls was in the continuity between the conceptual and the concrete. The junctions of structural elements were part of the same intellectual fabric as Foster's social and industrial ideals: both were the result of a happy conjunction of Foster's aspirations, those of his clients, and the more adventurous thinking of the time.

Rowan Moore

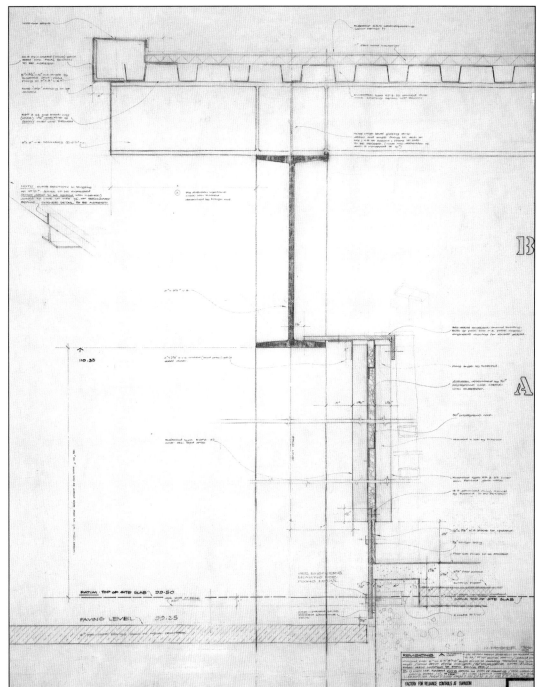

The south elevation of the building soon after completion, seen from a construction site on the opposite side of the main road. The simple, black-painted water tank and flue mark the end of the underfloor service duct.

The road elevation (right) of Reliance Controls looking west. The linked, welded frames in the east-west direction act as contiguous portal frames in which the cross-bracing is, in fact, redundant. Norman Foster, however, insisted the cross-bracing be applied to every bay, in both this and the north-south directions, creating a distinct device which laced the building together and established much of its individual character. Only at the entrance (below) and where escape doors were located in the glazed north facade (left) was the cross-bracing omitted, its absence signalling these bays' significance.

Looking south along the site access road towards the main thoroughfare. Landscaping around the building was minimal with simple grassed and paved areas. Dark grey brick walls, to which the company name was applied after the building opened, helped define the edge of the site.

Art and Architecture
an Interview with Ben Johnson

'Neoprene Gasket Supporting Curtain Wall Reflection'. Ben Johnson's painting (acrylic on canvas) of IBM Cosham was commissioned by Norman Foster in 1974. Based on a photograph by Richard Einzig (see page 126), the painting now hangs in the architect's home in Wiltshire.

Ben Johnson was born in Wales in 1946 and studied at the Royal College of Art in London. From an early age he kept an omnivorous scrap book of cuttings and pictures, some of them he distinctly remembers were of Bauhaus images and Mies van der Rohe buildings. Johnson's talent was recognised early and his first New York show took place when he was only 21. At that time he was not consciously interested in architecture, although he remembers buying a copy of Le Corbusier's *Le Modulor* at the age of 14 — but the experience of living in New York changed all that. Surrounded by an anonymous architecture of new buildings, and fascinated by the art of projected geometry, he rediscovered his old Bauhaus images.

Back in England in 1973 he made a painting of a section of the external cladding of Reliance Controls from a press photograph, never having seen the actual building. This picture was exhibited at the Institute of Contemporary Arts in the same year. It was in connection with that 1973 show that Johnson first met Norman Foster and from then on he began to specialise in High-Tech architectural subjects. One day in 1974, Norman Foster purchased two of his architectural paintings;

'Cross Bracing', the Reliance Controls painting, and 'Dock Reflection', a painting of the Fred Olsen Amenity Centre that Johnson had also never seen in reality. By now fascinated by Foster's work, Johnson went in person to the next Foster project. After discussing the architect's task at his (then) Fitzroy Street offices, Johnson made several progress visits during construction and was present during much of the fitting out of the Willis Faber & Dumas building in Ipswich, making uncommissioned paintings of it that were later to lead to a series of 100 prints commissioned by the Department of the Environment for exhibition in the House of Commons and embassies all over the world.

Since Willis Faber & Dumas, Johnson has painted many of Foster Associates' most important buildings. In 1978, Foster commissioned an edition of 75 prints of the Sainsbury Centre, and in 1982 the Renault Car Company commissioned an edition of 500 prints of the Renault Centre in Swindon, followed by a well-known painting called 'East Mast' in 1986. In 1990, Johnson painted a study of the Stansted airport terminal commissioned by the engineer Sir Jack Zunz. Based on a single structural support photographed eight times at intervals

Ben Johnson's most recent painting of a Foster project is this study of one of the structural supports for the new terminal at Stansted airport. Commissioned by Sir Jack Zunz, the painting was completed in 1990, well before the building was finished and "before anybody had a chance to ruin it".

'Willis Faber Escalator'. Impressed by Johnson's earlier paintings of the Willis Faber building, the Department of the Environment commissioned an edition of 100 silkscreen prints for exhibition in British embassies worldwide.

during a 24 hour day, Johnson believes that 'Stansted' shows the building as "pure engineering, before anybody has had a chance to ruin it".

What is it that fascinates Johnson about the work of Norman Foster? "There are two things really. First, the complex personality of Norman Foster himself, and secondly, the unique quality of light that is to be found in many of his buildings. In the end both these things are intangible, but as I came to know Norman better I think I came to understand that they are connected in some way. I have tried to analyse this elusive quality of personality and this sophisticated phenomenon of light in my paintings of his buildings, particularly the interiors of Willis Faber & Dumas. I do it by photography. For me taking photographs is a form of meditation and concentration prior to painting. I use a plumb line and a spirit level so I can set the camera up to produce completely axial views, but the verticals are always vertical. I do this in order to orientate myself to the building so that I can respond to both formal and human space.

"In the end you cannot separate Norman Foster from his work process. Once you have seen the way the office attacks a project you realise that enormous expenditure of energy is directed towards a social as well as a technical goal. I know that from his very earliest days in practice Norman has always been deeply concerned about the working conditions of the occupants of his buildings. I saw how this worked at first hand while I watched the progress of Willis Faber & Dumas. The employees would arrive from the old building in Southend and after only a few days in the new building you could see the physical change in them. Their quality of life had been transformed. The diffusion of light through the very walls of that building was only part of it. I think this is an aspect of what Norman Foster has achieved with deep-plan buildings that is not widely recognised.

"Light for him is more than a measurable quantity, if there is such a thing. I seem to remember the Sainsbury Centre has been described as 'a building about light and space never achieved before', and I cannot improve on that description. I remember once thinking that light in buildings must have had an importance for Norman that stretched right back to his childhood. He grew up in and around Manchester in the post-war years, surrounded

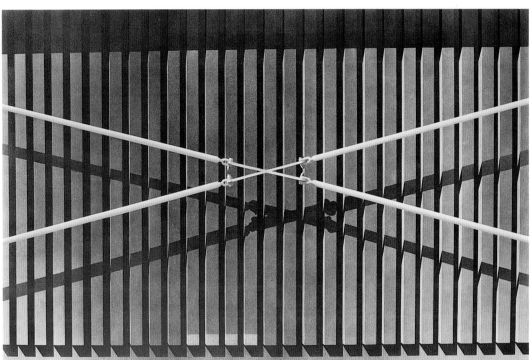

Painted in 1973 (acrylic on canvas), 'Cross Bracing' was Ben Johnson's first work that used a Foster project as its subject. Based on a press photograph, it was only later that Johnson found out that it was Norman Foster himself who had been the photographer (see previous page).

by a crumbling heritage of neglected, dark Victorian buildings. I think that part of the reason he seized upon glass as a material and pioneered such spectacular innovations in glass cladding was because of the memory of this older dark architecture and the grimness of the environment it created.

"When we come to his personality, I think that too betrays traces of his Northern background. He is a complicated person, part social and part professional, a diplomat in his ability to hold on to an uncompromising position without becoming embroiled in controversy, but also intensely private and personal. It is that private part of him that makes it possible for him always to think of the human involvement in what he is designing. To be always aware that particular people will use it, not just 'the workers' or 'the company'. The Northernness comes into it when you recognise this as a creative application of a 'them and us' view of architecture. Norman Foster does not have a chip on his shoulder, but neither does he behave as though he was born to decree where others should live and work. He has something more valuable than either attitude, and that is because he has never forgotten what it is like to be on the receiving end of architecture."

Newport School Competition
Gwent
Wales

A development of the SCSD programme, steel-structured systems-designed college buildings such as this Californian example of 1966 were used by Norman Foster as reference material to support his Newport School competition entry.

Foster Associates' 1967 Newport School competition entry can be seen as one of the most important buildings the practice never built. Not only was it their first major project, but it also demonstrated the value of using a theoretical project to advance the office's ideas. At the same time, it managed to impart something of the disciplined energy of a live project. A finalist in the competition, the project went on to influence and enable a succession of later buildings. Today, Norman Foster will go so far as to say that "without the knowledge that we gained from Newport, it wouldn't have been possible to do IBM Cosham. Arguably, Newport also made the Olsen Amenity Centre the very swift reality it turned out to be, and IBM Greenford, too, is more easily explained in terms of what we learnt there".

Certainly some links — notably those to do with the relationship of structure, services, skin and overall flexibility — are clearly traceable in these buildings. However Newport also symbolises another long-term Foster preoccupation, one which has been present in most of the practice's buildings but which has been given prominence here. That preoccupation has to

do with answering the brief on its own terms while at the same time seeking to smuggle in an extra social dimension. That dimension often surfaces as a possibility, as some encouragement to change the accepted order of things or at least to look anew at how people are treated by buildings that can too easily perpetuate outmoded attitudes.

On the surface the Newport competition brief did not encourage innovation. Traditional requirements, based upon conventional classrooms, had to be realised within the (then) Department of Education and Science cost limits. Foster Associates' response was a particularly imaginative one which used the school as a vehicle for exploring a systems approach to a multi-use building. Various alternative uses for the building as a whole were proposed and encouraged. Module-free flexible spaces were posited. New educational possibilities were enabled.

The building envelope conceived to achieve this was a compact single-storey structure with a constant-height roof umbrella incorporating all the mechanical and electrical services. A proportion of deep-planned teach-

As part of the competition entry Foster prepared several drawings to convey the *social* possibilities of the scheme. With top-down servicing (note projector) and movable partitions independent of a structural grid, these demonstrated that larger or smaller teaching spaces could be created at will.

"Newport Comprehensive School was used as a vehicle for further exploring a systems approach to multi-use buildings. The deep-plan form was a response to social aims and to the economics of flexibility. By rationalising the components, with a number of manufacturers and consultants, down to relatively few, highly repetitive elements, and balancing an expensive infill against a more straightforward low-cost enclosure, the scheme was priced within the then current cost limits."

Norman Foster, *RIBA Journal*, June 1970

At Yale, Foster learnt the importance of putting over radical ideas in a simple and 'friendly' way. The sectional perspective, mixing the technical and social aspects of a design, became a key drawing in the Foster Associates' repertoire.

ing spaces was assumed, although other possibilities were implied: for example, internal light wells and outdoor courts could be introduced where appropriate.

The whole building system was designed to stimulate an immediate sense of orientation and community. The main circulation mall was a social focus and, with its views into teaching spaces, promoted spectator involvement in a wide range of activities. Direct access to outdoors and a variety of internal spaces were intended to make for a pleasing mix of aspects in use. Whether consciously or otherwise, this planning arrangement was to serve as an accurate model for the IBM pilot head office which followed a few years later.

Norman Foster suggests that an important aspect of the Newport scheme, which has occasionally been overlooked, was the practical angle of creating adaptable spaces — areas which could be flexible because of their unusual design.

"The scheme meant that you could still have an orthogonal geometry", says Foster. "In other words you could have a school that would have corridors and classrooms and so on. But you could also have extraordinary geometries. I don't believe that we've done anything else, before or since, with quite that degree of flexibility. There was no module, and the idea of a very simple bungee rubber gasket

In an age before solar-reflective glass, full-height glazing required effective shading. Following the SCSD model Foster put this practical constraint to good use, creating a protected circulation zone right round the building.

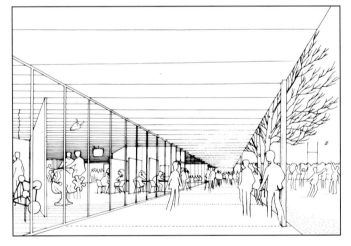

Removing the soffit from the circulation zone not only saved money, it also displayed clearly just how the building worked. This was amplified by continuing the external glazing above the internal soffit and thus displaying the services in the roof zone — a direct precursor of IBM Cosham.

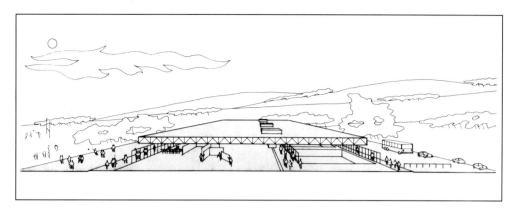

In response to a request by Cedric Price, who wanted a drawing of the Newport project for a special edition of *AD*, Norman Foster prepared this sketch in an attempt to capture the essence of the scheme in one image.

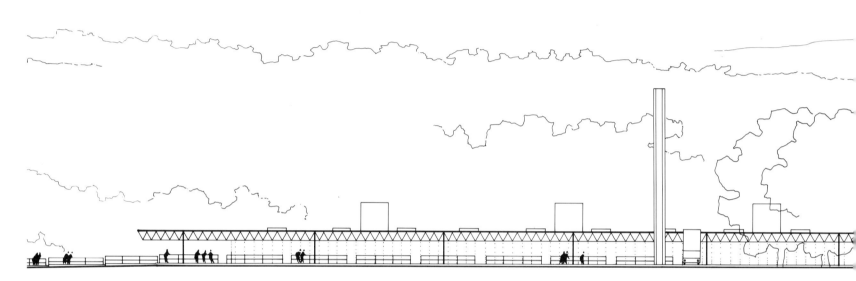

The immense 137 metre by 80 metre rectangle of the school was to have been covered by a uniform 1.2-metre deep space-frame roof of welded lattice trusses, whose edges would have been exposed on all sides. The only projections through this roof would have been the regularly distributed plant rooms and air-conditioning units that can be seen in the long elevation (above) and the short elevation (right). The structural grid of the building was to have been rectangular, reflected in the perimeter stanchion spacing of 17 metres on the long sides and 12 metres at each end. The shading effect of the deep overhang with its exposed truss was explored in detail elevations (above far right).

at the junction of wall and ceiling meant that we were freed from the grid. Architects — and we're no exception — can tend to get wedded to a grid."

Working closely with a number of potential manufacturers and consultants, the practice was able to reduce the building's components to relatively few. Those components contained highly repetitive elements and this whole approach, combined with the decision to balance an expensive interior against a simple low-cost enclosure, enabled Foster Associates to price the scheme within the current Department of Education and Science limits. Since those limits traditionally implied solutions which were cheap in the pejorative as well as the financial sense of the word, a scheme as sophisticated as this represented an unexpected level of quality.

The key was that it relied heavily upon lightweight steel construction and widely available components. This, combined with compact planning, simplicity, repetition and off-site fabrication, conferred cost and programme advantages.

The approach was one which clearly reflected the work of the SCSD (School Construction Systems Development) programme initiated by Ezra Ehrenkrantz in California in 1964, which had already embodied the notion of active participation by industry in this field.

Along with the free interior plan, a flexible heating and cooling system was proposed in order to respond to layout changes by means of precise zoning control. With all rooflights sealed, this was intended to achieve a highly controllable internal environment within a deep-plan building. In teaching and administrative areas the cooling target was to reduce internal heat gains on hot days to match external shade temperatures. While comfort conditions would not have been those of a fully air-conditioned school, they would

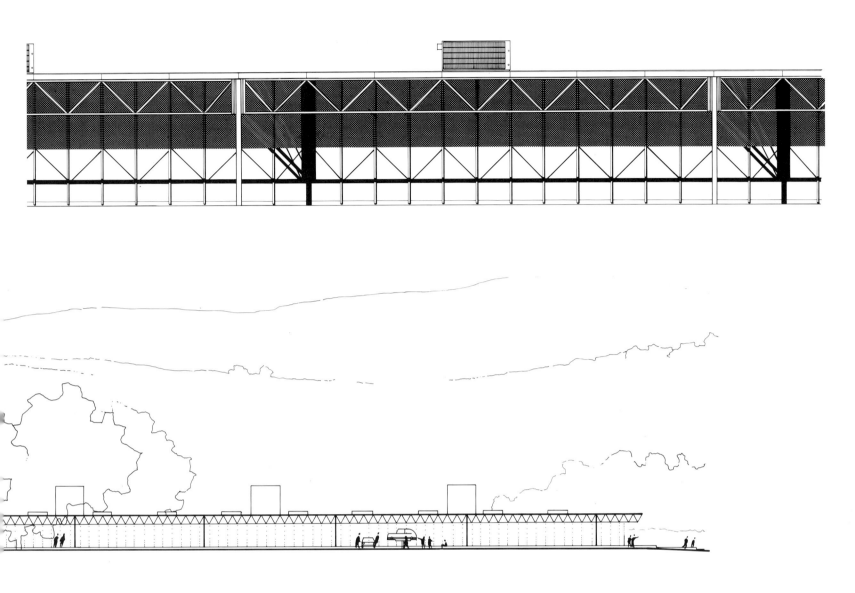

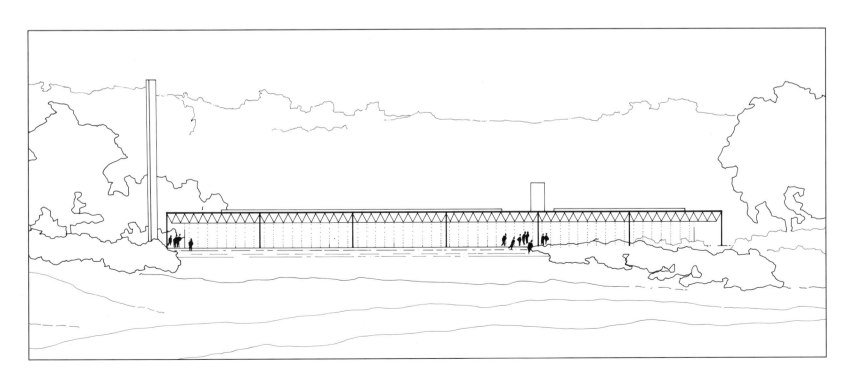

"The intention at Newport was to demonstrate that a generous roof umbrella could accommodate not only the specific requirements of the brief — which were absolutely traditional — but other approaches to education as well. If there had been a will to explore these other approaches — which were to do with newer technologies and the breaking down of the more rigid educational patterns associated with repetitive classroom units — then this scheme would have been very sensitive to such uses. It was more an educational tool than fixed building."

Norman Foster in conversation with Graham Vickers, 1989

Ezra Ehrenkrantz's prototype Californian SCSD (School Construction Systems Development) building of 1964. The ideas behind this industrialised, deep-plan building, with its high-level service distribution influenced many British architects.

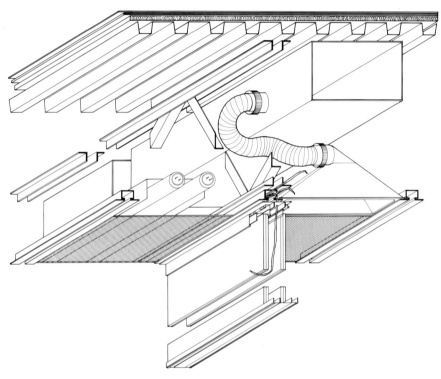

An assembly detail of the service zone beneath the roof decking, contained by its flush ceiling of Georgian wired glass. This transparent ceiling was to have served the synergetic purpose of permitting daylight to pass through the service zone from rooflights above without disrupting the service runs; providing the service zone with an immediate locatability of leakages or malfunctions; protecting the light-fittings; and securely receiving the foam rubber seals of the movable partitions.

A part section showing the air-conditioning ducting inside the roof service zone above one of the smaller, fixed-plan areas of the school. The large cowlings to the right are part of the ventilation and extraction system for the school kitchens.

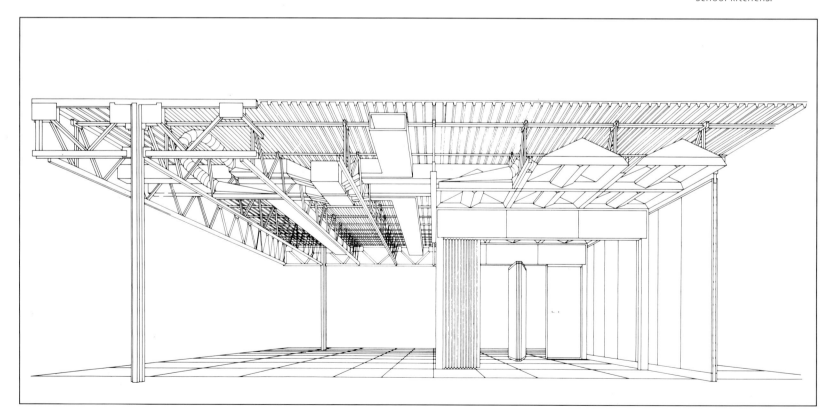

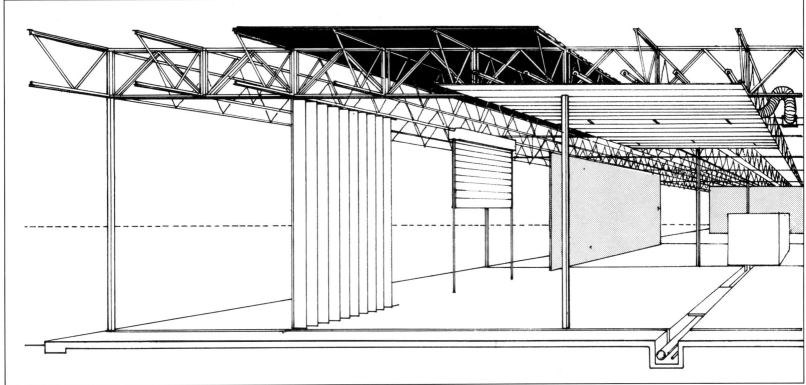

certainly have been superior to those provided in an ordinary side-glazed school with opening windows.

The building's basic construction was characterised by simple standard elements which would, in the scheme, be deployed to unusual effect. Based on a 6" deep raft foundation thickened to 1ft beneath columns, the steel structural frame consisted of lattice trusses of a constant 4ft depth on rectangular 6" x 6" hollow sections. The scheme used a large 40 x 56ft grid and standard metal roof decking with 1" thick expanded polystyrene and felt.

Internal walls were generally to have been of pressed steel, finished with pvc — otherwise formed by the use of a proprietary pvc-faced partition system.

The heating and ventilation scheme was to have used direct multi-zone system heating/ventilating/air-conditioning units handling eight zones per unit with eight flexible duct outlets per zone. Return air was via a plenum chamber in the roof void above the ceiling. Wet and waste services ran in a floor duct network

with a plug-in fitting facility. Power and communications, with a flexible plug-and-socket facility, ran in the roof service zone. Both internal and external glazing units were to have been sized in standard 4ft widths.

Three levels of operational flexibility were envisaged for the building. An immediate flexibility would come from the instantaneous rearrangement of partitions, bleacher seating, loose furniture and external barrier rails. Short-range flexibility — alternative weekend usage for example — could be achieved by the use of the demountable steel partitions. Long-range flexibility, such as vacation use, was enabled by altering what might normally be treated as immovable features: external doors could be repositioned, lavatories relocated at any point along the spine duct, and even the building itself could be extended.

Such provisions revealed the depth of the practice's early commitment to the notion of flexibility. Clearly that commitment went beyond ingenious 'quick-release' design solutions, and extended to the concept of a more elastic, creative and cost-effective use of the building all year round.

This cut-away drawing illustrates the evolution from Reliance Controls to Newport very clearly. The small service duct recessed into the ground slab is the only relic of the floor distribution system used at Swindon. Otherwise the roof space is designed to accept all the service functions of the building, including the support of the partitioning system below. The perimeter of the building, as shown here, could include horizontal and vertical sliding doors, and sandwich panel solid wall sections as well as the full-height standard glazing shown in other drawings.

"As a practice we began in a difficult period when the building boom had ebbed and the development boom had not yet started. In order to build, we poached on the traditional activities of the package dealers and contractors. We played them at their own game, but built better, more flexible buildings with a joy element. We took a progression of these techniques and applied them to a wider range of building types than anybody else."

Norman Foster, *Design*, October 1971

"You could have a school that would have corridors, classrooms and so on, but you could also have extraordinary geometries. I don't believe that we've done anything else, before or since, with quite that degree of flexibility."

Norman Foster in conversation with Graham Vickers, 1989

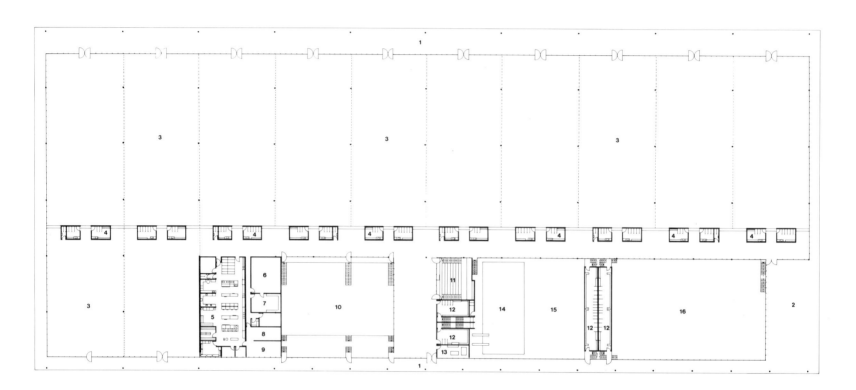

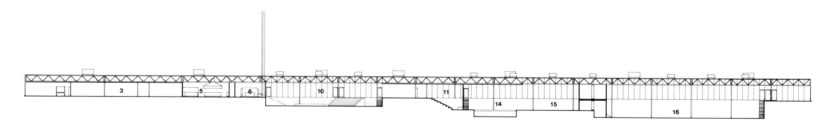

The plan and section of Newport School show at a glance how unlike any Victorian or 'finger pattern' school it was. Two-thirds of the enclosed area consisted of a vast perimeter- and top-lit teaching area (3) that could be subdivided in a limitless number of ways. The other third was separated off by a spine of cloakrooms and lavatories (4) above a long service duct. Beyond these was a kitchen (5); plant rooms (6 7) and stores (8 9); an assembly hall (10); lecture hall (11); a swimming pool (14) and gymnasium (15), with a larger sports hall (16) and changing rooms (12) between. The covered circulation area (1) surrounded the building with a larger entrance (2) recessed at one corner. All was accommodated beneath a fixed roof level, floor levels recessed into the ground where necessary.

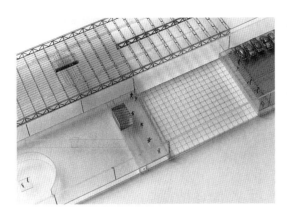

A photograph of the competition model of Newport School showing the basic structural frame, the roof service zone and some of the free-form planning possibilities partitionable beneath it.

The roof service zone seen in plan, with the air-conditioning and other service runs carefully standardised within the space-frame. The reduction in servicing load above the perimeter gymnasium and sports hall is clearly evident.

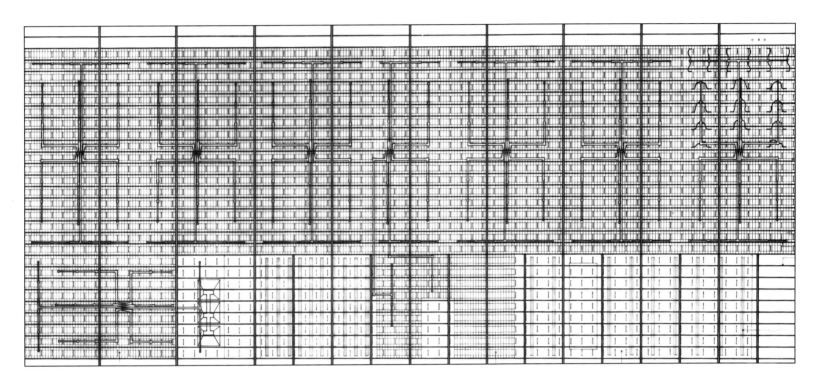

Like many unrealised projects, Foster Associates' Newport School competition entry, seen in retrospect, retains its radical idealism. Whereas, if it had been built, the new teaching methods the practice was seeking to encourage would themselves have eventually become outdated. This is an inevitable result of rapid social and technological change, but it does not vitiate the value of the attitude that sought to accommodate it. In more practical terms, the debt owed to Newport by later Foster buildings has already been acknowledged. Less easily calculated, but perhaps no less important, was the extra inspirational edge which the unrealised Newport School gave to these projects. Having been unable to translate their new ideas about integrating services and structure into deeds in 1967, the practice was primed to tackle future problems not only with a greater knowledge of integrated systems, but also with a degree of what might be called creative impatience, an eagerness to show just how well such systems could work that was soon to be rewarded.

Graham Vickers

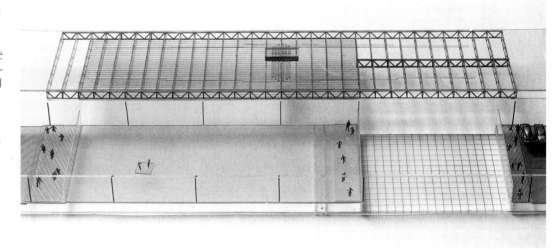

This alternative view of the competition model emphasises the structural simplicity of the design.

High-Density Housing
Radlett
Hertfordshire

"Our buildings will have to be planned for flexibility so that they can change, grow and adapt. As land becomes more precious we must reconcile these needs with buildings which are sensitive to areas of scenic beauty."

Norman Foster, *BP Shield*, March 1969

A cut-away drawing of a typically 'customised' interior space, using non-load-bearing partitions which could be erected in a number of ways. This interior planning freedom stemmed from the use of narrow frontage, cross-wall precast concrete construction. The large central floor service duct is an unusually advanced feature for the time.

This experimental project for a high-density development of 11 single-storey houses drew together concurrent ideas that were followed separately in the housing for Wates at Coulsdon and at Skybreak house for Mr and Mrs Jaffé, both designed while Norman and Wendy Foster were members of Team 4. It was Mr Jaffé's delight in the earlier house that led him to appoint Foster Associates for this scheme, initially proposed for a site adjoining Skybreak house but later explored in detail as a model for application elsewhere.

Like the Coulsdon project, cars are parked away from the houses, and vehicular and pedestrian routes are segregated. Here too, the progression from public to private follows the route into the scheme, from access road to car port, via a covered walkway to a protected entrance courtyard which gives on to individual front doors. Again, the influence of Serge

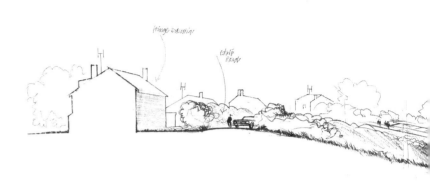

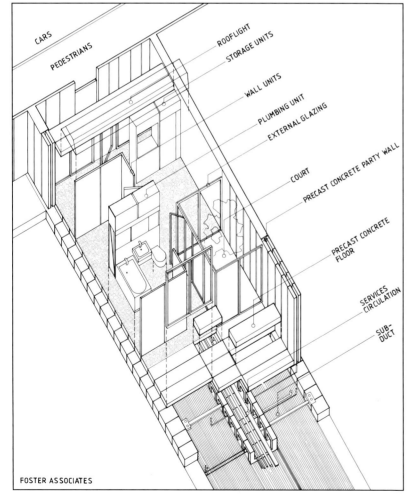

The sketch above by Norman Foster shows the essential topography of the scheme. Although all the structural elements are standardised, the entire project clings closely to the natural slope of the site.

A large degree of variation was possible within the standard pattern of narrow frontage houses. As each stepped down the site, a different arrangement of rooflights and small courtyards was intended.

Serge Chermayeff's seminal work *Community and Privacy* which had a strong influence on the planning of many of Team 4's early domestic projects. Chermayeff tutored Norman Foster at Yale University.

Bottom: The plan and section of the Radlett housing scheme seen in diagrammatic form. Eleven high-quality housing units with excellent green-belt views and privacy were to have been squeezed on to the irregularly shaped backlands site.

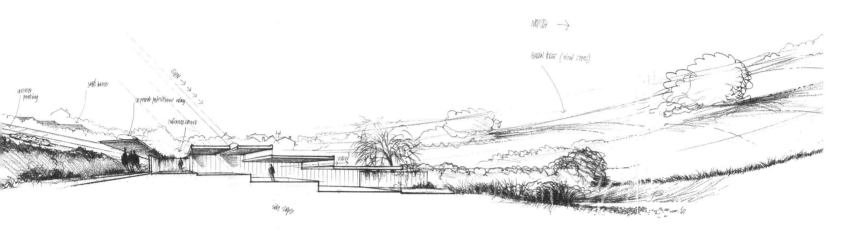

Chermayeff is clear. Chermayeff had been one of Foster's tutors at Yale and had involved the dedicated student in the final drafts of his polemical book *Community and Privacy*. Foster readily cites the importance of this work, and the early houses — most notably Skybreak — explore the ideas contained in that book in their most simple form.

Other recognisable themes from the Skybreak house are also present: the accommodation steps down in a series of platforms that follow the sloping site, opening out to views to the north, while, at roof-level, aluminium factory glazing is employed to allow sunlight into the long, thin plan. Here, this latter device is elaborated upon with the introduction of glazed internal courtyards.

The constructional system relies entirely on factory-made structural components and lightweight partitioning materials. Precast concrete units form the main party-walls and floors, allowing services to be ducted underfloor beneath a central circulation zone. These were intended to be the only fixed elements of the design; a shell within which each house could be 'customised' using varying layouts, materials and finishes to suit the purchaser's individual requirements.

David Jenkins

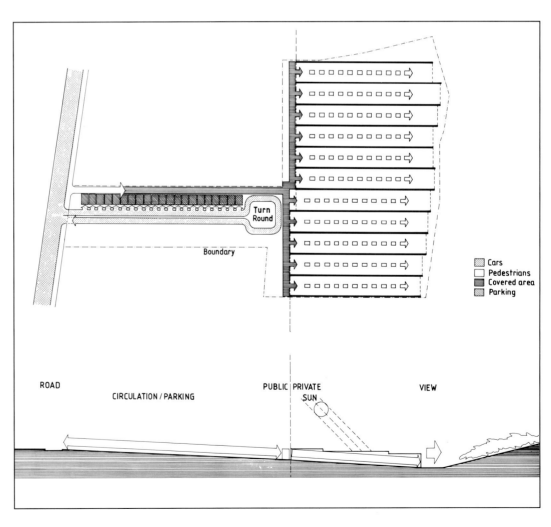

The different demands on a fully flexible factory system were itemised by Norman Foster in one simple diagram. Included are alternative roof structures of varying benefits and potential, as well as enclosed spaces with different industrial functions made flexible and compatible by design.

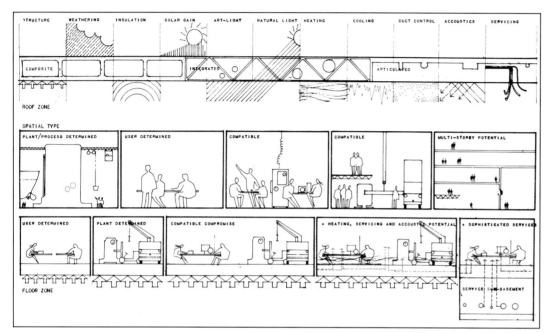

Approached by Tim Rock in 1969 to guest edit a special edition of *The Architectural Review*, Foster seized the opportunity to develop the ideas raised by the Newport School competition. Drawn by Foster himself, this cut-away sectional perspective quickly became a key image of the period, demonstrating in one immediately understandable drawing the office's total commitment and philosophy.

During 1969 when politicians and pundits were eagerly preparing for the 1970s, Norman Foster was invited by editor Tim Rock to guest-edit 'Manplan 3', one of a series of eight special issues published by *The Architectural Review* during late 1969 and early 1970.

With little work, Foster and his partner/wife, Wendy, were contemplating a move to the richer pastures of North America. There is a certain irony, therefore, that it was Manplan's aim to review the 'state of the nation', covering everything from education to religion and from housing to industry. Subtitled 'Town Workshop', Manplan 3 came out in November 1969 and was devoted to industrial buildings. It asked, "Is technology for or against us?", expressed alarm at the general acceptance of industrial squalor and proposed positive alternatives. Part of Norman Foster's contribution to the issue was a proposal for a multi-purpose industrial building system. In 1969 statistics showed that almost one in 10 people employed in manufacturing worked for companies that had either moved or opened branch factories since the War. It was primarily for these industrialists' needs that Foster's 'advance factory' was designed.

Much of the industrial expansion at the time was taking place in burgeoning new towns and development areas with the formation of industrial estates which might

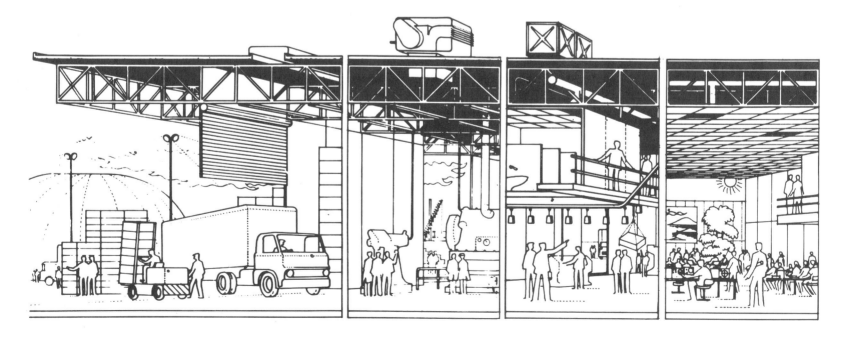

A typical unplanned, virtually undesigned industrial development of the post-war years. Through their factory systems studies Foster Associates were pioneers in the creation of a new, functional industrial image to replace this obsolete pattern.

Norman Foster's sketch of a heavy industrial exhibition unit proposed for Scottish Foundries. The elegant but massive steel beam structure supports a 25-ton travelling crane.

contain a wide variety of activities from light engineering to electronics or even office use. The prerequisite of the advance factory was that it "should never be taken by surprise, whatever activity the incoming firms want to pursue inside it". Norman Foster produced a composite perspective drawing demonstrating the logic of a multi-purpose system. Within a single structure he housed a factory with its production area, offices and storage, a teaching space, supermarket and a visitors' centre.

Foster noted that for every industrialist prepared to consult an architect in planning his company's short- and long-term needs, there were hundreds who were not. Most could be expected to haggle over the price and specification of a complex piece of plant to the last ball-bearing or nut and bolt, but buy an off-the-peg shed costing 10 times as much with no clearer brief than "a great big space at a rock-bottom price". Questions about maintenance, heating and lighting costs were often never even asked.

The advance factory unit was intended to compete economically with the package dealer's shed and accommodate these 'impulse buyers' as a government report had called them. In fact, independent studies in the USA had shown that a multi-purpose flexible pre-fabricated system could meet the requirements of 75 per cent of industry and obsolescence could be more or less eliminated. In the UK an

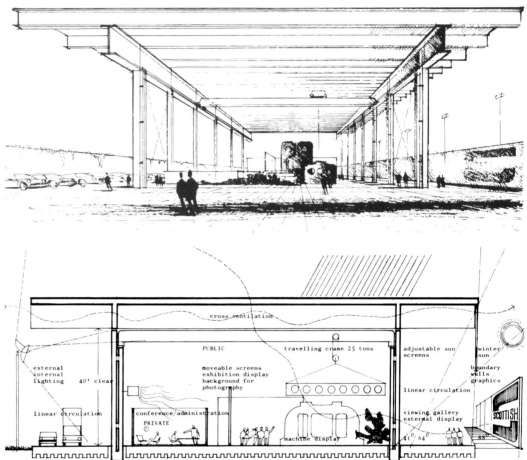

A section through the Scottish Foundries proposal. The display area is at ground level, 13 metres beneath the heavy steel roof beams. Ingenious features include external lighting and adjustable perimeter sun screens.

Embodied in the 'Manplan' drawing are all the key issues and concerns that would command the office's full attention over the next five years. Under a space-frame roof housing services, with roof-top tanks and air-conditioning units, a double-height space (allowing mezzanines) can be adapted to a multiplicity of functions.

An early application of the 'Manplan' factory systems studies, that also clearly showed the influence of the Californian SCSD programme, was the Cincinnati Milacron factory project of 1970.

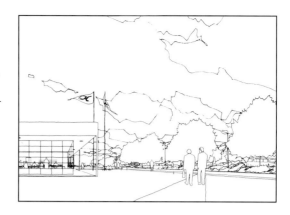

Cincinnati Milacron was a deep-plan project with cellular and open-plan elements deployed beneath a roof of long-span steel lattice beams supported by widely spaced columns. While this arrangement is similar to that achieved the following year at IBM Cosham, the elevation indicates that no attempt was being made at that time to develop a glass curtain wall cladding system.

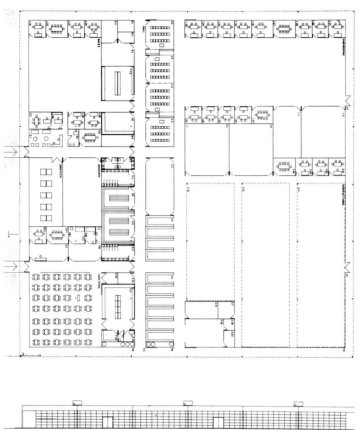

unpublished government-sponsored report had recommended investing in a prototype commissioned system akin to the California School Construction Systems Development (SCSD), but it had been shelved and forgotten.

In essence, the system Foster Associates proposed was the big brother of SCSD. The schools' prototype developed in the USA by Ezra Ehrenkrantz in the early 1960s had been a formative influence in the design of Foster Associates' Newport School competition entry in 1967. And the concept of a lightweight modular steel structure supported off a concrete floor slab, with services distributed horizontally in the deep roof structure zone using roof-top air-conditioning units and flexible trunking, is one that appears in many of their later buildings, most notably in the German Car Centre project of 1972 and the projects for IBM at Cosham, in 1971, and Greenford in 1980.

The key requirement of SCSD was flexibility so that the buildings could be expanded or modified over time to suit changing needs. This led to the identification of four basic design criteria: long-span structures, movable partitions, full thermal environmental control and an adaptable lighting provision.

The system also had to be used for a wide variety of applications by different architects and unknown contractors. The SCSD framework was consequently described as a set of basic 'rules' contained within a comprehensive per-

The similarities between Cincinnati Milacron and IBM Cosham are immediately apparent in these part section and part elevation drawings. Roof-zone servicing, typical of the factory systems studies, is coupled with a covered perimeter walkway inherited from the Newport School project. The roof-top air-conditioning units are located directly over the columns to minimise loadings on the beams.

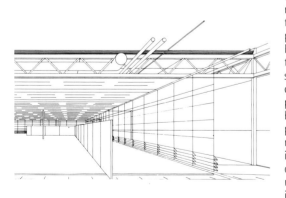

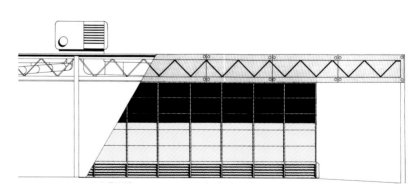

"The interesting thing about building for industry is that it is really a kind of 'no frills' situation; there is a crispness; there is a need to build quickly; a need to create generous uncluttered areas; to do it with a minimum of fuss; and, generally, to do it on extremely tight cost limits and on fairly demanding time scales."

Norman Foster, Arthur Batchelor lecture at UEA, February 1978

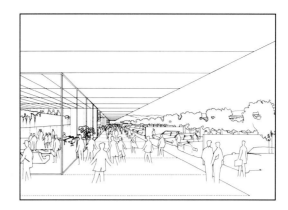

The debt to Newport School is evident throughout the factory studies, not least in the presence of covered perimeter circulation.

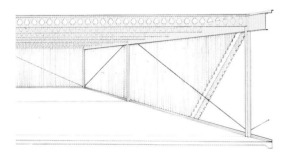

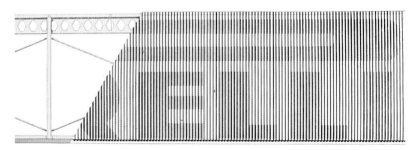

This 1970 warehouse project for Pirelli was more a development of the construction techniques employed at Reliance Controls than a use of the factory systems studies. In contrast to Reliance, castellated steel beams replace solid-web 'I' beams in the roof to permit service runs, while the diagonal bracing is relocated within the profiled-steel sandwich wall cladding.

formance specification. This allowed design details to be varied with ease, while still ensuring competitive tendering.

Structural, cladding and services subcontract packages were all covered by an integrated specification which ensured that the bidder was fully aware of the design implications of not just his own package, but of the context within which he would be working.

The advance factory embodied these basic principles but increased the scope and scale of possible modifications. Beneath the serviced roof 'umbrella', the space could be used as a single clear volume high enough to allow overhead walkways and conveyors above machines, or stacking with fork-lift trucks. Ancillary accommodation such as offices and canteens could make use of mezzanine floors above service cores, substations or enclosed environmentally-regulated areas. In response to each industrialist's particular brief, the basic shell could be fitted out or 'customised' by adding to or subtracting from a kit which included partitions, suspended ceilings, light fittings and heating units. The floor slab was designed to support a range of potential activities from heavily-loaded trucks to major pieces of machinery. And ancillary components or cores could be located anywhere within the modular framework and plugged into the services network like pieces of movable plant.

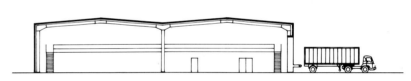

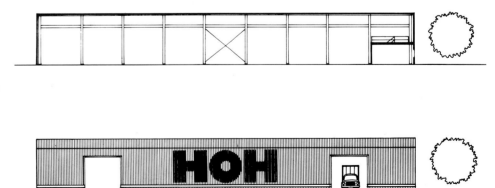

This 1972 double portal frame project, part of a sketch scheme for an industrial estate at Goole, was competitive with minimum cost level warehousing. In a refined single-bay form, this design was to reappear at Modern Art Glass.

One of the earliest applications of Foster Associates' factory systems studies was at Milton Keynes where a prototype 1200 square-metre multi-functional SBI (Systems Building for Industry) was erected for the Development Corporation in 1972.

An inverted view of a model of Ezra Ehrenkrantz's SCSD prototype in California. Part of Norman Foster's already extensive library of reference images, its influence on the early projects of Foster Associates is clear. The steel construction, corrugated decking and insertion of heating and ventilation trunking between the diagonal members of the lattice beams were all to feature in subsequent factory and office buildings.

In 1970, the newly-established Milton Keynes Development Corporation (MKDC) had a mandate to respond to a probable demand of some 50 000 square metres of industrial floorspace per year and required just such a system. Foster Associates were commissioned as systems consultants, with Anthony Hunt Associates as structural engineers, to work with MKDC's own architects' department on the development of the Systems Building for Industry (SBI). Foster Associates were also responsible for the servicing concept, its detail design and installation.

MKDC's research showed that, with few exceptions, the preferred factory was single storey and small in size. SBI offered a variety of solutions using a lightweight steel frame with 12 x 12-metre multi-directional spans, clear height options of 3.5, 5.5 and 7.5 metres, a roof service zone, increased roof and floor loadings, different cladding arrangements, a two-storey potential, and a range of environmental control, natural and artificial lighting possibilities. However, unlike SCSD, the SBI system was never intended to operate purely from a performance specification. SBI offered a 'constrained' performance specification, giving a degree of final planning control over materials and finishes to ensure continuity on large-scale developments.

To prove its economy, MKDC built a low-budget SBI prototype, the P70 unit at Wavendon, which was three bays or 36 metres square with a clear height of 5.5 metres. The latter was calculated to allow a central service core with a mezzanine level above. Metsec won the structural frame subcontract using a proprietary trussed girder system.

It was Foster Associates' first experience of a performance specification, but not of working with the successful subcontractor. The year before, Metsec had been responsible for the structural frame of the IBM pilot head office at Cosham and had already developed a close working relationship with Foster Associates. The new contract arrangement only formalised a working method developed on that earlier scheme, much to the advantage of the new building. A prototype of the structural system was erected in Foster Associates' Covent Garden office, allowing modifications to be proposed that would better integrate the services. All in all it was to prove a valuable — and influential — experience.

"Industrialists, if they think of an architect at all, regard him as a stylist who is engaged to titivate the more conspicuous parts of a structure designed by engineers or a contractor. The belief is widely held that the best industrial building is the most economical possible envelope to protect multi-million pound plant from the weather and conserve the heat which they are obliged to provide for their employees. Industrialists continue to manufacture precision engineering in dark satanic mills of indescribable squalor."

R.A. Bullivant, *The Architectural Review*, November 1969

Unit P70, the prototype SBI erected at Milton Keynes, was adopted by the Development Corporation and used to house their own architects' department. The extraordinary choice of colour was made by MKDC.

The cladding was a mix of glazed and flat, white, stove-enamelled insulated panels in a gasketed sub-frame assembly. The building was completed in 1972 and used as a drawing office for the architects' department before becoming a publicity centre, thus proving its flexibility. At Kiln Farm in 1973, the system was used in a courtyard arrangement which allowed the industrial flotsam that litters most estates to be contained within the confines of the building blocks.

But the full potential of SBI was never realised, partly because design tendering and production procedures could not be fully rationalised. And serial contracting in a fast-moving but sometimes erratic industrial development programme was made more difficult by galloping UK inflation and rising building costs. Derek Walker, who as Chief Architect and Planner was responsible for initiating SBI, regrets the loss. These obstacles, he believes, "baulked a very earnestly researched system that offered such a sensible and simplified service to the incoming industrialist".

David Jenkins

The design of Unit P70 shared the deep roof zone, low-level perimeter windows and high-level servicing of the Computer Technology building erected by Foster Associates a year earlier, but with a more open lattice roof structure instead of castellated beams.

Design for Living
by Norman Foster

This article was first published in March 1969 in *BP Shield,* the house magazine of the British Petroleum Company. The editorial in that issue noted that, "at a time of technical and social change, new materials, many of them derivatives of the petroleum industry, and new ideas are reshaping our approach to design." It is

a mark of the impact made by the Reliance Controls building — at that time Norman Foster's only major work — that he should be invited to write an essay on this theme.

There is a tendency for a certain mystique to develop around such words as 'design', especially 'good design'. This is unfortunate because it tends to cloud the importance that design decisions have in our lives. Virtually everything that is man-made has been subject to a design process involving deliberate choices and decisions; in our Western civilisation that means nearly everything that we see, hear, touch and smell. As in all things this is something that we can do well, badly or indifferently with corresponding end results. To this extent the very quality of our day-to-day living is profoundly influenced by the quality of our design.

Our environment is a compound of many tangible objects and enclosures whose designers may be anonymous, often hidden in bureaucratic and business organisations, or sometimes independent consultants. Their main role, in essence, is problem-solving. It is this fundamental aspect of their work which is so often overlooked.

The 'style' in which the problem is solved is far less important and it is unfortunate that this aspect is often over-emphasised. This dilemma can be seen in two current attitudes. First, there is a public apathy and indifference to the most fundamental aspects of design as they affect our very existence. Second, there is a tendency among designers to over-indulge in the more superficial aspects of their trade to the exclusion of the fundamental problems. The ensuing dialogue with its overtones of 'good taste' and mystique is largely irrelevant to a world going about its business.

As a random example of the above dilemma it is worth considering the 'tower block' of flats in the form which is currently designed and built in Britain. As a design for a family with young children it is chronically unsuitable. Despite all popular conceptions it is not the only way to achieve high densities; students of architecture were drawing-up low-rise, high-density schemes six or seven years ago. Nevertheless, it is commonplace for architects and critics endlessly to debate at the level of imagery and detail those 'tower blocks' which are 'good' and those which are 'bad'. Obviously some are better than others at a superficial

level, but fundamentally a tower block is a tower block, regardless of whether it is Neo-Georgian, mock-Tudor or plastic-faced.

It is amazing how long outdated design concepts can survive. At least our housing has attempted many new forms and experiments since the Industrial Revolution. By comparison, our design for industry has been virtually at a standstill since the 1800s. We still persist in building management 'boxes' and workers' 'sheds' even though this may actually conflict with the needs of processes, expansion, flexibility and management policies.

Obviously, some types of industries and processes are still rooted in a 'clean and dirty', 'we and they' social structure, but they are a growing exception. The traditional factory building and so-called industrial estate is currently one of our most unpleasant, uncomfortable, inefficient and expensive hangovers from the past.

These examples are only part of a totality. The family living in the tower block may be 20 miles from a major airport but deafened by one of its flight paths, traffic jams may separate the worker's factory from home, other facilities such as shopping, schools and recreation may be similarly unrelated. It is an indictment of our educational system that we accept such patterns almost without question as the mythical price of progress and frequently continue to regard good design as 'arting-up' or cosmetic treatment that can be applied 'after the act'.

At the risk of over-simplification, the designer's task could be summed up as analysing set problems in the widest sense and organising the best available resources to achieve the highest-performance solution in the most economical manner. It follows that the end result will have accommodated and integrated often conflicting and competing requirements. The very core of the problems and the way they are resolved will largely generate the style.

It should not be thought that so fundamental an approach is insensitive to the full range of our spiritual and material needs. Most of the historic places which today still continue to delight us were originally a calculated response to well-defined requirements.

For example, Bath was a speculative developers' 'New Town', based on a simple structural system of repetitive cross walls and repeated narrow window openings; an eloquent design totally embracing the social,

106

topographical, technical and financial aspects of its situation. It is interesting to compare the scale of our own opportunities and the quality of our resulting New Towns and speculative developments.

In our present time of social and technological change the designer's tasks become increasingly complex. The overlaps and interactions between the hardware and software of our time (cars, planes, television, communications, computers) and our building fabric make it increasingly difficult to conceive of architecture in terms of the traditional past.

The age-old definition of architecture as 'commodity, firmness and delight' is, however, still valid if the 'firmness' is realised by plastic and alloy instead of masonry, and the 'delight' is extended by current developments in electronic communications and climatic control.

The scope for new design solutions to meet both established and emerging needs is tremendous. It does not follow that we have to use untried techniques or ideas to innovate. Initiative taken on a prototype can determine vast potential on the open market. At one end of the scale new planning ideas allied with traditional techniques can often prove as significant as the utilisation of new materials and techniques in isolation. The real scope lies in the fusion of both, whatever the scale of assignment, from product design to city and regional planning, whether one-off projects or vast collective enterprises.

Design innovations which could change the appearance of buildings and make them more sensitive to our real needs can spring from a number of sources. These could be broadly classed under new techniques of planning, engineering and management. They can be separated out for examination in more detail, but in reality the design process itself would integrate these and other key factors.

First, new planning techniques. These are needed to satisfy today's rapidly changing social and technological patterns. Our spaces are becoming smaller but very highly mechanised. Like industrial plant it becomes uneconomic not to utilise them to the maximum effect. In planning terms this might mean spaces which have multi-purpose use. We also demand mobility and rapid change. Five-and-

a-half million people in the United States are living in trailer homes, which are increasing at the rate of 300 000 a year.

Obsolescence, whether based on fashion or real change, will have radical implications. Our buildings will have to be planned for flexibility so that they can change, grow and adapt. As land becomes more precious we must reconcile these needs with buildings which are sensitive to areas of scenic beauty. There is no reason why our present squandering of natural resources, both visual and material wealth, should continue. Intensive coastal development for housing and industry, for example, could be achieved without extending our present 'suburbia-on-sea'.

Similarly, by abandoning out-of-date planning forms which are currently based on hangovers from the past, we could preserve the genuinely historic parts of our cities and revitalise them with a modern, twentieth-century equivalent.

Second, new engineering techniques. Examples of these are new materials, structures, total energy concepts and the feedback of ideas from other sources such as the electronic and aerospace industries. At one extreme we have the large-scale potential. Vast areas can be enclosed with lightweight space-frame structures or inflatable plastic membranes. Full climatic control is feasible; the polar regions could be 'tropicalised' and desert areas cooled.

It is a sad reflection that it takes the stimulus of warfare to promote instant hospitals. A full surgical hospital unit, about our most complex building type, was dropped by helicopter on barren ground at Tay Ninh (Vietnam) quite recently. Complete with self-contained power-packs, its rubber-coated Dacron walls were inflated and the unit fully operational within a few hours.

Traditional site-based techniques are being replaced by factory-controlled components using new materials to achieve higher standards, speed and value-for-money. Some traditional materials like carpets are being completely reinterpreted by current technology. Mechanical equipment has become a major and fast-increasing proportion of the total building cost. Nevertheless, it is still in a very crude form (it is difficult to imagine anything more crude than our lavatories and waste disposal systems), and we generally insert it into an al-

ready obsolete shell, complete with traditional plumbing. At the present time we are still in limbo; half embracing a craft-based past and half aware of a new engineering potential.

Thirdly, new techniques of management. Increasingly complex organisations involved with problem-posing (clients, communities) and problem-solving (designers, contractors, manufacturers) can no longer rely on intuitive judgements. Skilled programming and briefing techniques are becoming increasingly important. Cost and time factors should be welcomed as further performance disciplines. Cost-in-use will become an increasingly critical factor. Our cost planning, often based on first cost in isolation, is quite misleading.

Although the framework for teamwork exists, all too often designers act in isolation, leaving other specialists to 'make it work' in a passive role. The scope for really integrated teams with wide-ranging skills is considerable. Current divisions between design and production will be reduced, involving the designer in new and exciting roles closely allied to industry. It will be a paradox that as the organisations involved get larger, the scope for small groups to innovate will increase, either from within or outside the organisations. Although greater rationalisation will produce sophisticated components and kits-of-parts, there is every reason to suppose that, as in the field of business and politics, key individuals will still play a decisive role in the field of design.

In many ways, the design process is probably one of our cheapest commodities. It allows us the scope to explore many alternatives and possibilities before making any actual commitment in reality. All too often, however, it is the subject of short-cuts; an unnecessary fringe benefit to which lip service is occasionally paid, or a luxury for those prestige occasions. The results we suffer surround us and the loss at all levels is entirely our own.

Fred Olsen Amenity Centre
Millwall Dock
London

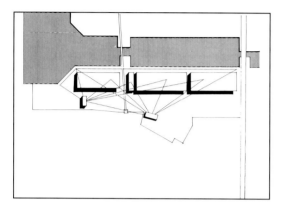

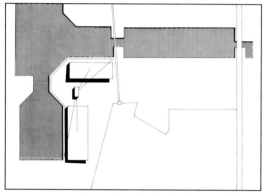

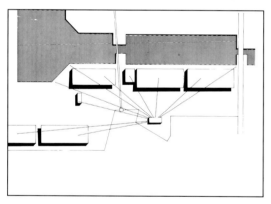

Foster Associates' first brief was for the construction of a small canteen and amenity centre for dock workers. Their analysis of where this would be best located and how it would relate to Olsen's other activities on the site convinced Fred Olsen to expand the brief.

The final scheme incorporated operations and amenity functions in a single building which bridged the firebreak required between two transit sheds then being constructed at dockside by the Port of London Authority.

The Fred Olsen Amenity Centre in Millwall Dock, London, was Foster Associates' first major building after the splitting up of Team 4. Indeed, shortage of work had been leading Wendy and Norman Foster to seriously consider emigration to the United States at the time they won the commission. Thereafter their place in British architecture was assured.

The project embodies the breadth of thought which has always given Norman Foster's buildings a freshness and originality, and made him valuable to his clients. Foster's contribution was never simply a matter of design, but also organisational and even political. The finished building, often deceptively simple, was the end product of wide-ranging and thorough analysis, with several possible solutions explored in parallel. With the Amenity Centre, the design developed from two main concerns: the building's role in improving and maintaining labour relations, and the need to organise the larger site within which individual works of architecture were placed. In addition, extreme demands of time and, to a lesser extent, money influenced the design and the organisation of the construction period. In this context Foster was as much an enabler and a mediator as a designer.

Although the Amenity Centre developed the same ideas of industrial democracy that had been central to Reliance Controls, the context could hardly have been more different.

Where Reliance Controls was for the youthful, rapidly expanding electronics industry, the Amenity Centre served the London docks, an industry in decline, subject to severe labour problems and dominated by arcane and out-of-date managerial practices that had only recently been reformed by 'decasualisation'. The standard of accommodation for dock workers was extremely low, exemplified perhaps – as Norman Foster found – by the provision of racially-segregated lavatories. Where, at Reliance Controls, innovative design and management was a reflection of growth, with Fred Olsen it was part of an attempt by an imaginative employer to reverse a desperate situation.

Foster Associates' original commission was for a small administrative centre and a separate amenities building, the latter, especially, to stand as a visible and practical symbol of good faith between management and unions. However, in developing the design it became apparent that the proposed location of the building at the periphery of Olsen's Millwall operation was far from logical, resulting in long walking times from the new building to the centre of activity on the quays.

Foster Associates' commission was, in fact, but part of a total redevelopment of the whole dock by Fred Olsen, which was to include the construction of several new warehouses alongside the quay. These had already been planned by the Port of London Authority but building

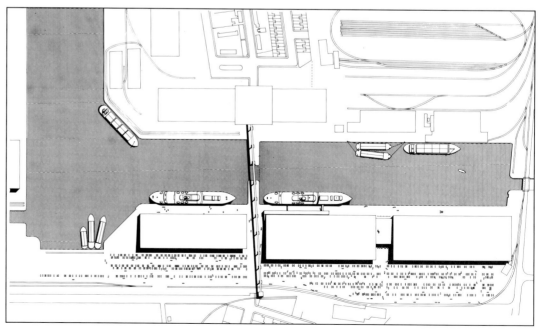

An alternative proposal in the early stages of the project suggested that the operations and amenity buildings, instead of being separate structures located behind the row of sheds, should be inserted, at a high level, directly into one of the transit sheds at dockside.

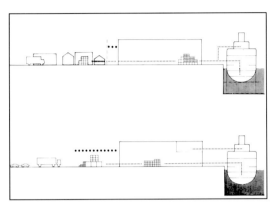

"Overall planning studies were carried out by the architects using a systems approach. These indicated new possibilities of achieving more intensive site utilisation together with improved communications and efficiency. All the company's activities were considered — administrative, servicing, cargo, passenger and vehicular.

This eventually led to a proposal whereby all these facilities were to be integrated with a large transit storage complex then being planned by the Port of London Authority."

Architectural Design,
May 1970

Right: with the location of the operations and amenity centre finally agreed, as a separate building to be located at dockside between the transit sheds, the design evolved in detail. The first version rose to three storeys with clear access to the quay for trucks at ground level.

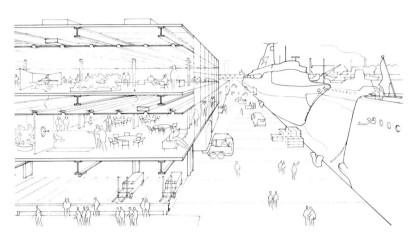

work had not yet commenced. It provided the opportunity Foster required and, after presenting the findings of his early research, Fred Olsen agreed that a reappraisal of the planning of the dock was appropriate. It became, therefore, Foster Associates' first master planning project, but its success was to prove only the start of a long involvement in that role, leading on to work at Gomera in the Canary Islands — again for Fred Olsen — and the reorganisation of St Helier Docks in Jersey.

Foster Associates quickly produced alternative studies for the organisation of the site, taking into account Olsen's techniques for handling goods and passengers, and the cross-sectional profile of their ships. In Foster's words, the main aims were "to improve communications and efficiency, to integrate related activities and to achieve maximum site utilisation". As such, any removal of either the administration or amenity centres from the quayside was seen as impractical and wasteful. Indeed, Foster's first inclination was to pull both facilities directly into the warehouses, possibly on raised mezzanine floors that would overlook the quay.

Fire regulations precluded this proposal as a minimum four-hour fire separation would have been required between storage and work or rest areas. Ironically, however, the same regulations now provided Foster Associates with a solution. It was discovered that a continuous warehouse would not be allowed along the full length of the quay; at least two warehouses were required with, between them, a statutory eight-hour fire separation. Nothing could be simpler, Foster proposed, than to insert the new facilities between the two warehouses, combining administration and amenity in the same building.

Organisation of the section of the three-storey proposal was very simple. The top floor was given over to operations (1), with the dock workers' amenity centre (2) taking over the entire middle level. The realisation that vehicular access (3) could be carried out through the adjacent transit sheds removed the need for this level and established the final two-storey scheme.

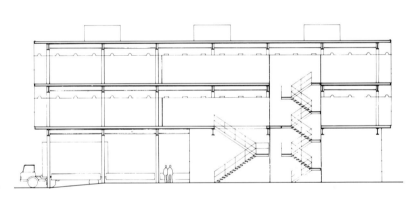

As this elevational treatment shows, the three-storey scheme would have risen above the transit sheds on either side. Glass cladding was intended from the beginning but the framing suggested here is more conventional than that finally employed.

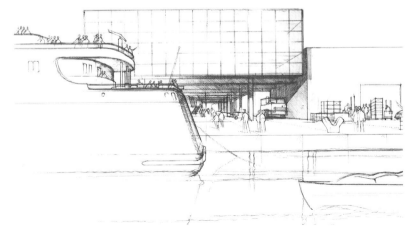

"Now the idea of integrating into one building those people who were concerned with operating the docks and those who were concerned with managing the docks, at that time was considered to be absolutely outrageous. But working with Fred Olsen in Norway, we proceeded with the project, very much against the wishes of the management in London who asked, instead, how we could possibly have dockers in the same building as the administration. 'They are dirty; they swear; the secretaries will walk out. It is unthinkable.'"

Norman Foster, lecture at the Aspen Design Conference, June 1986

Foster Associates' designs developed from an understanding of Olsen's operating techniques. The extensive use of side loading employing fork-lift trucks at dock level became an important element in the planning of the new building.

The Isle of Dogs before the construction of the amenity centre, and before the removal of the whole Port of London to Tilbury. The dock running left to right at the top is Canary Wharf into which, at right angles, is connected Millwall Dock. In this view, the Fred Olsen wharf is to the right of the dock.

At the very beginning of the project Norman Foster commissioned Tim Street-Porter to take photographs of dockers at work on the Olsen quays.

110

"The Port of London Authority's representative had announced that, basically, Olsen's were being led up the garden path and it wasn't possible to realise the kind of building that was being talked about in a 12 month programme. To reinforce the management's promises that had been made to the dockers, we became part of the large working group that included middle management from Olsen's which had direct representation with their Union. We all worked together and there was a lot at stake."

Norman Foster, lecture at Hille Seminar, July 1980

The sociological significance of the building's location at the heart of the Olsen complex, right on the quayside and within yards of the ships themselves, is not easy to understand in retrospect, but at the time it marked a revolution in labour relations.

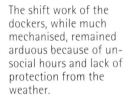

The shift work of the dockers, while much mechanised, remained arduous because of unsocial hours and lack of protection from the weather.

The building in its final two-storey form, rising to the same height as the adjacent transit sheds, as completed in 1970. The dockers' amenities are at ground level, immediately accessible from the quay.

Taken shortly after the building's completion, these photographs show dockers relaxing in the comfort of their new amenity centre. Like other facilities, it maintains a visual contact with the quayside and the ships.

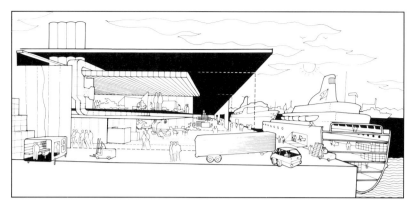

As Norman Foster's sketch demonstrates, the amenity centre relates directly to Olsen's dockside activities. Facilities for dockers are at ground level giving direct access to the quayside and cargo holds. Administration is above, relating to the ships' passenger and accommodation levels.

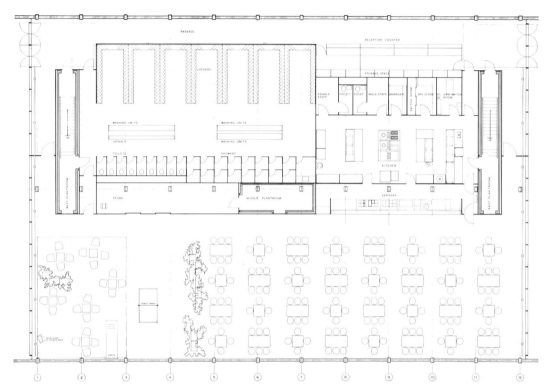

It was a radical proposal, not least because the integration of office and dock workers in the same space had never been contemplated. Many were initially alarmed by the prospect, but it was fully in the spirit of Fred Olsen's intent to bring a new way of life to the docks.

The floor plans of the building were drawn up after exhaustive consultations with both the dockers' unions and the clerical staff who were to occupy the administrative section. These consultations continually modified the provision of facilities and the layout of the interior throughout the period of design and construction. Foster describes his role as that of a 'middleman', someone whom both sides could trust.

The building was simply organised. The upper level housed the administration in deep-plan offices, landscaped into smaller units. Below was the Amenity Centre, which provided the dock workers with recreation space, a canteen, a rest area, lockers and washrooms. It also acted as a social centre for the neighbourhood at night. As far as possible, floorspace was left unobstructed to allow maximum flexibility of use, with a single row of columns downstairs and the roof spanning from wall to wall above. The plan was divided into served

The ground-floor plan showing the facilities available to the dockers in the amenity section of the building. What is effectively a large service core is isolated from one party-wall (top) by the direct route through the building from the quay to the parking area, and from the front and back glass walls by the two enclosed staircases to the upper floor. The core itself contains locker, lavatory, washing and storage areas for up to 240 dockers (to the left) and kitchen, servery and plant rooms to the right. The rest of the space is taken up with a restaurant, table-tennis area and television room.

The dock workers' restaurant was finished to an extremely high standard – as were all their facilities – and, like the rest of the building, it was air-conditioned. The servery remained open 24 hours a day.

The tinted glass cladding of the amenity centre seen from the deck of an Olsen ship berthed at the quay. At the time of its completion, the building's pristine quality stood it apart from any other building in the docks.

The entire first floor spans the full 27 metres from party-wall to party-wall without internal columns, allowing clear vistas to the dock-side and parking area at each end of the building. As at the ground floor, all services — including air-conditioning duct-work — are installed in the ceiling zone, deep castellated beams allowing the penetration of services where required.

The first floor is mainly given over to administrative offices, open-planned to accommodate up to 60 people. Managers and clerical staff share the same space, with planting and cabinets carefully arranged to mask meeting areas and managers' offices where greater privacy may be required. A small service core, with plant rooms and lavatories, runs along one party-wall.

and servant spaces with services running horizontally through castellated beams, again to minimise obstruction and maximise flexibility. In this the building anticipates a recurring Foster theme, the simple, unobstructed enclosure sheltering a wide range of different and changing needs. The Sainsbury Centre was to develop this idea on a more spectacular scale. The integration of structure and services into a single layer can also be traced back to Ezra Ehrenkrantz's SCSD concept, which Foster had himself explored and reinterpreted with the Newport School competition of 1967. As in many of Foster Associates' buildings, the success of the Amenity Centre was based on the application of earlier theoretical studies.

Throughout the Amenity Centre, the detailing and finish were of uniform quality. There was no question of different standards for different classes of employee. Furthermore, the interiors were of a colourful, air-conditioned, well-detailed lushness in deliberate contrast to the monochromatic bleakness of the rest of the docks. Outside, visible through

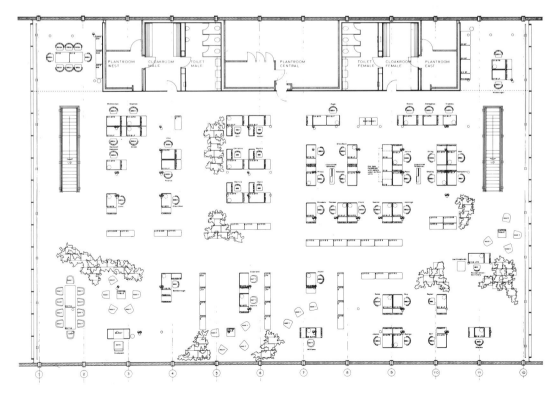

"The aim of the architects has been to reflect, as it were, in terms of bricks and mortar, the progressive policies of the owners, both in their management and in the design of their ships."

Journal of Commerce, February 1970

"Inside colour has been used with an exquisite sensibility — quite unlike the typical killjoy 'architect's interior'. Grass-green floor surfaces, warm brown facings to the service core and peppermint-green linings in Swedish melamine are the ground elements. Other details, such as purple stair rails, yellow edge tinted

Perspex menu holders and bold semi-abstract paintings provided by Fred Olsen himself add up to an environment more in tune with limp-wristed aesthetes than with the brawny, matter-of-fact *habitués* of the London docks."

Alastair Best, *Design*, May 1970

The interior of the upper operations floor at Fred Olsen, with all environmental services concealed in the roof zone above the perforated metal false ceiling. The concentric circular air-conditioning diffusers can be clearly seen. Return air is extracted through the light fittings into the plenum formed by the roof zone itself. In order to offset the long and deep shape of the building, special attention was given to light levels and internal finishes, including carpets and furniture which were deliberately brightly coloured.

The passage between the glass cladding and the upper floor access stairs on the dockside elevation of the building. The slot between the edge of the upper floor and the continuous glazing mullions can be clearly seen. The door at the far end gives on to the tv 'lounge' and restaurant.

"It is the reflective glazing of the amenity building – usually connected with the rich executive pastures of Manhattan and Chicago – that is its most unexpected feature. By day the glass, which was made in Pittsburgh to the architects' specification, throws back a rippling image of the dockside scene; by night the picture is reversed and the eye has an uninterrupted view of ground-floor canteen and landscaped first floor offices, separated by castellated steel beams."

Alastair Best, *Design*, May 1970

the tinted glass walls, all was battered, corrugated greyness. Inside, surprising but successful colour combinations – blue chairs and mauve railings against a grass-like green carpet – created an oasis of richness and warmth. On the walls, to the possible perplexity of the dockers, were examples from Fred Olsen's collection of contemporary art. Meanwhile, washbasins, lockers and showers were given the level of design for which international fashion houses will now pay enormous fees.

The philosophy extended to the exterior, with the even, seamless facade making no distinction between upper and lower floors, and introducing a delicacy and level of finish which for the docks of the period – or, indeed, anywhere – were astonishing. At that time, Foster Associates were the only private architects working in what is now known as Docklands outside St Katharine Dock, a fact almost impossible to believe in the light of subsequent development. That this sophistication should be for the benefit of dock labourers was even more remarkable, but was entirely in keeping with his own beliefs, and Fred Olsen's. Associate Birkin Haward has since summed up the philosophy as "shininess for all".

Ships reflected in the neoprene-mounted, two-storey glass dockside facade of the completed amenity centre. The steel kerb structure at ground level prevents damage to the glass by fork-lift trucks working on the quay.

The first-floor arrival point of the enclosed stairs from the amenity level. Subtle indirect lighting, simple steel detailing and complementary carpet, ceiling and furniture colouring created a calm atmosphere in the operations centre, emphasised in this photograph which was taken before the building was occupied.

Bottom: As at IBM Cosham, the ceiling service zone remains exposed behind the glass facade and is clearly visible in the evening. Castellated beams span between party-walls constructed within the cladding line of the structurally independent transit sheds.

Manhandling one of the sheets of glass into position. Despite the largest possible sheet size of 4.25 x 1.8 metres being specified, tolerances of the order of plus or minus 1.5 mm over 10 metres were achieved on the glazing frame.

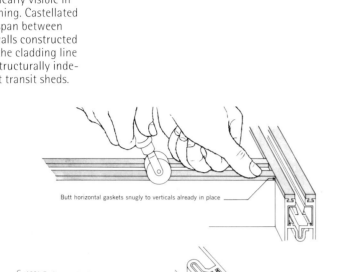

Butt horizontal gaskets snugly to verticals already in place — 2.5 2.5

#1921 Back-up gasket for ⅛" glazing
#1922 Back-up gasket for ¼" glazing
#1923 Back-up gasket for ⅜" glazing

End view of temporary glazing gaskets

#1920 Blank Filler Gasket

Shaded area shows recommended coverage of #4040 non-sag sealant

90

The implications of air-conditioning on the design of the two glass walls at Olsen were very carefully studied, and various combinations of internal shading, venetian blinds and drapes, external louvres and heat-absorbing glass were evaluated. In the end a low heat and light transmission American glass called Solargray was chosen, 6 mm toughened panes with 24 per cent light transmission being specified. It was supported by a two-storey, silver-anodised aluminium box-section frame with a linear neoprene gasket fixing system developed by Pittsburgh Plate Glass of Kokomo, Indiana. The hand sealing sequence for the gasket strips is shown here.

The pristine fragility of the Amenity Centre's exterior was offset by the crude sheds on either side, by the machinery and cranes reflected on its walls, and by the fork-lift trucks roaring up and down the quay. Indeed, the contrast of delicacy and vigour was a major theme of the building, from the castellated steel beams visible through the glass, to the bare steel and corrugated-sheet walls set against the carpeted interior. The Amenity Centre was also the first building in Britain to use reflective glass for its curtain walls, a device which, by night, set its own glossiness against the guts of the interior. By day, the contrast was with the chaotic surroundings.

However, the construction of the Amenity Centre was not just governed by appearance, but also by the demands of programme. The building was designed and built within a year, which led to an early use of multiple prime-cost contracts, under which detailed design overlapped with construction, a technique now known by the American name 'fast track'. Thus the structure went up before the rest of the design was complete, and so had to allow for flexibility and change. Similarly, the curtain-wall system was prefabricated by an American company, Pittsburgh Plate Glass (PPG), and zipped together with a minimum of on-site labour. In this reaction against traditional 'wet' trades, one can detect the same aversion to the messy and constricting past that pervades the design, and informed both Olsen's and Foster's approach to labour relations.

The success of the curtain wall was, in fact, a late addition to the design. With its deep plan and blank side walls, a maximum of glazing to the Amenity Centre's end walls brought many advantages: daylight could penetrate deep into the space, while those within could now enjoy the dramatic views. As with the later Willis Faber & Dumas building, the use of a relatively luxurious 'skin' was made economically possible by the low ratio of exterior wall to floor area provided.

PPG's timely introduction of an elegant new system that also incorporated their recently developed, solar-reflective mirror glass offered, Foster realised, the perfect solution. The system, however, had only been designed for use over a single storey. Without awaiting approval, Foster decided to fly directly to America where he was met by a somewhat bemused executive of the company. The same day he was installed in PPG's own design office

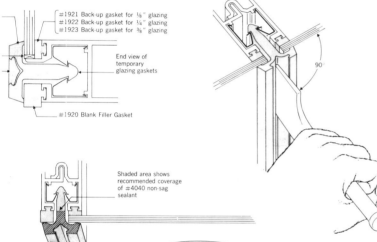

"Over the duration of its life, Olsen's did not suffer from unofficial strikes or, indeed, any kind of industrial action for which the docks are notorious. I don't know how you quantify that in terms of cost plans."

Norman Foster, lecture at the Construction Industry Conference, May 1980

An oblique view of the glass cladding: the unprecedented combination of light penetration and reflectivity makes the castellated structure within appear to float in space.

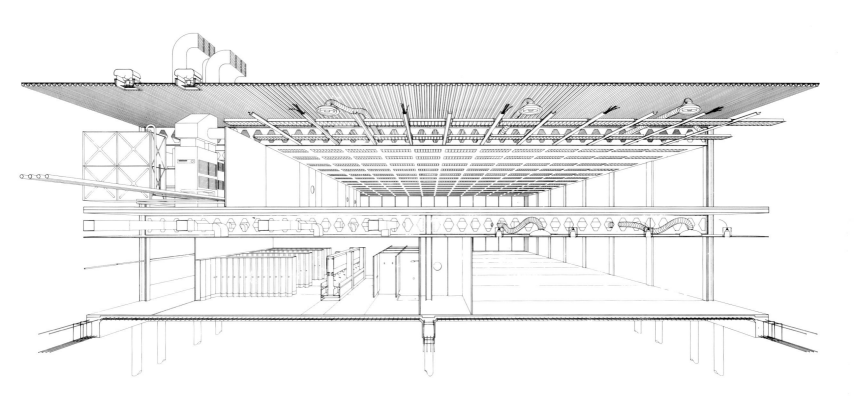

The building's structure could hardly have been more straightforward. One metre deep castellated beams span the 27 metre space between the transit sheds, supported on their own steel columns. To provide the required four-hour fire separation, the columns were encased in concrete with brick infill panels. All servicing was distributed through the two ceiling zones, supplied from plant installed at first-floor level.

One of the earliest glass curtain-walls in Britain, the PPG system was also the most elegant available, with only 25 mm wide neoprene gaskets showing on the external facade. The entire assembly floats in front of the structure, spanning from concrete ground slab to a capping beam cantilevered from the top of the main roof beam.

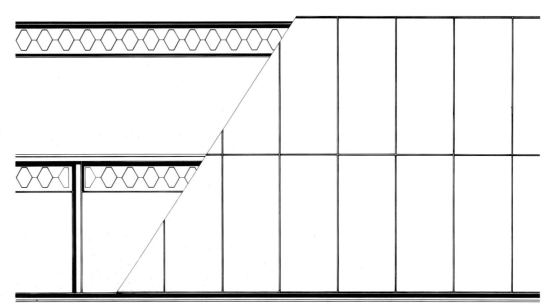

At night the reflectiveness of the tinted glass gives way to a dramatic transparency, exposing the inner workings of the building in all their detail.

With a tolerance of millimetres, the first floor cantilevers out to touch — but not support — the curtain-wall's aluminium framing. A simple freestanding handrail offers security.

and a week later he returned to London with complete working drawings for a two-storey system. The prefabricated sections arrived in London a few months later where they were assembled by the newly established, specialist contractor Modern Art Glass. A year later the system was used again, in its original form, for the IBM pilot head office at Cosham.

In the event, Foster Associates' and Fred Olsen's brave attempt to civilise and modernise the docks was overtaken by events beyond their control. The London docks were soon containerised and moved to Tilbury, and Olsen relocated to Southampton. The Amenity Centre eventually fell victim to the redevelopment of Docklands and, after several years as offices for the London Docklands Development Corporation, it was demolished and nothing now remains. Yet, for nearly two decades, the Amenity Centre constituted Foster Associates' only major work in London and, in spite of the vast amount of construction that has since taken place in Docklands, few of any recent buildings there have matched its rigorous quality.

That the newer work is for international bankers where Foster Associates' was for soon-to-be-redundant dockers, makes this fact all the more striking and poignant. The fact that, during the period of the building's occupancy, Fred Olsen suffered virtually no labour disputes, is a testament to the building's success in fulfilling every aspect of its brief. Certainly, the building's quality was not lost on Sir Robert Sainsbury. On seeing the building a few years after its completion, he was immediately determined that Norman Foster receive the commission for what was to become the Sainsbury Centre for Visual Arts.

Rowan Moore

1969-1970 **Fred Olsen Passenger Terminal**
Millwall Dock
London

Close to the threshold that separates architecture from mere industrial enclosure, and erected in only three weeks, the Olsen passenger terminal was a remarkable exercise in structural minimalism.

The first version of the terminal was a relatively heavy affair relying on a cantilevered structure of tapered steel frames, the weight-reducing holes in their webs doubling as service runs. Horizontally profiled aluminium sheeting was to have been wrapped around the 'tube', with purpose-made windows inserted into the sides.

In spite of obvious formal differences, the Fred Olsen passenger terminal is a product of the same planning study that lay behind the Amenity Centre, and shares the same clear-sighted approach to the organisation of the site. That study was greatly concerned with the movement of goods and people, and with the separation of activities. The terminal is, accordingly, legible as built circulation, as a set of 'tubes' raising passengers above the turmoil of the quayside, taking care of their baggage, and delivering them to the ships at the correct deck level. The section of the terminal, with its accommodation held in the air above the quays, shows how it connects directly with Olsen's ships, with passengers above and freight below.

It is an open question whether it was a building in any conventional sense, as opposed to either a built diagram or a piece of equipment. It had more moving parts than a typical building, including a baggage-handling device made from customised agricultural machinery. It was, in a sense, itself a moving part, being supported on pin-jointed columns and deriving all its stability from another building, the adjoining transit shed. It might also be said that the architecture of the Olsen projects

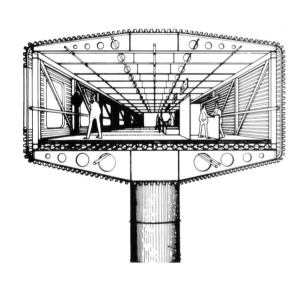

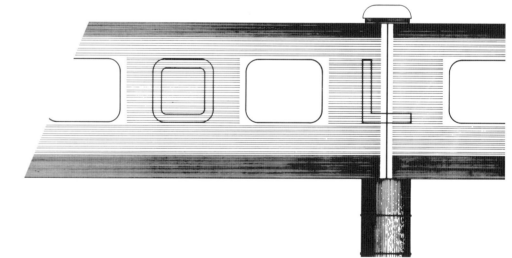

A mobile maintenance platform, originally designed for servicing jet aircraft, was adapted to support a simple adjustable gangway linking terminal to ship.

"The passenger terminal has a simplicity of approach and clarity of structure which belies the level of thought and research behind its design."

Jose Manser, *Design*, January 1971

The relationship between the terminal and the cruise liners it served could not be simpler. Raised up to permit uninterrupted cargo operations at quay level, the tube links horizontally with the passenger decks of the berthed ships.

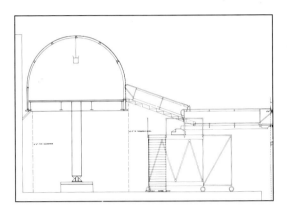

In its final form, the terminal is little more than a 6.5 metre wide, 70 metre long steel beam floor framework, supported on steel stanchions pin-jointed to the quayside and stayed against the existing transit shed. The cladding is a single skin of ribbed aluminium.

resided not in the terminal or the Amenity Centre individually, but in the combination of the two, their relation to the rest of the site, and in the organisation of the site as a whole.

In the years since the Olsen projects were completed, the definition of architecture has tended to narrow into a set of formal ideas, and it is hard to imagine a building of the late 1980s as open or relaxed as the passenger terminal, or with plans and elevations so bare and uncomposed. Now it would tend to fall victim to imposed hierarchies.

That said, the terminal has plenty of the qualities one would expect of a good building of any period. Like most of Foster Associates' early buildings it was built to an exceptionally tight budget and programme, and each element was used to its fullest effect. The primary element was the long, narrow passenger and baggage tube supported on pillars, these standing on massive bases designed to withstand any chance impact from the heavy traffic of the quay. Seen from the outside, the tube clearly belonged to its quayside setting, its formal and material qualities echoing the warehouses to one side, the ships to the other, and even the packing cases in between. At the

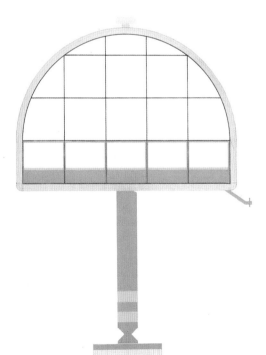

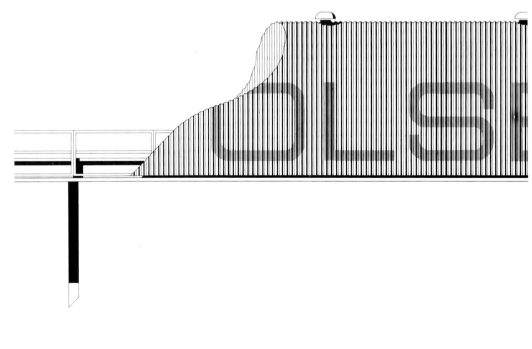

The interior of the finished terminal. The aluminium cladding was supported on a minimal steel frame. Simple square-cut 'portholes' provided access to the ships, with roller-shutter doors, fitted externally, sealing the openings when not in use.

"There is a rising breed, amongst whom Foster Associates are a notable example, who are on easy terms with contemporary conditions, have a decent working relationship with industry and commerce, and who are in their seemingly relaxed way producing some of the most interesting and appropriate modern architecture. Foster Associates, particularly, are doing it with a steely dedication and disregard for prescriptive methods that makes all those prima donnas look like flabby leftovers from another age."

Jose Manser, *Design*, January 1971

same time its elegance, the precision of its detailing, and the freshness of its logic set it apart as something exceptional.

Internally, the integrated design of exposed structure, services, and natural and artificial lighting established a calm rhythm differentiated by individual events: a customs and ticket office made from truck sections; a spiral stair rising from the quay and wrapped in mesh; dramatic square openings at access points to the ships; and a carefully detailed balustrade. Against a generally grey background these elements were picked out in primary colours, with the stair and offices in yellow, and customs desks in blue. As in the Amenity Centre, the effect of the colour scheme was to introduce a sense of luxury to generally bleak surroundings.

The terminal was characterised throughout by an interplay of permanence and transience suitable to its purpose. The tube in which passengers waited to board embodied an in-between state, belonging to both the stable world of the ground and the moving world of the boat. The satisfying curve of the roof evoked stability, while its construction was revealed as lightweight and bolted together, keeping the memory of the building site fresh. From the outside the confident shape of the tube seemed precariously balanced on its single row of columns, and glass walls at each end revealed precisely how thin the structure actually was.

The Fred Olsen passenger terminal demonstrated just how much Foster Associates could achieve with limited resources, simply by observing the brief closely and finding a fresh and imaginative solution to every problem.

Rowan Moore

The simplicity of the final design was approached through a long process of refinement. Sliding doors to access ports, indicated in this early elevation, were later replaced by roller doors: the logo was retained but on naturally finished aluminium.

An axonometric drawing of the terminal in its early colour plastic-coated skin. Designed to fit tightly round the corner of the existing warehouse, the terminal was approached via a long shallow ramp (also covered) which kept cars and buses well away from the chaos of the quay. Lavatories, and luggage-handling and customs facilities were neatly contained in the main tube.

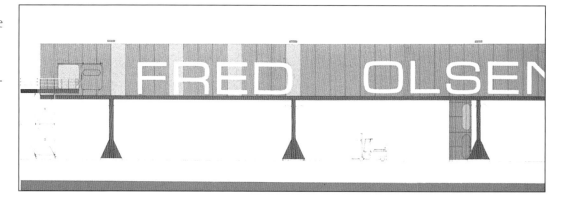

Lighting (centre below) was a combination of daylight – via translucent corrugated pvc sheets which replaced the aluminium at regular intervals – and fluorescent tubes positioned in a suspended metal trough running the length of the terminal.

To compensate for an otherwise windowless tube the two ends of the terminal were fully glazed, offering spectacular views of the working dock below. A transitory space, the fit-out was elegantly resolved – most often with off-the-peg components – but minimal.

Together with the Fred Olsen name, the shipping line's flag, which is the company logo, was also painted on to the aluminium cladding.

Mainly used as a staff link, the spiral staircase – encircled in perforated steel sheet – gave access to the quay below. The free-standing cabin beyond contained lavatories and washroom facilities.

Seen from a moored ship, the barrel-vaulted terminal blended imperceptibly with the sloping aluminium roof of the transit shed beyond.

The world's first inflatable office building, designed to house 70 Computer Technology personnel for a 12 month period. The nylon-reinforced pvc envelope was secured to perimeter beams laid directly on the surface of Computer Technology's car park.

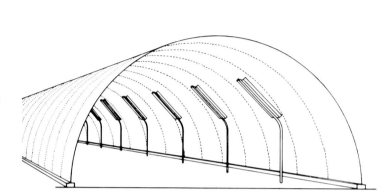

In its final form, the plan of the air structure presented a spacious office arrangement, with a central aisle and a main 'air-lock' entrance at one end. Three further escape doors were installed for use in emergencies only. The external generator and twin inlet fans not only pressurised the envelope but also supplied warm air for space heating.

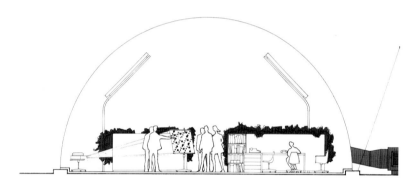

The notion of an 8000 square-foot office building being delivered to the site in a single compact bundle is something of a novelty. Seeing that structure take shape in less than one hour may even hint at a slightly capricious architectural response to a client's office overspill crisis. In fact, nothing could be further from the truth. The famous air-supported office proposed and realised by Foster Associates for Computer Technology in 1970 not only demonstrated the office's commitment to appropriate technology and the solving of problems by a return to first principles, it was also a highly rational and cost-effective solution.

In the late 1960s, Computer Technology was a dynamic young company driven by the sudden and rapid success of their 'Modular One' computer series. But the speed of that success had brought with it some unusual accommodation problems.

Foster Associates had already converted for office use a canning factory on the company's Hemel Hempstead site and was about to build an adjacent new permanent headquarters when unexpected planning permission difficulties made the provision of temporary office space an urgent priority. Work space for 70 employees over a period of 12 months was required within 12 weeks.

Foster Associates were asked to carry out comparative studies on a number of different options. Contractors' huts, portable cabins,

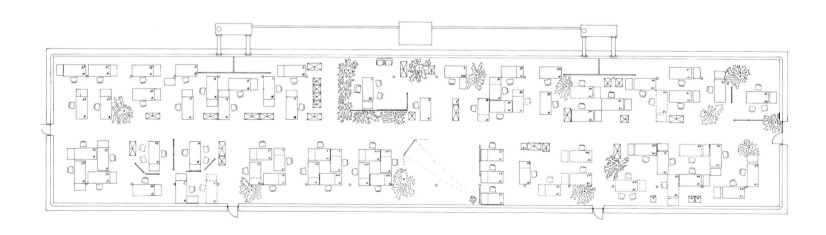

The lighting stanchions supported standard fluorescent tubes which reflected their light off the inner surface of the nylon/pvc envelope. They also provided practical emergency support in the event of sudden deflation.

Delivered as a 2 metre diameter bundle, the 70 metre by 13 metre envelope was craned into position on the heavy-duty-polythene covered car park, and then un-rolled and connected to its perimeter beam prior to inflation.

dome structures and other conventional and unconventional solutions all proved far more expensive than the one which Norman Foster preferred: a purpose-designed inflatable tent. No one was in any doubt that this was the cheapest solution, but still unanswered were questions of stability, security, temperature control and lighting. Inflatable structures in themselves were hardly new, but their previous industrial use had been limited to warehousing; it was the office-space application that raised the key questions — and simultaneously offered the opportunity to re-examine a number of more familiar problems in this new unfamiliar context.

The location of the inflatable structure was the area destined to become the car park for the final building. On to this rectangle of tarmac the structure was anchored by means of a concrete perimeter ground beam. Electrical and telephone cabling ran around the top of the beam, encircling the 200 x 40ft enclosure and supplying all the internal equipment, none of which, incidentally, required a current exceeding 2 amps. The subsequent economies

made in wiring and insulation exemplified an approach which at no point sacrificed cost to innovation.

The translucent envelope itself, made from a nylon and pvc fabric purchased from the company Swedish Polydrom, remained something of an unknown quantity in certain respects, despite its obvious structural suitability. Twin inlet fans inflated the structure via baffles designed to minimise noise and distribute the air evenly. By heating the inflation air to 90°F, an internal temperature of 70°F could be maintained in winter — the structure was erected in January — although an unpredictable variation in the insulation value of the envelope's skin took some time to identify. The presence or absence of daylight, it was eventually found, caused a perceptible change in the material's U-value: loss of heat by radiation being significantly greater at night. Further fine-tuning was also required when it was discovered that a slight slope in the car park was causing noticeable heat stratification.

Instant office space. The envelope was inflated in 55 minutes to the condition seen above, satisfying the client's requirement for immediate overspill office space in a manner that was both dramatic and rational. Subsequently, the polythene over the car park was simply covered with underfelt and carpeted.

Iann Barron, managing director of Computer Technology, moved into the air-supported office worried that his staff might object if he remained in the apparent luxury of his old office. In reality, they were incensed at the speed with which he laid claim to the best spot in the new space.

"Its semi-transparency to light, including internal light, gave it a delicate air of transience, yet its form (like that of many other inflated structures) was not so different from that of, say, a long heap of clay piled up at its natural angle of permanent repose. That particular form makes functional and economic sense (something more bubble-like would have enclosed wasteful amounts of volume) but it still left a powerful sense of visual ambiguity, which is perhaps proper to an 'impermanent' structure."

Reyner Banham, *Foster Associates*, RIBA Publications 1979

The Computer Technology inflatable in the snow of winter, 1970. Throughout the one-year occupation period the crucial issue was thermal performance. Cold radiation through the thin envelope was controlled by twin 500 000 BTU/hr oil-fired warm air heaters and the creation of a no-go 'reservation' around the perimeter of the open-plan office. Summer overheating was prevented even more simply by the evapora-tion of water from the external surface of the envelope, sprayed on by nothing more complicated than a standard garden sprinkler.

The central aisle proved the most efficient form of circulation for the space, while also providing the most direct means of escape in the event of fire or rapid deflation.

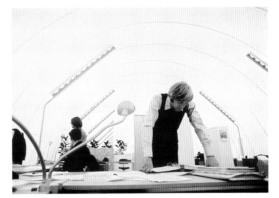

Concerned that the thin membrane might act as a cold radiator, task lighting was provided at every desk, as much for the local heat it generated as its light. In fact, these concerns proved unfounded due to the substantial solar gain even on overcast days.

Lighting and safety considerations were happily united in a single elegant solution: a double row of canted steel tubes, cantilevered out of the floor slab and supporting standard fluorescent fittings, would act as supporting ribs should the structure collapse.

The lights themselves, directed on to the inner surface of the envelope, provided 35 lumens per square foot of background lighting. At work-station level, tungsten desk lighting added another 40 lumens per square foot and this combined with the specially chosen, bright red broadloom carpet to bring a sense of

The furniture and service layout in the air structure was landscaped and divided into activity and group work zones. Meredew and Ryman-Conran office furniture was evaluated in use.

warmth to a translucent structure which, perhaps inevitably, carried psychological overtones of coolness.

Psychological reactions were also a concern with regard to the structure's lack of windows. In reality, the very openness and height of the space seemed to allay any sense of being closed in for most people. Curiously, the space was more responsive to the outside environment than most traditional structures, changing dramatically when sunny or overcast and responding directly to the sound of falling rain.

When summer came, the need to reduce temperatures inside the temporary structure resulted in the installation of 'an evaporative cooling system' or — more prosaically — 10 lawn sprinklers which were draped over the structure. The simplicity of this solution perhaps detracts from its remarkable effectiveness and its almost absurd cheapness. The same might be said of the whole air tent itself. Before the structure was finally sold off, to be superseded by the planned permanent building, Computer Technology had enjoyed a pioneering piece of 'instant' architecture at a fraction of conventional costs. As for Foster Associates, the experiment had provided a focal point for a long-standing area of fascination while making its own unique contribution to the cumulative knowledge of the practice.

Graham Vickers

The perimeter 'reservation' was used as an additional circulation route, with work-station screens positioned to act as baffles in front of the air inlets. The fluorescent tubes supplied such a good standard of ambient light — supplemented during the day by a 10 per cent transmission of daylight through the translucent envelope — that the task lights were rarely used.

IBM Pilot Head Office
Cosham
Hampshire

Typical proprietary temporary buildings of the type that, in 1970, had already been used by IBM at their nearby Havant site.

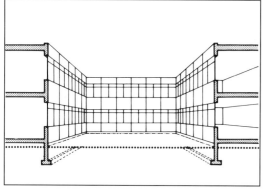

A two-storey proprietary office system was also considered for the Cosham site. Although covering much less site area, this solution would have required deep foundations in reclaimed land of poor bearing capacity.

Though the IBM brief called for no more than the use of the 'best' temporary buildings available, Foster Associates' research proved a deep-plan permanent structure would offer better value. This sketch from the initial report bears a strong resemblance to the final building. The tinted glass was retained but the large logo was dropped.

In March 1970, Foster Associates were invited to consider the feasibility of providing a pilot head office for IBM at Cosham in Hampshire. The proposed site adjoined land designated for the company's main UK offices, and the need for what, in effect, would be a temporary headquarters building was brought about by the scheduling of a land reclamation programme on the main site that would delay occupation.

That 8.9-acre site lay just north of Portsmouth. Formed by refuse-tip reclamation in the 1930s, it was bounded by playing fields and Cosham Park to the north-west and east, and lay adjacent to the (then) proposed M27 south-coast motorway linking Havant, Portsmouth and Southampton.

As was common for many rapidly expanding companies at that time, IBM were happy to rely on a mixture of permanent and temporary accommodation. At some locations as much as half their office space was provided in proprietary prefabricated buildings. It was no surprise, therefore, that Foster Associates' first brief required little more than to research the best of these available systems and propose their suitable arrangement on the site. It was exactly the situation Foster had argued against in his factory systems studies and 'Manplan' articles of the year before. He raised his objections again.

While agreeing that something fast and low-cost was required, Foster argued that any new building should also embrace very high architectural and environmental standards. As a building which, it was hoped, would attract existing London staff as well as new recruits, the pilot head office would need to take on something of an ambassadorial role.

Accommodation for 750 employees was needed, with expansion potential for up to 1000. This, and a two-thirds parking requirement (for 660 cars), suggested a gross floor area of 150 000 square feet, with possible future expansion pushing this up to 200 000 square feet. Furthermore, a capacity to accommodate change was also required; there was some uncertainty as to the detailed use of the building over its expected life-span, and so maximum flexibility was specified.

An extended two-month discussion period elapsed before the commission was finally awarded, leaving Foster Associates, in effect,

In response to IBM's request for proposals for a similar building on a smaller site, Foster Associates proposed raising the entire building so that cars could be parked underneath. Little more than a verbal discussion, the scheme did not proceed.

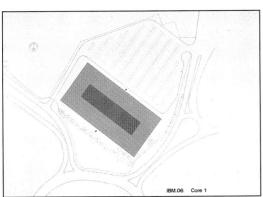

IBM.06   Core 1

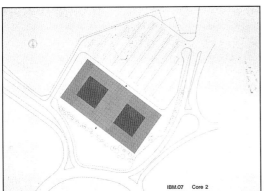

IBM.07   Core 2

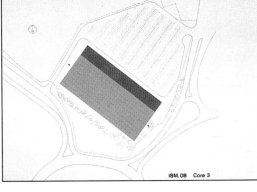

IBM.08   Core 3

Service zones of identical size were overlaid on similar plans for comparison. IBM agreed that central service cores reduced flexibility and accepted Foster Associates' preferred option (bottom) to run all highly-serviced areas along the north side of the building.

only four months in which to develop a design solution. Important concessions had been made by IBM during this time however. Most importantly, following a visit to Fred Olsen's Amenity Centre at Millwall Dock, Gerry Deighton, head of IBM's estates and construction division, had agreed to Foster Associates drawing up a new systems building.

In deference to the initial brief, however, Foster Associates were asked to evaluate a complete range of possible solutions with regard to phasing, expansion and site utilisation. The cheapest option, an air tent as used at Computer Technology, was rejected as being unsuitable on security grounds for the valuable equipment that it would house. Quickly, for the purposes of the initial report, the options were narrowed to three. Foster Associates preferred a new building but two 'temporary' solutions were included as a means of comparison.

The first proposal used the same solution as was currently being employed at nearby Havant: a single-storey Youngman patent pre-fabricated timber system, shallow-planned on a 40 x 40ft office bay with courtyards giving natural through ventilation. This scheme was

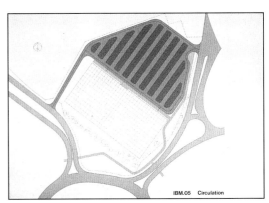

IBM.05   Circulation

The site layout proposed in the 1970 report is remarkably close to its final form. Primary road access and parking is to the north of the rectangular building. The Portsbridge intersection, to the south, was subsequently linked to the M27.

Illustrations of the building's interior, as given in the initial report, emphasised how the deep-plan approach promised flexibility greater than was possible with any short-span temporary building.

IBM.14   Reception/Restaurant area

"The brief was to provide space for computers, offices, restaurants and a communications centre. Now, normally this would sprout a multitude of separate buildings, each, say, with connecting corridors. In this instance, the solution was to put them all under one umbrella. In this way the activities can flux and change over a period of time, and that is what has actually happened. Over a period of 10 years the building has been subject to constant change."

Norman Foster, More with Less lecture, February 1979

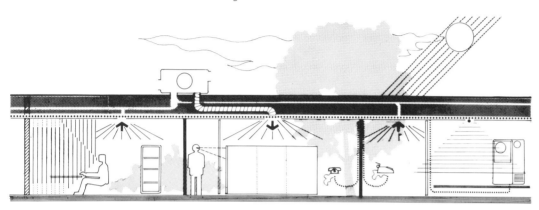

rejected on several counts: it did not allow sufficient space for car parking and possible expansion; it required opening windows which would result in traffic noise disturbance; and electricity and phone distribution were restricted to the perimeter of the bays. Also certain services and facilities could not be incorporated without expensive and complex conversion of the standard units.

The second proposal — essentially a two-storey version of the first — was rejected for much the same reasons and because the extra parking space advantage gained was offset by expensive pile foundations, necessary because of the low bearing capacity of the reclaimed land of the site.

The third solution — Foster Associates' preferred option — was for a custom-designed, deep-plan building with full environmental control using lightweight industrialised components. Its advantages were clear. The lightweight structure would need no deep foundations as it could sit on a thin raft of concrete. The elimination of the internal courtyards for ventilation meant that a compact building form was possible, and the large, uninterrupted internal space allowed the gross building area to be reduced. Air-conditioning would allow sealed glazing to eliminate traffic noise and, finally, the use of an open industrialised component system would allow design and selection to suit specific standards within the costs and time available. This last proposal was adopted and within days work began on site.

A diagrammatic representation of some of the service systems of the building. Roof-mounted air-conditioning units — positioned over the columns — connect directly to high-level flow and return ducting. All services are supplied from the roof zone, telephone and electrical cabling being run down the columns to worktop height. Eye-level height partitions allow privacy for individual work-stations.

In this exploded isometric the roof, complete with its air-handling units and chillers, is 'removed' to expose the network of air distribution ducts and the internal planning arrangement of the building as it was on completion in 1971. Over the years this arrangement has been extensively altered, but the possible extension indicated has never materialised.
1 car park
2 general office
3 managers' offices
4 reprographics dept.
5 boiler room
6 lavatories
7 kitchen
8 restaurant
9 reception
10 computer room
11 control section
12 plantroom
13 telephone exchange
14 stationery store
15 key punch operators

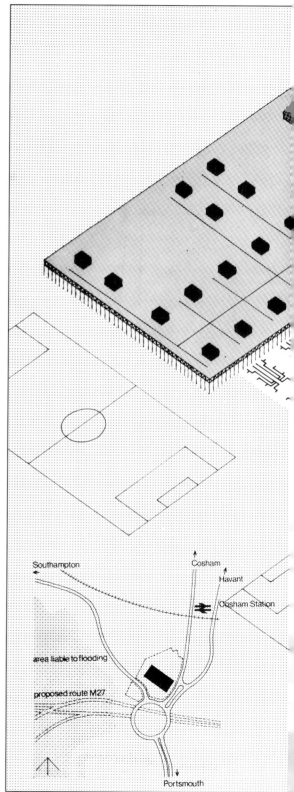

In an unlikely coincidence, it was discovered that IBM Cosham and Crystal Palace shared an identical structural grid and construction period. A drawing was found which showed that even construction techniques were similar, though, at Cosham, a fork-lift truck superseded the horse.

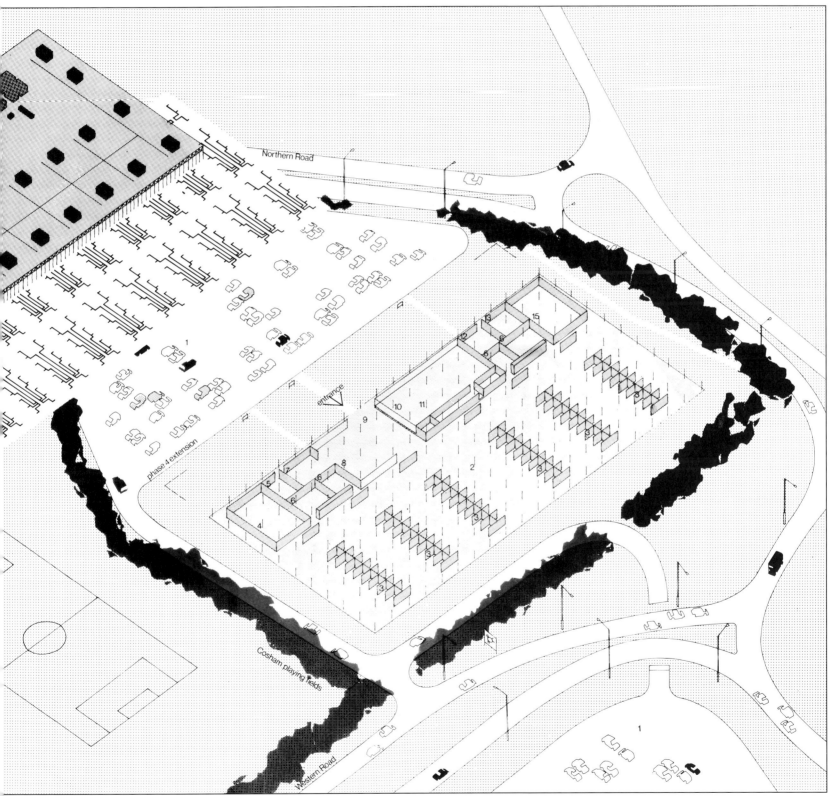

Northern Road

entrance

phase 4 extension

Cosham playing fields

Western Road

Engineer Tony Hunt presented a series of alternative structural systems ranging from heavy 'I' sections, as used at Reliance Controls, to an omnidirectional space-frame. In the event Foster Associates chose 7.5 metre Metsec lattice beams at 2.4 metre centres (centre bottom).

The corner condition of IBM Cosham under construction and complete. Cosham consists of the lightweight structure of earlier projects, but this time enclosed by a transparent glass skin revealing the edge of the whole roof service zone.

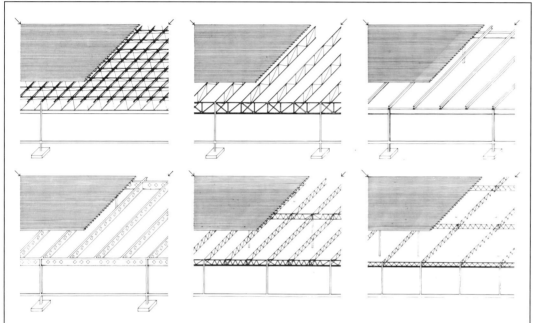

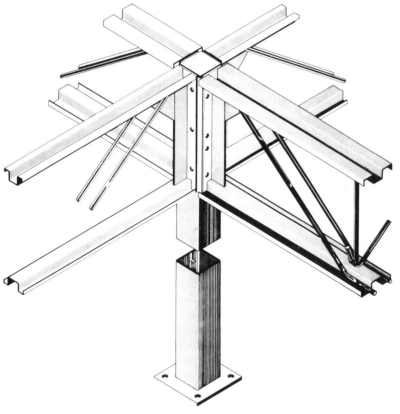

This standard intersection of 600 mm welded-steel Metsec lattice girder beams bolted to square steel columns is the key to the construction of the building. The large openings between top and bottom chords created a service area deep enough to permit the easy suspension of cables and ducts, while allowing the whole roof zone to serve as a return air plenum for the ventilation system. Even the square tube stanchions serve a second function as cable drops for power and telephones, and as supports for outlet boxes above floor level.

What is missing from this analysis is a theme which Norman Foster still considers to be a central and radical aspect of IBM Cosham. Again, as at Reliance Controls or the recently completed Fred Olsen Amenity Centre, here is evidence of the practice introducing a psychological reading of the brief below the surface of the pragmatic one.

"We were very much entrepreneurs of the concept", Foster explains. "You must remember that for this client at that time it would have been far more usual to have made three separate buildings — an office building, an amenity building and a computer building. Of these the computer building would have been the 'shrine', and the ground slab would have been customised for it. The idea that you could put all those buildings under one roof umbrella and then have this capability for moving them around beneath it has its roots in the Newport School competition and before. It is a recurring theme. The Sainsbury Centre did exactly the same thing for a very different kind of institution, and the same thinking can be seen as late as the Renault Distribution Centre and as early as Reliance Controls too."

More demanding at the time must have been the extreme speed demanded by IBM, especially as it quickly became clear that there would be no set brief. The ramifications of this are apparent in the practice's report at the time: "The building is considered as a synthesis of systems — the integration of structure, environmental control, movement and location. These systems are organised specifically as a direct response to a brief which is typical of a company with a high growth rate.

"It is in the nature of such a brief that requirements can only be defined broadly at the time when design is initiated and will develop and change during the design and construction period. This is particularly evident with a fast overall programme. It is necessary that the internal space and accommodation should be capable of adaptation, change and growth during occupation."

Engineered so as to be entirely behind the glazing line, each box section of the glazing frame is slotted on its outside edge to receive a thin neoprene extrusion designed to hold two sheets of glass.

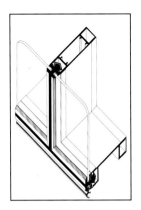

The glazing projects out over the edge of the floor slab with an aluminium drip inserted into the lower horizontal neoprene extrusion. Beneath is a neat perimeter drainage strip of pebbles.

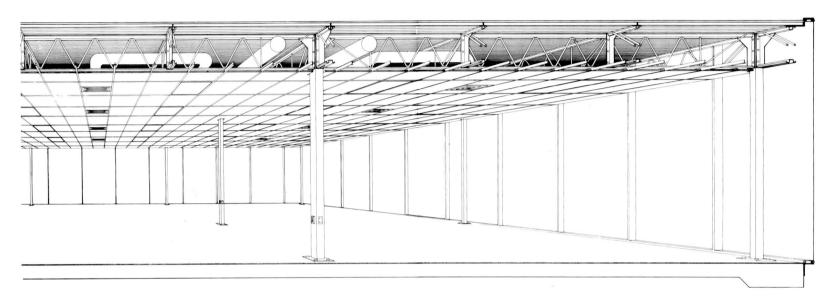

The building's structure and servicing system explained in one straightforward drawing. The corrugated steel roof decking is supported by Metsec lattice beams bolted to square stanchions, themselves bolted directly to the reinforced-concrete ground slab. The roof zone above the false ceiling, and the hollow columns, carry ducted services and wiring.

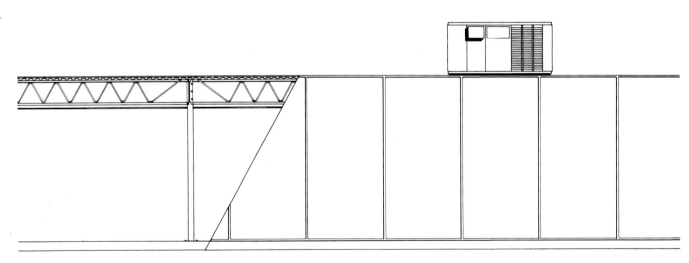

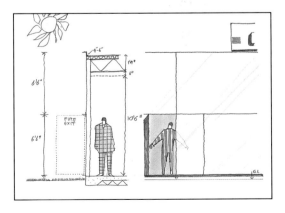

An early sketch for a possible escape route proposed an outward opening fire door inserted into the cladding system as a half-height door hung between the mullions. Within a more formal frame, this system is used on the completed building.

The glass envelope at Cosham is formed using aluminium box section glazing frames, the vertical mullions spanning from slab level to the top chord of the perimeter lattice roof beams and supporting 4 x 2 m bronze-tinted solar glass panels.

"It had been standard practice at IBM, up to that point in time, to treat a computer room as something sacred, rather like a chapel."

Norman Foster, lecture at Hong Kong University, February 1980

"Our earlier school systems studies showed the perimeter of the building as a lattice structure, giving an overhang for circulation with the glass wall set back. On the IBM project we introduced the glass skin on the outside and took advantage of that same perimeter walkway, but now inside the building itself. What is interesting is that this edge has now become the popular location for *ad hoc* conferences and the actual conference rooms provided are not used."

Norman Foster, lecture at Hong Kong University, February 1980

The interior of the computer suite, originally labelled the machine room. Apart from extra air-conditioning requirements, it was treated much as any other part of the building, the standard ceiling treatment being made possible by the installation of a 300 mm raised floor system to accept the extra cabling.

Even with solar glazing, the edge zone of the building cannot maintain the same environmental standards as the main office areas, becoming warmer, for instance, in bright sunshine (note the open fire doors). Using this area for circulation overcame the problem and proved so successful that the same solution was integrated into the planning of subsequent buildings, most notably Willis Faber & Dumas.

The glass-enclosed cafeteria was initially placed adjacent to the reception area, and circulation mall that runs east-west across the building. When the computer room needed to expand, it was easily relocated to the northwest corner of the building.

A variety of office layouts was created in the building. Low-level partitions throughout the general area maintained a sense of openness, while desks close to the edge of the building almost seem part of the landscape. Only the computer room needed a more contained environment.

Four-way power and telephone service outlets were fixed to (and supplied via) each column. Alternative distribution systems from these were drawn for comparison, the fixed desk-height trunking (top) quickly giving way to a more flexible floor-level arrangement.

In the final design the four-way service outlets, now mounted near the foot of each column, were augmented by free-standing satellite outlets known as 'dice boxes'. These were fixed to the floor where required and fed by tough, flexible metal conduits.

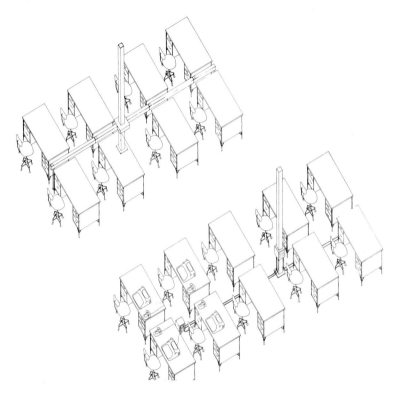

Early plans offered a rich variety of space-utilisation arrangements for the offices, including open and partitioned work-stations, inner cellular management offices, and small conference facilities. The strictly observed perimeter circulation zone is punctuated by intermittently used conference areas shielded by indoor planting.

Engineer Loren Butt, who was to have a long association with the practice, joined soon after IBM Cosham was under way. He recalls the remarkable speed with which the pilot building was erected. "The way the activities overlapped on site was very interesting", he notes. "At one end the structure was being put up whilst at the other end internal finishes were already starting — it was almost as if the building were coming out of an extrusion machine."

Butt also points out an elaborate and unlikely coincidence of construction between IBM Cosham and the Crystal Palace. "I worked out, at one point, that the construction period was the same, the same structural bay module was used (24 feet), and that the start and finish dates were exactly 120 years apart, almost to the day!" To complete the parallel, two remarkably similar site photographs exist of the two buildings under construction.

IBM Cosham introduced the notion of using the peripheral areas of the building for secondary circulation and meeting places, later to be used at the Willis Faber & Dumas building in Ipswich. No desks are pressed up against the windows, where local solar gain might prove too uncomfortable. Instead, the circulation zone allows the external views to be enjoyed by the office workers as well as their managers. Again one suspects that Foster rather enjoyed the social inversion here: the enclosed managerial offices, traditionally the 'prime' spaces closest to the windows, are in this instance located towards the middle of the building, away from the views.

Such manipulation indicates a desire for social integration that has proved every bit as much a recurring theme as many of Foster Associates' structural or practical philosophies. At Reliance Controls and the Olsen Amenity Centre, workers and managers had been brought together under the same roof, but in carefully delineated areas. At IBM, for the first time, Foster introduced a much closer integration, in the process reversing social convention. It was to provide an exact model in the planning of the Hongkong Bank's new headquarters — an institution that might be considered a bastion of such convention — and was even further exploited at the Willis Faber & Dumas building in Ipswich where separate managerial offices were almost totally eliminated.

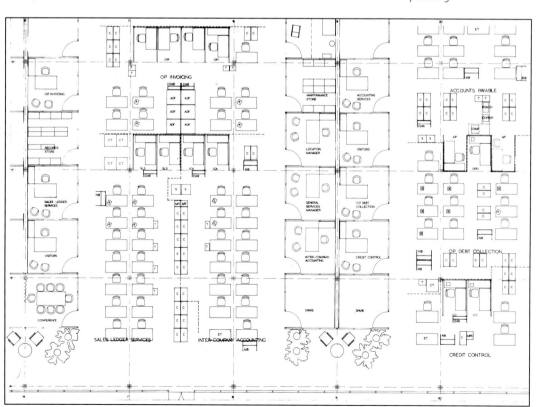

In the finished building, semi-private work-station areas were installed, using low-level partitions to provide privacy for desk work while allowing extended views across the building from a standing position.

An early plan of the space utilisation at Cosham, much as when the building first opened but omitting to show the low-level partitions used throughout the open-plan office areas.
1 main entrance
2 reception
3 restaurant
4 kitchen
5 lavatories
6 cellular offices
7 central 'street'
8 open-plan offices
9 circulation zone
10 computer suite
Soon after opening, the main entrance was moved to the east side of the building, at the end of the 'street', and the computer suite extended through to the restaurant area.

A conceptual view between cellular offices of one of the large open-plan office areas. Over the 20 years of IBM occupation, the proportion of open office space has been greatly reduced as specialists have replaced clerical workers.

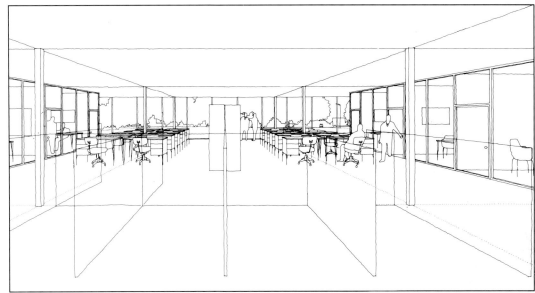

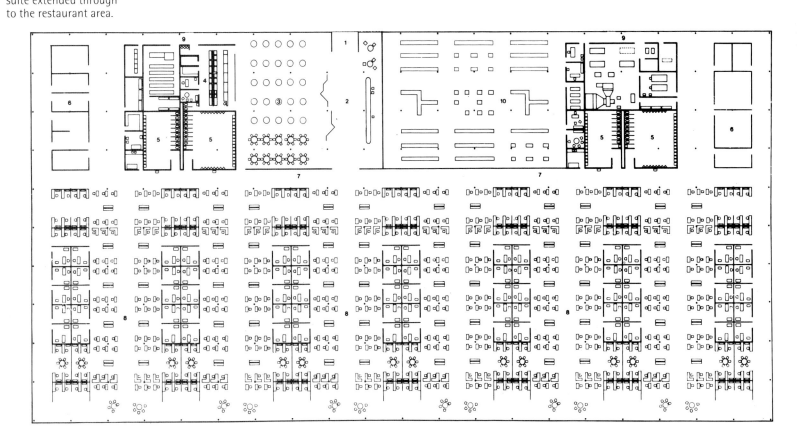

"Part of my brief was to read (Lance Wright's) appraisal and show visually the points being made. With its bronze glass cladding reflecting clouds and trees, this shot aimed to bring out the point, 'a building which virtually disappears', although at second glance the duplicated sun does give the game away."

Richard Einzig, *Industrial and Commercial Photography*, July 1973

"When you drive up to the IBM building it isn't there. All you find is a duplication of reality: two parking lots, two sets of trees, a symmetrical sky and yourself doubled — most of it disappearing to infinity."

Charles Jencks, *A&U*, September 1975

"The building is not disguised in any way. It is an honest, straightforward glass box. But when you look at it you don't see a glass box, you see the surrounding trees and things like that. This is probably carrying self-effacement to the point of lunacy, except, of course, it has given the building a very powerful image of quality — of a curiously negative or back-to-front kind — which Foster was to exploit brilliantly, I think, in his Willis Faber building."

Reyner Banham, the Yellow Bicycle lecture at UEA, June 1985

The long tinted-glass south elevation of IBM Cosham, reflecting the grass and trees that separate it from Portsbridge Road.

"We have never really
had the luxury of that
utopian vision where a
client isolates a brief and
hands it over to a design
team who then, in glori-
ous isolation, design a
fixed building and hand
it over to a contractor
who produces a fixed
building. In our experi-
ence life is not like that.
The only constant is
change."

Norman Foster, lecture
at the Construction
Industry Conference,
May 1980

The south side of the
building in bright sun-
light, showing the tran-
sparency of the tinted
glazing under these con-
ditions.

Another product of Foster Associates' integrated
approach was the location of the machine or
computer room. Conventionally, the solution
would have been to provide special construction throughout this area. At Cosham, however,
the machine room has the same ceiling detailing as the rest of the building; provision of a
raised floor and standard internal partitions
satisfy the special services and humidity control such spaces need.

Ingenious, cost-effective solutions within
an elegant office building are easy to miss,
despite its size. When Cosham was completed
and in use it was acclaimed for its efficiency. At
a senior management seminar, an IBM executive once introduced Norman Foster as the
architect of the only IBM building which, if it
burned down, would be instantly re-commis-
sioned without alteration.

Such assessments are justifiable, and yet
it is important to remember that IBM Cosham
was also built very quickly and cost very little.
This was an award-winning building achieved
for the sort of money normally associated with
mediocrity. However, if the cost limitations

An informal sitting area
located in the perimeter
zone and given privacy
by indoor plants.

At the edge of the build-
ing the suspended
ceiling is stopped un-
ashamedly short, expos-
ing the steel structure
above.

Yellow roller-blinds were installed along those elevations where the deep penetration of sunlight may have proved distracting or uncomfortable, but they are rarely used, the office workers preferring the extensive views offered through the full-height glazing.

The east-west circulation 'street' running from one side of the building to the other. Glass partitions separate it from the service and computer areas to the north and the office zones to the south.

Bottom: under certain light conditions the ephemeralisation of the building envelope can be remarkable, and has proved a colour photographer's dream.

proposed to overcome the restrictions imposed by the slab construction. It was not without its advantages however. When the computer room had to be expanded, IBM was surprised to find that the cost of the operation was half of their estimate based on past experience.

The internal layout of the building was a model of clarity. A main circulation corridor, known as the 'street', connected all the facilities: restaurant, computer room, lavatories and word-processing areas. From the 'street', smaller subsidiary 'lanes' led down between the work spaces. With the extensive use of low-level partitions and occasional full-height glazing, where privacy of sound was required, it was more or less impossible to become disorientated. Interestingly, the design could eschew the notion of a grand entrance and a fixed circulation pattern aligned to it. "For a long time the entrance was at one end of the building", says Norman Foster. "Then one day we popped it out and moved it down to the other end. It seemed to work better that way."

IBM Cosham must now be considered one of the most influential buildings in the Foster Associates *oeuvre*, an extraordinary position

failed to compromise the structure's overall quality, they did at times pare certain features to the bone.

"To do what we did was possible only by being quite ruthless", Norman Foster recalls. "You laid the ground slab as if it were a road and put a carpet straight on to it knowing that this would have repercussions on flexibility of services." But overhead servicing proved to be the answer, with cables routed down through the columns. Access to telephone and power lines, it was originally assumed, would then be via flush-mounted points at the mid-point or base of each column. As the design progressed, however, increased demand necessitated the addition of what came to be known as 'dice-boxes'. Mounted on the columns, these could be directly accessed or, more usually, could feed cables to free-standing boxes positioned nearer the equipment to be used.

The raised floor in the computer room, one of the first installations of its type, was an early design decision by Foster Associates

"IBM takes this (Paxton) tradition to its logical conclusion and makes the whole building a window. Of course the roof and floor aren't glass, but one assumes Foster Associates will solve this rather minor inconsistency in time."

Charles Jencks, *A&U*, September 1975

"From the economics derived from the simple envelope the architect has found money to pay for complete air-conditioning, carpet throughout, and a high standard of equipment. He has clearly fulfilled his task of giving good value for money, and the building demonstrates that architecture can be produced from a tough commercial situation by the exercise of ingenuity and imagination."

Extract from the assessors' report for the RIBA Award, 1972

when its tight budget and short time-frame are considered. Its standing was apparent on completion. IBM's UK management was put in the embarrassing position of explaining to the American head office just why so much supposedly cheap, temporary accommodation had been commissioned in the years before Cosham, when they had now clearly proved that far better results could be obtained just as quickly and for less cost.

More impressively, the building has fully stood the test of time. It was expected to last only three or four years, until a permanent headquarters building (by Arup Associates) was completed on a site nearby. When that time came, however, the Cosham building had proved so popular that IBM decided to retain it as an independent research office — expanding the computer room significantly to do so.

In 1988, 17 years after completion, the building interior was completely refurbished by Foster Associates, following almost exactly the design intentions laid out all those years before. Major planning changes have been implemented without problem, and of the major elements only the flat roof has been upgraded and the air-handling units replaced. The building's structure and reflective glazing, on the other hand, have survived as good as new.

Graham Vickers

The internal roller-blinds are shown lowered in this view of one corner of the building. Attached to the outer edge of the top chord of the perimeter structural beam, the yellow blinds are completely hidden from the office areas inside, but are able to drop through the slot left at the edge of the building between the ceiling, structure and glazing. The blinds are electrically operated — via a manual switch — so that a perfect alignment is maintained along the whole elevation.

Under strong sunlight the rich bronze tinting of the solar-reflective glass becomes very apparent and, with their minimal neoprene fixing beads for head, foot and mullion, the individual panes seem almost to float in the landscape.

The building at night, seen through the surrounding belt of trees. The depth of internal illumination visible shows the extraordinary transparency of all but the northern service core areas.

With a low evening sun illuminating the interior, the edge condition of the building is clearly seen. There is no corner mullion, the two abutting sheets of glass being joined instead with an early form of silicone sealant. Two stainless-steel clips provide extra support.

In at the Beginning
by Tony Hunt

Below: Norman Foster's photograph of the assembly area in the completed Reliance building. With special fixings to the secondary beams, the metal roof deck acts as a structural diaphragm, eliminating diagonal bracing.

A highly respected engineer, Tony Hunt has pursued an active interest in steel structures for more than 30 years. After qualifying he worked with Felix Samuely before establishing his own practice, Anthony Hunt Associates, in 1962. He has collaborated with many of Britain's leading architects and was consultant engineer for all the Team 4 work, as well as many of the early projects of both Richard Rogers & Partners and Foster Associates.

In 1988, he went into partnership with the architects YRM and is now chairman of YRM Anthony Hunt Associates and a director of the YRM Partnership. He was elected an honorary Fellow of the Royal Institute of British Architects in 1989.

As part of a costing exercise for Reliance Controls Tony Hunt prepared this drawing, comparing all the structural systems suitable for an industrial building with the 'preferred' solution.

I first met Richard Rogers at a dinner party held by a mutual friend, Neave Brown. Richard was there with Su and, as I remember, they had only recently returned from the USA and were in the process of setting up Team 4. I had just arrived in London too, also to set up my first office. But unlike Richard and Su, who had only just completed their university education, and although we were contemporaries, I had already been working for a number of years.

Looking back now, I can see I was very lucky to have had my first job with the structural engineer Felix Samuely. This was the late 1950s and they were doing some good work, innovative work, with some of the best architects of the time. A lot of my earliest projects were for the Lyons Israel Ellis Partnership, a lot of reinforced-concrete, and it was through them I got used to working closely with architects. This happened very naturally, so I have tended to take that idea of a working relationship very much for granted. It certainly was a great surprise, later, to come across architects who seemed happy to just send you their finished design drawings to 'engineer' up.

In those days though, we were all in it together. They were exciting times: we were all young and we were building the new Britain, which, even then, was still recovering from the Second World War. We thought we could do anything. Lyons Israel, too, were one of those firms that seemed to spawn budding architects destined to go off and set up on their own. Neave Brown was there, as were Jim Stirling and James Gowan — that's where they met. There were quite a few others — John Miller and Patrick Hodgkinson for example — and some, of course, who did not become 'household' names, even if good architects. All this stood me in good stead because, when I set up on my own, it was these people who gave me some of my first jobs.

Working with architects was a real bonus for me. While training, I had considered switching to architecture but, following my father's advice, good advice too, I decided to complete the engineering first. I had also got

used to working with services engineers. This was partly a necessity of working in reinforced-concrete. I remember especially working on the new lecture hall for the post-graduate medical centre at Hammersmith Hospital — one of my first major projects at Samuely's — where the precast concrete was to form stepped seating through which would run all the ventilation ducting: the architecture, engineering and services were inextricably combined and had to be right first time.

This interest in teamwork and design continued after I left Samuely's in 1960. For six months I actually worked for the formative Conran Design office as a furniture designer, but it wasn't really the success I expected, so I quickly accepted the opportunity to go into a joint practice with two architects interested in setting up a multi-disciplinary office. This was

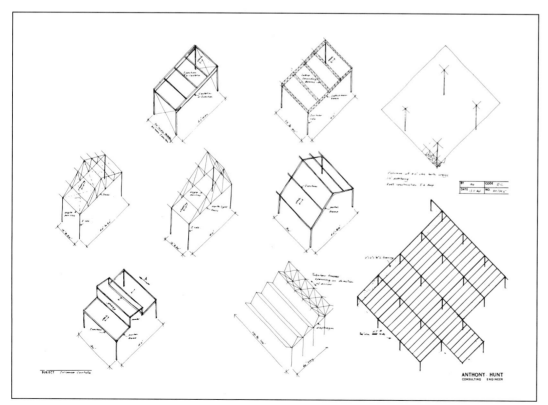

ANTHONY HUNT
CONSULTING ENGINEER

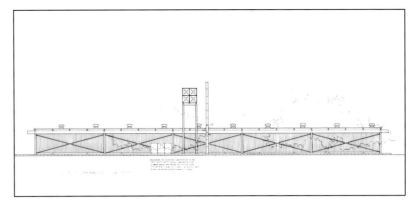

Structural engineering as architecture. At Reliance, with its exposed structure and minimalist detailing, the dividing line between the two is impossible to define.

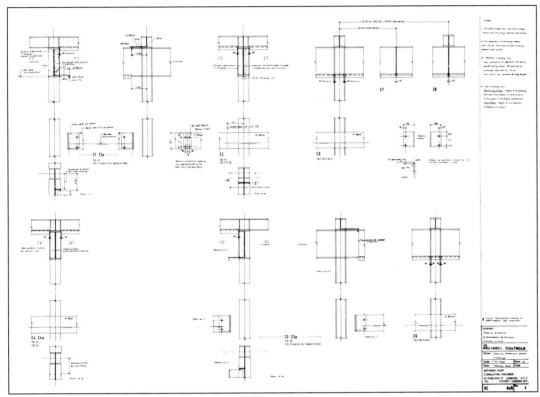

in Berkshire and I worked there for two years before getting caught in the crossfire of a partnership break-up. It was then that I realised it was time to set up on my own.

I had got on very well with Richard and Su at the dinner, but it was some months later before we met again — and this time to work together. I was working then with an architect, John Howard — another great friend of Richard's and mine — on a block of flats in Hornsey, and either he or the quantity surveyor on that job, who had also done some work for Team 4 by then, recommended me to them. This was for the Retreat, though then we referred to it as 'the Hut'. I think they had thought they could do most of the engineering themselves but then decided they needed a professional opinion: one way or another, I ended up doing some detail drawings for them. I met Norman and Wendy, of course, enjoyed their company and it was the start of a long and happy relationship.

I worked on all their early housing projects; sometimes officially, sometimes as a friend. We all got on very well and between work — we were all doing long hours in those days — we often met socially. Richard and Su,

The simplicity and clarity of thinking behind Reliance Controls is no less apparent internally. Full-height glazed partitions allowed the layout of the whole building to be understood at a glance.

With intense effort and careful analysis, Tony Hunt was able to reduce the number of structural elements — and their various connections — to an absolute minimum.

myself, my first wife Pat and several assorted kids even piled into my rather tired Volkswagen Variant one summer and set off to Italy for a holiday together. The quantity surveyor, John Walker, appeared on the scene at this time and quickly became an ally, always willing to try his best with any direction we wanted to pursue.

The Retreat naturally led on to the Creek Vean house itself. At this stage, it was still seen as an extension to an existing Victorian building on the site. It was clear Norman and Richard would have preferred to remove the old building but didn't know how to suggest the idea to Marcus Brumwell, the client — it was a remarkably undistinguished building. Eventually, it was decided I should do a survey of it and I was able to report, honestly, that retaining the building would present major problems: it was in poor condition and differential settlement would have been difficult to control.

In many ways, however, all these early houses were structurally 'traditional' buildings, and it was not until Reliance Controls came along that there was a project in which I could become truly involved. For Norman, Richard and myself this has to be one of the major turning points of our careers. It was the first time we used an appropriate technology for the time and building type. After Reliance, we could go forward, developing these ideas together and separately and, I believe, it was the start of a whole new concept of architecture and engineering for industrial buildings.

It was our first 'industrial' commission and the challenge was exciting. Factory buildings at that time were almost all of the office-at-the-front, shed-at-the-back type, mostly with saw-tooth north-light roofs. With a very small budget we set out to break this mould and produce a building which would reflect our different thinking: no 'front and back'; one entrance for all; and a democratic working environment. Our aim was a simplicity and clarity of structure, a flat roof, the maximum repetition and precision of elements, and an ease of assembly using as much prefabrication as possible.

The team of Norman, Richard, John Walker and myself was now so well established that, if we didn't quite read each other's minds, we certainly worked together using the simplest of 'shorthands'. It's very difficult, now, to remember who made which decision or how. We met once a week and were joined, at quite an early

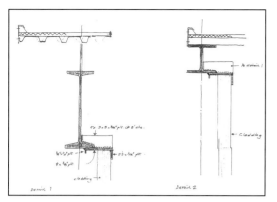

Tony Hunt's working sketch of the relationship between main and secondary beams, and cladding. All structural connections at Reliance, whether made off- or on-site, were welded.

Below: though far from necessary, cross-bracing was included on all four sides of the Reliance building, in every structural bay except that which marked the main entrance.

stage, by Loren Butt, a services engineer then working for Haden's, but he, too, quickly became an ally and launched himself into our collaborative ways.

Initially, we tested a number of building forms and structural options which we reviewed at our weekly design sessions, but the direction of our preferred solution became clear very early on: steel frame, a single cladding system from floor to roof — either profiled steel sheeting or glazing — and a profiled steel roof-deck, all within one envelope. The important feature of this simple assembly was that through intensive thinking the steel frame

all the options to prove to the client our solution was the best and cheapest. Services coordination was just as important. At Reliance, the services were not too complicated: there was no cooling or ducting, for instance — the building was naturally ventilated — and electrical requirements were light. Loren decided

The original design included full-height glazing running the whole length of the building's north elevation.

ing was extended, all this work paid off with the whole of phase two being constructed without disruption to the existing building.

Of course, the point that I always have to answer for now is the multiple cross-bracing, not only along the sides that would have required some diagonal support anyway, but also along the two elevations — one facing the main road — that did not require it at all. I am still a little embarrassed: it is not a 'pure' structure, so the engineer in me can never be entirely satisfied. The designer in me, however, tends to agree it makes the building look better. The real irony — and for me a far more difficult problem — was that Norman, who had used all his charm to persuade me to accept multiple cross-bracing for the building, then decided the water tower would be better without it. As a very tall, very slender portal frame, this really did present some problems!

Despite the structural anomalies, Reliance was a great success and we felt we had made our mark. Certainly, I was now very busy but, sadly, Richard and Norman parted and for a while neither had much work at all. But just when Norman and Wendy were ready to give up on England, a sudden rush of projects turned up in quick succession which allowed us to build on the groundwork we had established at Reliance. Fred Olsen's Amenity Centre, Computer Technology — an early use of high-strength friction-grip bolted connections — and IBM Cosham followed each other over a period of just a few months it seems now.

The team came back together, Richard's presence being replaced by Birkin Haward who had recently joined what was now Foster Associates, as had Loren, bravely leaving the security of Haden's. Each project brought its own successes and challenges. More complex services had to be integrated, different cladding and structural systems could be explored.

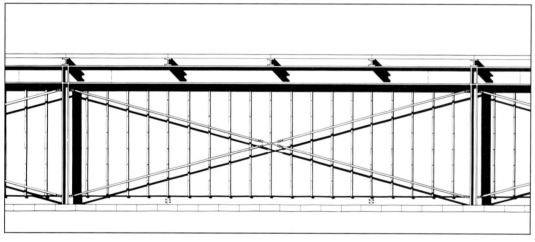

could be reduced to only four elements: the main column and cross-head welded together; a main beam; a secondary beam; and repetitive diagonal bracing.

We approached the design of the cladding and roof in the same minimalist way, although this was not a word in our contemporary vocabulary. Traditionally, metal-clad sheds had sheeting rails and posts. We threw them away and designed the cladding to span top to bottom as its own structure, double-skinned with insulation between. Similarly, with the roof, we made the metal deck work twice as hard by turning the whole roof into a diaphragm with special seam fastenings and extra fixings between deck and secondary beams, thus eliminating any wind-bracing members in the roof. The resulting structure and cladding thus became a fully engineered stressed box.

We all worked incredibly hard; Norman did many of his own working drawings, I did all of mine. John Walker worked his way through

heating and electrical distribution were best handled in the floor, so only lighting was required in the roof. But even this was carefully considered and the secondary beam spacing was specifically chosen so that the fluorescent tubes would fit exactly.

The omission of high-level ducting certainly simplified the structural design. It could be light, and straightforward 'I'-beams could be used. There were long discussions about the positioning of the cladding but the brief's insistence on the possibility of extension made an 'exposed' structure the best option. This suited my preference for an all-welded structure since all difficult-to-protect, mechanical joints were avoided. In fact, there are no fixings into the structure at all in the final design. Site welding, of course, is not that easy, all too quickly disrupted by bad weather, but for our purposes it worked well and we achieved our elegant solution. When, eventually, the build-

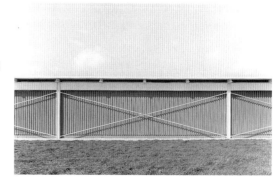

The structural frame at IBM Cosham was put up in three weeks and required only one fork-lift truck for its erection. A two-way portal structure, primary and secondary beams are of the same depth.

The ground slab at Cosham is a reinforced-concrete flexible raft that was constructed using road-laying techniques. Construction of the slab and structural frame were carried out simultaneously in an overlapping sequence.

Design sessions were intense, we searched hard, experimented, but always we were learning.

And the learning paid off with IBM's pilot head office. Getting this job was a saga in itself. I had just moved into new offices in Bedford Street, Covent Garden. A four-storey building, it was far too large for me then but offices were difficult to come by and I intended to sublet. I was still unpacking when Norman phoned in some agitation to say that IBM had rung and would like to visit his office. At this time Norman and Wendy — and half a dozen others — were still working out of their flat in Hampstead Hill Gardens, effective but rather chaotic. We agreed he should borrow one of my floors and, virtually overnight, a nameplate appeared on the door, screens were found, Zeev Avram lent us some furniture and Foster

Castellated beams at the Fred Olsen amenity centre.

Associates' Bedford Street office was in operation. Gerry Deighton of IBM was impressed enough to give us the job and, though not intended, Foster Associates became my tenants.

IBM's brief called only for the organisation of whichever 'commercial' temporary system we thought best. We researched these but all proved totally unsatisfactory to our way of thinking, being inflexible, nasty and not cheap. Our experience told us we could do far better with a new building, still meeting the tight budget and programme limits. Much to our surprise, the client agreed with us.

The building was to be single-storey again and structurally there were only two options — a long-span structure on pile supported columns or a short-span structure on a raft. The short-span solution won on the three factors of simplicity, cost and speed of construction — we had a nine month programme to complete 115 000 square feet of floor area. We were so short of time that we decided to write a closely

defined performance specification for the structure. This was an American method that Norman had been studying and considering for some time, but it was new to me. With little alternative we optimistically pressed on and, somewhat to our relief, it worked very well.

The specification for the structure was issued to six firms who specialised in light-weight-steel prefabricated systems, and the tender was won by Metal Sections (Metsec). The structural solution was the simplest — one column type, one primary lattice girder and one secondary lattice girder of the same depth, with the whole frame braced from corner to corner as two 240ft squares. Air-conditioning units were positioned over the column heads to avoid loading any of the beams, thus ensuring that they were as light as they could possibly be. Cross-bracing was avoided in the vertical plane by developing the structure as a two-way portal frame.

Since the column spacing was close (24 feet in each direction), the foundation loads were light and we found it possible to design

Cincinnati Milacron, designed at the same time as IBM Cosham and incorporating an identical structure.

an overall flexible raft to the allowable bearing pressure of quarter of a ton per square foot, mesh reinforced and constructed on load-laying principles. The frame itself was put up in three weeks as an overlapping sequence with construction of the raft, needing only fork-lift trucks for its erection.

For me, IBM Cosham has always seemed a masterpiece, totally co-ordinated, yet with a simplicity I doubt we could better today. It was the culmination of four exciting years of intense teamwork. Foster Associates and Anthony Hunt Associates were now firmly established. Before IBM was completed Willis Faber & Dumas was commissioned, and before that building opened we started work on the Sainsbury Centre. Great buildings too, and just as exciting as projects, but times were changing.

Both companies were expanding rapidly. Within two years, Norman outgrew Bedford Street and moved on to Fitzroy Street: I was grateful to take over the space he vacated. Other responsibilities were accumulating, teams grew, work had to be delegated. The days of our regular design sessions were drawing to a close. Despite our later, better-known achievements, the work we carried out in this period still brings immense personal satisfaction. It is always best to be in at the beginning.

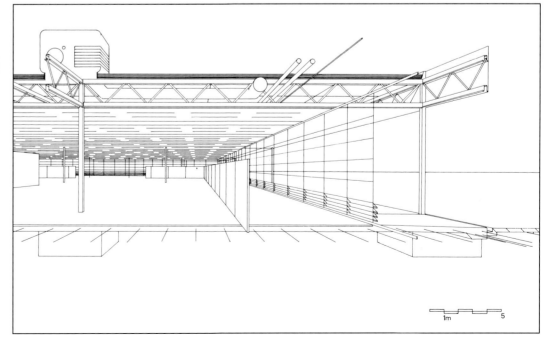

Computer Technology
Hemel Hempstead
Hertfordshire

The reception area of Computer Technology's first building, a converted canning factory modernised by Foster Associates in 1969.

The ground floor of the canning factory. The ceiling lighting is crossed by cable trays that provide a flexible network for the vertical service distribution. Foster Associates' most important innovation, however, proved to be the installation of fitted carpet throughout the work areas.

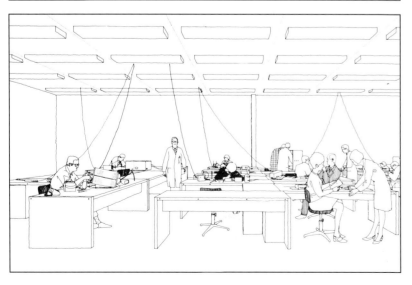

An omni-directional 'service zone' was created beneath the canning factory's new suspended ceiling, with all services dropping vertically down to the work-stations.

If IBM Cosham achieved a minimalist elegance in the face of a tight budget, Foster Associates' next permanent building in Hemel Hempstead was to be visually much bolder. Even so, the Computer Technology permanent building, which was to work in conjunction with the company's earlier canning factory refit and succeed the well-known temporary air structure, was also realised on limited finance. Here again Foster was to provide a flexible internal space, serviced entirely overhead, leaving the maximum floor area clear of structure.

For the final stage of their involvement with the young computer company, Foster Associates proposed a single-storey, deep-plan building enclosing a generous air-conditioned and landscaped space. From the beginning, Computer Technology's managing director, Iann Barron, had enthusiastically agreed with Foster Associates' proposal that there should be a single enclosure for varied activities, with a common entrance. Internal divisions would be totally flexible and their location determined only by operational demands. Apart from a few enclosed spaces which had to take account of special acoustic or other requirements, there was to be a single dynamic space in which all activities, from basic research analysis to the physical assembly of computers, could take place. Barron had enthusiastically endorsed Foster Associates' earlier proposals for the air-supported office and had worked there for 12 months. Norman Foster's own preoccupation with the social benefits of breaking down traditional barriers within the workplace had, at last, found overt support from his client.

The new building, linked to the original converted canning factory by a glazed corridor, was to be both a continuation and a more satisfactory realisation of intentions hastily proposed there. In the old building some features already enshrined the spirit of the new building to come: its wall-to-wall carpeting symbolised a flexible, socially integrated and humane working space. Extending through the assembly workshops, the carpet had actually improved work practices which were now far tidier and cleaner.

It had even prompted Foster Associates' first venture into furniture systems; associate Martin Francis had designed furniture for the

The office and workshop furniture for the canning factory modernisation was designed by Foster Associates – the first to be specially designed for a building by the practice.

original conversion and later repeated the exercise for the new building. Assembly benches, internal walls, desks, tables and kitchen worktops were all made from a simple system of knock-down components and partitions.

The building itself demands to be assessed not only in its physical context – a visually uninteresting Hemel Hempstead industrial estate – but also in terms of its cost and time-frame. The heady days of the (then) burgeoning computer industry demanded the sort of flexibility of approach which made Foster Associates the ideal choice of architect, but which also brought unusual conditions, not least from the company's financiers.

Engineer Loren Butt explains: "The spacing of the structure was interesting because the financing of the building came from ICFC (Industrial Construction Finance Corporation) who were very concerned about future uses of the building, beyond the time when CT might be using it. So the structural bay, the heights and structural spans were all influenced by financing. We looked at all that with glee, because future flexibility was what we were always talking about. It is true to say that Computer Technology was a firm changing

In the late 1960s Computer Technology represented one of the earliest of a new breed of 'clean' industries whose precision work and highly qualified staff required a different approach to conventional industrial building. Printed circuit board design and assembly was not an activity that could take place in a traditional factory. Foster Associates were one of the first firms of architects in Britain to see the design opportunities inherent in upgrading the workplace to new standards, providing the same comfort conditions for both workforce and management.

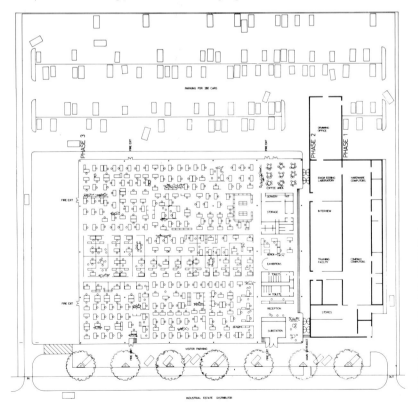

The permanent new Computer Technology building, seen to the left in this plan, linked to the converted canning factory, at right, by a glazed corridor. The contrast between the traditional two-storey, shallow-plan factory building and the new single-storey open-plan structure is striking.

The exterior of the new Computer Technology building. The grassed area outside the glazing actually aligns with the floor level inside. Only the vehicular access ramp and car park are set down at a lower level.

An early drawing by Birkin Haward of the rapid reconfiguration work-station arrangement at Computer Technology. Designing the fixtures and fittings as well as the building created true flexibility.

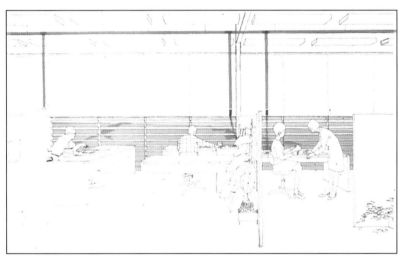

As in the earlier canning factory conversion, a vertical servicing system from the ceiling zone was prepared for the new building. As Norman Foster observed, the one great advantage of high-level servicing was its visibility: redundant sections could not be ignored as they might have been in underfloor ducts.

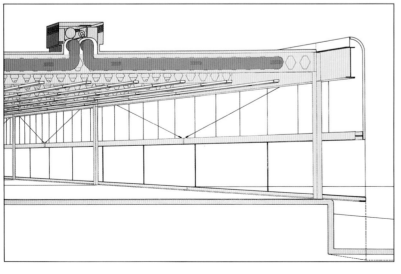

A part-section through the new building. Air-conditioning units were roof mounted on castellated roof beams which permitted free passage of all services and ducting. Unlike IBM Cosham, this service zone was hidden from the passer-by by solid cladding panels fixed above the glazing.

rapidly at the time. The degree of change in this building was far in excess of anything that happened in an IBM building. The mix of office and design space, and assembly areas was very flexible. One weekend, I recall, they took all of one department out and simply extended the assembly area — all in the same building. Computer Technology were using the flexibility that had, at least in part, been designed for future users at the behest of the financiers who paid for the building."

Despite this happy meeting of aims, cost limitations meant that the facility's practicality and visual expression of intention often needed to be extremely simply stated. Loren Butt suggests that in terms of temperature control, although the Computer Technology building represented an advance on the system installed at IBM Cosham, it was still not ideal. "Here we had the roof-mounted package solution that I would have preferred at Cosham", he says. "Even so, initially it had to go in with only heating and ventilating capability. The facility to add a cooling unit came later on, when more money became available."

The idea that there would never be any need for full-height partitions inside the building meant that there would be no need for a ceiling to provide a junction. This led to the notion of expressing the services throughout the building and exposing them in a way which would be both practical and visually exciting.

Between steel columns at 11-foot centres, castellated steel roof beams would permit the free penetration of a multi-coloured display of service lines: blue for cold water and sprinklers, red for hot water and heating ducts, yellow for rainwater pipes, orange for telephone cables, green for gas conduits. As a result, the interior of the Computer Technology building was to achieve a visual boldness that might not have been appropriate for a more traditional client.

Concern about insulation resulted in a much better standard than full-height glazing could have provided: only the lower section of the walls was glazed to retain an outside view. This lower band of Pilkington's umber-tinted Spectrafloat glass, which sat above a plinth of bolted concrete panels, contrasted dramatically with the highly insulated, snow-white panels above in a solution, in a way, prefiguring that of the Sainsbury Centre. Indeed, the Computer

"The exterior of this single-storey building is simple, direct, yet distinctive in expression. A large trade symbol fulfils its purpose while at the same time forming an interesting part of the appearance of the building seen as a whole."

Financial Times Industrial Architecture Award, 1971

"We were able to muscle in on that non-architectural field (of low-cost fast-build proprietary systems) by demonstrating that not only could we build at the same cost, but also that we could operate, if anything, faster, by using techniques of prefabrication, by introducing design concepts of flexibility, and by recognising that, for most of our commercial clients, the only constant was change itself. There are still a number of projects which go through the office that wouldn't be described as architects' architecture."

Norman Foster, *A&U*, September 1975

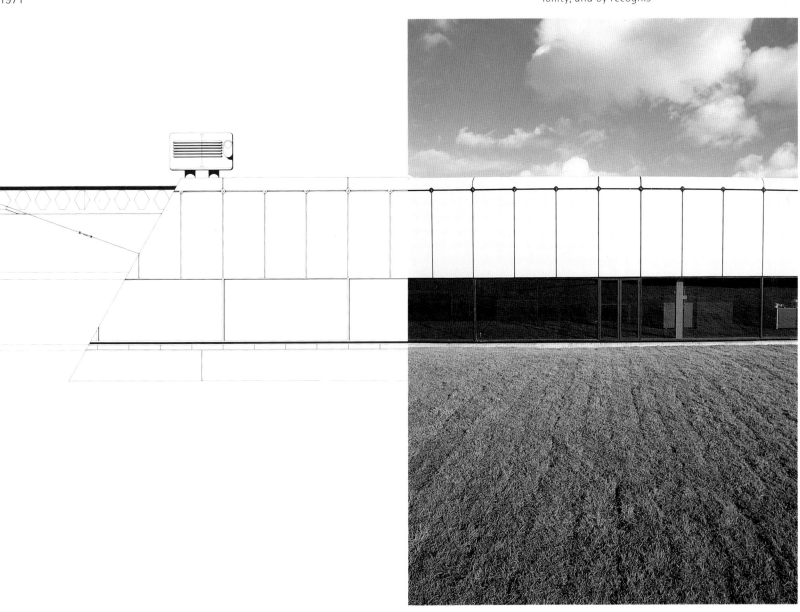

This cut-away elevation of the facade of the Computer Technology building exposes the castellated beam roof structure and diagonal bracing wires behind the white-painted, aluminium-faced polyurethane cladding panels. Derived from freezer-truck technology these panels, separated by neoprene strips, provide what appears to be a sealed 'umbrella' above the glazed lower section of the walls. In fact, the curved 'cornice' section merely conceals a traditional flat felt roof.

"There is nothing soft about Computer Technology, except its software and the fact that its Hemel Hempstead plant is the first factory in Britain where the production area is fully carpeted. The computer men were keen to break down the traditional white collar/blue collar division of British industry. Architecturally they agreed whole-heartedly with their architects that there should be only one shed with one entrance for everyone, and that divisions within the shed should be completely flexible without distinction of class or collar."

Nicholas Taylor, *The Sunday Times,* 5 May 1968

Iann Barron, Computer Technology's managing director, at work in the new building after its completion. It was Barron's enthusiasm for Foster Associates' innovations that made the entire sequence of jobs for Computer Technology possible.

The interior of the new building showing the vertical servicing system in operation. The exposed two-way castellated beams support and permit the passage of colour-coded electricity and telephone cables, air-conditioning ducts and air-pressure lines, while the fluorescent lighting is suspended on continuous tracks below.

Like the roof, the naturally finished internal face of the cladding panels is left exposed. Lateral support for the panels is provided by a steel section at window head height, supported at mid-span by diagonal cables. The low head height of the windows themselves was designed to restrict views to the landscaping in the foreground, avoiding longer views of an otherwise dreary industrial estate.

Technology building marked the first time the practice had ever used composite sandwich panel cladding.

The Alply cladding panels used were made of aluminium-faced polyurethane, with finished interior and exterior faces and a vapour barrier laminated into a single prefabricated unit. Being light and demountable, the panels were ideally suited to phased building operations. The junctions between panels, derived from container construction techniques, used neoprene and aluminium extrusions to make airtight joints — essential in an air-conditioned building.

Interestingly and, for Foster Associates, atypically, the building employs a minor trick of visual deception, again necessitated by the low budget. Seen from ground level, it looks as though its sides continue up and over the building in an unbroken line, as was the case

The interior of the Computer Technology building at the time of the Financial Times award. All Foster Associates' innovations can be clearly seen: vertical servicing from above, carpeted floor, low-level glazing and purpose-made furniture.

in the later Sainsbury Centre. Here, however, there is a disguised flat roof. The illusion of continuity is created by curved panels at the eaves and the corners of the walls. The slight visual disappointment, however, is limited to the rarely seen aerial view.

Computer Technology were early in addressing questions about the organisation and operation of deep-plan, barrierless office spaces. The inclination of users to clutter a generous space is one which the architect can only discourage, never prevent. However, in this case, Foster Associates' decision to use an overhead electric power distribution to drop power cables directly from the roof zone suggested an interesting self-regulating solution.

Norman Foster: "The idea of dropping services from the ceiling in a factory is a long-standing industrial tradition. To extend it, to help blur the edges between office space and production space, was, I think, an interesting idea. Of course, there is a very real risk of visual pollution in use, especially when there are high concentrations of connections and wiring. In defence — or, perhaps, if I wanted to play devil's advocate — I could argue that such a system might be more self-policing. What tends to happen now is that the average highly-serviced building has probably got more redundant wiring hidden out of sight than it has current wiring. 'Out of sight, out of mind' gets you into bad housekeeping habits that might not happen with a more visible system."

Graham Vickers

1971-1972 **Fitzroy Street Office**
Bloomsbury
London

Reg Bradley

Norman and Wendy
Foster

Loren Butt

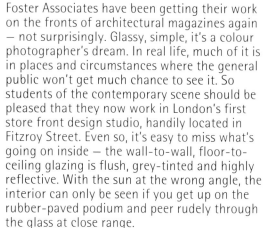

Mickey Kuch

Jamie Troughton and David Bailey

A champion of Norman Foster's and Richard Rogers' work since their earliest days in Team 4, Reyner Banham was inspired by Foster Associates' new Fitzroy Street office to write an article that started as a critique of this project alone, but quickly developed to become an appreciation of the practice's work to date.

First published in *New Society* on 9 November 1972, this article is reproduced here in full, starting below and continuing on page 148 immediately after this section.

LL/LF/LE v Foster

Foster Associates have been getting their work on the fronts of architectural magazines again – not surprisingly. Glassy, simple, it's a colour photographer's dream. In real life, much of it is in places and circumstances where the general public won't get much chance to see it. So students of the contemporary scene should be pleased that they now work in London's first store front design studio, handily located in Fitzroy Street. Even so, it's easy to miss what's going on inside – the wall-to-wall, floor-to-ceiling glazing is flush, grey-tinted and highly reflective. With the sun at the wrong angle, the interior can only be seen if you get up on the rubber-paved podium and peer rudely through the glass at close range.

Inside you'll see a fully carpeted open-plan office *à la mode*, divided into work spaces by Herman Miller AO-2 'advertised in *Scientific American*' system furniture, in a colour gamut that tends to yellows and acky greens. A ditto-green wall down one side is punctuated by snub-cornered spaceship doors, giving access to kitchen, lavatories and the usual etceteras. On the other wall leans the boss's racing bike (yellow, naturally), and the staff tend to affect basic Brook-Street-temp gear, tan jeans, moustaches-of-the-month, and accents that span the globe.

It's a success scene; it's an architectural office doing its thing for fun and profit. The work style suits them, the product visibly suits the sort of client who wants to project a keen liberal image without ceasing to turn a fast buck. Typically it was said of one client: "Every time he opens his mouth, a quarter of a million comes off the budget." But the building made all the magazines, and still attracts architectural pilgrims.

154

"The wall-to-wall, floor-to-ceiling glazing is flush, grey-tinted and highly reflective. With the sun at the wrong angle, the interior can only be seen if you get up on the rubber podium and peer rudely through the glass at close range."

Reyner Banham, *New Society*, 9 November 1972

James Meller

Michael Hopkins

Mark Sutcliffe

Loren Butt and Chubby Chhabra

Frank Peacock

Jo van Heyningen

155

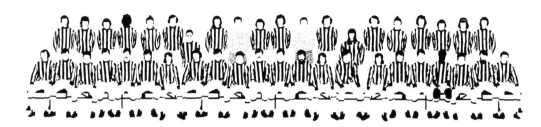

The full-height glazing on to Fitzroy Street was built twice. The first installation, which employed aluminium mullions, was destroyed by an IRA bomb planted in the nearby Post Office Tower. Foster seized the opportunity to improve on this with a second attempt which used, instead, Pilkington's newly developed, all-glass system.

By enclosing all service requirements along one side wall, the plan of the Fitzroy Street office became a rectangle inside a rectangle. This was then occupied with a molecular structure of Herman Miller furniture and fittings, augmented and arranged in ways its inventor had never imagined.

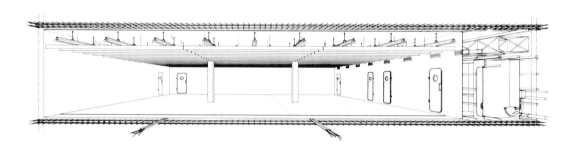

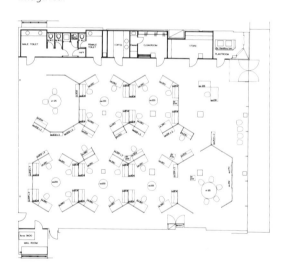

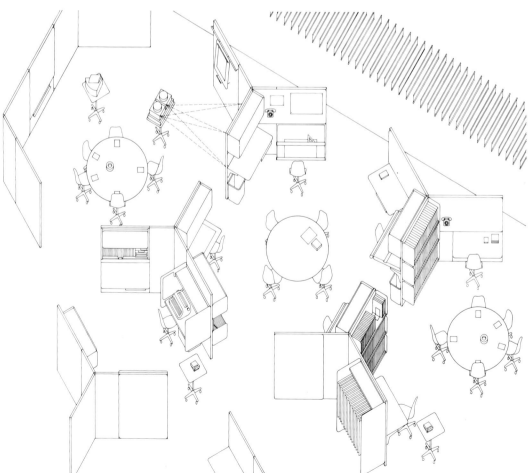

"With its aciduous lime-green paintwork and jet-black service core reached by submarine doors, rimmed, inevitably, in neoprene, Fitzroy Street resembled the offices of an advertising agency or even an airline, rather than an architectural practice."

Alastair Best, *Designer*, June 1983

Ian Ritchie

Birkin Haward

Tony Hunt

Martin Francis

Max Aiken and Diana Goddard

John Walker (centre)

LL/LF/LE v Foster
by Reyner Banham

Foster Associates' kind of architecture — lean, elegant, shiny, mechanistic — is the kind of thing that, for half a century, the Modern Movement believed itself to be about. Lightweight, standardised, advanced-technology stuff that the Masters of Modern Design kept trying to build all through the 1920s, '30s and '40s and finally got round to in the 1950s (except Le Corbusier, who'd given up trying). It seems that the professional establishment in architecture recognises that Foster Associates have achieved at least one of the ideals of the Movement, because one of their jobs — for IBM (of course) at Portsmouth — received the 1972 Royal Institute of British Architects architecture Award for the southern area of England, and duly appeared on the cover of the RIBA *Journal* last July. Its appearance, in so prominent a place in that particular *RIBAJ*, involved an irony so cutting as to be satirical, and has had architects tittering everywhere.

To explain why requires a short excursion along the frontier between technology and envy. The converse of that RIBA award is architects wondering out loud how Foster 'gets away with it?' Nothing to do with financial skulduggery, but about sheer nerve in making buildings. The walls of that IBM building consist of sheets of glass over 12 feet high, held in place by almost nothing; just aluminium glazing bars about an inch wide.

On 12 July, the good old *Architects' Journal* published Working Detail No 408 (in a series that seems to have been running since Christopher Wren was a lad) which revealed that Foster had achieved this skinny detail at the top of the wall by securing the aluminium bar to a flat capping-strip of steel along the concealed edge of the roof behind. On 19 July a baffled reader writes to *AJ*, expressing admiration for the way Foster Associates are developing "invisible structures", but adding that, "There seems to be a perfect vehicle for condensation . . . in the uninsulated mild steel roof capping. Perhaps Mr Foster would care to comment before we all start doing it."

Certainly the absence of the usual clutter of gaskets, sealing strips, foamed polyurethane and general gunge at this point was impressive. Foster Associates clearly didn't see this as an inviolable trade secret. On 26 July, Loren Butt, their mechanical engineer, wrote, in a short, businesslike letter to the *AJ*, that the movement of conditioned air under this detail removed any risk of condensation; but that if they had applied anything to the under side of the steel, there might have been condensation between it and the metal, and "the insulation has been specifically omitted in order to prevent a condensation problem occurring".

One week later, the full import of Butt's explanation dawned on 'Astragal', the *AJ*'s Pendennis: "IBM's air-conditioning plant has to be on all the time at night, and during the weekends, to prevent condensation . . . heat has to be thrown at the glass wall — to be radiated outwards in vast quantities — to keep the building habitable. The process can only be extremely wasteful. Foster might now turn his back on lightweights and try to design heavy buildings which have many advantages — including an inbuilt resistance to condensation." Anybody who has tried to cook in the kitchen of a Glasgow tenement with condensation streaming down its (heavy) stone-built walls, anyone who has battled with black mould growing in the standing water on the walls of a tower block built in the once-vaunted 'heavy prefabricated concrete panel' systems, is bound to wonder how Astragal can be so morally positive about so unreliable an 'inbuilt' quality — except that you can never be morally positive in the real world without ignoring contingent factors. Who or what is Astragal that he can presume to ignore factors quite as consequential as these?

A crypto-LL/LF/LE is what he is! He, or one of his semi-independent writing limbs, must be an unavowed member of this new and officially sponsored amalgam of (mostly tame) young ecological radicals and good greying architectural liberals in waistcoats. The official backing comes from the RIBA (it's all a bit like the Festival of Light, somehow) and the unusually modish set of initials stand for Long Life/Loose Fit/Low Energy. This means that buildings ought to last rather longer than the current expectation of about 60 years; that they should not be too tightly tailored to their present functions, so that they can be adapted to other uses over time, not scrapped; and that they shouldn't consume heat, light and other kinds of energy at the wasteful rates now tolerated (not to say encouraged by present tax structures and the like).

All this high-sounding stuff was launched with due presidential pomp and circumstance in a lead editorial in the *RIBAJ*. That's right, irony-spotters, the self-same issue that be-laurelled Foster's IBM building.

The PRIBA commended Long Life/Loose Fit/Low Energy to the membership as a "study . . . an attempt to work towards a set of professional ideas to meet the environmental crisis". That may be how the President sees it. Some hairier adherents to the idea seem to see it as something of a crusade, not a study, and the initials as a kind of magic formula for 'solving' the environmental crisis.

Others, understandably, see it more cynically. Disgruntled RIBA members tend to regard it as an attempt to distract attention from the internal political mess at the institute's headquarters. Trend-watchers saw it as a last desperate scramble on to Raine Dartmouth's environmental bandwagon before it rolled off to the Stockholm Conference with a nude at the prow and not a solitary architect on board.

All are agreed (me, too) that in plugging Long Life/Loose Fit/Low Energy as a quasi-political nostrum, the RIBA is attacking exactly the kind of architecture which it rewarded at IBM. That was specifically a temporary facility, tightly fitted round the client's functional needs, and consuming quite a lot of energy (chiefly because it is virtually impossible to run computers except in air-conditioned environments, and Foster Associates were capitalising on this fact to economise on structure). So either the RIBA is speaking with a forked tongue or a split personality.

Not that there's anything wrong with the RIBA doing some serious work on environment problems. If the present alleged study has diverted talent into designing a Long Life-etc campaign emblem (bearing an unintendedly ironical resemblance to the trademark of Kimberly-Clark paper, who have done so much to contribute to the world's waste-disposal crisis), it has also provided an establishment platform for serious eco-radicals like Andrew

Peter Reyner Banham (1922-1988) was one of the most prolific and admired architectural writers of the twentieth century. Born in Norwich, he served a wartime apprenticeship with the Bristol Aeroplane Company but later studied at the Courtauld Institute. His doctorate, published in 1960 under the title *Theory and* *Design in the First Machine Age*, marked him out as the definitive English language historian of modern architecture. Later books included *The Architecture of the Well-Tempered Environment*, *The New Brutalism* and *Megastructure: Urban Futures of the Recent Past*.

McKillop. But in going bullheaded for the slogan concept of LL/LF/LE, the RIBA must appear to be (as the President himself was admitting, almost as soon as that issue of *RIBAJ* came out) "wanting to pre-empt the result of our study", and making serious research almost impossible. How could a well-intended operation (as I know it to be) have managed to get up the proverbial gum tree so fast?

One reason is the well-known polarisation effect, which eliminates third (fourth . . . nth) alternatives in all quasi-political debate, and is very marked in architectural polemic. We go straight from high-rise to low-rise, from permissiveness to determinism, from scientism to intuitionism, Classical to Romantic, monumental to ephemeral; you have to be *for* or *against* Le Corbusier, the New Towns, pneumatic structures. Utopia is always the opposite direction to the way we are headed. If people like Foster are building lightweight, short-life, energy-consuming, highly precise structures, and we are heading for an energy crisis, then the only salvation lies in the exact opposite of *everything* Foster Associates are doing.

I exaggerate, but not that much. There is another factor at work. In architecture, as in other arts of the possible, a problem is rarely perceived until the answer to it already exists. Architects, understandably, and for good reason as often as not, tend to work from example. When they see others doing it, they call it cribbing. When they do it themselves, it's called a fact-finding tour, or the 'study of typologies'. If the RIBA is plugging LL/LF/LE as the 'solution', the institute must have actual buildings in mind that exist.

They do. The original submission to Lady D made it easier to guess what they were, because it also mentioned heavy construction and less complicated exterior forms. And if ever there was a type of building that had tidy outlines, heavy construction, has lasted a long time, was designed to consume very little energy and is a loose fit on what goes on inside it now, it's the kind of building most of Britain's most influential architects were trained in — the Georgian terrace house! At Liverpool, Cambridge, Edinburgh, Bristol (I can't remember the full list), and above all at the Architectural Association, generations of students have been conditioned by up to seven

years of daily exposure to accept Georgian as a kind of universal environmental fail-safe. The Loose Fit myth, in particular, has been bred in the bone at the AA, which is located in Bedford Square, where other similar houses contain, without strain, functions as seemingly diverse as publishing, moral welfare and various other administrative all-sorts.

So, radical eco-chic and greyheaded eco-told-you-so can unite on almost the only premises that all the generations of English architects hold in common. United, they have been saying some pretty alarming things already: one of the greyheads, who is now delighted to find himself "leading the profession from the rear", told this year's RIBA conference that for years "we've been saying you could build buildings simpler, cheaper, better ... with fewer drains (spend the money on important things like decent brickwork)". Did he really mean that architectural values are more important than health and life-support? He's a nice guy, a humane man. It just shows how silly the debate can get.

Each term of the LL/LF/LE slogan contains a potential silliness of this sort. If we are really going to be as short of land as is currently being doomsaid, then we shall need shorter-life buildings that can all be cleared away when they're not needed, to free the land. Loose fit may be fine for fundamentally similar functions like sitting at office desks in Bedford Square. But how many swimming pools, blast furnaces, cold stores, lifeboat houses and Anglican cathedrals are there in those admired purlieus? And how many cold stores, for instance, could be a loose enough fit to serve as Anglican cathedrals — though plenty of the latter might work wastefully as the former!

The biggest potential silliness concerns the relationship existing between loose fit and low energy. Holding forth about this kind of thing lately to a student audience at the Architectural Association, I was suddenly struck by the visible fact that adapting two Georgian front parlours into the lecture hall where we had found ourselves — a simple enough piece of loose fitting, you'd think — involved quite a startling amount of electric lights and similar gadgetry, whereupon a well-informed non-student voice from the floor volunteered the most up-to-date figures available: that the AA pays £900 a year rent and £2000 a year for

electricity. Even allowing that the AA currently pays a less than economic rent, the disparity should give the LL/LF/LE campaigners a pause.

Quite a long pause, we architecture-consumers must hope. Long enough for serious reflection, and genuine study. Such research may well show that the kind of adaptability looked for in the Loose Fit concept can only be bought at an expenditure of energy that is too high to be acceptable when our energy sources are under strain; and that it would make better sense to design Tight Fit buildings that can take better advantage of the energy that's got to be used anyhow, Foster-style.

For the fact remains that there is no habitable building at all that doesn't use energy of some sort, and quite a lot of it. In Georgian terrace houses the energy source was called Serving Wench, and the fact that she doesn't appear on the architect's plan doesn't mean she wasn't there.

To go back to where we came in. You can only prevent humidity-saturated atmospheres from depositing moisture on walls by having warm enough walls, by throwing heat at them sometime, in the manner Astragal found so shocking. That is why you have put an infra-red heater or a hot towel-rail in your tiled bathroom: right? And if your bathroom has thick brick walls, you may dissipate less heat to the outside world than IBM's glass ones do. Except that you've also opened the window to let the bloody steam out, taking heat with it, and IBM has a closed and controlled air-conditioning system that knows, pretty accurately, where all its heat is going.

If the LL/LF/LE concept is ever properly studied, and the balance of trade-offs between its elements fully understood, it could be that someone is going to have to apologise to Norman Foster. They may have to, since he'll probably be PRIBA by then. If there's any RIBA left to be P of.

Officially considered ineducable until 1971, mentally handicapped children had only just begun to receive special educational care when the Hackney special care unit was built. It was a pioneering design.

Special Care Unit
Hackney
London

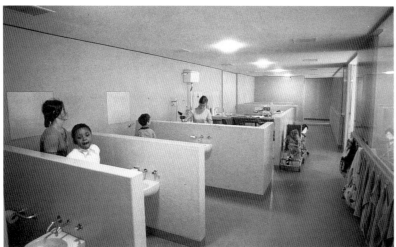

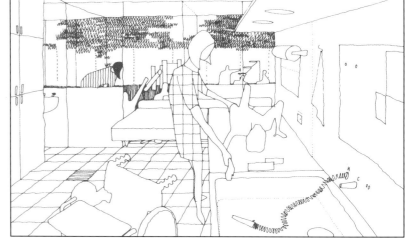

The walled south-facing court (top) and, inside, the carefully planned lavatory areas (centre). As all the children were doubly or singly incontinent, a clear view into and out of this area was considered an important design innovation.

There is a fine tradition in British school building to do with the inter-relationship between technically advanced modern architecture and progressive educational philosophies. In the 1930s, the combination of Walter Gropius and his aims for an architecture which was simple, practical, universal and imaginative, and the egalitarian educationalist Henry Morris, found expression in Impington Village College. From this collaboration developed the notion of a non-assertive architecture of steel-framed buildings and light, colourful interiors complementing and reinforcing new pedagogical ideals. The Hertfordshire schools of the 1950s and the highly acclaimed Consortium of Local Authorities Special Programme (CLASP) system in the 1960s followed in this tradition and, in turn, influenced the Californian School

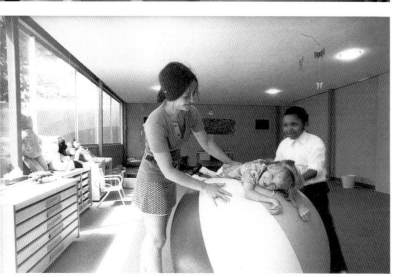

Birkin Haward's concept drawing of the sluice room clearly shows the intended view across the activity area to the outdoor courtyard, as well as the specially designed washing and dressing facilities in the foreground.

Construction Systems Development (SCSD) building programme.

In the early 1970s Foster Associates designed two schools for special needs in which the practice's now established architectural philosophy was applied to low-cost public/voluntary sector educational buildings. The brief for each building was evolved under the sponsorship of the Spastics Society and both were, to a large extent, experimental in concept and design.

The late 1960s had seen a radical reappraisal of primary level schooling culminating in the Plowden Report with its emphasis on

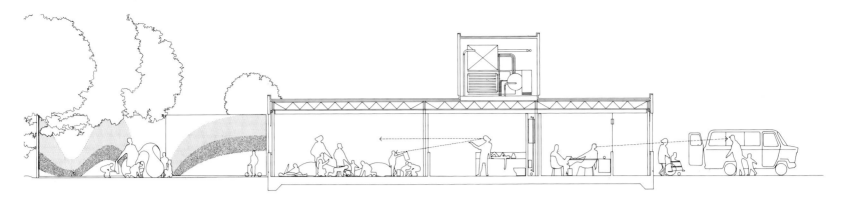

informal, child-centred learning derived from the ideas of educationalist pioneers such as Froebel and Peztalozzi. Mentally or physically 'handicapped' children were, however, considered "uneducatable" and were dealt with under the jurisdiction of Medical Officers of Health whether in psychiatric hospitals, residential homes, junior training colleges, special units, or under the care of parents. In 1971 the Education (Handicapped Children) Act brought the then categorised 'educationally subnormal' under the Department of Education and Science and the concept of special schools was introduced.

The aim of the first school Foster Associates designed, which formed part of a research project initiated by the Spastics Society, was to develop an experimental prototype that could be monitored in use, and a standard set of parameters to be applied to future projects, whether conversions, extensions or new buildings. The architects were interested in developing a standardised 'kit of parts' to this end.

In 1970, the London Borough of Hackney was approached and agreed to provide land on the site of an existing junior training college in the residential area of Ickburgh Road. A special care unit was proposed for 14 to 24 severely mentally and physically disabled children who were either unable to talk or walk, were incontinent, or were generally thought to be unresponsive to any sort of stimulation. Their education needs would involve an attempt to provide such stimulation through play and dedicated care.

In addition to consultation with the Spastics Society, Foster Associates were able to draw on experience in the field from Hackney and the Inner London Education Authority who would take over the running of the school. The architects' investigation of existing provision showed it to be woefully lacking, rigid or inappropriate. In the face of an innovative and changing educational climate, the approach which had been developed by Foster Associates in terms of flexibility and user choice, appropriate technology as a means to a social end, and the disengagement of structure and services from space seemed highly appropriate. Their reputation for imaginative analysis and lateral design thinking was also brought to bear, particularly with regard to the problem of incontinence and lavatory design. Incontinent children spend more time going to the lavatory

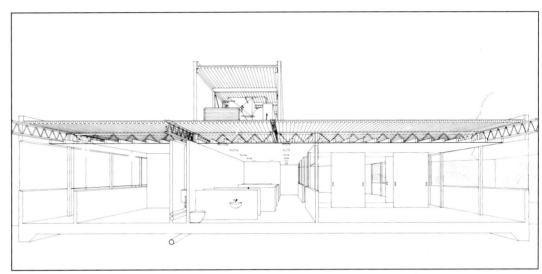

The basic structure of the building consists of Metsec steel lattice joists supported on square tubular-steel stanchions as at IBM Cosham. All servicing systems were housed in a large, cross-braced plant room above the roof deck.

Beneath the metal roof deck, a false ceiling carried radiant heating panels, a safe heat source for handicapped children. The glazing consisted of sliding glass panes matching the sliding doors separating the activity areas. The plan of the building facilitated observation:

from the central washroom through to the outdoor play area; and from the offices to the arrival car park and entrance lobby.

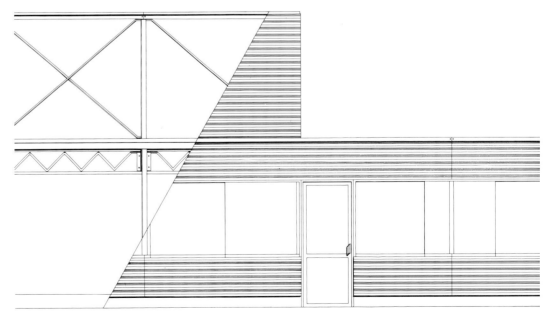

Foster Associates' staff contributed to the completion of the special care unit in person by painting the walls and concrete ground slab of the outdoor play area in bright yellow and blue patterns.

"The architects may be right: one can't in this case ask the customers. They may get more than one suspects from the warmly coloured scene. The bright yellow walls, the orange stanchions and the vivid pink sliding doors are certainly visually compelling."

Selwyn Goldsmith, *Design*, July 1973

and require constant supervision. Traditionally, lavatories were in remote, badly-lit latrine blocks. Foster Associates reversed this arrangement and the lavatory area forms a key element in the adopted plan form.

The new single-storey unit was conceived as three linear zones extending right across the site to leave an enclosed play court in the south-facing corner. The first (public) zone contained the main entrance, reception, medical and therapy rooms; the second (service core) provided lavatories, laundry and storage; and the third (private) zone comprised the activity/teaching areas leading on to the court. The lavatories were conceived as open, light areas with internal windows which functioned both in terms of views out and for ease of supervision from the teaching areas. Certainly,

The special care unit in use, shortly after its completion. Indoor activities took place on a big carpeted area equipped with a special 'landscape' of large inflatables designed and made by the Psychiatric Rehabilitation Association.

Two rows of sliding doors separated the larger activity areas from a central 'wet play' area, which had additional sliding-folding doors to the outside play area.

when the building first opened, it was immediately liked by both teachers and children. Changing attitudes over the intervening 20 years, however, have tempered these views. These are considered at the end of the next section, another special school for the Spastics Society at Palmerston, Liverpool.

Louis Hellman

The building occupies the full width of the site. Two large activity areas, with a 'wet play' area between, overlook the protected outdoor play area with its patterned 'floor'. A central office/service core contained the open-plan lavatories and sluice room – adjacent the activity areas – as well as store-rooms, a laundry, offices, staff and therapy rooms, and a small doctor's surgery. A 'quiet' room occupies the angled corner space, with a separate circulation corridor leading from it to the main entrance and reception area.

The low-level lavatory stalls were specially coloured yellow to avoid an institutional appearance. Extract fans in the ceiling drew smells directly into the plant room overhead where they could be dissipated easily.

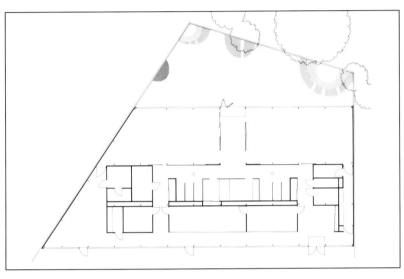

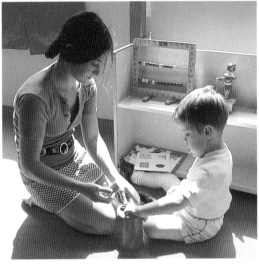

The strong orange and yellow colour scheme was maintained throughout the building, with an easily cleaned nylon carpet, yellow painted walls, and yellow roller-blinds to cover the windows at night or in bright sunlight.

The 'wet play' area (above) separated the two large activity areas and could be closed off with full-height sliding doors. All heating and lighting was confined to ceiling level, well away from the innocent hands of the children.

Bean Hill Housing
Milton Keynes
Buckinghamshire

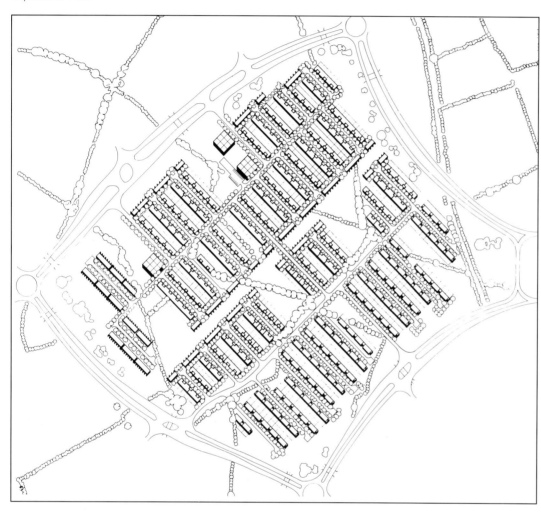

The plan of phase one at
Bean Hill is in marked
contrast to the earlier
high-density Team 4
housing schemes. Laid
out at only 11 dwellings
to the acre, the 569
dwellings are arranged
in short terraces orient-
ed at 90 degrees, north-
west/south-east and
south-west/north-east.
These terraces were to
have been cleverly cut
through by existing
hedgerows of the
original fields on the
site, which were then to
have been reinforced

with additional planting
to form informal new
routes for cycle paths
and pedestrian ways.
Where these footpaths
crossed the vehicle cir-
culation system, a varie-
ty of outdoor spaces was
created in anticipation
of community services
intended to be built at a
later date.

The most urgent problem facing the newly
established Milton Keynes Development Corporation in the early 1970s was the need to
build sufficient housing to draw settlers to the
embryonic city.

As Chief Architect and Planner from 1970
to 1976, Derek Walker also set out to establish
a positive identity for Milton Keynes by promoting new ideas in housing. He pursued an
energetic and enlightened commissioning
policy, allocating 40 per cent of the design
work to outside architects and selecting innovative firms to meet this challenge. Late in
1971, Foster Associates were among the very
first to be chosen, when asked to prepare a
scheme for Bean Hill, a 100-acre grid-square
site at Woughton, south of the city centre.

Bean Hill re-investigated many of the
concepts explored by Norman and Wendy
Foster in the early Team 4 houses and housing
schemes which were variously concerned with
the notions of privacy, flexibility and adaptability. The single-storey Skybreak house, for
example, relies on the use of sliding partitions
to open up a range of spatial options, and splits
the living accommodation into living and
sleeping areas with a central zone acting as a
'noise buffer'.

This idea was taken further in the high-
density housing project for Radlett where clear
main services and circulation zoning allowed
the freedom to fit out each house to suit individual needs. In the Wates project, the houses
were organised into parent and children realms,
allowing each a degree of independence.

Significantly, these schemes all employed
'heavy' *in situ* masonry or precast construction
techniques. The shift away from this at Bean
Hill can be seen as an inevitable part of the
Milton Keynes brief. Derek Walker now charac-
terises the city in the early days as a 'frontier
town', with almost no indigenous industry or
labour force. Most of the building workers were
bussed in from nearby towns like Stevenage or
Northampton. And operating Britain's largest
house-building programme, with a goal of
3000 houses per year, suddenly turned traditional building materials into a very rare commodity: systems building seemed to offer the
only short-term answer.

But the Corporation was also committed
to providing low-rise housing. It had found on
most sites that a two-storey development was

At street level, lush planting was intended to offset the hardness of the houses' facades.

A Helmut Jacoby rendering of one of the single-storey sections of Bean Hill. The short rows of houses were to have been grouped orthogonally around cul-de-sac roads, yet penetrated irregularly by the wandering 'reinforced hedgerow' lines of the pedestrian and cycle routes. Old people's houses were to have been placed at the ends of each terrace overlooking green spaces, and all the houses were planned so that the living rooms looked out on to private gardens. Unfortunately continual cost-cutting led to the abandonment of the important additional landscaping and planting needed for these pedestrian links.

The plan below is of an early proposal with continuous pitched roof terraces and individual driveways, neither as finally built. The penetration of the irregular pedestrian ways through the strictly arranged terraces can also be seen here in more detail. The boxed area at the top left of this plan is magnified in the lower drawing to show the arrangement proposed for covered shared driveways that would have provided a link between front and back gardens. This was abandoned in the final version when the houses were close-coupled.

"We face a crisis in housing which most of us working on the subject on a day-to-day basis view with increasing pessimism. It is not just that we cannot build enough — it is also about the quality of what we can build."

Derek Walker, *The Architecture and Planning of Milton Keynes*, 1981

the one most likely to meet stringent government cost yardsticks. However, at Bean Hill, the poor load-bearing soil conditions and the relatively low suburban density of only 11 dwellings per acre raised the possibility of achieving a single-storey scheme within similar cost limits.

Engineer Tony Hunt's structural studies confirmed this, showing that only part of the site could accommodate two storeys without the use of deep foundations and in fact, when costed, proved that a single-storey solution could be more viable provided that a lightweight constructional system was adopted.

A variety of off-the-peg steel-framing options was considered, from agricultural cowsheds to package-deal industrial structures, but none was available within the budget. Foster's instinct for "going direct to industry" led the design team to further research with manufacturers in the UK and Scandinavia, and to the conclusion that a timber frame offered the best value for money. The outcome was the adoption of the Walter Llewellyn 'Quick-Build' prefabricated system which allowed relocatable internal walls and could satisfy a wide range of plan types, including two, four, five and six person units.

The timber frame comprises load-bearing party-walls and partitions supporting a stressed plywood roof deck, all sitting on a reinforced-concrete site slab. The external walls also have a plywood skin, but now faced with bitumen-impregnated insulation sheaving and clad with dark grey, stove-enamelled profiled aluminium sheet. Foster now believes that a timber panel cladding might have been more appropriate, his elaboration that this might have been a self-weathering wood, turning a silver-grey colour with time, only emphasising this shift of attitude.

In Foster Associates' first proposals, the single-storey solution was explored to open up related plan areas, making the most of the restricted Parker Morris space standards. By introducing clear openings between dining, kitchen and living rooms, the full width of the house was revealed. And by using sliding partitions in the family houses, the dining space could be enlarged into a daytime play area by joining it to the children's bedroom.

Similarly, the living room could be linked to the parents' bedroom; the house being zoned into 'quiet' and 'noisy' areas on either

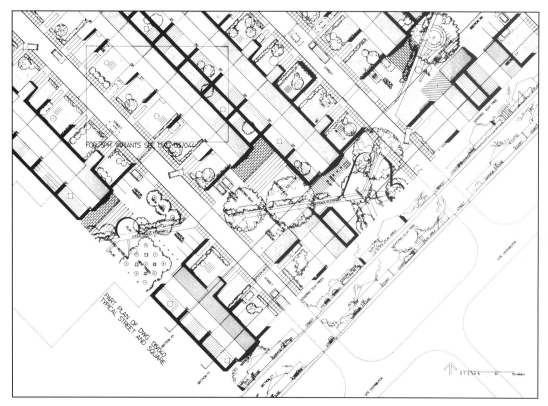

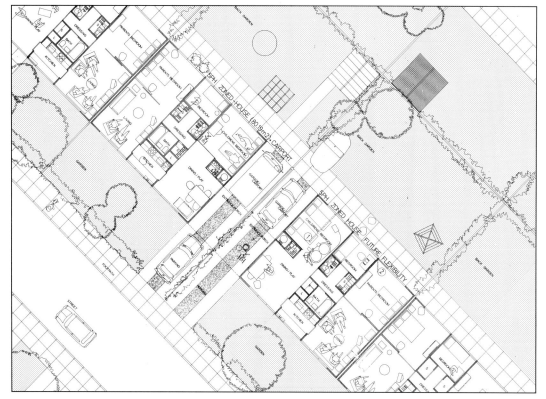

Pre-assembled timber frame components from the Walter Llewellyn Quick-Build system being lowered by crane during the construction of Bean Hill. Using this system each shell could be erected and roofed in a single day.

A cut-away drawing of the front wall of a typical Bean Hill house showing stud framing and windows with the outer dark grey corrugated aluminium sheet cladding to the right.

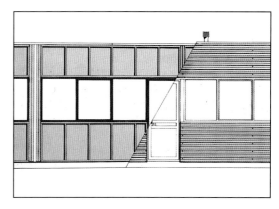

side of a combined kitchen and bathroom service core which provided acoustic privacy. It also offered the traditional advantages of the bungalow — adaptability with minimal physical alteration and ease of management for a young family or the elderly.

Derek Walker remembers this scheme as "a remarkably ingenious solution which maximised every square inch of space, keeping circulation to the absolute minimum". However, there was a great deal of resistance to the scheme from others within the Corporation and, in the face of pressure to cut costs, the layout gradually stiffened from its early spatial freedom to a much more conventionally organised *Raumplan* with car ports notched into a continuous terrace rather than between paired units as originally envisaged.

This reduced the building envelope and was no doubt more economical in terms of site use, but destroyed the visual link between front and back gardens. Foster believes that the first version came closest in spirit to the aims of the motor-generated garden city, in the way it reconciled house, garden, green space and car.

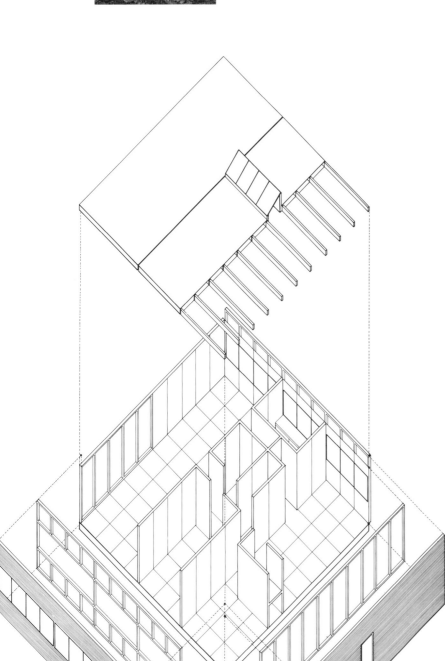

An exploded axonometric showing the prefabricated timber elements used at Bean Hill. The adapted Quick-Build system comprised load-bearing, stud frame gables, and party and partition walls supporting a composite stressed roof deck of plywood, all resting on a concrete ground slab.

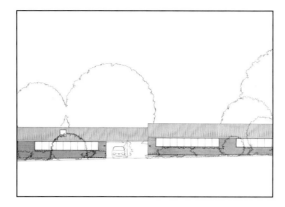

An early elevation of a
single-storey Bean Hill
terrace, complete with
its monopitch roof.

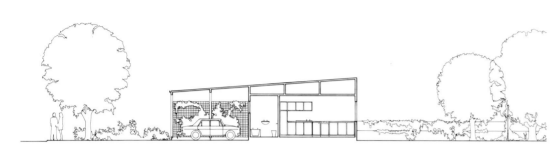

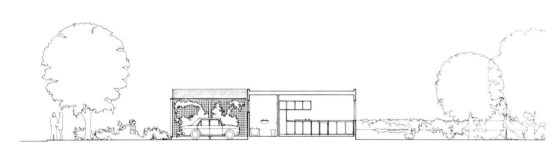

Comparative cross-
sections through typical
terraces were prepared
for two alternative roof-
ing options. The mono-
pitch proposal was
rejected in 1972 by the
Development Corpora-
tion on cost grounds.
The flat aluminium-
covered roof was used
instead, with fateful
results.

As completed in 1973, phase one of Bean Hill
(phase two was built later under the Corporation's supervision) consists of 492 single- and
77 two-storey family houses, grouped in terraces around short cul-de-sacs which give on
to open spaces. Old people's houses are distributed throughout the site in groups overlooking more generous green spaces.

The houses relate comfortably to the
gardens and the landscape as a whole. All the
rooms have direct views of a private plot, and
the existing trees and hedgerows which weave
through the site have a greater visual impact
in the context of a single-storey layout.

Where necessary the hedgerows have been
reinforced with additional planting to delineate
cycle paths and pedestrian ways. Where the
routes cross, a variety of outdoor spaces has
been created to form sitting and play areas.
These were intended to relate to a later *ad hoc*
infill of corner shops, clubrooms and the like
which the Corporation intended to build over
a period of time.

One of Foster's great regrets is that the
lush landscaping scheme prepared by John
Allen was never carried out. Helmut Jacoby's
aerial perspective offers the clearest picture of
how Bean Hill might have looked, the low terraces nestling among dense planting.

The Foster Associates design team was
also frustrated in constructional terms. Preliminary sketch schemes had explored the use of a
continuous pitched roof for the terraces, a
solution which, although it caused intense
philosophical debate within the office, was
again finally ruled out by the Corporation on
cost grounds: an ironic decision in the light of
the later re-roofing. Foster's preference for a
flat built-up felt roof was also rejected in spite
of the office's proven success with the method
on other projects. The Corporation insisted on a
proprietary low-pitch aluminium system that it
had specified at Netherfield with, it later trans-
pired, similarly problematic results.

With hindsight, it is clear that relentless
cost-cutting to meet an over-tight budget lies
at the root of many of Bean Hill's subsequent
shortcomings. These can be traced in a number
of separate but cumulative strands. The roofing
system was undermined by poor subcontract
workmanship and in some cases failed, allowing rainwater to back up through flooded or
blocked valley gutters into the houses. Insulation standards were also very poor, although

A child's climbing frame, one of the few communal facilities provided by the Development Corporation in the final scheme.

The final layout approved by the Milton Keynes Development Corporation, featuring shared driveways but with no passage between mid-terrace houses to link front and back gardens. This plan reduced overall costs, but lost many of the important amenities of the earlier layout.

conforming with the minimum standards of the day. This led to a high incidence of condensation and expensive heating bills.

Other problems resulted from spending too much money unnecessarily. The Corporation would not accept Tony Hunt's raft foundations and insisted on deep footings at the slab edge. The access roads too were heavily structured to take account of the marshy ground, only adding to the escalating infrastructure costs and reducing the amount of money available for the houses themselves.

The final irony is that the scheme was eventually found to be 10 per cent under budget, a discovery that caused justifiable anger in the Foster Associates office. The Corporation and their quantity surveyors had been dramatically over-prudent. But even this was not without consequence.

It was a set policy to fix new rents as a proportion of build-costs. Because Bean Hill was so far under budget it naturally became one of the cheapest estates and attracted a high proportion of 'disadvantaged' families; a situation compounded by the decision to reduce the mix of houses for rent and for sale from an initial ratio of 60:40 to a final 75:25.

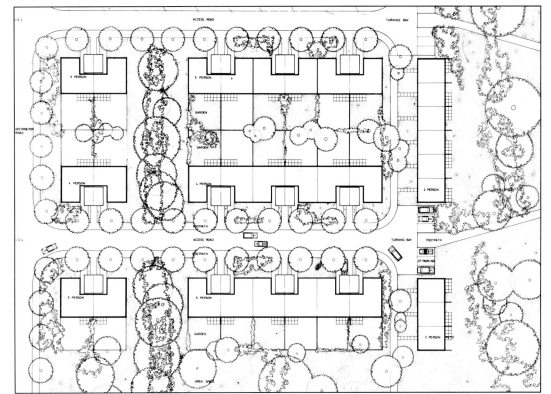

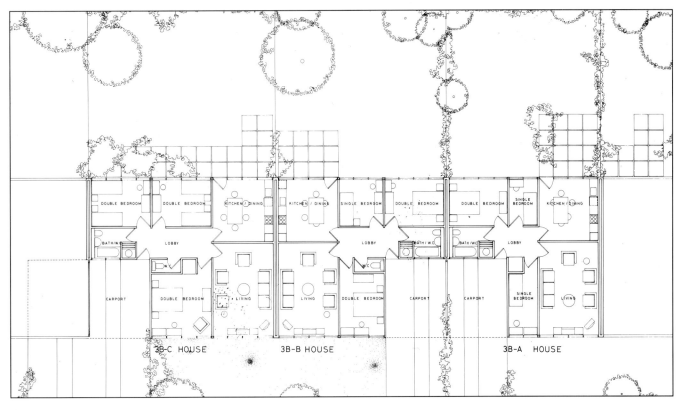

3B-C HOUSE   3B-B HOUSE   3B-A HOUSE

Detailed plans of the final arrangement at Bean Hill. The timber-frame cavity party-walls can be clearly seen, as can the ingenious planning that reduced circulation areas inside each house. Earlier prefabricated core units, consisting of kitchen and bathroom plumbing sets intended to be installed complete with hot and cold water supply, were now replaced by back-to-back installations in adjoining houses.

"For all its regularity, Bean Hill makes a notable contrast with its bloody-minded neighbour, Netherfield, in the grid square immediately north-east. But as the John Betjeman has shown with equal sensibility, the essence of suburbia (which is surely what Milton Keynes has raised to the pedestal of official approbation) is that, however banal, its physical components allow an infinite variety of individual expression. Even if the 'mature hedgerow structure' guides late party-goers back to their own particular cul-de-sac, will Foster Associates' eminently rational design provide for this irrational human need?"

The Architects' Journal,
9 May 1973

The Corporation had, largely through their own efforts, turned what was once a housing problem into a stock of problem housing, eventually having to spend more money on its refurbishment than it had cost to build.

Derek Walker acknowledges that in the first few years of Milton Keynes' life, the learning curve was too steep. The scale and speed of the housing programme demanded financial management skills and expertise that no one in the Corporation really possessed. He now accepts that the optimum number of units that can be successfully built at one time is probably 100: at Bean Hill there were nearly 600 in the first phase and quality control became impossible. "If it had been built five years later, when these problems were more familiar", he suggests, "we might have pulled it off."

Here, Norman Foster offers his favourite analogy of the architect as aircraft pilot to illuminate the Foster Associates/Milton Keynes relationship. "We were under ground control for most of the flight but, as always, the pilot must bear responsibility for the safety of his aircraft whatever directions he has been given." In this context, after the unqualified successes of Foster Associates' earlier work, Bean Hill can be seen as a bumpy landing.

By October 1984 an out-of-court settlement for more than £3 million had been agreed as compensation for defects. Most of the money was paid by the scheme's roofing and cladding subcontractor, Roberts Adlard, and Foster Associates.

In the two decades since Bean Hill was commissioned, the pioneering ideas that drove Milton Keynes have been trampled underfoot by private sector house builders and a fashion for the neo-vernacular: Bean Hill is not alone in being abused as much for its looks as its leaks. Reporting in March 1989 on an RIBA seminar on the repair of post-war buildings, 'Astragal', in *The Architects' Journal*, noticed how the speaker responsible for the wholesale imposition of pitched roofs at Bean Hill had described in detail how the new roofs were deliberately varied, with a choice of slates or tiles and a hipped or gabled form. "Altering the image", observed Astragal, "seems almost to have been the primary objective."

David Jenkins

Included in phase one of Bean Hill — as completed in 1973 — were 77 two-storey family houses. Because of their narrow frontages these were allocated separate garaging instead of integral car ports. The skyline view below shows a uniform roof-line with aluminium-capped parapets to the corrugated cladding. The lush planting originally intended has never materialised.

Three of the 492 single-storey houses built at Bean Hill, in their original form showing the shared driveway configuration with its lower roofed car ports.

Photographed 17 years after completion, the scheme is now virtually unrecognisable after re-roofing in variegated slates and tiles. Carried out for the Development Corporation prior to sale to owner occupiers, the Bean Hill neighbourhood has now been renamed 'The Gables'.

This view through a cluster of the two-storey houses shows the crisp aluminium cladding details at roofline, window and corner conditions. Embryonic tree planting can be seen between the terraces.

One of the pedestrian and cycle paths passing between two-storey houses in a terrace. In earlier, less economical versions of the layout, this passage would have been wider and less forbidding with more planting to soften the otherwise hard edges of the development.

Close-carpeted, open-planned from front to back and easily reached from any part of the school, the common play area at its centre was daylit from two glass-clad gable ends and through rows of overhead skylights.

Roughly 3000 handicapped children are born in the UK each year. Of these, some 15 per cent will be in need of special care. All these children will be severely mentally handicapped: and some may also suffer from one or more physical disabilities.

Before April 1971 all such children were beyond the educational pale. Some were cared for in hospitals or residential homes, others were looked after by their parents under the eye of the Medical Officer of Health.

In April 1971, the Education (Handicapped Children) Act brought all educationally subnormal children under the care of the Department of Education and Science.

Against this background of changing attitudes, the Spastics Society and Foster Associates started to plan a new special care unit for Hackney. We read the (all too little) available literature, spoke to the (all too few) specialists and visited the (all too rare) built examples. With a tight budget, we determined on a systems approach using readily available off-the-peg components.

With no fixed rules for special care, we concluded that any new building would have to be able to adapt readily to new roles. We developed an arrangement, for Hackney, that placed the maximum amount of flexible space around a fixed service core.

Now, with Palmerston Special School on the drawing board, the DES has published *Design Note 10* on designing for the handicapped in special schools. With its emphasis on flexibility and simple plan forms, it seems to confirm many of the design principles we developed for Hackney.

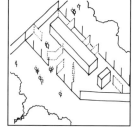

Unlike Hackney, however, the DES publication makes a strong case for integrating the special care aspects of education into the general running of a more broad-based special school. So at Palmerston, handicapped and severely handicapped children will be cared for side by side.

Our first designs assumed one large open-plan space flowing around four fixed service cores, all under one simple 'single-pitch' enclosure.

The structural form of the single-pitch design, however, has not proved to be the most cost effective. We now propose a multi-pitch building based on a series of smaller linked portal frames. The low-profile structure will be lighter and easier to construct. A variety of straightforward cladding systems are currently being considered.

Internally the open-plan arrangement of the first scheme will be retained, though with possible variations in the location of service cores.

Most importantly, the building is being designed around the simplest (and cheapest) available systems for structure and enclosure, so as to release as large a part of the budget as possible for fitting out the internal environment.

Our research is now continuing, notably on how best to service the building; not only with regard to comfort but also to future maintenance.

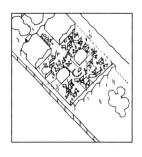

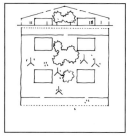

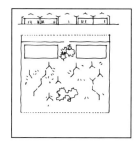

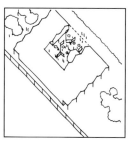

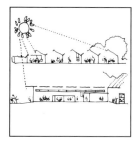

Palmerston Special School
Liverpool
Merseyside

The school sits in its field like a luminous, five-gabled row of agricultural barns. Inside, ample light and a large, connected open-plan space made for a flexible, functional environment.

The innovative approach to the design of schools for mentally and physically disabled children initiated by Foster Associates at Ickburgh Road was to be developed and refined by the practice at the much larger Palmerston Special School in Liverpool. This building was a joint project commissioned by the City's Education Department and the Spastics Society to provide facilities for 60 disabled children between the ages of 14 and 16, with a special care unit for an additional severely and doubly disabled group.

While Palmerston was on the drawing-board, the Department of Education and Science (DES) published its *Design Note 10*, 'Designing for the Severely Handicapped'. This recommended that 'handicapped' and 'severely handicapped' children be educated in special schools which provided flexibility in teaching spaces, simple spatial relationships, a friendly and reassuring atmosphere, freedom of movement, covered play areas and the integration of special care units into the same building. This guide also drew on a report by Kenneth Bayes, an architect with the Design Research Unit in London, published in 1964 entitled 'The Therapeutic Effect of Environment on Mentally Handicapped and Emotionally Disturbed Children'. This theory of the therapeutic environment held that space, light, colour, pattern and texture could be manipulated to help elicit a response in passive children and to calm those who are hyperactive.

In essence, these various findings were in accordance with Foster Associates' conclusions following their investigations prior to planning the Hackney school and were in line with the architects' general design philosophy.

In contrast to Ickburgh Road, the Liverpool site was an open wasteland on the fringes of the city, punctuated by housing estates and edged to the south by grass and a long belt of trees. The structural system proposed was a typical Foster Associates 'umbrella' steel-frame solution linking five hollow section portal frames in six bays with the stanchions canti-levered vertically from concrete slab footings thereby obviating the need for cross-bracing. This arrangement allowed a flexible deep-plan form roughly square in shape with freedom to dispose the plan elements in any desired pattern. Wrap-around, yellow-coloured corrugated cladding to the roof and sides confined

Birkin Haward's early concept sketch is for the large 'single-pitch' building, but the planning principles remain the same. Flexible screens and movable furniture would allow the staff to experiment with a variety of arrangements within the single space, restricted in the completed building only by the four fixed service cores.

windows to the two five-bay ends. Following criticism of the high sills and lack of protected outdoor space at Ickburgh Road, these ends were fully glazed from floor to ceiling and set back from the structure to provide sheltered paved areas. The resulting 'extruded' form was reminiscent of Foster Associates' Modern Art Glass factory at Thamesmead (itself owing some debt to Gropius and Meyer's 1914 Werkbund Pavilion), and was a precursor to the even more sophisticated variation, the Sainsbury Centre, being designed in the office at the same time.

This concept of an open-plan, flexible shed was earlier applied to a school building by Maguire & Murray at Bow Common. Not only does this solution allow flexibility of planning, but it provides both more usable space and a higher proportion of the budget for fitting out the internal environment. At Palmerston the latter represented 75 per cent of the total budget as against a 66 per cent norm.

"The single gable at Thamesmead here becomes a series of five portals; and the glazing, which for Modern Art Glass formed a very appropriate shop window outside the steel frame and flush with the cladding, is now recessed to the depth of one bay, allowing the skinny steelwork (one of Anthony Hunt's most ele-gant structures) to form a kind of covered arcade at either end. The effect of all this — a typical Foster Associates' device — is to convey the impression of a section cut through a seemingly endless building envelope; steel portal frames, cladding rails, cladding, all sharp and distinct. Quite simply, when it comes to (humble shed) buildings of this type, they are among the best in the business."

Alastair Best, *The Architectural Review*, November 1976

"The chief interest of the interior is the contrast between the relatively massive, rounded forms of the high-level ductwork (fed by air-handling units in one of the northern cores) and the spindly, square-section outline of the structural steel frame. The steelwork, in fact, is something of a minor *tour de force*; the hollow section portals are cantilevered off continuous strip footings, obviating the need for additional bracing: a really elegant use of steel."

Design, December 1976

The enclosing envelope of the school is supported by 12 structural bays, each of five contiguous portal frames. The pitched roofs give a domestic scale, while the openness to daylight is matched only by the night-time transparency of the gable elevations.

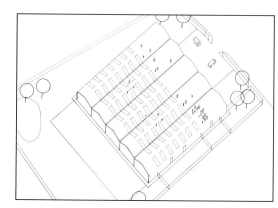

An early axonometric. To maintain a bright atmosphere in the deep interior a high degree of top-lighting was always envisaged, with up to 25 per cent of the sloping roof surface being given over to fixed rooflights.

The deep-plan, open-ended form at Liverpool related to the site, enclosing or revealing aspects as required, and the planning of the building represented a more subtle variation of the 'zoning' approach at Ickburgh Road. One glazed end adjoined the approach road to the north and formed the main entrance. The relatively rigid service core zone at Hackney was here broken down into four nodes. Two flanking the main entrance contained staff and service areas, and two provided internal lavatories and cloakrooms allowing easy access for incontinent children from the open-plan teaching areas. These themselves were linked with private outside play spaces through the south-facing glazed end wall. At Palmerston the public zone extended through the centre of the building under a translucent roof to accommodate entrance, dining, resource areas and central activities.

Following the DES *Design Note 10* recommendations, the special care unit was fully integrated within the building envelope as one of the four teaching areas. This was in contrast to the same facility at Ickburgh Road which was segregated from the junior school and without a link of any sort.

Related to the lavatory cores were four open-plan teaching areas intended to allow flexibility and choice for teachers experimenting with different teaching methods. Each area was distinguished by being equipped with 'Y' plan screens of a different colour — green, yellow, orange and blue — which could be arranged to vary spatial requirements and create specific areas: quiet, practical, play, wet or general. Integrated both by colour and size with the screens was a furniture system providing storage boxes, work surfaces, cupboards, trolleys, school and play equipment. The contents of the teaching area thus aimed to provide both mobility and stimulus for children and teachers.

Given the experimental nature of these two schools it might be appropriate, almost 20 years on, to attempt some appraisal and assessment of the assumptions underlying their design. Were the hypotheses proven? When the buildings were initially in operation they seemed to work well and were liked by children, teachers and parents alike. Norman Foster particularly recalls letters from grateful parents of children attending the Palmerston school. Today the staff at both schools have

A simple solution to the problem of producing a small covered area for outdoor activities, the one-bay recessed glazing line on the north and south elevations gives great elegance to what would otherwise be a banal industrial configuration. The simple plan, with multiple exits on all sides, obviated the need for fire protection to the steel and resulted in a remarkable lightness of structure.

Corrugated asbestos roofing and cladding, once a very common material, could not be sharply detailed because of its thickness, rigidity and poor dimensional tolerances. At the eaves, the coarseness of the curved lapping section is offset by the precision of the inset steel portal frame.

"We took the heart of the school, the core of the school, and created an area that was generous, that was light, that had good views and that was well placed for supervision. We put the money – the special school's allowance – not into architectural gymnastics, but into the cheapest structure so that you could improve the building services, making the heart of the school the freshest place in the building."

Norman Foster, lecture at Hong Kong University, February 1980

The effect of the completely glazed elevation, coupled with the carefully articulated separation of the asbestos cladding from the steel structure, was to create the appearance of a simple thin plane of roof floating over a complex interior.

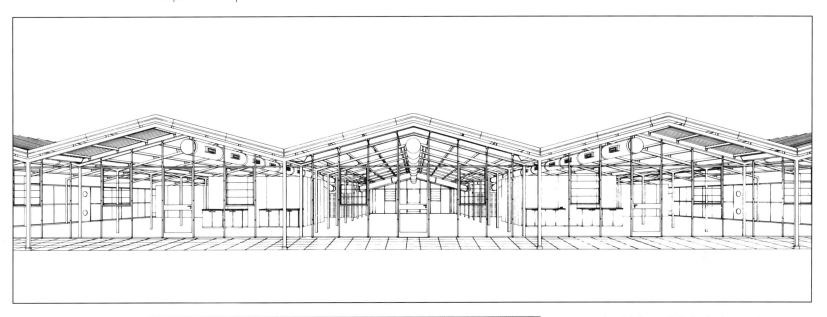

A model of Palmerston special school, with the roof cladding removed, demonstrates the free plan-form that was possible using simple movable 'Y'–shaped screens.

The model with roof surfaces in position. The bright yellow colour scheme was an early decision, as were rooflights though these were not included in this model. The concentration of flues and vents indicates the position of plant rooms below.

expressed criticism of their design and appropriateness. However, it is not clear how much this is conditioned by the progressive running down of resources for public sector education during the 1980s. Today there is insufficient money for basic essentials such as books and materials let alone for building maintenance or adaptation. Ickburgh Road particularly has been affected by the blight resulting from the recent abolition of the ILEA. In any case the fact that neither of these schools was ever monitored as initially intended means that any assessment must remain subjective.

The internal open wc arrangement has been questioned, particularly at Ickburgh Road. This may be due to the changed status of disabled people during the past two decades. Today it is recognised that even severely disabled children have as much right to privacy as so-called normal people. Again the very idea of special schools was a progressive innovation in the early 1970s, whereas today they are seen as divisive and the impetus is towards the integration of disabled children into mainstream education. By current standards too, Palmerston would be considered too large for its purpose.

Today's emphasis on user participation might have helped to temper such criticisms, but what of the architect's claims for flexibility? Should not the buildings have responded to changed circumstances? For one reason or

A small hydrotherapy pool stands next to the perimeter wall of exposed asbestos sheeting. Above, perforated steel acoustic panels span above the structural purlins and between rooflights. The use of exposed asbestos finally spelled the building's demise.

In a drab neighbourhood, at the edge of an industrial estate, the bright yellow exterior was a conscious decision by the architects to introduce an element of joy. Surprisingly, this was supported by the local authority.

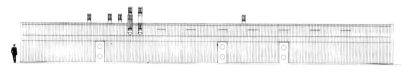

The contrast between end and side elevations reveals the design of Palmerston at a glance. In the spirit of flexibility, flues appear in response to internal needs.

1 entrance portico
2 staff room
3 medical centre
4 kitchen
5 entrance/dining area
6 headmaster
7 caretaker's flat
9 audio-visual room
11 secretary
12 plant room
13 junior teaching area
14 special care unit
15 senior teaching area
16 nursery
17 covered play area
18 internal court
19 activity area
20 pets
21 lavatories
22 teaching bathroom
23 teaching kitchen
24 changing room
25 laundry
26 quiet room

The concentration of axial baffled asbestos flues and vents over the main internal plant room. The exact slope of the roof was determined by the angles of standard asbestos radius sheets readily available at the time of construction.

another the built-in potential for internal re-arrangement resulting from the disengagement of structure and services from functional space was not exploited in either school. Llewellyn Davies, in his research into growth and change in hospital buildings in the early 1960s, concluded that flexibility in terms of the re-arrangement of internal walls was not feasible either economically or operationally. He proposed instead the notion of indeterminacy, the provision of a range of inter-connecting optimum spaces whose use could alter according to changes in requirements. Recent developments in educational buildings have reached similar conclusions.

Unhappily, Palmerston today is a vandalised ruin, abandoned because of its asbestos cladding, and Ickburgh is shabby and under-maintained. It is unfortunate that these pioneering buildings should be allowed to fall apart from neglect. If they are no longer appropriate for their original function they could surely be renovated and new uses found for them.

Louis Hellman

Self-coloured yellow heavily profiled asbestos sheeting, with matching acrylic rooflights and lapped radius junctions between roof and walls, provided a simple but effective cladding for the school. Neat details, like the ramped perimeter paths for wheelchairs, demonstrate a thoughtfulness of design applied throughout the building.

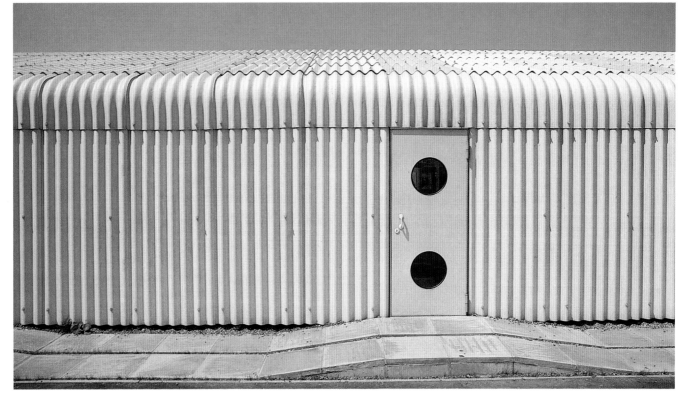

Palmerston special school in use. The internal space is subdivided by four service cores, two major and two minor, which define the various zones of activity. Unlike the exterior — and unlike the interiors of the Hackney special care unit — internal structure and cladding is white, colour being provided only by the movable low-level screens, colour-coded to define the four main teaching areas, and an olive green carpet. High-level ducting, running below the ridge in each of the five structural bays, provides ventilation. Fed by air-handling equipment in the main plant room, the ducts withdraw warm air in summer and supply it in winter.

"Spaces around the cores flow pleasantly into one another, but have been roughly demarcated into four zones by means of simple coloured screens, each zone, in turn, being furnished with play equipment and boxes."

Alastair Best, *The Architectural Review,* November 1976

"This school for handi-capped children reveals an objectivity in solving the requirements of the brief that is often lacking in more complex buildings. This approach to the design is equally apparent in the selection of the structure, materials and service systems which, although utilitarian in appearance and unconcealed within the building, are combined with the furnishings and colour there to create an environment of sparkling warmth and interest. The building obviously works well and is enjoyed by the staff and the children."

Extract from the assessors' report for the RIBA Award, 1977

Systems Thinking
by Francis Duffy

Below: the newly established National Coal Board was one of the first major British corporations to embrace systems thinking.

Combined Operations command centre for the Western Approaches, photographed during the Second World War. Systems analysis appeared in rudimentary form to tackle the industrial problems of mass production during the 1920s and '30s, but it was the pressures of war that saw its first major advances and a growing acceptance of its methods.

which turned out to be so empty an inspiration for so many architects, into an utterly convincing architecture? These questions need to be answered if the foundations of Norman Foster's particular architectural contribution are to be properly surveyed and understood. With the right answers Foster's early career can also be used to illuminate what is likely to become an increasingly evanescent and hard-to-understand episode in cultural and technological history.

Systems Thinking

Related to the interdisciplinary thinking which in the early 1940s was the basis of the invention of operational research, systems thinking carried the aura of big public sector programmes like the Tennessee Valley Authority scheme of the Roosevelt era, wartime Combined Opera-

In a Word

Francis Duffy is an architect with a special interest in how organisations use space over time. Born in 1940, he studied at the Architectural Association and later at the University of California, Berkeley. With John Worthington and Luigi Giffone he founded DEGW in 1973. He is now chairman of the firm which has offices in London, Milan, Paris and Madrid, and specialises in user requirements, space planning, information technology and research for major corporations. Francis Duffy is editor of *Facilities* magazine and co-author of *Office Landscaping: Planning Office Space* and *The Changing City*.

If one word can encapsulate a whole quarter of a century, 'systems' sums up the years from 1950 to 1975. Disciplines ran riot, renounced conventional boundaries, sought interconnections between phenomena, thought big, started again from scratch. They began, in short, to connect the kneebone to the thighbone. Architects, never backward in such pursuits, sought throughout this whole period a fresh vision. Many expected this to emerge from a radical analysis of their clients' needs. For most the vision never quite materialised; for some, as the skylines of innumerable cities testify, an all too concrete imagery emerged in the form of a thousand tower blocks. Norman Foster, in contrast, wholeheartedly embraced the idea of systems architecture and came away in 1975 with a clutch of buildings which were not only different but obviously superior.

Why was this idea of systems so attractive to architects in this period? Perhaps more important, what is it about Norman Foster which has enabled him to turn the systems thinking,

tions and the Manhattan Project implicit within it. The very word was worth a lot: it had the effect of a simultaneous claim to intellectual respectability and practicality.

Eric Trist of the Tavistock Institute was a typical systems intellectual of the period. In the late '40s, when British social science still meant something, he demonstrated that systems thinking could be profitably applied to designing the interface between men and machines in the newly nationalised collieries. Trist showed that it was essential not just to import wholesale the latest American coal-cutting technology but to introduce it in such a way that it did not destroy the mutual support in risk-taking between miners which had grown up over centuries in the Durham coalfields. Men and machines were, in effect, an 'open socio-technical system'. Social systems, reward systems, technological systems, all had to be carefully

interwoven to make it possible for the newly founded National Coal Board to achieve its organisational objectives.

Architectural Antecedents

Four key examples are enough to show how similar systems ideas were introduced into architecture.

The earliest and best innovators in this field were American: Charles Eames, who created a brilliant metaphor of systems thinking in his own house — all standard components from builders' catalogues and *objets trouvés* — not to mention his highly innovative product design and exhibitions; and Buckminster Fuller whose whole career is in itself a core study of the abolition of intellectual boundaries and the search for systems solutions.

In Britain the obvious contemporary parallel was the post-war work of the development groups in the old Ministry of Education, so well described by Andrew Saint in his book *Towards a Social Architecture*. At that time resources were scarce and demand for school places was heavy: how could a miracle in the procurement of school buildings be achieved? By systems thinking, of course: bringing architects and educationalists, physicists and builders, scientists and quantity surveyors together to rethink not just how to build the old kind of school faster, but how to build new schools, with new curricula, new plan forms and new ways of teaching. The logic was simple: relax the old constraints, bring intellect to bear, rethink the problem, and out comes new teaching, new architecture and a bright new world.

Not only in Britain and not only in education did such miracles of the Modern Movement happen. In Germany in the mid-'50s the Schnelle brothers began to think about office buildings from first principles. The same conditions applied: great economic stringency, a heavy demand for office space because of the rapid rebuilding of the German economy, a crossing and intermingling of disciplines, the urgent need for cheap physical solutions to pressing organisational problems. The result was the dazzling new concept of *Bürolandschaft*, the famous open-plan office layouts that were designed to maximise organisational communications and which, from the inside out, determined the shape of a totally new generation of office buildings. *Bürolandschaft*

instantly encapsulated generations of management thinking from Taylorism, to Human Relations, to Cybernetics — all by way of systems.

Equally important to the success of these precursors was memorable imagery and a fully articulated intellectual programme.

Foster Associates' work is best understood in the context of this dualist tradition. They can be compared, for example, to contemporaries who seemed in earlier phases of their career to be equally promising for the same reasons. Cedric Price is the best British example, with his eloquence, radicalism and rage for a more soundly based, more rational architecture. Ezra Ehrenkrantz, who had absorbed the radical British tradition in his years at the Building Research Stations, appeared as a star in the Californian skies in the early 1960s with his innovative 'performance specification' approach to procuring school buildings called School Construction Systems Development (SCSD). In fact certain images from the SCSD programme were present as icons in Norman Foster's earliest office in Covent Garden.

However, neither Cedric Price's nor Ezra Ehrenkrantz's built work ever succeeded in capturing the systems idea strongly enough in architectural terms, ideology always seemed

Ezra Ehrenkrantz's SCSD prototype of 1964 is still standing in Stanford, California.

stronger than imagery (and, in the case of Ehrenkrantz, the ideology too seems to have faded with time).

A Late Starter?

Norman Foster had all the advantages of single-mindedness and a late start. The position from which he began, in the late '60s, allowed him to establish quickly his own vision of what systems buildings ought to be like. The models were available, an architectural language existed, and an appropriate ideology had already been worked out. The extent of Foster's acceptance of this inheritance is abundantly clear in the Newport School competition of 1967.

Billed as a "sophisticated package within Department of Education and Science cost limits", the proposal manages to combine the lively and imaginative interest in users so characteristic of the best DES work of the time (compare Foster's sketches with those in contemporary *Building Bulletins*); with an enthusiastic acceptance of the deep open-plan (owing a lot to North American influence, for example, from schools being publicised at the time by the Educational Facilities Laboratories); and with an energetic and practical sense of the way buildings should be put together (that owed as much to the engineer Anthony Hunt as to the example of SCSD).

However, there is a toughness and rigour about the Newport plan which is new. Care is taken to demonstrate that the rigid rectangular

Open-plan offices date from the turn of the century, but it was not until the 1950s, with the concept of *Büroland-schaft*, that their stark unpleasantness was much improved. Compare this American example of 1942 (right) with Foster's Fred Olsen amenity centre below.

"I wonder how Paxton would react to systems building now, to the opportunities and achievements of a new age? He had the confidence and optimism to produce a systems building for an industrial exhibition — the Crystal Palace — which was later reassembled on another site for a different use. If only we had the same confidence to continue in his tradition with today's systems."

Norman Foster, More with Less lecture at RIBA, July 1976

building envelope can accommodate both the 'traditional' classroom layout and a "plan arrangement based on new educational techniques". While the sketches hint that the latter style is preferred, the basic systems network will accommodate both. Something of what Newport promised for school buildings was achieved in the Palmerston School for Handicapped Children.

This is a school building conceived as a shed — five linked portal frames, to be exact, with four service cores "to define the various zones of activity". The project combines typical

features of the period – a glum unpromising site; the severe, deep plan; the taut, nervous, almost aerodynamic building skin; the construction kit grid; the visible integration of services and structure; and relatively loose, almost rhapsodic interior planning. Somehow the children and all their paraphernalia are independent of and yet counterpoint the architecture.

Similar features can be found in the Hertfordshire and local authority consortium schools of the 1940s, '50s and early '60s illustrated by Andrew Saint. But in none of these buildings do the various elements fuse in the almost obsessive, holistic way that has already become the touchstone of Foster's genius.

Beyond a Social Architecture

The first commercial building Norman Foster ever built (with Richard Rogers at Team 4) carried this holistic passion into a different world, one that had previously tolerated very low standards of building and design. This was

the steel-framed electronics factory for Reliance Controls at Swindon built in 1967 — for which Peter Paul-Huhne was the enlightened (and fortunate) client.

Foster and his colleagues in Team 4 rose to the challenge of a dynamic client in an emerging industry with a combination of fast track design, speedy erection, low cost, flexibility to accommodate growth and change, and a progressive image. In plan, the distinctions between office and factory were swept away. Throughout the design, provision for adaptability and for service was the priority.

Three factors indicative of the future direction of Foster's work are present in this building: first, stretching the use of familiar components far beyond the conventional view of their capacity (*eg* the use of corrugated deck

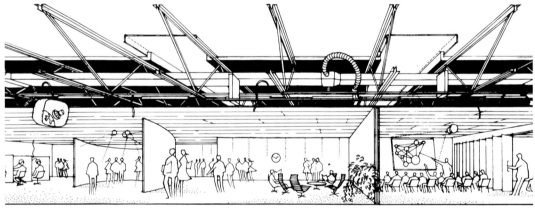

Foster's 1967 Newport School drawing demonstrates his complete understanding of SCSD and that he is already developing on it.

units with no intermediate supporting rails); second, the integration of all components into a comprehensive system (for example, the reflective nature of the underside of the roof decking doubling as a ceiling); and third, the extreme, practical, minimalist elegance of the construction. Nothing superfluous; everything deft; all components working together. This is why Foster's perspective section through the building is an important drawing: it is a heuristic device to eliminate redundancy but explaining, after the fact, what was done.

The projects for Fred Olsen at Millwall Dock follow directly in this line. Now the architect has the bit between his teeth — the pencil flying over the pages of the notebook, diagramming, reducing, explaining all at once. The new challenge (in what was then a real Docklands) was operational — how to move large numbers of people from taxis and coaches, through ticketing and customs on to ships; and how to provide amenities for Fred Olsen's staff. In the design of the passenger terminal (1970), the shell design is simplified into a search for the least number of the simplest possible components. The planning equally becomes a process of remorseless simplification. Nothing is left unresolved, everything is made into an intellectual challenge — an opportunity to think laterally, to cut the Gordian knot, to reduce, to solve the problem with the least expenditure of energy in the most elegant way.

Nothing Will Come of Nothing?

'Less is more' was already a famous axiom by the 1970s, but nothing in the work of Mies van der Rohe prepares one for the nervy, obsessive, impatient quality that was already characteristic of Foster's work by the time the Fred Olsen buildings were completed. In Chicago, Mies van der Rohe was attractive to developers because his view of architecture did not particularly contradict theirs. Foster, in a much more positive way, had become by this stage highly attractive to certain sophisticated industrial 'user' clients, because it had become obvious

that he was capable of exploiting scarce resources to achieve organisational objectives through the design of buildings in very much the same way as they did in their various businesses. The Fred Olsen amenity centre and the later passenger terminal, showed how Foster was able not just to build economically but also to plan intelligently with management to achieve operational goals — which, in this case, meant working collaboratively with the dockers as well as anticipating passenger requirements.

IBM is the epitome of the enlightened client. For an architect to work with IBM is to experience excellent project management — just as capable in procuring buildings as in developing new computer systems, of using the corporation's immense experience, as well as seeking innovative ways of solving new problems. So it is not surprising that in 1970 IBM picked Norman Foster, given his recent experience in the electronics industry, to design what were originally to have been temporary offices at Cosham. These temporary offices are still there today as crisp and sharp as ever.

The plan form at Cosham is almost exactly that of the Newport School — if you are Norman Foster you never waste a good idea — a

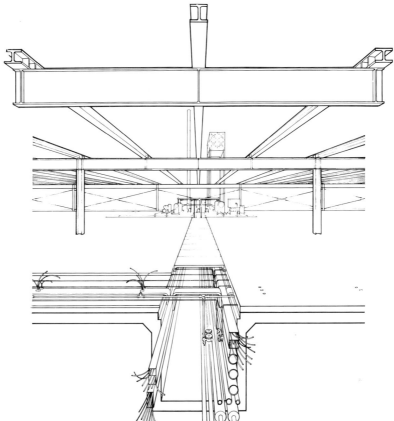

huge single-storey rectangle (146 × 73 metres) with absolutely clear access and circulation, served by asymmetrically placed cores and highly serviced areas.

Here again is the ghost of Hertfordshire schools, but with their wayward planning exorcised and their clumsy detailing transmuted into the most exquisite delicacy and lightness of construction. Birkin Haward's drawing of the section is itself a masterpiece rivalling Ehrenkrantz's, and one of the great architectural images of the period. The slowly accumulated

experience of two decades of public sector work has been captured and raised to another level for the service of the most sophisticated computer company in the world. And this was achieved not by elaboration but by reduction, by the simplest, most intensely focused means.

Clarity is everything. The brochure produced by Foster to describe the scheme is itself a didactic masterpiece. Data and electrical services are integrated into the column grid which in turn neatly complements the layout of desks and of internal rooms. The distribution of air-conditioning units on the roof follows a precise and confident modular plan — so unlike the clutter that still disfigures buildings today in dozens of so-called business parks. Site planning, services, structure, construction, layout,

all have been comprehended and ordered. So simple, so direct that it is still possible to ask 20 years later — why isn't all building like this?

Progressive Refinement

Two other deep, commercial projects of this period should be mentioned: the 1973 building for Modern Art Glass at Thamesmead and the earlier building (or rather degree zero building) for Computer Technology Ltd, built at Hemel Hempstead in 1970.

What Modern Art Glass — a warehouse and office/showroom — demonstrated again was Foster's capacity to seize any opportunity to develop component design as far as he could take it. The client had been a subcontractor on earlier Foster Associates' projects and wanted

185

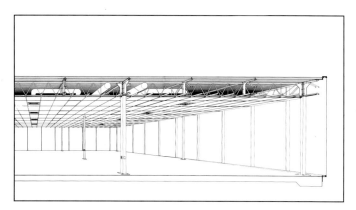

"One of the great architectural images of the period", Birkin Haward's perspective section of IBM Cosham accommodates in one seemingly simple drawing virtually all there is to know about the building's construction and assembly.

to use his own building as a showcase for glazing technology. Foster rose to the challenge — "12 mm bronze-tinted toughened glass positioned on lugs welded to tubular steel supports, with vertical mullions of bolted neoprene and horizontal joints filled with silicone — all pretty impressive". Modern Art Glass may be a showpiece but it is also unabashedly still an industrial shed. In the end it is the extraordinary way in which ordinary components have been put together which impresses. Unlike, for example, Richard Rogers' much later Lloyd's building, where innovation proceeded grandly on a hundred fronts simultaneously, Foster was content, in 1973, to focus on the smallest number of most feasible means to improve one assembly — the glazing system.

That such synergetic improvements quickly raise building components to a totally different level of quality has direct parallels with

from *Architectural Design* which tacitly claims, project by project, a Darwinian line of refinement very much in the Buckminster Fuller tradition, from Reliance Controls to the 'ephemeralised' air structure for Computer Technology. D'Arcy Thomson author of *Notes on the Synthesis of Form,* would have been proud to display this as an example of progressive adaptation and improvement in one of the most basic components of architectural enclosure.

Note, however, the extent of understatement in the Foster style — by a sleight of hand, technological progress is made to look imper-

Stansted Airport terminal. Its integrating and reductionist disciplines can be traced back to Reliance Controls.

relevant to achieving clients' operational goals in the fastest growing sector of the economy at that time;
— he could use individual projects as a means to achieve the equivalent of a continuing programme of development; and finally
— that building components could be as easily and effectively developed as building types themselves.

That all this was possible in a series of low budget projects on dismal industrial estates — unfashionable locations at best — simply adds to the magnitude of the achievement. The groundwork had been done and the objectives established for subsequent far more conspicuous and complex projects such as the IBM Technical Park at Greenford and Willis Faber & Dumas in Ipswich. If one analyses Foster Associates' major achievements of the last decade, such as the Hongkong Bank and Stansted Airport terminal, the genesis of the approach can be traced back to the same integrating and reductionist discipline that led to the success of Reliance Controls.

Foster found very early in his career a system-based ideology which combined satisfying client requirements with innovatory thinking about how to put buildings together. It was a severe, puritanical, purging kind of ideology with little scope for sentimentality or second thoughts. Under its scorching, excoriating glare, there was little room for the wilful self-indulgence of *Bürolandschaft* layouts — a tougher, service-based discipline had to be found. Nor could there be any sympathy for the romantic elaboration of heavy concrete construction that lies at the heart of Hertzberger's contemporary attempts to reconcile long-term corporate culture with short-term individual worker discretions. The objective is always to do the most with the least. There is, in fact, scant evidence of tolerance, or of whimsy or choice on the part of the end users — corporate clarity always tends to dominate.

There is no attempt to emulate the growing German interest in complex building forms intended to articulate and reinforce group spaces — it always seems more important to stress the rationalist, corporate orthogonal than to explore the potential of unusual grids. Steel is the ideal material given its lightness and precision. In this way, Foster avoids at a

Japanese industry today. Corporations like Sony, Toshiba and Nissan concentrate on the continuing improvement of the quality of ordinary things to produce some of the most refined products in the world.

Norman Foster's most radical exercise in minimalist design at this period was the temporary air structure for Computer Technology at Hemel Hempstead: 8000 square feet of space was commenced, erected and occupied in eight weeks, providing basic office accommodation while the more permanent (and, one has to admit, rather less memorable) structure was built.

Summing up this extraordinary period from 1968 to 1974, we can see a process of progressive refinement during which Norman Foster turned the industrial shed into an art form. This is conveyed perfectly in the diagram

sonal and inevitable. In fact, such continuing refinement can only be the consequence of an individual vision, of one man's overriding drive.

All Heaven in a Grain of Sand

By 1975 Foster had demonstrated in the unglamorous and highly competitive and commercial arena of the design of deep-plan industrial sheds that:
— he had not only learned everything that there was to know from two decades of patient development work in the public sector schools programme, but was capable of transferring it to another sphere;
— his particular architectural skills were

Mies van der Rohe's unbuilt design for the Mansion House site. Mies' elegant detailing of the surfaces of his buildings masks a traditional approach to office construction and planning that can be dated back to Daniel Burnham's Flatiron building of 1902.

With the Hongkong Bank, Foster went back to first principles, questioning every aspect of how an office building is used. Hidden by the more eye-catching advances in construction technology, it is as much the development of *social* systems in his early projects that made this building possible.

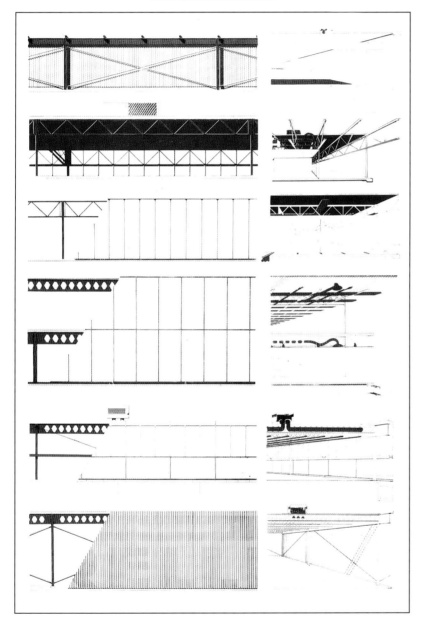

In this drawing, specially prepared for a profile of the office by *Architectural Design* in May 1970, Foster tacitly acknowledges an almost Darwinian line of refinement through all the early projects, from Reliance Controls to Computer Technology. With the air structure — also for Computer Technology — the process of ephemeralisation was brought to an absolute peak. That Foster was able to establish so much in this, a series of essentially low-budget projects, only adds to the magnitude of the achievement.

represented at this time an ideology, a particular, no-nonsense, approach to building design. Breaking down barriers between offices and workshops, between front and back, between high and low status was very much an open systems attitude of the time: "long life, loose fit, low energy". Second, and more important, the radical simplification that open planning entailed allowed Norman Foster to concentrate on the development and refinement of certain recurrent constructional details — in the sense that he removed planning from the problem: all the plans of his early commercial buildings are the same. Third, and most importantly, deepness and openness allowed Norman Foster to make 'visible' his intention to integrate systems. There is a strong, partly unconscious, didactic programme which runs throughout all these buildings — "systems integration is good; therefore it should be seen". For this mission, smaller, more fragmented building types would not have suited Norman Foster's purposes at all. In a sense, the accident (or the singlemindedness) of being commissioned to design a series of similar buildings made Norman Foster the architect he is. These buildings, in a very real sense, both chose and made him.

Did Norman Foster really need the intellectual baggage of systems thinking? The answer is undoubtedly yes. Without this open-ended, conceptual framework his energies would have been both dissipated and too narrowly channelled. Would systems thinking in itself have been enough to create what Foster has achieved? The answer is certainly no — the legacy of the schools' programme is sufficient testament to the weakness of good intentions without great talent. Foster's reductionist genius required a starting point. In the end, this series of projects leaves one breathless at the intensity of imagination, at the alchemy which could reduce such ordinary material, such temporary and mundane projects, into purest gold.

stroke the overcomplexity and rigidity of attempts to integrate services with concrete structures. Meeting short-term objectives is always more challenging than catering for vague notions of long-term capacity. There is no attempt to follow Louis Kahn's love of the articulation of building form to express served and servant spaces except in the most abstract terms. Understatement is more attractive to Foster than an architecture which needs mass to expound its meaning. There is no playful-

ness, no waste, no redundancy, no attempt to speak in any regional dialect. Simplicity is the thing.

All the buildings discussed in this essay have deep open plans. The significance of the deep plan is not just that such plan configurations are sensible for the purposes these particular buildings serve (as they certainly are) but for three underlying and much more important reasons. The first is that the deep open plan

A perspective section through the 2200 square metre phase-one building for SAPA. Warren trusses, 1.8 metres deep, span the 21-metre width of the factory floor, securely bolted to square, hollow-section columns to form a portal structure. Lightweight metal sheet roofing supports roof-top plant. The structural frame was sized so as to permit modular expansion in any direction and the building was eventually extended to triple its original floor area.

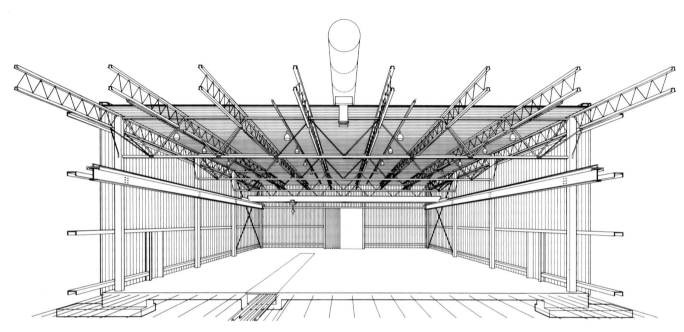

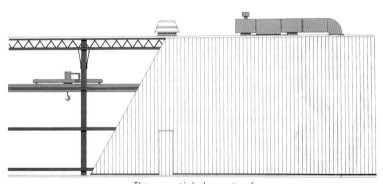

The essential elements of the SAPA 'shed' in the colours used on the final building. White profiled-steel sandwich cladding panels rise full height to a flat roof on which sits green servicing equipment. Internally, dark blue steel framing supports the cladding and an orange overhead travelling crane.

In the spring of 1972 the Swedish metal extrusion company Scandinaviska Aluminium Profiler AB (SAPA) commissioned Foster Associates to undertake joint preparatory production engineering studies and site searches after committing itself to building a British manufacturing plant; a decision made on the basis that nearly 20 per cent of its total output was already being exported to the UK market. Investigations into plant and layouts were carried out in Sweden and Holland, then related to equipment available on short-lead delivery times. Eventually a suitable 4.26-acre site was found in a newly designated industrial estate just off the M1, outside the Derbyshire town of Tibshelf.

Once the site was chosen, no time was wasted. Foster Associates were briefed in July 1972 and, by November, the previous SAPA sales base in Slough was closed and moved into temporary inflatable warehousing and pilot office units installed at Tibshelf, by Foster Associates, in just five days. Within six months the complex plant and 2200 square-metre shed had been completed, ready to start full production early in June 1973.

On top of this already tight schedule, the Foster Associates design team met a full production-engineering brief that involved liaising

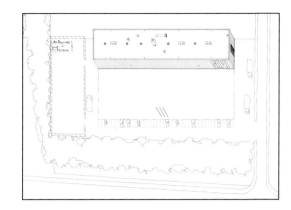

The 4-acre SAPA site close to the M1. The project included a large fenced storage compound at one end of the building and space for future phased construction. Extensive tree planting was planned.

A clear head-height of 6 metres was required beneath the travelling crane to carry it over all machinery and racked storage. The high capacity ventilators, crane, machinery, walls and even the concrete floor slab were colour coded inside the building.

with SAPA and the machinery manufacturers in the detailed layout of the plant: the contract included ordering and installing manufacturing equipment. Items that are normally outside the building brief were drawn into the 10-month period allowed for design and construction.

Initially, fragmenting some of the plant's activities and housing them in temporary structures was an essential part of the strategy for meeting SAPA's deadline. A variety of instant enclosures was considered, including Abstracta domes, pneumatics and even Porta-kabins in advance of the main building; economy and availability being the chief criteria.

SAPA intended the new factory to house a single extrusion press and associated machinery. This was to form the first phase of a planned development which, by March 1977, four years later, consisted of two presses, an anodising plant, a fabrication shop and additional staff facilities. Foster Associates were responsible for this later expansion. Ultimately the site can accommodate expansion of up to four times the original building volume.

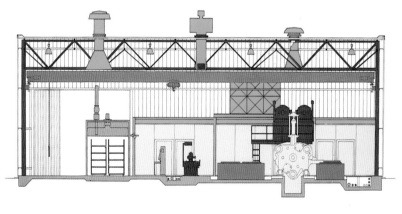

Production engineering became an inseparable part of Foster Associates' design approach; the manufacturing process determining the basic plan form of the phase-one building. Located east-west on the site, the enclosure follows the process in its essentially linear progression, beginning in the east with service cores, vehicular entry and ingot storage. This is followed by the extrusion press, water and air quenchers, and the run-out table, with production offices located alongside.

The full scale of the 100-metre long phase-one SAPA 'supershed' could only be grasped from a distance. With no views in or out, its white rectangular shape is seen here beyond a green field and a waterway on the edge of the Derbyshire industrial estate. Apart from the doors and the servicing elements on the roof, all colour was confined to the inside of the building. To relieve this starkness when phase two was completed, the company logo 'SAPA' was painted to the full height of the building at one end of the long elevation.

Green-coded ventilation equipment, yellow cabin walls, blue-painted steel trusses and red equipment, the contrast with the building's exterior could hardly be more extreme.

Aluminium extrusions stacked next to one of the two aluminium extrusion presses.

The high temperatures of aluminium extruding and pressing machinery required the large-scale movement of 'quenching' air through elaborate 'octopus' ducting. Its form was to influence later Foster Associates designs, notably the exposed ducting at the Renault Centre.

Packing, weighing and despatch are then carried out at the western end of the factory.

An internal clear height of 6 metres allows the incorporation of two overhead electric travelling cranes for moving aluminium sections and servicing machinery. It also offers the potential for adding further mezzanine-level staff facilities at either end of the building. Services are distributed in underfloor ducts and at roof level, where most of the mechanical plant is located. SAPA's own liquefied petroleum gas installation supplies heating for the building and the various stages of the extrusion process.

Structurally, the building is divided into 10-metre bays forming a shed 100 metres long and 21 metres wide, with the clear span demanded by the extrusion process provided by welded-steel primary trusses bolted to 254 mm square hollow-section steel columns. Trussed purlins bolted to the primary trusses at 3-metre centres support the roof deck. This steel skeleton was designed to allow a modular expansion in any direction.

The cladding is off-white, stove-enamelled steel double-skin profiled panels, each 8 metres high by 900 mm wide, with a foamed

polyurethane core. This, together with the ready-felted roof panels was the first British use of a then newly developed Italian system. Only four fixings were required to secure the tongued-and-grooved panels to the cladding rails, which means they can be easily erected or dismantled in a matter of minutes and re-used as the frame grows.

The phase-two expansion, carried out during 1977, tripled the factory floor area by adding a further 20 structural bays along the southern side of the existing building, to form two building bays 21 metres wide and 100 metres long. With a project lead-time of only four months, it was still possible to have the new plant fully operational within a nine-month period. The new machinery was installed while the building itself was being completed, and full production in the existing factory was maintained throughout the entire period — a measure of the efficiency of the operation and the goodwill of the SAPA workforce. SAPA is a company with a progressive attitude to industrial democracy. Its declared objective is to

The plan of phase one was determined by the needs of the extrusion process. Vehicle entry was at the eastern (left) end, next to storage and service cores. The extrusion press and a long run-out table filled the central space, with storage racks located next to the west exit.

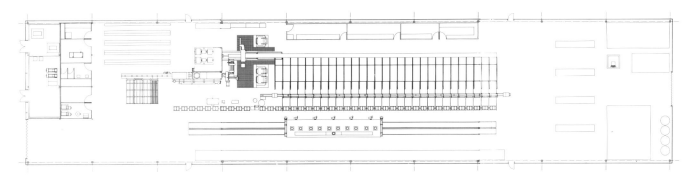

A grand dinner for over 200 guests and employees was given in the SAPA shed in September 1977 after the opening of the second phase of the plant by Eric Varley, the then Secretary of State for Industry. An indication of the size of the building can be gained from the diminutive heavy trucks in the background and the fact that the area shown is only the south-west corner of the enclosure. The original phase-one factory can be seen beyond the columns on the right.

"make profits and have fun doing it". All workers are involved as closely as possible in its financial plans and have a profit share.

Creating a high-quality working environment is seen as central to this approach. SAPA intended that the whole factory, including changing rooms and canteen, should be designed to a higher standard than any other comparable plant in the country. With the company's encouragement, Foster Associates consulted employees at all levels as part of the design process prior to the phase-two expansion. Some operatives, for example those in the die shop, were even allowed to define their own requirements.

In contrast to this vocality, the building itself is quiet, taking the 'undecorated shed' to the nth degree. The smooth-running 'industrial machine' as Norman Foster describes it, ticks over regularly under a plain bonnet, relieved only by the large, bright blue SAPA logo emblazoned along the southern elevation of the building.

Like the factory process, which is self-sufficient and contained, the building is closed. There are no windows and no views in or out. The working environment is colourful, introspective and entirely artificially lit.

The lighting incorporates mercury vapour lamps derived from those developed in Germany for colour television coverage of the Munich Olympic Games, and the colours of the production plant, handling equipment, piping, structure and services were all chosen to respond to the visible spectrum of their light output. Internal core partitions are chrome yellow, the floor is light blue, and services and machines are picked out in primary colours. The primary structure is painted mid-blue, meshed overhead with orange gantries and the drooping, silver octopus arms of the fan-driven air quenchers.

From outside, the structural frame is concealed, a decision which can be seen as a move away from the structural articulation of, for example, Reliance Controls completed six years earlier when Norman Foster was still with Richard Rogers and Team 4. There the notion of extension is explicit, the projecting beam ends clearly indicating the possibility of future growth. With SAPA, the potential for both the

Because of the complexity of the equipment, Foster Associates became involved in the whole production engineering process at SAPA, from purchasing to installation.

Aluminium processing machinery in use at SAPA. The plant was designed to a higher standard than any competitor at the time.

"At the SAPA factory high levels of insulation both stiffen the tall steel cladding panels and keep the process-generated heat inside the building, virtually obviating the need for additional heating in winter."

Barbara Goldstein, *RIBA Journal*, January 1978

"Gaunt shed and crude office, the SAPA building certainly stands out. Amid general numbing environmental pain just a sore thumb would go unnoticed. But the view from dismal surrounding suburbia may anyway be concealed in two decades, for the site edges are banked and unusually generously planted. Perhaps the bland factory exterior is a fair reaction to the brief and to the site, while it hides the surprise of the brightly (and entirely artificially) lit interior. Under the pallid skin are green and red, blue and orange arteries and muscles, sinews and heart."

The Architects' Journal, November 1973

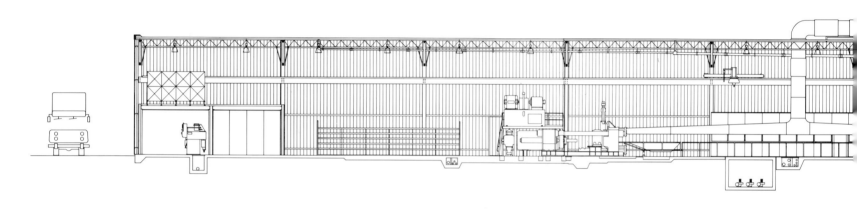

Process machinery inside the SAPA plant. The necessary light levels inside the artificially lit factory were carefully calculated, and achieved using high-level mercury vapour lamps capable of good colour resolution under all conditions.

building's and the company's expansion remains hidden, though such expansion was an inherent part of the brief.

As such, the building marks the beginning of a strong interest in the concept of the 'smooth skin', to be realised with such success in the gleaming silver 'extrusion' of the Sainsbury Centre. It is interesting to note that following these successful experiments, however, Foster Associates were to return to an increasingly dramatic structural expression, culminating in the bold yellow structure of the Renault Centre and the muscular gymnastics of the Hongkong Bank.

Since it set up a manufacturing base in the UK, SAPA's business has steadily improved and its approach to growth has been pragmatic. The 'temporary' prefabricated office facility was finally replaced by a permanent block in 1979 and a second factory opened at Holmewood in 1980, both designed by local architects. SAPA envisages that a third press will be needed and a further addition to the Tibshelf plant will be made early in the 1990s.

David Jenkins

"It is seldom that the flexibility of modular buildings — so frequently a central concern of designers — is made use of in reality. When it is used it is even less often that is works. Yet the expansion of SAPA's factory shows that this is possible."

The Architects' Journal,
September 1977

The basic module for SAPA was a 10 x 21-metre clear-spanning rectangular box, repeated 10 times to create a building 100 metres long. The section below shows the full length of phase one with its large extrusion press installed. The roof and wall cladding system was design- ed to be installed in five weeks using ready-felted roof panels and 8 x 0.9-metre stove-enamelled sandwich cladding panels with a 50 mm core. Periodic underfloor ducts service specific machinery, fed from one major supply duct which runs the full length of one side of the building.

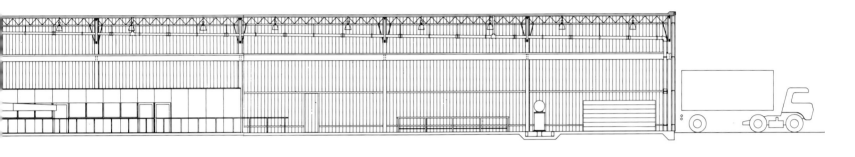

The SAPA factory in use: run-out tables and stor-age racks, and the 'oc-topus' nozzles of an air quencher in front of yellow office cabins. A glazed canteen area (below) was provided at mezzanine level in the phase-two expansion.

1972-1973 Modern Art Glass
Thamesmead
Kent

The Modern Art Glass warehouse and show-room at Thamesmead, in its original blue profiled-aluminium factory finish with one glazed double-height vertical roller vehicle door, strip roof-lights and projecting fan intakes and outlets. At one stage objections from planners at the Greater London Council raised the possibility that the building would have to be painted grey, but on appeal Foster Associates won the right to retain the bright blue.

Foster Associates' working relationship with Modern Art Glass began in 1970 when the company was appointed erector of the glazed curtain wall at the Fred Olsen Amenity Centre in Millwall Dock, Norman Foster's first glass-walled building. That was followed by a second successful partnership at IBM Cosham in 1971. Both of these early projects successfully adopted the Pitco 'T'–wall mirror-glass and neoprene curtain-wall system. In the summer of the following year, Modern Art Glass commissioned Foster Associates to design its own building at Thamesmead.

The brief was for a low-cost warehouse with supporting offices and showroom, to replace the company's existing southern regional base at Plumstead which it had out-grown. Modern Art Glass was at the time (it has since been taken over) one of the largest privately-owned glazing contractors and im-porters of glass wall assembly systems in the country, with a head office in Leeds. It recog-nised the need for a building that would per-form efficiently, provide a high standard of working conditions and act as a showcase where clients — architects, designers and build-ers — could view its products.

The site was 0.66 acres of flat, windswept reclaimed marshland on the Greater London Council's (GLC) Thamesmead East Industrial Estate. As landlord, the GLC laid down strict planning guidelines for the estate including the use of materials, colour and building height, with the aim of harmonising new development.

In some respects this was a pioneering move. Aesthetic controls rarely figure largely in the detailed design of industrial estates. Most

"There is something sur-
real about the industrial
estate at Thamesmead.
Some dull factories,
some pylons, a lot of flat
space waiting for some-
thing to happen, and the
massive Ford complex
across the river giving a
different industrial scale.
There are also fields of
horses and a battered
sign saying Manor Farm.
It is a confused no-

man's-land, the sort of
area that Gertrude Stein
had in mind when she
said 'There is no there
there'. Now it has ac-
quired a 'there', a land-
mark, Foster Associates'
big blue box for Modern
Art Glass."

John Winter, *The Archi-
tectural Review*, July
1974

Two early axonometrics
show the building in
what might be its final
form. Wrap-over clad-
ding envelops a simple
portal structure, with
only the south-facing
end elevation glazed.

such sites are a jumble of ill-conceived development. But at Thamesmead the controls
themselves had an adverse effect, inducing a
banal and grim monotony. To conform, the GLC
wanted the new building to be not more than
5.5 metres high and to be faced with Stafford-
shire blue/grey bricks like its (then very few)
neighbours.

This presented immediate problems.
Norman Foster summarises his objections to
the statutory bricks: "We started off in the
middle of a brick shortage and, in any case, we
should have needed extra piling and monumental brick piers to hold the walls up. Added
to which quality control over bricklaying is
practically nil nowadays." Fortunately, it
proved possible to negotiate a path through
the rules. Foster Associates made a strong case
for cladding the structure in profiled sheet
aluminium and for going higher than the
recommended limit to accommodate an overhead travelling crane in the warehouse, thus
allowing room for a mezzanine-level office
above the showroom at one fully-glazed end of
the building. The GLC agreed, with the proviso
that the cladding be painted blue/grey in lieu
of the brick, and construction began in March
1973. The building was in use by the following
October, after only six months on site.

Once completed, it became apparent that
shades of colour are, of course, open to degrees
of interpretation. Foster maintains that the
deep-blue factory-coated cladding represented
"a more appropriate interpretation of the spirit
of the controls". The result stands out from its
bland surroundings, confident and colourful.

Bexley, the local planning authority concerned, disagreed stating firmly that the
planning permission specified dark grey. An
enforcement notice was eventually served,
ordering that the building be repainted to the
correct colour. Louis Hellman wryly observed in
a cartoon in *The Architects' Journal* at the time
that to fit in with the existing environment, the
Modern Art Glass building would have to be
"grey and drab". "I would say this is probably
the only building with which we've ever had
any snags on the planning side", Foster recalls.
"I think that our relations with planning
officers have been very fine indeed and this is
the only building where we really came close to
coming unstuck."

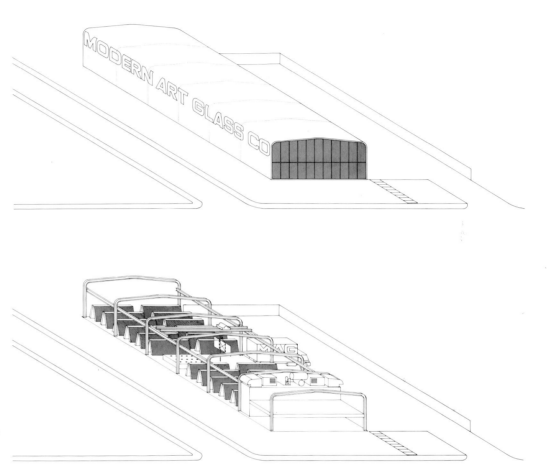

Inside the warehouse, a
simple volume with the
only equipment a special
travelling crane for lifting large panes of glass.

Internally, a two-hour
fire wall incorporated all
mechanical services, as
well as an escape stair
and lavatory accommo-
dation.

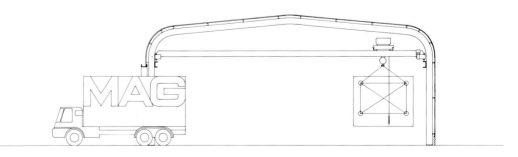

The essential elements of the Modern Art Glass shed in the colours used on the final building. Blue profiled-aluminium cladding and roller door, yellow steel framing with purlins and diagonal bracing, and the rails for the orange overhead travelling crane.

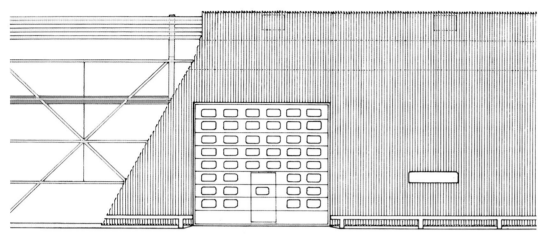

Modern Art Glass' modest new building quickly became a reluctant *cause célèbre*. An appeal was lodged but Foster reassured the client: "I said if it has to go grey then we'll paint it grey. And he asked if I would give him that assurance in writing. I said there was no question of that — he either took my word for it or not, and he did. If it had gone grey then it would have done so at our expense". Had the appeal been lost, Foster was prepared to arm the whole office with spray guns and take them to Thamesmead, television cameras in tow, and personally help with the repainting. The huge amount of press coverage the case had so far received would have guaranteed them a slot on the evening news.

However, the problem quickly evaporated once the inspector visited the site. He liked the building and its colour and judged it "the best kept blue/grey building on the estate".

With Modern Art Glass, Foster Associates also pursued a direction that can be observed in other projects of the period — the concept of the wrap-around skin. Here the corrugated aluminium cladding envelops the flank walls and roof; the wrapping and the configuration of the shed-like structure prefiguring the form of the Sainsbury Centre.

Structurally, the building is conceived as a series of rigid steel portal frames forming eight 7-metre bays, standing on a comprehensively piled, reinforced-concrete raft foundation. There is room on the site for the building to be extended by two further bays. Diagonal tubular strutting in the second and seventh bays provides wind-bracing and regularly spaced purlins span between the frames to form a substructure for the cladding.

The cladding itself is a double-skin sandwich system with a glass-fibre core, colour-coated externally and natural-finished aluminium internally. The cladding kit consists of four basic panel types, two for the pitched roof and two for the walls, with capping pieces running along the ridge and panels curved to the smallest practicable radius forming the corner detail at the eaves.

Rainwater is allowed to run off the roof and down the walls to collection in a gutter at ground level, thus doing away with the paraphernalia of high-level gutters and downpipes; another idea developed further at the Sainsbury Centre a few years later. In the few cases where the cladding is punctured, for fan in-

The double-height vertical roller vehicle loading door was a standard proprietary component, chosen from a catalogue, but specially painted blue to match the cladding. At its base, a warning strip of blue and yellow stripes matches 'crash' barriers that protect the building from parking cars.

Internally, the vehicle loading door is left in its natural aluminium finish, as is the inner skin of the cladding. The structural frame was painted yellow, with the different services colour-coded for ease of identification.

The completed 605 square metre warehouse from the south-east. External landscaping was minimal, with only a small car park and a wide grass verge beside the main access road.

takes and exhausts and the loading bay door, the housings and frame, respectively, are detailed to run the water to the sides of the openings. The generous vertical rolling door is itself punctured by long formatted windows, giving views out across the Erith Marshes. Tough steel barriers at ground level, dazzle-painted yellow and blue, protect the cladding from accidental impact damage by cars and trucks.

Inside the 650 square-metre warehouse, which takes up seven of the structural bays, the bright yellow steel frame is revealed. Overhead, the crane gear, which has a special glass-handling attachment, is picked out in a vivid orange. The warehouse once had facilities for glass storage, cutting and racking but is no longer used as originally intended, since Modern Art Glass moved out when it was taken over. The space is heated by gas-fired, warm-air units and lit by mercury vapour lamps. These give a brilliant daylight quality during the darkest winter days, though its generous rooflights alone have allowed the building to operate safely during power cuts.

Between the warehouse and the 190 square metres of office and showroom, the required two-hour, fire-resisting wall was 'fattened' into a circulation and service core with white-painted plaster walls which houses lavatories, utility and store rooms. This creates a densely planned filter between the two major accommodational elements, and an effective fire lock. The same planning device was used at the Renault Centre 10 years later. An escape staircase from the upper-level office leads directly to the open air, while a free-standing, steel spiral stair provides the main internal link between the ground-floor showroom and offices above.

These special areas occupy a shallow, single-bay zone behind the fully-glazed southern wall, but have neither opening windows nor air-conditioning. There is no problem with overheating or discomfort, however, due to a careful combination of passive and active measures. The glass has a reflective bronze tint to reduce solar gain and the first-floor slab stops 120 mm short of the glazing, allowing air movement between the two levels. Mechanical ventilation assists the natural stack effect; warm air is drawn out at high level while fans push in fresh air at a comparatively low level.

The entire south elevation is a wall of bronze-tinted glazing carried on tubular mullions inside a blue-painted fascia. Behind this are located the building's showroom and mezzanine-level offices.

The structural frame is built off a short-piled ground slab because of the poor ground conditions. It consists of eight structural bays, each defined by welded portal frames. These are connected by purlins which also provide support for the cladding. Two bays are cross-braced for lateral support.

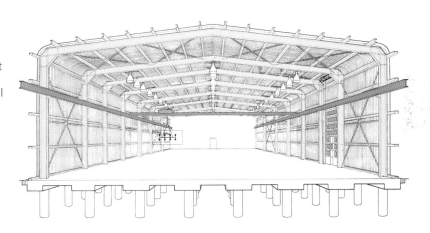

The glass curtain-wall at the south end stretches from cladding line to cladding line, passing in front of the portal frame and mezzanine steel-work. The whole assembly was designed by Foster Associates.

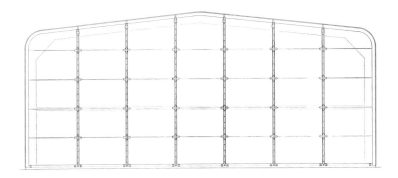

Staff access between the ground-floor showroom and offices above is provided by a simple spiral staircase. The showroom and offices were fully carpeted, its colour matching that of the structure exactly.

The edge of the office mezzanine floor level is set 120 mm inside the glass cladding line permitting the tubular glazing mullions to pass uninterrupted from the concrete ground slab to special top connections cantilevered off the portal frame.

The rate of air flow and temperature can be adjusted to suit the user's requirements.

Both the offices and showroom have downlighters recessed into suspended, metal acoustic-tile ceilings. Task lighting was integrated with Herman Miller's Action Office 2 furniture system, creating a comfortable ambience for the office staff. Providing an attractive environment for the workforce was a key move in meeting the challenge offered by the brief; taking what was essentially a low-cost industrial shed and building character into it.

At the time, Foster insisted that the design was not expensive when lined up against the typical package-deal shed which proliferates on most industrial estates. The 'square-foot' prices that might initially be quoted by a package dealer do not include 'under the line expenses', as an industrialist would discover sooner or later to his cost. For example, the extensive piling and raft foundation, and the office fit-out would all have been extras. So too would the glass wall which Modern Art Glass itself erected as a test-bed installation.

This wall was, in fact, a dry-run for the system that Foster Associates thought they might be forced into using at Willis Faber &

The exterior of the south wall presents a finely detailed flat glass surface with all fixings hidden inside apart from the vertical clamping strips. The cowls in the cladding at ground and first floor levels are for ventilation.

Tony Hunt's preferred design for a welded junction for the portal frame, following the curve of the cladding, was economic but difficult to erect. A simpler but less elegant bolted connection, with site-welded gusset, was used instead.

The edge detail around the glazed wall is formed with a blue-painted 200 mm deep steel gable angle inside a neoprene trim stop. The perimeter toughened glass sheets are restrained inside this by means of a neoprene seal and clamping strip.

Dumas where a solution for the glass curtain wall did not emerge until late in the day. To force the pace on both projects, Norman Foster worked closely with Martin Francis, an expert solver of construction and manufacturing problems who had last worked with Foster Associates on the Computer Technology building in 1970.

The aim at Willis Faber & Dumas was to achieve a mullion-free glass wall. Martin Francis initially approached Pilkington Glass who already had an all-glass system but this was ground-supported and not suitable for Willis Faber & Dumas' three floors. Pilkington were also experimenting with a suspended system using toughened glass with patch plates at the corner of each sheet and silicone-sealed joints, but this too had only been used for straight runs over a single storey. Adapting it for three storeys required the development of special intermediate supports. A further complication was the requirement for tinted toughened glass: toughening large panels of tinted glass still presented technical problems.

Pilkington were reluctant to commit themselves. And so a fall-back system was detailed — by Martin Francis and Foster Associates — that relied on suspended stainless-steel mullions to give the glass structural support. It was this system that was manufactured by Modern Art Glass and installed on their own building. The mullions have projecting flanges with lugs on which each 12 mm-thick panel of glass can rest. Simple, vertical steel and neoprene sandwich strips provide a weather seal and hold the glass in position.

Helmut Jacoby's early perspectives of Willis Faber & Dumas show how the serpentine glass wall might have looked had the Modern Art Glass solution been applied. Norman Foster admits that the building would have lost something — the vertical joints tending to bunch on the curves, spoiling the clean lines.

Eventually, at the last possible moment, Pilkington agreed to be included on the tender list for Willis Faber & Dumas, returned the lowest tender and finally accepted full design responsibility using many of the details developed by Martin Francis and Foster Associates. Modern Art Glass brought the story full circle by then being appointed erector for this glass wall also.

David Jenkins

The Modern Art Glass gable wall is an important evolutionary step in the journey from the proprietary Pittsburgh Plate Glass system used at the Olsen amenity centre and IBM Cosham, and the Pilkington 'Planar' system developed by Foster Associates for the Willis Faber & Dumas project in Ipswich. At Modern Art Glass the aluminium box mullions of the PPG system were replaced by suspended tubular-steel mullions which restrained the glass panels vertically with the aid of an external clamping strip held in place with stainless-steel fixing nuts: an assembly that was daringly minimal at the time but now looks surprisingly heavy-handed. Built while the Willis Faber project was on the drawing-board, it was initially assumed that this system would be used there too.

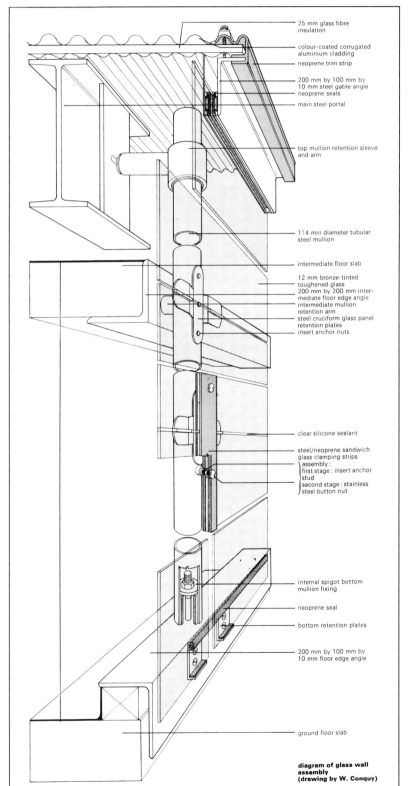

25 mm glass fibre insulation

colour-coated corrugated aluminium cladding

neoprene trim strip

200 mm by 100 mm by 10 mm steel gable angle neoprene seals

main steel portal

top mullion retention sleeve and arm

114 mm diameter tubular steel mullion

intermediate floor slab

12 mm bronze-tinted toughened glass
200 mm by 200 mm intermediate floor edge angle
intermediate mullion retention arm
steel cruciform glass panel retention plates
insert anchor nuts

clear silicone sealant

steel/neoprene sandwich glass clamping strips
assembly:
first stage: insert anchor stud
second stage: stainless steel button nut

internal spigot bottom mullion fixing

neoprene seal

bottom retention plates

200 mm by 100 mm by 10 mm floor edge angle

ground floor slab

diagram of glass wall assembly (drawing by W. Conquy)

"With new advances in technology — whether in glues, glass- or carbon-fibres — the glider has evolved so it can now cover greater distances at higher speeds. One thousand miles in nine hours: all solar energy, with greater safety and greater pilot comfort. But more importantly, as it has evolved it has become more beautiful.

This prospect of greater beauty, allied with improved performance and higher satisfaction, offers, I believe, an important lesson for the future of architecture."

Norman Foster, More with Less lecture, February 1979

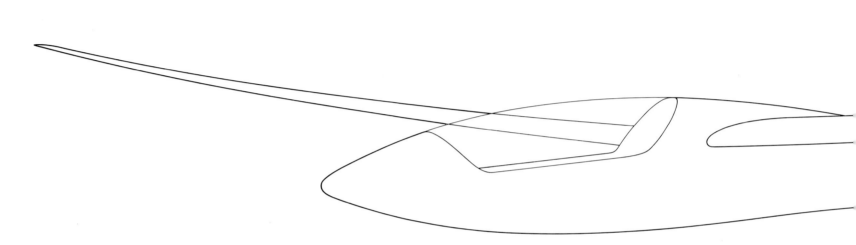

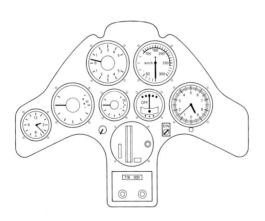

"The Caproni sailplane does what it does without consuming any energy at all once it's up and flying. It flies almost on pure intellectual power. Seriously. It takes brains and sensibility, but not gasoline to fly a glider."

Reyner Banham, the Yellow Bicycle lecture at UEA, June 1985

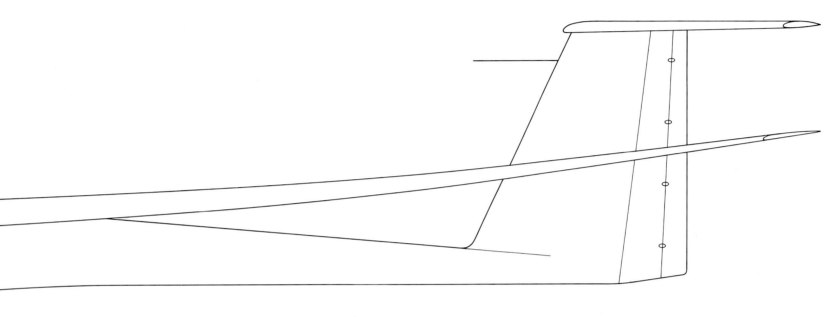

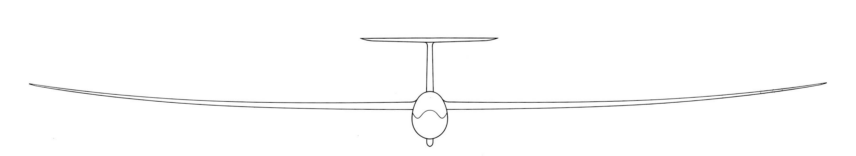

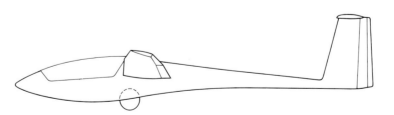

"When the Vestby project in Norway was presented, laden with signs of energy conservation, many assumed an about-face had occurred in Foster Associates' attitudes to technology. For on close inspection the raised pavilions, that silently infiltrated the forest and so deceptively looked like High-Tech boxes, proved to be Pandora's boxes packed with appropriate technology surprises."

Architectural Design, March 1976

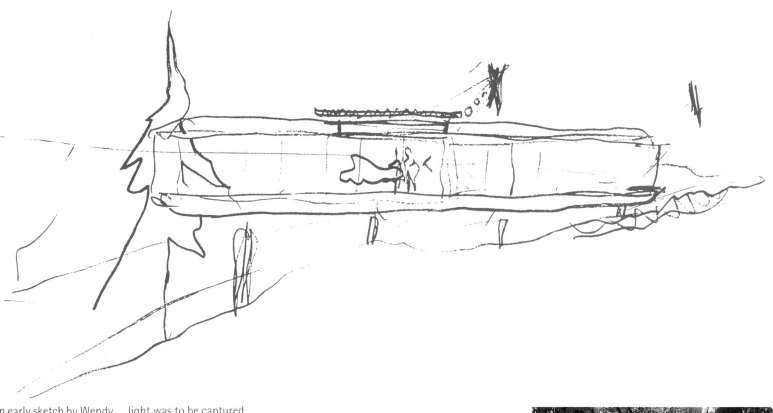

An early sketch by Wendy Foster demonstrates how the energy-conscious principles of the Vestby project formed the basis of its design. Raised on pilotis because of the steeply sloping site, each unit was to have made maximum use of this feature by drawing in a large volume of cool ventilating air from below and expelling it through the roof. In addition, sunlight was to be captured in every way possible using reflectors reminiscent of the sunscoop designed for the Hongkong and Shanghai Bank a decade later. Finally, the flush, reflective skin of the buildings was designed to minimise wind resistance and heat loss.

Circulation within the Vestby forest complex was to have been entirely on foot, with all cars left at the perimeter. In this way the natural features of the site were to have been as little disturbed as possible.

Country Offices
Vestby
Norway

The Vestby project was one of a number of studies carried out by Foster Associates for Fred Olsen in the years following their successful association on the Millwall Dock buildings. It was in response to a proposal by Fred Olsen and two related companies, Akergruppe and SRS, to move their offices out of Oslo to a forest 45 kilometres to the south, overlooking Oslo Fjord. Foster Associates' proposal was for a series of pavilions loosely arranged within the forest, which could be increased in number to accommodate the companies' growth.

The wish to exchange life in the city for virgin countryside is both powerful and recurring, and it has inspired many of the best-known works of modern architecture, most notably the Farnsworth House and the Villa Savoye, with which the Vestby project has clear formal resemblances. Like its distinguished forbears, it aims to disrupt its setting as little as possible by lifting the building on to pilotis. The building is seen as little more than a frame, with nature flowing round it and through it. The main difference is that Vestby pursues these ideals more thoroughly: now the building is wholly raised off the ground and it is almost completely transparent.

In addition, construction was to have been prefabricated, with a minimum of excavation and building work taking place within the forest itself, and vehicular traffic was to be stopped at its edge. Circulation about the site was to be entirely pedestrian, on walkways following its contours. These walkways covered service connections immediately underneath. Again, excavation would be minimal.

Another important influence on the Vestby project was the 1973 Arab-Israeli war and the oil crisis. At Vestby, Foster Associates determined to turn their technological inventiveness to problems of saving energy and minimising environmental impact. Typically, they came up with a wide range of solutions, so that the ideal of minimum interference is enacted at a practical as well as an aesthetic level. By lifting the building off the ground, they allowed the circulation of air all around the envelope, which obviated the need for

Norman Foster's sketch for the forest paths. Laid out along the routes of existing ski trails, he proposed that they be supported above ground level so as to permit water, power and communications services to run beneath them where they would be concealed but easily accessible.

The proposed solar reflector systems were designed to track the low northern sun and thereby maximise natural lighting.

A large air volume and stack-effect assisted ventilation were utilised to promote natural ventilation and thus avoid the high energy consumption of air conditioning.

Birkin Haward's sketches were used to explain to the client the benefits of appropriate technology. The structure at Vestby, a long-span steel lattice system, called for minimal ground support to reduce environmental impact.

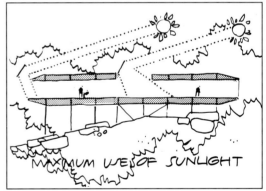

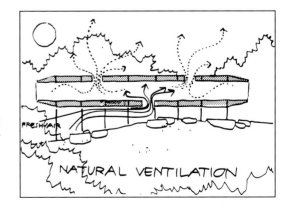

"Designing buildings in this energy-conscious time poses quite new problems, and these problems are not about how to achieve low energy designs; much greater is the difficulty of making value judgements which maintain a balanced view of energy in relation to all the other factors surrounding a building project, thereby avoiding the comfortable refuge of reliable looking technical calculations which sometimes deceive people into believing that building science is exact — it isn't!"

Loren Butt, *Foster Associates*, RIBA Publications 1979

The structural and service components of the pavilions had to be relatively small and extremely lightweight to minimise access and construction damage on site. A steel lattice-beam construction was proposed, supporting wraparound profiled-steel decking above and below a single-storey office. The roof and perimeter envelope was then enclosed in a reflective metal skin.

In this Helmut Jacoby perspective, the Vestby pavilions seem to float above their wooded site south of Oslo. High performance glass cladding was to have been used, as at the Olsen amenity centre and IBM Cosham.

mechanical air cooling. The external skin was to be well insulated and reflective, with louvres designed to respond to external weather conditions. On the roof, mirrored sun scoops were to follow the winter sun with the help of tracking devices, introducing warming sunlight into the centre of the building, and using the sun's heat directly to melt winter snow along its north elevation. Although Vestby was not implemented, the sun scoop idea was eventually put to use at the Hongkong Bank, bringing light into its central atrium.

The scheme would also have derived its water supply locally, and its waste was to be recycled. It would have been as self-sufficient as a modern office can be. What Vestby demonstrated, simply but completely, was that the technological approach developed by Foster Associates in their earlier projects could have been taken much further into the sphere of energy without being destructive to the environment. Modern techniques and the ideals of the log cabin are not mutually exclusive.

Rowan Moore

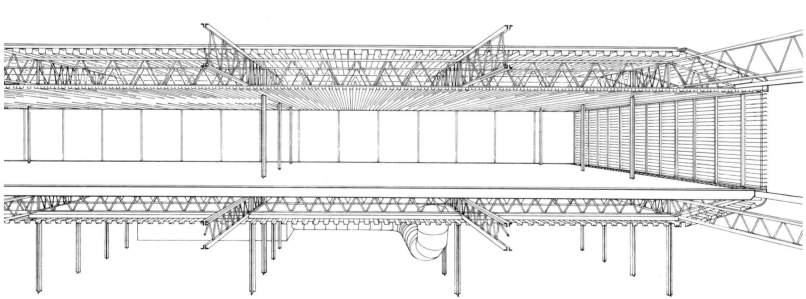

Adjustable external thermal louvres – which automatically responded to changing weather conditions – were to have been installed, maintenance access being provided by a mobile gantry moving on rails recessed into the cladding.

"In this large-scale side elevation of one of the Vestby pavilions, for example, we are trying to demonstrate the chameleon-like characteristics of the building. Depending on how the external blinds are activated the building can read as a solid form – coloured metallic or ribbed – or, at the throw of a switch, the whole elevation can become a reflective mirror. We are also exploring how that whole side might open up – so that you could almost touch the forest outside."

Norman Foster, *A&U*, September 1975

The south elevation of a Vestby pavilion, in model form. Aerodynamic roof-mounted reflectors were designed to direct sunlight through rooflights and into the north-facing elevation.

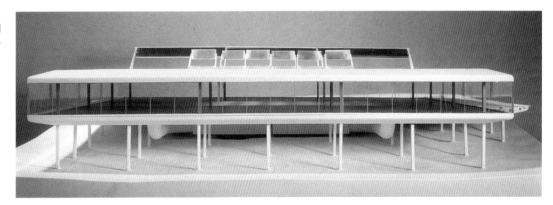

The east elevation of the Vestby model shows raked reflector mountings and the large-volume air-movement heating and ventilation equipment that was to have been installed beneath the building.

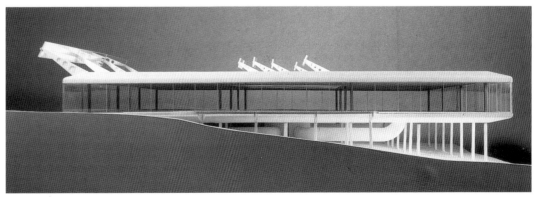

Son Recreation Centre
Vestby
Norway

The site model of the Son country club and marina, situated on a peninsula projecting into Oslo Fjord 50 kilometres south of the capital. The project included the adaptive use of existing barns as well as new buildings, boatyard facilities and a heliport.

The country club proposed for Son in Norway grew out of the proposals for the nearby Vestby site. Son was to provide recreation facilities for employees at the relocated offices there, and form a social centre for the entire local community. It could also have been used as a conference hotel, while Foster Associates' own studies for the site added a possible yacht marina and converted an existing barn into a picnic base.

Where the Vestby pavilions were generic and repeatable, Son was to be a unique construction, specific to its setting and orientated towards views of the fjord which it overlooked. It was a variation on the Vestby theme of minimum interference with the landscape, but differently enacted. As at Vestby the structure was to be lightweight and prefabricated, but the accommodation, rather than floating above the ground in a single plane, was to be placed on a series of terraces that followed the contours of the hill.

Son is a singularly clear example of Foster's continuing interest in the single enclosure sheltering a multiplicity of changing uses, which has close affinities with the ideas of his friend and inspiration Buckminster Fuller. It

Birkin Haward's sketch interior of the Son recreation building proposed column-supported balconies projecting into an open-plan space on which facilities for different activities could be easily intermingled.

A sketch section through the principal Son building, a discreet large-scale glazed dome at the water's edge. Terraced internally and tucked into the contours of the land so as to be inconspicuous despite its size, the structure would have provided unrivalled views of the Fjord.

Location plan showing the relative positions of Son, Vestby and Oslo, home of the existing Fred Olsen shipping line offices.

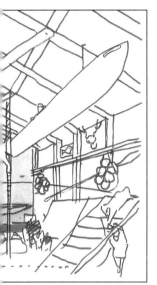

also embodies a recurring duality in Foster Associates' work: of the lightweight super-structure floating above a solid, well-serviced base hollowed out of the ground. Indeed, in many ways, the Son recreation centre can be seen as little more than the sophisticated re-building of the Retreat at Feock, but on a far grander scale.

Foster Associates' comprehensive studies for Fred Olsen's Norwegian operations also included proposals for the Oslo city block in which their headquarters were situated. This project gave Foster Associates a relatively rare opportunity to work with a historic building, a nineteenth-century, timber-frame structure which occupied one part of the site, and had housed Olsen's original offices.

Although so much of their work had been on green field sites or industrial estates, Foster Associates produced what would have been, if built, an original and valuable contribution to the emerging conservation debate. Foster now calls it the "no hands approach", the construc-tion of a wholly new building next to the exist-ing, with minimum contact between the two. The historic fabric of the city is given the same treatment as the landscape at Vestby: it is re-spected and left alone.

But this does not mean that it is ignored. The existing building forms the centre-piece of the glazed atrium mediating between the old work and the new, while the framed structure of the new building has a conceptual affinity with that of its predecessor. The atrium is it-self an echo of the glazed central courtyard characteristic of many traditional Oslo build-ings, including the existing Olsen offices. It is also, like its historic models, a response to the extremes of the Norwegian climate, providing a sheltered, internally landscaped space that mediates between the private offices and the public world of the city. Foster Associates' commissions had not, at that stage, been given much occasion for such spaces, but in outline the Oslo atrium looks forward to comparable spaces in the BBC Radio Headquarters project, the Hongkong Bank and, most recently, the new headquarters for ITN.

Rowan Moore

This drawing, by Helmut Jacoby, was prepared as part of a proposal for an extension to the Fred Olsen offices in Oslo. One of Foster Associates' very few opportunities to refurbish a historic building, they proposed turning the adjacent street into an enclosed arcade and leaving the existing nineteenth-century timber-framed building intact. The Oslo refurbishment was to have been linked to the move to Vestby and was abandoned with that scheme.

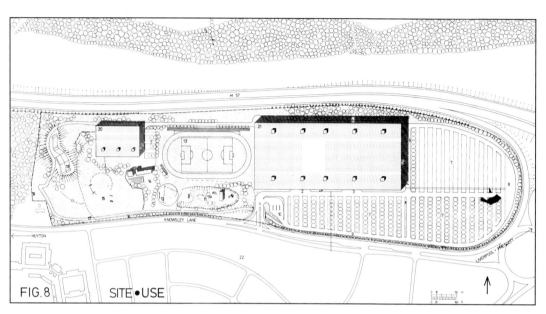

FIG.8   SITE•USE

When in 1972, Foster Associates investigated the concept of integrated shopping and leisure centres, there were few out-of-town developments of any kind in the UK and nothing as novel elsewhere in Europe.

The integrated concept had been formulated by MPC & Associates, a firm of marketing and planning consultants who spent five years researching retail and leisure trends in Western Europe and the USA. They recognised the fact that people were now working fewer hours for more pay, and that catering for personal recreation was quickly becoming a growth area.

Peter James, who headed MPC's subsidiary management company, Pavilion Recreation Ltd, commissioned Foster Associates together with landscape consultant John Allen to produce feasibility studies for two prototype centres with sites at Knowsley, near Liverpool, and Badhoevedorp in Holland.

In the UK there was still widespread opposition from planning authorities to the hypermarket idea and the route to out-of-town approval could be long and expensive. It took Carrefour, for example, five years to complete the whole process from planning submission to opening its superstore at Eastleigh in Hampshire. At the outset of the project, Peter James, quantity surveyor John Walker and Norman Foster made a four-day study tour of superstores in France, including Carrefour.

Recognising the prevailing hostile climate, the Pavilion concept responded by using the hypermarket as a catalyst for creating a wide

Long and short sections through the leisure centre proposed for Knowsley show perhaps the most literal of all the 'umbrella' buildings. Beneath the broad overhanging eaves of a space-frame roof any variety of commercial and leisure activities could take place.

The site of the Knowsley project was a curious strip of land isolated by the construction of the M57. Near a major interchange, however, the site was ideally situated to draw on a potential catchment area of 1.5 million people. Anticipating such developments as the Gateshead

Metro by many years, the scheme shows extensive sports, leisure and play facilities in addition to the 288-metre long superstore and parking for 2500 cars.

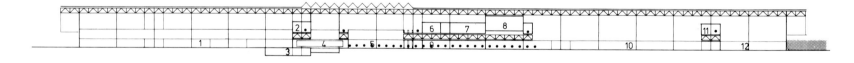

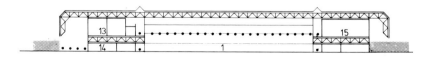

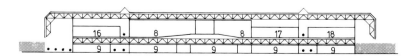

Helmut Jacoby's perspective of the proposed Knowsley superstore seen from the tree-planted car park to the south. Typically, the planting was designed to minimise the building's great size.

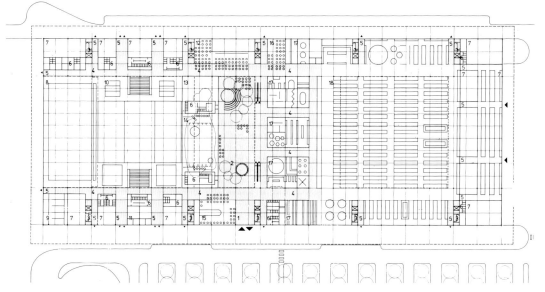

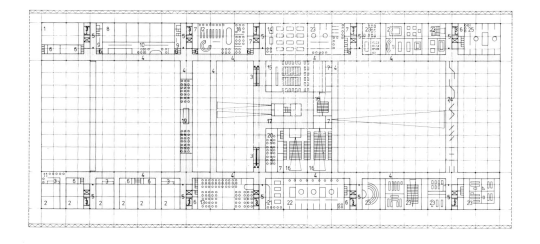

Ground floor	14 leisure pool	8 gymnasium	22 administration
1 main entrance	15 bar	9 sauna	23 lecture halls
2 plaza	16 cafeteria	10 fitness centre	24 exhibitions
3 lifts	17 shops	11 club bar	25 offices
4 circulation areas	18 superstore	12 library	
5 exits		13 discotheque	
6 lavatories	First floor	14 snooker hall	
7 storage	1 gymnasium	15 bingo hall	
8 roller-skating rink	2 squash courts	16 cinemas	
9 golf practice centre	3 lifts	17 reception	
10 sports hall	4 circulation areas	18 restaurant	
11 medical centre	5 exits	19 performance area	
12 restaurant	6 lavatories	20 steak bar	
13 crèche	7 storage	21 pool hall	

range of social and recreational facilities, some of which would be subsidised by the commercial operation. This made the proposition more attractive to the planners and, more importantly, provided a valuable and comprehensive amenity for the local community.

At Knowsley, the site was a 50-acre section of Lord Derby's country estate, seven miles east of Liverpool city centre, that had been isolated from the main park by the construction of the M57 motorway.

In commercial terms the Knowsley Pavilion was dominated by a 12 200 square-metre Associated Dairies (ASDA) superstore. At the time, ASDA, whom MPC was advising on its expansion programme, was the leading UK superstore operator with branches throughout the north of England.

Of the total floor area of 47 000 square metres, just under half was taken up by recreational facilities which comprised: a public swimming pool and sports hall, a roller-skating rink, squash courts, golf and archery practice ranges, bars and restaurants, a library, and adult education and medical centres. Outside the main building, the site also contained soccer pitches, athletics and cycle tracks, a dry ski-run, a riding school based in retained estate farm buildings, and a petrol station.

The Badhoevedorp Pavilion was designed for a smaller gridded field site close to the Amsterdam/Haarlem motorway and contained a similar but less ambitious recreational element combined with a hypermarket that was to be operated by Miro, a major Dutch supermarket group. The proportion of retail/recreational/circulation and ancillary uses was 50:22:28 per cent compared with the less commercial mix of 32:41:27 per cent at Knowsley.

Finding the right ingredients for this mix was fundamental to what Norman Foster describes as, "retranslating the hypermarket as an individual building operating solely for commercial gain, into a centre for all the family". The strength of the mix on offer, from shopping to active and passive sporting pursuits and places to rest and eat, meant that there was something to encourage everyone, young and old, to make the journey out of town and spend a day there.

At Knowsley it was envisaged that the sports and recreational facilities might also be used by local schools on a part-time basis, for

The Lord's Hill shopping centre, in Derby, was a competition entry based on the earlier leisure centre work for MPC. With its branching structural 'trees' supporting the roof, the project can be seen as a direct progenitor of the Stansted air terminal started a decade later.

A photomontage of the proposed leisure centre at Badhoevedorp in the Netherlands. Though smaller than Knowsley, it possessed excellent motorway access and included extensive facilities in addition to shopping and parking.

example on week-day mornings when the centre might expect to have few visitors. Getting there would be easy: the locality was already well served by local transport, and a bus terminus together with parking spaces for coaches and 2500 cars was planned.

All the facilities would be available to the public without a membership fee, and some things such as the crèche, adventure playground and swimming pool would be free, thus broadening the centre's appeal to the community as a whole and preventing it becoming a 'club' for middle- and high-income families.

Like their more orthodox hypermarket counterparts, both projects employed shed structures, conceived as wide-span 'umbrellas' sheltering a variety of accommodation. At Knowsley the envelope was 288 x 126 metres in plan and 15 metres high, and employed a large-span steel space-frame primary structure to support a lightweight insulated roof deck. A secondary steel truss structure, spanning 21 metres, supported the upper floor level. All internal spaces were air-conditioned, plant being located at roof level and services distributed via ducts within the roof zone.

Large facilities — the superstore, sports hall, pool and plaza — were located in a central full-height zone with smaller spaces arranged in two floors along each side. On the long southern face overlooking the car park, the building enclosure was pulled back to form a generous sheltered promenade below the overhanging roof.

Movement patterns through the plan were designed to ensure that every unit was given maximum exposure to passing shoppers. The superstore and smaller retail outlets were all entered via a plaza from which escalators led to the upper-level galleries. These were dominated by a three-screen cinema and bingo hall, arranged around a central foyer that incorporated an audio-visual projection facility capable of relaying still or moving images on to screens, adding an extra dimension to the double-height plaza and transforming it into a public arena.

The Badhoevedorp Pavilion was similarly organised but within a smaller 186 x 96-metre envelope on a 24-metre square grid. Like Knowsley, it had an arcaded elevation facing the car park with covered service and delivery bays on one short side, and the plan organisation followed an ordered sequence along its

A Jacoby drawing of the proposed interior for Badhoevedorp. Here, a swimming pool and large landscaped atrium were to be included beneath the 15-metre high space-frame roof.

length from service area, hypermarket storage and sales zones to the plaza and recreational facilities.

At both centres, the recreational facilities were to be operated by individual tenants who would control their day-to-day running, while overall responsibility for the centre itself would be retained by the resident Pavilion management team. This gave the tenants a high degree of control, in the hope that the impersonal service and character offered by similar 'municipal' facilities would be avoided.

The centres would function almost round-the-clock, the shops opening at 9am and closing late at 10pm, with restaurants and discos staying open even later. They would be lively, welcoming and attractive places to visit at any time of the day and, unlike most out-of-town sites or 'New-Town' city centres, there would always be things to do and places to go.

In addition, the Knowsley Pavilion, for example, was expected to provide over 400 full-time jobs and employ 450 people part-time: in all a very impressive set of credentials to present to the planning committee. In fact, presenting the schemes became a regular event. Ian Ritchie, who worked most closely with Norman Foster on the centres, remembers travelling with the 'Pavilion roadshow' — a multi-visual production that relied on a host of slide projectors and other hired kit. The show reached Lord Derby, ASDA, planners, councillors and potential tenants in the North and their equivalent bodies in Holland.

Foster Associates and MPC also consulted a variety of interest groups including local chambers of commerce, the Sports Council, youth-club leaders and a cross-section of inhabitants within the Pavilion catchment area. This area was potentially very great. At Knowsley, a survey showed a population of 77 000 living within a five-minute drive of the centre, and up to 1.5 million if the travel time was extended to 30 minutes.

It seemed that economically and socially the Pavilion centres had everything to offer and that success could be guaranteed. But MPC could not make the leap from initiating the concept to funding the buildings in spite of the enthusiasm shown by ASDA and Miro. And even though their feasibility was proven, they were not taken further.

David Jenkins

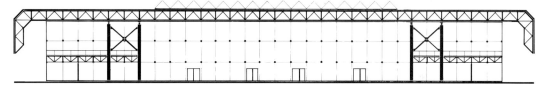

Full-height glazing would have provided internal areas with spectacular views of the surrounding park.

The structure of the building was to be a large-span umbrella space-frame, with a cantilevered eaves overhang

providing an extensive covered set down and pick up area.

Orange Hand Shops
England

An early cut-away perspective and section illustrate the kit-of-parts approach Foster Associates developed for the Orange Hand chain of shops. Anticipating contemporary retailing practice by many years, the 'kit' proposed high-level servicing and removable display units instead of fixtures. The full width of the shop opened on to the street — security being offered by fold-away glazing and a roller shutter. Storage areas were separate, possibly in a basement, while air-handling equipment was suspended undisguised from the ceiling.

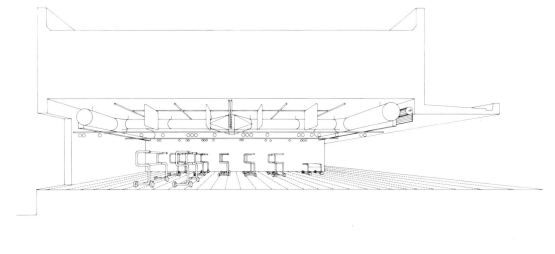

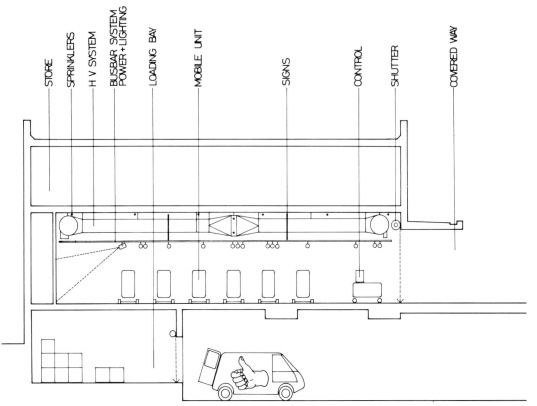

Orange Hand was a retail shopping concept created in the early 1970s by the Burton clothing group, under managing director David Thomas. It was Thomas' aim to establish a nationwide chain of shops specialising in 'trendy' clothes for boys between the ages of 5 and 15 years, thereby breaking Burton out of its '50-shilling-tailor' High Street image.

The concept had been tested with varying degrees of success in three prototype shops, but these had little unifying style or recognisable identity. David Thomas' brief to Foster Associates was to "develop the retailing concept further by design innovation". Norman Foster was initially approached by Burton's chief architect, Gerry Deighton, who had moved to the company from IBM's estates and construction division where he had been project manager for the pilot head office at Cosham, completed only the year before. Impressed by Foster's radical reworking of the IBM brief and the fact that the building was completed ahead of schedule, Deighton wanted to employ the same skills to get the Orange Hand shops up and running.

In May 1972 Foster Associates were given a crash programme to realise the first five shops in time for that year's peak Christmas sales period. The company also wanted to reduce their typical opening costs by up to 50 per cent. Foster Associates were given a wide-ranging brief which included providing project management to monitor progress; defining cost and programme targets; and, most importantly from Orange Hand's point of view, "breaking through the opening late syndrome".

The initial sites were five standard shop units, each of approximately 1000 square feet in major shopping centres; one in central London situated on Sloane Square and four in regional locations at Brighton, Nottingham, Reading and Uxbridge.

As a first move, the existing operation was analysed in depth and the 'rag trade' in general investigated. It became apparent that most chain stores' units were fitted out on a one-off basis which meant that a high proportion of fittings were often permanent and therefore lost at the end of the lease. In the prevailing volatile retail market, and with the burgeoning of new city shopping centres leading to a surplus of short-lease sites, Foster Associates concluded that it made no sense to custom-fit

Elements of the mobile demountable retailing system. High- and low-level hanging racks and shelving units were assembled from chrome or painted steel tubing and pressed metal sheets. Dressing cubicles could be formed with additional acrylic panels.

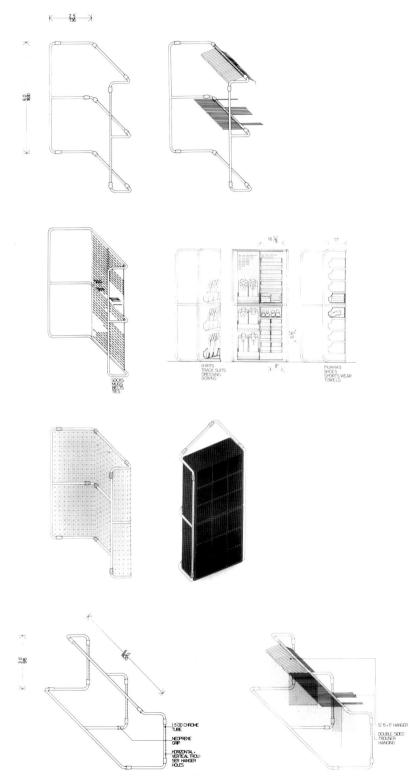

One of a series of Burton clothing group advertisements for Orange Hand. The target customer profile was active boys between 5 and 15 years old.

Birkin Haward's concept/presentation sketch of a standard Orange Hand shop unit shows all the components of the project in all but their final form. Working to a tight 27-week programme, there was little time to reconsider once approval had been given, only to refine.

each individual shop. This only discouraged mobility which might otherwise be commercially desirable.

Instead, Foster Associates proposed a standardised kit-of-parts, applicable to any number of shops that could be assembled quickly and, if necessary, relocated. The kit included shop-front and fascia, heating and ventilating equipment and a flexible display system. "Keep it in the family — don't give it to the landlord", became the Orange Hand motto.

The shop-front was designed for maximum transparency allowing the clothes inside to make an immediate visual impact on the passer-by. Consisting of 8-foot high glass panels capable of sliding away partially or completely, it also eliminated any physical barrier between shop and customer. A glass panel above filled the remainder of the opening, with a flashing neon Orange Hand logo suspended behind it. This too could be quickly demounted and cost only half as much as Burton's original fixed sign. However the Orange Hand clenched fist symbol, designed by Wolff Olins, proved controversial. All the local planning authorities apart from Reading, which had a relaxed attitude, considered it offensive and it was not used on any other fascia.

There were two exceptions to the standard shop-front. At the Sloane Square shop, which occupied a prominent corner site, the front was fully glazed but without sliding doors, very much like Foster Associates' later Fred Olsen

The Orange Hand symbol devised for Burton's by Wolff Olins. Intended for all shop fronts, this neon sign version was used on only one of the five stores as objections were raised by local authorities to its resemblance to a clenched fist.

The completed Sloane Square store in 1972. The tubular steel display units and exposed white-painted ceiling void with suspended services are exactly as Birkin Haward's concept sketch intended. Only the suspended display signs are missing.

Travel Agency in Regent Street. At Nottingham, where the shop was off an enclosed mall, there was no shop-front at all, merely a retractable grille which could be lowered at night.

Work to the shell itself was reduced to an absolute minimum: floors were finished with vinyl travertine tiles, and the walls and ceilings spray-painted white to form a neutral back-drop against which the bright-yellow-framed shop fittings and service ducts were super-imposed. In this way, the budget was directed away from what Norman Foster terms 'cosmetics' towards refining the essential components all of which, including the major services elements, were left exposed. A suspended ceiling hiding the duct work was tried in the Uxbridge shop, but Orange Hand agreed that it was better without it.

All the mechanical and electrical services were designed in house; one of the first projects undertaken by engineer Loren Butt on joining Foster Associates. Working the scheme and the services design up together was the only way that the whole package could be progressed within the tight timescale. The suspended duct work housed a reversible heating and ventilating system — "a simple

idea designed from scratch" as Loren Butt describes it — which could produce a curtain of warm air across the open shop-front in cold weather or be switched over to extract warm air from the back of the shop in summer. Mechanical cooling could be incorporated when needed. The lighting was Rotaflex high/low voltage spots on a ceiling track, a system chosen for its accurate colour rendition.

The shop fittings were the most flexible and adaptable parts of the kit. Initial research showed that there were no suitable fittings on the market which would allow low display rails in the centre of the shop and higher units at the perimeter. As a result a prototype 6 x 3ft, tubular-steel unit was developed. It could be used either vertically against the wall or horizontally on the floor, allowing staff an overall view of both the shop and customers.

This basic unit was adaptable into a series of options, the frames combining in a variety of ways with slotted Dexion back-plates and brightly-coloured industrial storage bins to form hanging or rack display stands, and changing cubicles. The movable cubicles were infilled with metallised acrylic panels, fitted mirror-side out to stop young customers

The Nottingham store. The kit-of-parts approach was an ideal solution, offering fast erection but maintaining an instantly recognisable 'look' whatever the location.

Lighting in the shops was a high/low voltage spot system selected for its flexibility and accurate colour rendering.

"The Foster Associates' system is cheap. It also provides visual unity and allows staff to move units to suit daily needs, even moving them on to the pavement. Also, because the units can be used vertically or horizontally, only one type of unit has to be considered, ordered and deployed according to the merchandise avail- able. But this very flexibility is a drawback: a visually unaware sales- man can move units to such a degree that the clean line of the design becomes muddled. The architect is considering a systems manual; a humorous solution which might just work."

Ilse Gray, *Design*, May 1973

Every element in the fit-out kit was exposed, including the ductwork for a specially developed reversible heating and ventilating system supplying warm or ambient air to the back or front of the shop.

The Orange Hand symbol on a check-out counter and cash desk in the Reading store. Movable acrylic-panelled dressing cubicles stand against a recessed wall in the background.

Brightly coloured standard industrial warehouse storage components were adapted for use as a low-cost shop display system that could contain anything from shoes to shirts.

spending too much time admiring themselves. The cash desk was designed as a special item within a customised tubular frame with a black rubber top and sliding plastic drawers.

Signs were rationalised down to a simple system of cards held between acrylic sheets bolted together and fixed to the display units using black anodised-aluminium clamps secured by Allen bolts. The signs could be changed or rewritten by shop staff using dry transfer lettering. All of which allowed the units to be moved around and signage altered to suit new sales techniques or changing stock.

All five shops were complete at the end of a 27-week programme which included proto-type research and development, detail design and an average nine weeks on site. They traded successfully and proved very popular but no further shops were built due to management reshuffles and a consequent change in marketing strategy, resulting in Burton's decision to close down Orange Hand only three years later.

David Jenkins

German Car Centre
Milton Keynes
Buckinghamshire

"Milton Keynes has lost through ill-luck, over-optimism, international recession and timidity, a number of projects that would help make the city beautiful: Stirling's Olivetti headquarters and Foster's German Car Centre (among them)."

Derek Walker, *Unbuilt Milton Keynes*, 1981

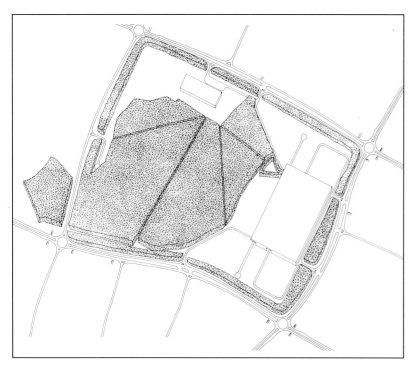

The full 1 square kilometre Linford Wood site. A separate amenity centre (at top) was to be connected to the main building by footpaths running across the site. This structure, to be shared by the three car companies, was designed to expand to a maximum 800-metre length, its compact 'footprint' making it possible to preserve as much of the natural woodland as possible.

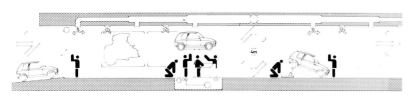

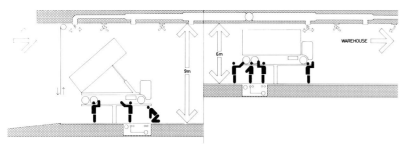

In response to extensive handling and storage studies – that involved research trips to Germany and the USA – Foster Associates proposed a 4-metre high motor workshop area, a 6-metre high commercial vehicle workshop and a 9-metre high area for heavy goods vehicles. All workshops could be serviced from the same constant-height roof zone. Similar exhaustive studies were carried out for warehousing systems.

"New city building", observes Derek Walker, "is remarkably like a post-mortem on a fishing trip: the most significant fish are inevitably the ones that got away." In the first half of the 1970s when Derek Walker was Chief Architect and Planner, and Milton Keynes was enjoying its peak building period, the city lost a number of projects that would have become landmarks, among them a sculpture park, James Stirling's Olivetti headquarters and Foster Associates' German Car Centre.

Foster Associates were commissioned by Thomas Tilling Ltd, the UK franchise holder for three separate German motor manufacturers – Volkswagen, Audi-NSU and Mercedes Benz – who planned to build a central headquarters on a site at Linford Wood. The scheme was to include offices, workshops, training facilities, warehousing, staff amenities, and short-term residential accommodation for trainees.

Thomas Tilling had been introduced to Norman Foster in the summer of 1972 by Derek Walker, who convinced the company not to accept the design/build package-deal it had been offered. When the Milton Keynes development plan was first conceived, Linford Wood was designated as a nature sanctuary within an area zoned for light industrial development. A mature wood, 850 years old and covering 100 acres, it provided a natural habitat for numerous animals and plants. It was seen as a place where local residents could walk in unspoilt surroundings, and also as an environmental backdrop for exemplary industrial buildings.

Working with the PE Consulting Group, who were engaged by Tilling as management consultants and distribution systems experts, Foster Associates evaluated alternative building forms and the resulting site organisation. The conventional approach, which VW had followed in its new American headquarters in Massachusetts, would have resulted in a 'campus' with each of the three companies occupying separate parts of the site, fragmenting accommodation and duplicating many functions.

Foster and other members of the design team also undertook extensive study tours – often travelling in VW's own Islander aircraft – to the three companies' existing operations in Germany and the USA. These showed that strong inter-connections between their prime activities were possible. Indeed, many of Foster Associates' observations were taken up by

A Helmut Jacoby perspective of the Volkswagen section of the proposed German Car Centre. Open-framed around the perimeter of the building, the immense 24 metre square structural bays were used to form large covered parking areas. Perforated steel roof walkways, with impressive downward views, were provided within the depth of the 3-metre deep steel trusses, while the inset full-height glass cladding passed outside an inner column line to which were connected castellated steel beams supporting mezzanine-level open-plan offices.

VW/Audi who were then implementing their own rationalisation plans. Foster Associates' goal was to develop a single architectural form that would optimise these relationships while reinforcing significant design, financial and operational advantages.

The overall site, an entire grid square north of the city centre, was dominated by the wood, leaving two areas for development. It was proposed that the smaller area to the north be given over to amenity and residential functions, connected by footpaths to the major warehouse and administrative building on the large site to the east. Car parking was located between the two.

The concept for the main building followed directly from Foster Associates' early factory systems studies, where a flat-topped, repetitive modular frame allowed a range of infill solutions with services distributed horizontally in the deep roof structure zone.

Investigations in Germany into warehousing systems showed that the optimum clear height in these areas was 8 metres, with a wide 24 x 24-metre bay size giving maximum flexibility for various aisle options, permitting a mix of bin, pallet and rack storage with either motorised picking or fork-lift handling. This, in turn, generated the overall structural umbrella

enclosing a simple rectangular volume within which easy interrelationships between the various activities of the brief were possible.

In typical cross-section, the building divided vertically into two principal components. The full-height warehouse volume ran alongside a two-storey, multi-functional area arranged with the 4-metre high motor workshop and training school area on the ground floor for car access, with a 3-metre high open-plan office floor above. Separating these was a 1-metre deep serviced floor zone. A narrow, densely-planned services, storage and fireproof circulation core was placed between the two major areas.

This cross-section was then uniformly extruded to accommodate all three companies' requirements, and could be extended to cope with future expansion. Mercedes Benz were located at one end of the building with VW and Audi-NSU (who were in the process of harmonising their operations) placed together at the other end, allowing either section to grow independently.

In January 1973 Tilling's Mercedes Benz franchise ran out, and Daimler Benz announced that it would extend the British concession

Early sectional studies put forward a variety of options. Mezzanine floors carry offices and training centres, with vehicle maintenance and lecture rooms below. Rooflights bring daylight to double-height atria and internal streets serving the extensive warehouse areas.

Helmut Jacoby's perspective of a double-height showroom overlooked by open-plan offices on the mezzanines. Essentially a utilitarian structure to enclose large volumes of warehouse space, Foster was keen to explore the dramatic possibilities in the few public areas of the building.

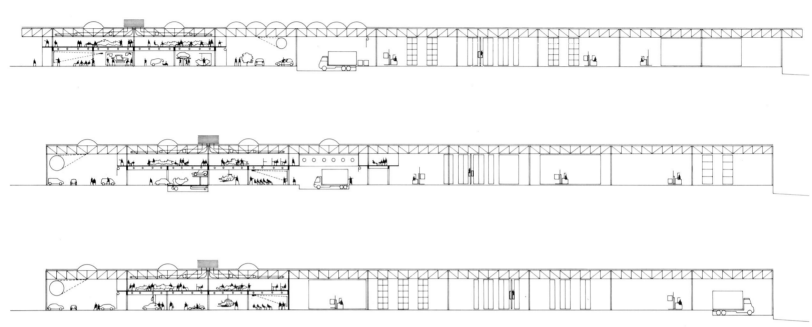

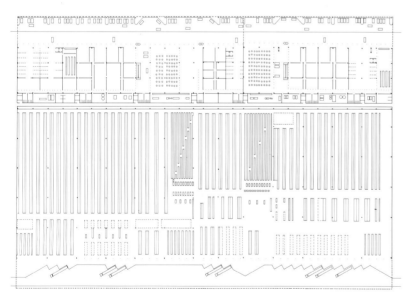

The ground floor plan of the Car Centre was developed into a highly rational diagram. A strip of training rooms and motor workshops (under an administration mezzanine) was separated from the larger warehouse racking area and loading docks by a fire separation service core housing plant rooms, escape routes and lavatories. The same planning strategy was used at the distribution centre for Renault nearly a decade later.

for only one year before establishing its own dealership network. This immediately put the brakes on the Milton Keynes project, and Tilling was forced to reappraise the situation. By March, Tilling had finally merged its VW and Audi-NSU holdings, in line with moves already completed in Germany, to form VW (GB) Ltd, making it Britain's largest motor importer, with annual sales of more than 80 000 cars.

Sharing common facilities at all levels, from design to manufacture, became a key part of VW-Audi's forward strategy for the 1980s. The two marques would offer complementary model ranges using interchangeable parts. Only marketing would remain separate.

Establishing a combined VW-Audi base in the UK was still a high priority and, in October, Tilling announced that Foster Associates would work with Demag, VW's German warehousing systems' supplier, on a new facility using the northern corner of the original Linford Wood site. This would accommodate a centralised administration and an intake of 5000 trainees a year, from workshop mechanics to dealership proprietors. But it was dominated by a heavily automated 19 500 square-metre warehouse which required a substantial 20-metre high-bay area to allow for an overhead crane retrieval system. Smaller, semi-automated sys-

A Helmut Jacoby perspective of the VW-Audi project that succeeded the German Car Centre in 1973. Using only part of the Linford Wood site, the scheme was smaller but featured a 20-metre high warehouse section.

tems for small parts handling could still utilise the original 8-metre clear height, but the structural grid was reduced to 17 x 17 metres in line with Demag's optimum requirements for the high-bay area.

A variety of structural and cladding solutions was considered before the adoption of a low-cost panel system with a curved eaves detail similar to that used on the Sainsbury Centre. The cladding was stretched tight over roof and walls — unlike the first project where the roof structure was clearly expressed — the roof generously projecting out along one elevation to give shelter and create a public space for arrival.

The final scheme also made other fundamental concessions to cost and the limitations of its more restricted site. To reduce ground works, part of the services core was dug into the sloping ground, allowing the building to step from a 4-metre high single storey, accommodating offices and the training school at one end, to an 8-metre high warehouse at the other, keeping a constant eaves line above which only the high-bay area projected.

It was an elegant and economical solution, although far more modest in scope and content than the three-company centre. But it was not economical enough. In September 1974, Tilling faced a dramatic slump in its half-year profits, falling car sales and a reduced market share — down from 4.1 per cent the year before to 2.9 per cent. Like other German car importers, it had been hit badly by the falling value of sterling against the Deutschmark. This, combined with the effects of galloping inflation, forced Tilling to shelve its building programme and cut back stocks, facilities and staff, and eventually to sell VW (GB) Ltd to Lonrho.

Once the market recovered, Lonrho went ahead with the Milton Keynes Centre, but on another less sensitive site. Ironically, it was designed and built by the same package-deal company whose offer Thomas Tilling had turned down three years earlier. For Foster, however, the experience was not wasted, as ideas established here would be realised only a few years later at IBM Greenford and the Renault Distribution Centre.

David Jenkins

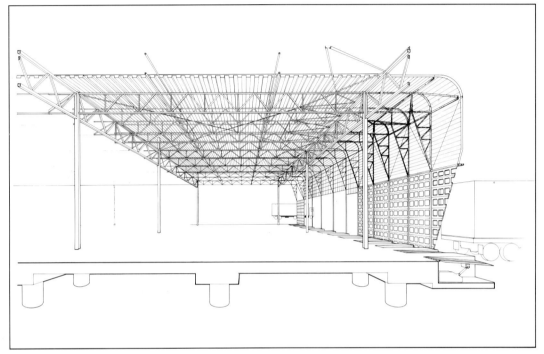

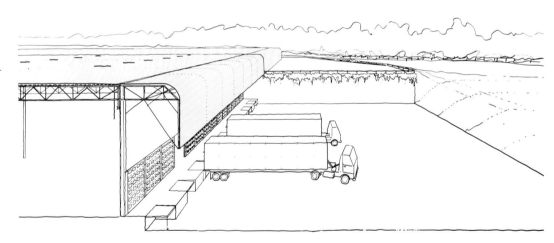

The structural system of the VW-Audi building was a much simpler affair. The structural bay was reduced to 17 metres square, allowing straightforward warren trusses rather than the earlier space-frame. Profiled metal cladding wrapped over the building created, on one side, a covered loading bay.

To reduce its impact on the surrounding area, the entire building took advantage of a natural fall across the site and was dug in as much as possible. The project was still at the early sketch design stage when cancelled.

219

Norman Foster
Foster Associates

I always thought this first book, showing our earliest projects, would be the most interesting of all the proposed volumes on our work, and seeing the pages as they were mocked up more than confirmed this impression. Much of what we now take for granted as architects is made explicable by the strivings of these early years.

In 1963 I returned to England, after studying and working in the United States, to join Richard Rogers and two architect sisters, Georgie and Wendy Cheesman. We formed a practice based in Wendy's London flat, called Team 4 Architects, which lasted for some four years, before, as Richard explains elsewhere in this book, there was a parting of the ways. Almost from our first meeting Wendy and I had become inseparable, so there was a certain inevitability in our forming a new practice together: after much agonising we chose to call it Foster Associates. The name, with its overtones of a larger plurality, was a gesture of confidence in an uncertain future. Not only were there no associates, there were no commissions to build either.

The first Team 4 projects were mostly for friends and relations. It is only now, looking back, that one can marvel at the courage of those clients, subjecting themselves to a level of social idealism which was matched only by our lack of real experience. Perhaps the most important asset for a designer, though, is the ability to recognise and accept the limits of personal knowledge, because this leads to the process of posing the right questions to the right people. In those early days this was a relatively slow and linear process, rooted in traditional trades and attitudes. However, the factory for Reliance Controls, the last Team 4 project, extended this challenge by introducing the commercial reality of time — in addition to financial and engineering constraints — as a fixed and limited resource. It set the stage for a way of working that has since become second nature.

Although all the work of Team 4 received wide publicity, and even national awards, we were still part of a vicious circle. Without the right kind of work to show, we lacked credibility; but how could we demonstrate credibility without first being given the opportunities? By the middle of 1968, after nearly a year occupied with small-scale conversion work and part-time teaching, Wendy and I — now with two very small sons — were talking about emigrating to a more receptive and open society. In the event, an established contact with the Fred Olsen company in London's dockland came to the rescue. After long months of 'stop-go' — in competition not against other architects, but with contractors offering a package deal of design and build — Fred Olsen decided to commission us to design his new buildings, a decision which became a major turning point for us and helped establish Foster Associates.

The buildings which arose from this commission were born out of painstaking research into the operational processes of the company and the hardware of its ships, but they were also realised on extremely short time scales. These structures were later to be visited by potential clients such as IBM, Sir Robert Sainsbury and Willis Faber & Dumas, proving instrumental in securing new opportunities for the future.

Typical of these visits was the occasion when the senior management of Willis Faber came to see the buildings. The outgoing chairman, Johnny Roscoe, was accompanied by Julian Faber, who was soon to take over. I introduced them to Mike Thompson, the then dock manager, who was later to become a director of the Olsen company. We sat down in the open office space, contemplating the ships beyond and the paintings from Fred Olsen's personal collection which adorned the walls. Johnny Roscoe, an outspoken individual, came to the point quickly. "Well, is he any good?" he said, pointing at me. Mike Thompson squirmed with embarrassment and I got up to try and leave them to a private conversation. The chairman, persistent and visibly impatient, waved all this aside. Mike Thompson then entered into the spirit of the interrogation and conceded that, perhaps, I rated an 'A minus'. "That's fine", was the reply, "anything better and I wouldn't have believed it, anything less and it wouldn't be good enough." Fred Olsen put it a different way; when quizzed about the nature of Foster Associates he said merely: "They ask the right questions".

Trying to talk about these early days reminds me that Wendy was supposed to have written this piece. Much to my surprise Ian Lambot had persuaded her at a time when it seemed very far off, yet looking back it was barely two summers ago. I teased her about what she might write. "I'll say that you are a juggler", she replied. "You throw the balls higher than anybody else, and you let them fall lower before catching them."

This analogy of the juggler is useful to explain the component of time in the design process, and is perhaps best illustrated by an anecdote, also about Wendy, that I recalled in the second volume of this series. It was at a regular weekly team meeting of architects, engineers and cost consultants involved with the design of the Sainsbury Centre. The meeting was to monitor what had come to be accepted as the final design. However, between that day and the previous team meeting there had been a design breakthrough of great magnitude. It was as if the original concept had suddenly flowered. To anybody who had felt the pulse of the project it was the culmination of all the work that had gone before. The other side of the coin was a transformation of such magnitude that it required the complete reworking of the many specialist drawings and schedules. To hold to the original date for starting on site would require a supreme effort by everyone. The meeting was emotional. One of the engineers, while conceding that the new scheme was far better, suggested that it should be reserved for some future project. Wendy polarised the discussion by saying that such an opportunity might never occur — each scheme had to be the best thing we could achieve in the time, so "let's do it now". It pushed everybody to the brink but unlocked a creative energy that improved the design even further. Looking back it was obviously the right course of action and no party to the project, particularly the client, would ever disagree. In the logistics of striving for the ultimate achievable quality within the fixes of time and cost, it was a supreme juggling act.

The story does not tell of the camaraderie between the members of a team which made possible such heroic efforts. The present teams associated with the office, like those of the past, extend from a design-based core to embrace clients, users and a network of consultants and manufacturers. In the larger, more complex projects, which have evolved progressively from the earlier works in this volume, it is sometimes necessary to first design operational structures to bring the right people into the process at the right point in time. Without a clear definition of needs, there is no basis on which to design. But often an honest 'don't know' is a far more precise acknowledgement of the reality of a situation than some spurious attempt to quantify an unknown future. Unlike the design of artefacts, buildings are conceived in the present for a volatile future but, culturally, they cannot be separated from the context of the past.

Despite the differences between architecture and artefacts it can be helpful to draw comparisons to illustrate a point. Consider the helicopter for example. To fly a helicopter you have four controls. In front of the pilot is a stick called the cyclic, you push it forward to go forward, back to go backwards, to the side to go sideways and so on. Next to the seat is a lever called the collective; you lift it up to ascend and push it down to descend. Depending on the movements of the helicopter it will require continuous adjustments of power, which in the most basic models are achieved by a twist grip throttle on the end of the collective stick: you wind it up for more power and release it for less. All these control inputs act on the main rotor which is overhead. Finally, the pilot's feet can move pedals connected to the tail rotor which enables the helicopter to swivel on its own axis.

The helicopter, unlike a fixed wing aircraft, can describe almost any three-dimensional sequence of movement in space. To do so involves the movement of all the controls simultaneously; the adjustment of one input has consequences on all the others. You can pick apart the theory of this on paper or on a blackboard, but until the physical co-ordination of all these variables together, at the same time, becomes second nature, you simply cannot fly the machine. The relationship between the four controls is totally interactive.

To return to the design team and the issue of posing the right questions. If the development and realisation of a design are seen as a dynamic process in time, then all the variables — for example massing, materials, inside, outside, structure, heating, lighting, cooling, cost, time — are, like the control inputs to that helicopter, entirely interactive. You cannot change one without affecting some or all of the others. To be able to pose the vital questions and assess the consequences requires a team of specialists, who can come together and who are, each in their own way, able to share a

vision. There is the potential for much misunderstanding in all this. Such an approach is far removed from the grey world of design by committee. Although each individual may become committed to a common point of view, it is the personal chemistry and mutual respect that enables anyone to challenge anything and everything — nothing is too sacred. It is the opposite of much that has been academically taught. The architect is not handing down from above, passing the parcel to the specialists who wait in line to be told what to do. Each individual has the potential for a creative input. Paradoxically, the architect comes closer to the heart of the project because he is integrated into the 'how and why' of the making of the building. So the process extends out from the architect's office, to the workplace where real people are making real things. And this must be right, because that surely is the essence of our culture — the making of things.

I told only one part of the story of flying a helicopter; it is of course a much more complex interplay of all the senses. Aviation like architecture is also subject to legislation and prejudice. The flight can be linked by hidden lines of command with ground controllers who have the right of legal authority, although the ultimate responsibility is still said to rest with the pilot. When disasters occur, whether in airborne or ground-based structures, they both offer a field-day for the media as various parties are individually pilloried, with scant regard for the total system which created them and of which they are an integral part. A flight, like a building, is only the visible tip of a vast iceberg of infrastructure.

When I fly an aircraft I can, in the same way that I analyse architecture, rationalise the event. Such factors as weight, load capacity, speed, range, fuel consumption and cruising altitude can be quantified into flight times and cost factors. I can even explain an aerobatic flight with blackboard theory, but the striving to produce a graceful three-dimensional sequence of manoeuvres in space requires not only a grand design but continuous in-flight decisions to refine the performance. The poetic ingredient of flight can lie close to the surface, even if it never emerges in conversation. In the same spirit, every decision in the design of a building is touched not only by reason but also by those intangible and poetic influences.

Although unspoken, and often taken for granted, it is this fusion which may explain my own passion for architecture. Like any love affair it is difficult to separate the heart from the mind.

Wendy's response at that design team meeting of "let's do it now", with the emphasis on the 'now', also explains much about the nature of Foster Associates. John Walker, writing elsewhere in this volume, recalls my spontaneous dash to the United States when British industry could not produce the goods to maintain the tight time schedule on the Olsen project. It never occurred to us to wait for time-consuming authorisations. Taking the initiative to solve the problem rather than proffering apologies was very much in the spirit of 'doing it now'. That approach possibly explains the relatively youthful cross-section of the office as well as the early integration of other skills, especially model-making. It is also about the endless quest to improve a working life style.

I am reminded of a group who recently visited our new studios which overlook the Thames. "Where do you work?" I was asked. I explained that I had the same amount of space as anybody else at one of the vast workbenches. "But why don't you have your own grand office?" I was asked, almost in disbelief. I tried to explain that it was exactly what I did have, but I shared it with everyone else — I could never have had a space as grand as that just for myself. What I did not say was that the space was symbolic of the team. This has nothing to do with any theoretical attitudes: it is simply a good place to be, to work alongside inspiring people. This grand dimension has taken many years to realise but, like all previous spaces that we have occupied, it was envisaged well ahead by Wendy. It is sad that she did not live to see it realised. I am sure she approves.

Site development explained diagrammatically on an early model. The first stage shows the UK Distribution Centre (UKDC) on its own.

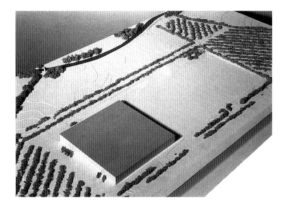

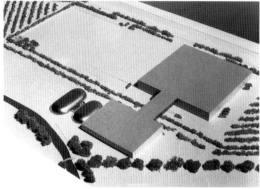

Seen from the north, the UKDC is now joined to the future Installation Support Centre (ISC) by a link bridge over a central access road.

As at Computer Technology, inflatable structures were proposed as a solution to temporary accommodation problems.

The line of sketches to the right is Norman Foster's own site analysis presented to IBM in 1975. The availability of nearly 40 acres in Greater London, less than five miles from Heathrow, clinched the IBM land purchase, but all existing buildings (shown in second sketch) were to go, the new plan being derived from the topography. For reasons of access and outlook Foster favoured the north-west corner of the site, overlooking the canal, for the 'people dominated' accommodation, and the lower south-western area for the 'machine dominated' distribution centre. Future expansion would be to the east on either side of a spine road.

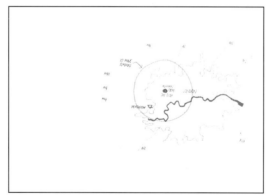

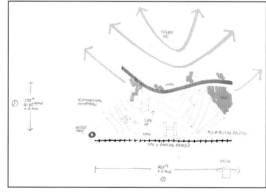

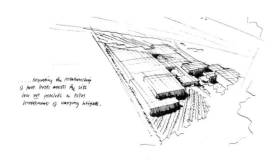

Worried that a strictly linear arrangement may seem too rigid, Norman Foster explored the possibility of a more random growth pattern, filling in the corners and accepting varying roof heights.

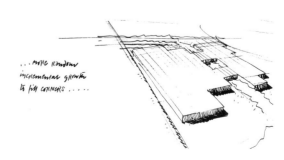

1975-1980 **IBM Technical Park**
Greenford
Middlesex

Future site expansion was to be a strictly linear process following the established east-west axis.

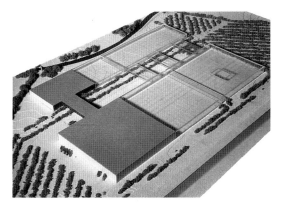

In the west London Technical Park for IBM, we see a satisfying conclusion to the sequence of architectural ideas, techniques and preoccupations that inform buildings such as IBM Cosham, Computer Technology and other descendants of the pioneering Newport School competition. This is in no way to suggest that all these buildings were taken as opportunities to apply the practice's theories, rather it is to identify Norman Foster's developing awareness of the architectural possibilities presented by a section of British industry which was prepared to look outside traditional architectural attitudes, and which had declared itself ready to commission buildings that reflected this spirit.

The 40-acre site, 15 miles from central London and four miles from Heathrow airport, had been occupied by a previous tenant — Rockware Glass — using buildings very much in the haphazard and anti-social tradition so depressingly typical of British industrial estates. Management boxes and worker sheds, with their concomitant social implications, had been dotted around a site disfigured by outdoor storage dumps and a complete absence of visual care. Stranded in an unlovely landscape, the Greenford site had hitherto enshrined the

kind of industrial attitudes which Norman Foster abhorred and which, in various (and sometimes surreptitious) ways, he had tried to combat in earlier industrial buildings.

In 1975 Foster Associates were asked to prepare a feasibility study for the site which IBM had acquired in order to build a distribution centre for its range of business machines. IBM's own ambitions for the site were to create a technical park — not in the now familiar sense of the phrase, but rather in the sense of siting a good industrial building in park-like surroundings. Clearly, this was an idea very much in tune with Foster Associates' commitment to create high-quality working environments, both inside and out.

Early discussions between architect and client were focused on the provision of a single enclosure incorporating double-height and mezzanine spaces within the same building. This would have formed phase one of the site development and would have allowed for subsequent smaller buildings to be placed to the north of it. Intended to contain a warehouse, repair shop and small parts storage, this original building was approved, and design work was duly begun.

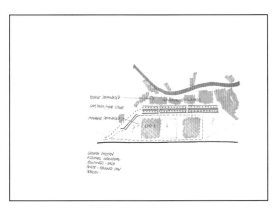

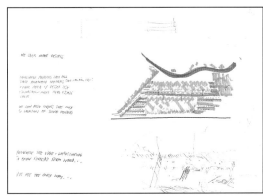

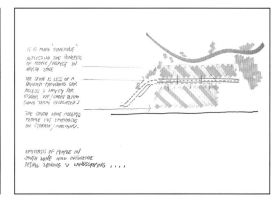

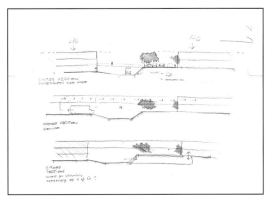

In sketches remarkable for their similarity to the final scheme, Norman Foster explores different ways of accommodating and linking the various functions to be included in the building under a constant-height roof.

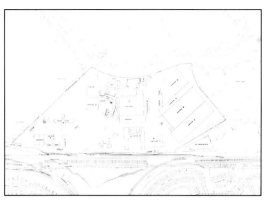

The existing site plan showing the full 37 acres formerly occupied by the Rockware Glass factory, complete with its own railway spur. The northern boundary is the canal, and the southern the road and railway. Demolition made possible a new south-west access road.

The first scheme (right), proposed before the ISC was added to the brief, includes only 'education' offices to the north of the distribution centre, though the site arrangement is otherwise similar to the final scheme.

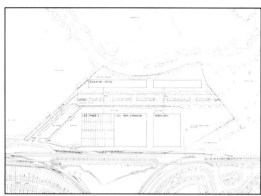

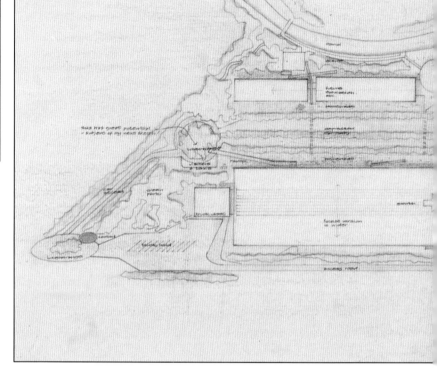

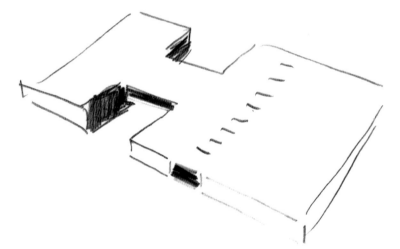

One early sketch by Norman Foster explores the possibility of introducing daylighting into the deep-plan UKDC by means of a glass-clad wall section and roof-lights running west to east. Foster's sketchbooks from this time contain numerous sketches of the project — now with the ISC in place — exploring the building from every angle.

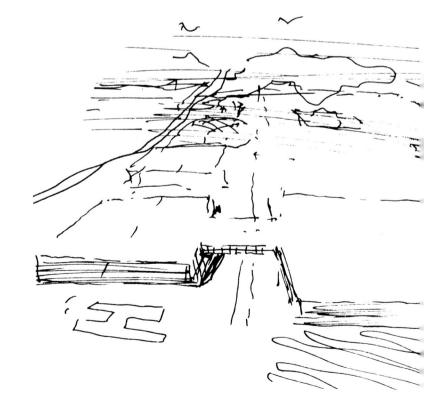

Dated February 1975, Norman Foster's early presentation sketch shows the first scheme. As he points out, it is only a diagram, but all the main elements are now in place. Only the broad central mall, including the car park, would be lost in the final scheme.

An early site model, again exploring the possibility of random growth, and including 'finger' units extending north to follow more closely the curve of the canal. The relative crudeness of the model indicates that it is more a means of proving the concept wrong than a serious alternative.

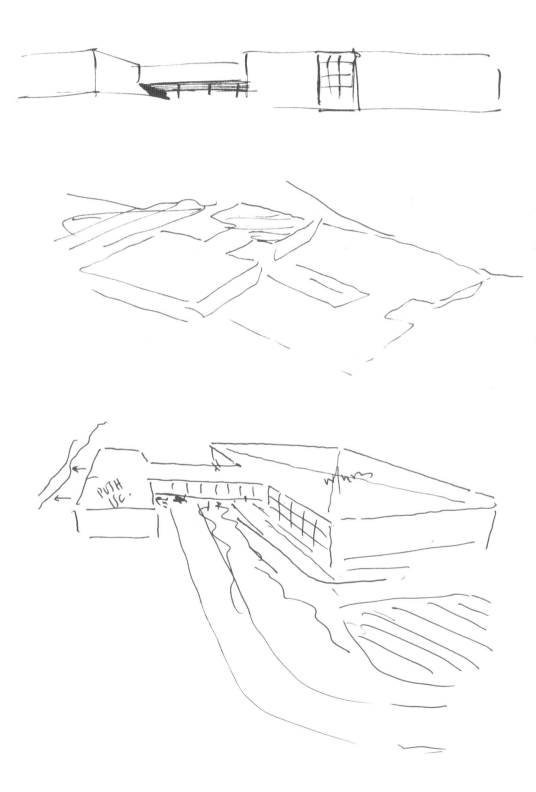

"IBM came to the office and said: 'Forget the London Distribution Centre, we need to get the Installation Support Centre going. If it can be built in nine months we can build it here in London. If we can't it will have to go to the Continent. We don't think we can get it built for two years. What do you think?' We said we could build it in the nine months, knowing we could put the same components together in a different way."

Loren Butt to Graham Vickers, October 1989

Not the mall between the two buildings, but an early proposal by Norman Foster to introduce open courtyards into the top floor of the UKDC, so that office workers might enjoy a landscaped outlook even though in a deep-plan building. The idea was not taken up — indeed, in the final design, even rooflights were a late addition — but considering future developments (see page 232) it was a remarkably perceptive observation.

A section and elevation of the UKDC in its earliest form, before the addition of the office link bridge over the road to the ISC. In its place an open footbridge provides access to and from the car parks. In other respects the arrangement of space is well advanced: double-height warehousing — with 27-metre spans — is separated from workshop areas and three levels of offices by a central fire-resistant service spine.

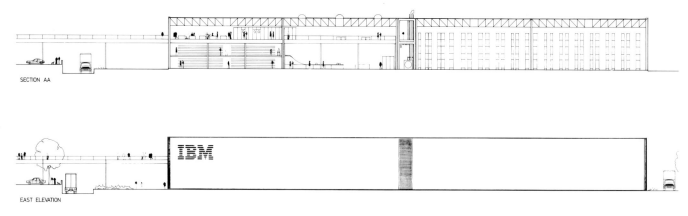

SECTION AA

EAST ELEVATION

An east-west cross-section of the UKDC through the workshop and packing areas, which are overlooked by high-level mezzanines.

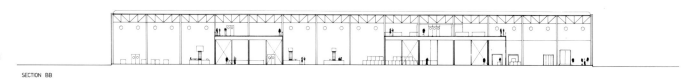

SECTION BB

Once accepted into the brief, great care was taken to integrate the new ISC into the original scheme, a physical link being proposed by means of a high-level office bridge. The distance between the two service spines and the mall was determined by fire regulations.

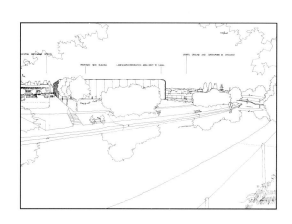

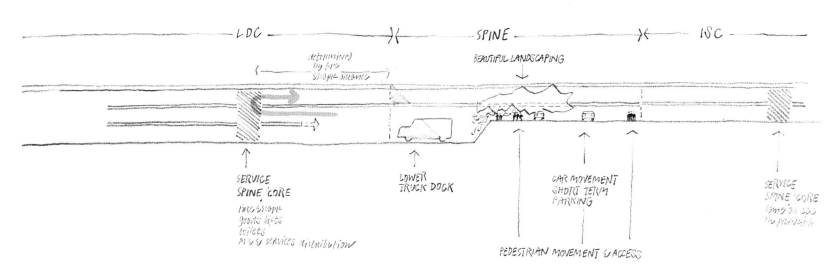

The feasibility study involved Foster Associates in 18 months of design work before a new element was abruptly added to the brief, superseding the original building in urgency. Incremental acquisition of the site and changing business patterns had resulted in new instructions from IBM in the United States. This, in turn, meant that there was a sudden opportunity for IBM to build an additional building on another part of the same site.

The Installation Support Centre (ISC), as it was to be known, would house the company's very large computers for demonstration purposes. Crucially, the chance to build the ISC at Greenford only existed if it could be realised within a year — otherwise it would be built elsewhere in Europe. Initially few people thought this was feasible, least of all the client, and indeed in a sense it was *not* possible to build such a structure from scratch in such a short time.

Foster Associates' design work on the original United Kingdom Distribution Centre (UKDC) building, however, had been once again characterised by great flexibility of planning, occupancy and provision for future changes of use. This meant, invaluably, that the design work already undertaken on the distribution centre could be usefully applied to the task of

From the same page of Norman Foster's sketchbook as the section above. As ever, the implication of a design decision is explored quickly in three dimensions, further possibilities becoming apparent in the process.

"The new building was placed to the north of the warehouse and joined to it by a bridge across the now central service road. The resulting 'elementarist' composition is, coincidentally, the same as that of the Dessau Bauhaus."

Christopher Woodward, *The Architectural Review*, August 1980

A sectional perspective of the 27-metre wide workshop bay of the UKDC from the first scheme. The same space is incorporated in the final scheme with additional full-height glazing inserted into the long side elevations.

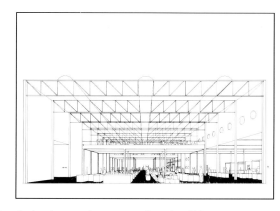

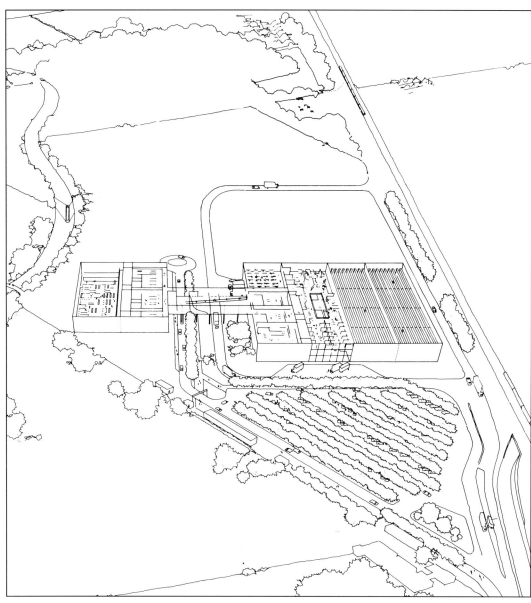

Birkin Haward's cutaway perspective of the final Greenford scheme illustrates the interrelationships of all elements. Separate truck and car circulation has now been made possible by moving the car parking to the western side of the UKDC. The warehouse building itself consists of four 27-metre bays side by side, one of which — housing the workshop areas — is glass sided and supplied with rooflights. The ISC is linked to the UKDC by a high-level bridge building, with a footbridge below providing ground access only.

designing and constructing the ISC, even though it was to be a building of quite different function.

This crucial fact was what enabled the realisation of the ISC to a remarkable timetable: Foster Associates were formally instructed by IBM to proceed with the ISC building in February of 1977. During the following month of March, management contractors were organised on site and they commenced preliminary works. Planning permission was granted at the end of that month. The contract period was 32 weeks and the building was handed over at the end of October in the same year. The time span for the ISC part of the complex, from inception to occupation, was less than nine months.

Early sketches and plans prefigure this flexible and dynamic process. Norman Foster was anxious to explore a number of possibilities for the original building which, he believed, could be treated in a variety of ways. It did not need to be rectilinear, it did not need to adhere to the single roof-line which was, in fact, to become a reality. This preoccupation with fluidity of concept seems to have been prompted by certain worries that the practice's philosophical approach was being seen in some quarters as having only one form of expression. "I wanted to show that the master plan was about zoning and movement", Foster explains. "Because our earlier buildings had certain edge lines, certain roof-lines, I thought it might have been felt that this was a dictate in our work, but I wanted to show that things could be much freer."

In fact, that freedom was eventually to be realised not in the asymmetrical perimeter shown in some of Foster's early sketches, nor was it to be expressed in differing roof levels or the introduction of atria: it was to be shown in the skilful accommodation and promotion of mixed uses within the building. The final scheme was a building with a single roof-line and integrated services, a building designed to be expandable in its east-west zones, one which responded well to its surroundings, drawing in service vehicles and visitors rather than segregating them, and one which encouraged and endorsed new patterns of social and industrial change.

"The location, 15 miles from London's West End and only four miles from Heathrow airport, was typical of the blighted and outmoded industry of the United Kingdom. In contrast to this the brief from IBM has been translated into a technical park which seeks to give form to new patterns of social and technological change reflected in high environmental standards, generous landscaping and the recognition of democratic influences at work."

A&U, February 1981

The second floor of the IBM Greenford building is dominated by the central office area that links the two buildings. This takes the form of a single room of open-planned workspaces, loosely articulated by islands of glass-partitioned meeting rooms. In the ISC, a corridor through the central service core leads to a dramatic viewing gallery overlooking the computer hall. In the distribution centre, similar corridors lead through to a generous open-plan workshop area positioned on the top floor so as to benefit from existing rooflights.

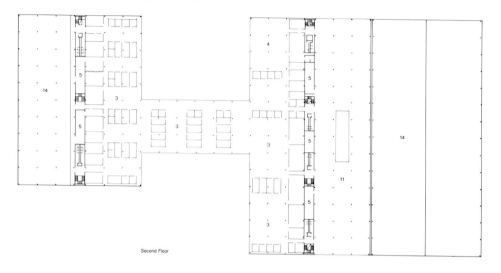

Second Floor

The first or mezzanine floor of the UKDC. Access from ground level is by a footbridge (15) across the mall from the vehicle drop-off point. A secondary access for staff, this level of the building — no corresponding floor exists in the ISC — incorporates only a small parts store (7) and reception area.

1 reception
2 visitors' parking
3 offices
4 restaurant
5 plant rooms
6 secondary plant
7 small parts store
8 dispatch
9 warehouse 1
10 warehouse 2
11 workshop
12 computer hall
13 loading dock
14 void
15 footbridge

First Floor

The ground floor. The floor plans of both the ISC and the UKDC are arranged around a constant 9 × 8.1 metre grid, the only exception being the two warehouse bays of the UKDC which are 9 x 27 metres. In both buildings a fire-resistant service core separates the more heavily-populated office and administration zones from workshop/ storage areas or the computer hall. Requiring an eight-hour fire separation, the warehouse areas are isolated from the rest of the building by adjacent walls and a double row of columns supporting separate structures.

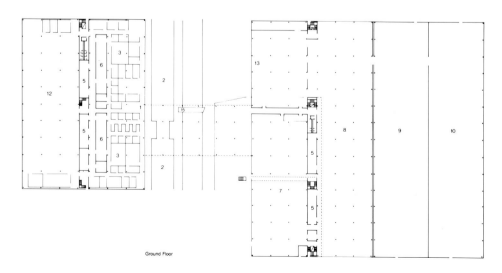

Ground Floor

The Greenford site, irregularly shaped and incrementally acquired, also sloped upwards towards a canal. This meant that in order to maintain an unbroken roof-line (a feature which soon came to be accepted as a visually satisfying solution), internal spaces would necessarily vary in height. The treatment of that variation was to become one of the strong points of the design. Further limitations were imposed by the need to accommodate potential expansion in the east/west direction; if the building were to have the capacity to extend in strips, Lego-like (so, perhaps, eventually to gain an irregular perimeter determined by specific needs), then it would need to have the space in which to do so.

With the ISC and the UKDC now forming the brief, a plan was evolved to connect the two buildings by means of an upper-storey link spanning a central mall. The eventual form they were to take was recorded by the practice in its final report to IBM in these terms:

"The ISC is realised as a large-span steel structure clad with ribbed-aluminium sheeting combined with fully glazed facades. The frameless, glazed entrance and exit doors are suspended from the structure without support from the external walls. Inside, the highly serviced computer room, in the form of a machine hall, is a double-height space fully glazed to the north and designed so that an intermediate floor can be added if required.

"Both the machine hall and the office spaces use a 900 mm modular partitioning system. That system is pressed into unusual service in the machine halls when used in the horizontal plane to provide a roof for single-storey cabins within the double-height space.

"The UKDC is both larger and more complex in construction than the linked ISC building. The cross-section varies structurally, reflecting the variety of activities being carried out under one roof. The 12-metre high 'very narrow aisle' warehouse spaces are steel-framed with lattice beams on an 8.1 x 27-metre grid. The office area, small parts storage and workshops are a two-storey reinforced-concrete frame topped by a single-storey steel roof structure running contiguously with the ISC building.

"Although the external skin is continuous, two primary structures within the UKDC are separated by adjacent walls to afford eight-

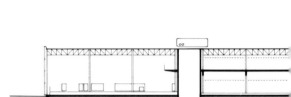

The machine hall — a showroom for IBM's main-frame computers — is double-height, with a raised floor and fully glazed north facade. Air-conditioning is supplied at high level from roof-mounted plant over the adjacent service core.

As well as offices and general administration areas the ISC houses staff facilities that include a bank, newsagent and travel agency. The visitor drop-off point and entrance is at ground floor level.

Including all the building's functions on one 'typical' drawing can be misleading. The outdoor loading docks are, in fact, offset in plan from the overhead office link bridge, and not beneath it as implied here.

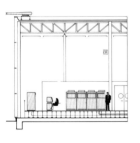
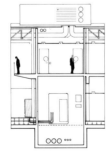
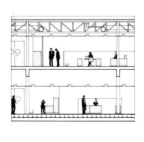

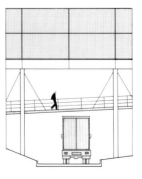
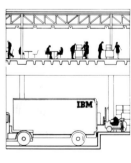

"In a capitalist economy the conventions of industrial design consider aesthetic surface as no less important than functional and economic efficiency. By treating architecture as industrial design Norman Foster legitimises his search for aesthetic excellence along with technical competence. Architecture is reduced to a client-directed package, but the package includes architecture."

Robert Maxwell, *A&U*, September 1975

The west elevation and corresponding section of Greenford show the integrity achieved by maintaining the same roofline and virtually unbroken cladding in two such widely separated buildings. The final design forces the circulation mall between the buildings to resolve all problems of height difference, neatly handled by the separation of car and lorry routes at different levels. The complex of bridges and steps then securely ties the two parts of this large structure together.

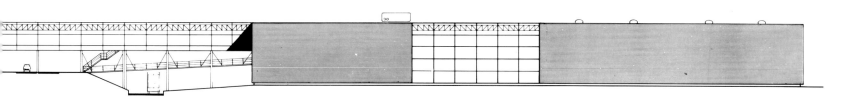

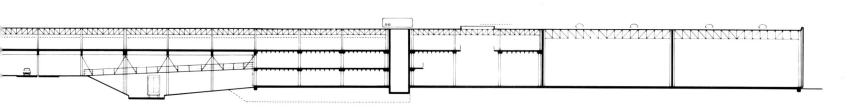

The three levels of the UKDC — offices above and small parts stores below — are linked by a glass-enclosed hydraulic lift around which spirals the main access stair. Incorporated into the main service spine, rooftop plant is mounted above. The bay to the south of the spine houses a double-height packaging and dispatch area with roof-lit workshops above.

A double-skin eight-hour fire wall separates the automated 'very-narrow-aisle' warehouse areas from the rest of the building, access ways being protected by automatic fire shutters.

The walls of the long east and west elevations, as well as the warehouse's south elevation, are typically clad in horizontally ribbed aluminium panels.

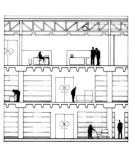 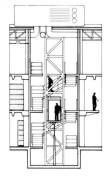 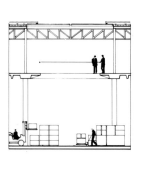 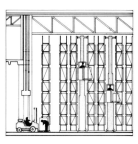 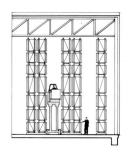 

231

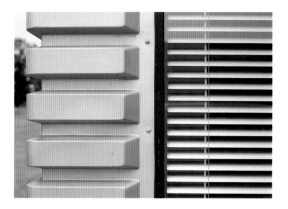

The special corner pieces
were moulded in glass-
fibre — metal tooling be-
ing too expensive — and
are fixed in place with
hexagonal skirting bolts.
At the glazed facade the
connection is made
directly to the curtain-
wall framing, a simple
neoprene strip sealing
the gap between panel
and glass.

hour fire separation. A number of other technically demanding stipulations were laid down
by the client's insurers. Within the 'very narrow
aisle' areas extremely high tolerances in the
level of the floor surface — 1.2 mm in 1.5
metres — were demanded and achieved.

"The servicing of the complex is integrated with the structural systems throughout.
Necessarily, it too varies in response to the
activity zones. At the northern end, the highly-
serviced zone of the machine hall changes to
the simpler comfort-cooled office area which
employs a basic system of fresh air exhaust and
replacement. Unit heaters provide an appropriate degree of environmental control to the
large warehouse spaces.

"Throughout the complex, servicing is
both centralised within the 'core' areas as well
as decentralised with externally-mounted
locally positioned plant on the roof. The track-
supported roof plant permits flexibility of
movement in tandem with changes in building
use and fabric."

Useful as such summaries may be in
grasping the overall nature of the building,
they belie a design process which needed to be
highly responsive to change right from the
start. Foster Associates' wish to introduce
natural light to the middle of the building was
initially frustrated by the client, only to be
reinstated when some of the employees expressed concern about the lack of external
awareness. A rooflight and end glazing were
eventually introduced to the relevant zone to
ameliorate this condition.

Financial restraint precluded the practice's
favoured solution for cladding the building: a
panel system. In this case the solution was to
use what must be considered an unexceptional
profile cladding. However, in an exceptionally
well-judged piece of detailing, special corner
pieces were devised to create the impression
that the profile ran unbroken around the corners. This simple idea — which had to be expressed in two different forms, one corner
piece to join profile to profile, another to butt
profile to glazing — greatly enhances the
building's appearance.

Engineer Loren Butt recalls that the double-height space in the machine hall proved to
be a sensitive issue with IBM, who at one stage

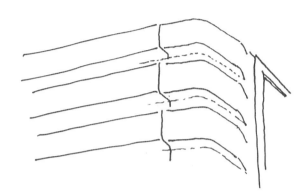

A more-or-less standard
panelling system, Foster
Associates brought a
new level of refinement
to the metal cladding by
careful control in the
positioning of vertical
joints and fixing bolts.
That the glass-fibre
corner panels are not a
perfect colour match
was not considered a
problem; in fact, being
slightly darker, they help
define the end of the
elevation.

Norman Foster's sket-
ches explore ways of
bringing together the
heavily corrugated
panels and the smooth
areas of glazing, and
propose a special corru-
gated panel element to
wrap round the corner.

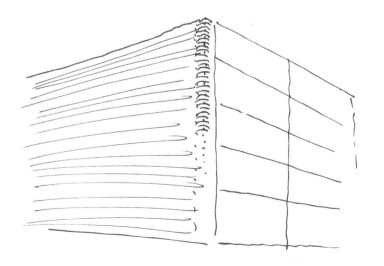

The roof zone of the workshop area in the distribution centre. The perforations of the curtain-wall mullions are repeated in the rooflight supports to create a delicate lace-work of green-painted steel framing.

A detail of the glazed curtain-wall, applied here to the three-storey UKDC. A development of the Pitco 'T'-wall system used at the Olsen amenity centre, the aluminium framing has been stretched to its limit at Greenford to accept panes of glass 2.4 x 4.05 metres in dimension.

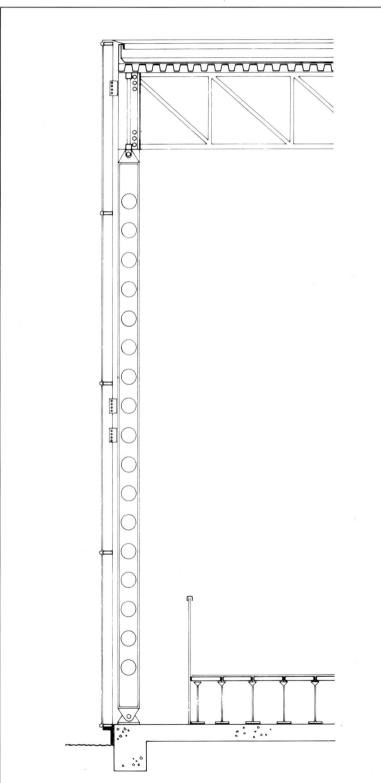

Left: a section through the glazed north facade of the computer hall. The principle of exposing the mechanics of the building's structure and servicing, introduced with the use of full-height glazing at IBM Cosham, is taken one stage further at Greenford where the edge of the non-standard computer floor – capable of very high loadings – is also exposed, set back from the facade and sealed with a glass hand-rail. Housing secondary air-conditioning ducts and computer wiring, the raised floor void also acts as a return air plenum.

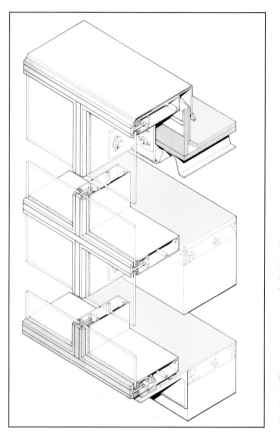

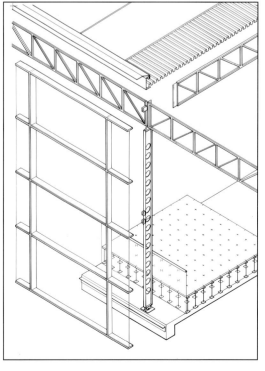

An axonometric of the major elements of the machine hall. A metal-deck flat roof is supported on 1-metre deep warren trusses, bolted to universal steel stanchions to form a two-way portal structure. Structurally independent, the glazed curtain-wall framing is wholly supported at ground level; connections to the stanchions and intermediate pierced-web mullions, at mid-height and roof level, providing lateral wind-bracing only.

Two views of the corridor that runs along the east side of the bridge link. Through the glass (below left) can be seen the stair from the mall below, while in action (below right) is IBM's branch of the National Westminster Bank.

Roof zone air-movement ducting and other services over the machine hall in the ISC. The ducting and insulated services are finished in natural aluminium as is the underside of the roof-decking. The structure and other services are painted green.

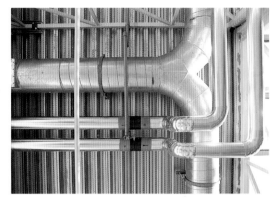

Offices on the second floor of the UKDC looking out over the mall with the bridge building and ISC beyond. Colours are generally muted, dominated by the matching beige of the carpet, desks and cabinets. Highlights of blue are restricted to chairs, doors and the handrail.

Looking north-west from the restaurant on the second floor of the distribution centre towards the bridge building and the ISC.

felt it was an unnecessary waste of space. "One reason that the provision for another floor level was made", he says, "was to forestall any suggestion from the client that the roof-line might be broken at this point to reduce the height of the machine room."

Both Norman Foster and the architect in charge of IBM Greenford, Graham Phillips, stress the unpredictability of the project. Foster points out that, "the clarity of the diagram was always difficult to achieve. IBM bought the site in increments and they were forced to act expediently, so it was never the ideal linear sequence where you would have a known site, do a master plan and then implement it". This created severe practical problems as Phillips explains: "We had to order all the steelwork and put in the foundations before we even knew what was going in the building."

Even the low cost of the final building — although naturally a source of satisfaction to begin with — had its negative side too. The final result was so successful and so prestigious in appearance that the parent IBM company, distanced from the realities of the situation, used it as an example to express dissatisfaction with other IBM buildings which had taken longer to achieve, looked inferior and, more often than not, had cost more.

Despite all these restraints, there was little evidence of compromise in the finished building. If a raised floor was revealed for what it was by side glazing which extended below it, then no attempt was made to disguise the exposed supports — instead they were painted bright yellow. Only one early proposal, incorporating a broad central mall in which cars could be parked, was eventually abandoned when increased building size squeezed the available space. In retrospect, Loren Butt feels that something of the technical park atmosphere was lost when this early mall went and parking was pushed to the ends of the site: "The concept became subsidiary to site utilisation, with some inevitable environmental loss."

A view of the computer hall from the mezzanine-level viewing gallery. With its full-height glazing — looking north towards the Grand Union Canal — the space follows in the grand Victorian tradition of halls for machinery.

Rooflights and air-movement ducting in the roof zone of the daylit workshop bay of the distribution centre.

The glass enclosed lift-shaft and its surrounding access stair in the distribution centre. Butt-jointed glass panels are set-screwed to the welded steel enclosure.

The interior of the vast machine hall at Greenford where IBM computers are displayed and demonstrated. The glass clad wall, to the right, shows alternating main structural stanchions and full-height perforated steel mullions, both used to restrain the box-aluminium glazing frame. Vertical conduits run between the flanges of the centre rows of green-painted stanchions up to the roof zone and the exposed underside of the roof decking. Knowing that computers will become ever smaller, the structure of the machine hall was sized to allow the future installation of an intermediate floor.

235

In 1985, five years after the completion of the UKDC, IBM came back to Foster Associates with a request for a revised masterplan and, more importantly, a new administrative building. Zoned as a deep-plan structure to be built to the east of the ISC, Foster returned to an earlier idea for top-lit courtyards and atria introduced for the original UKDC building but never implemented.

A broader building than the ISC, Norman Foster's comparative sketch shows how atria running across the new building, parallel to a central service spine, would bring sunlight into the heart of the office spaces.

And yet IBM Greenford, as built, remains a re-markable achievement. The complexity of the internal activities it successfully accommo-dated, together with the satisfying realisation of the continuing services/structure integration theme and the quality of its detailing belie the uncertainty of its genesis.

Neither was this Foster Associates' final involvement with the Greenford Technical Park. Flexibility and future growth had always been assumed, and in 1985 the practice was again invited to look at the site.

By this time IBM's requirements had changed significantly. It no longer required the originally assumed style of extension to an open-plan 'shed'. Instead a cellular solution was proposed in which an additional building would be sited to the east of the ISC and nomi-nally linked to it. Various explorations of this

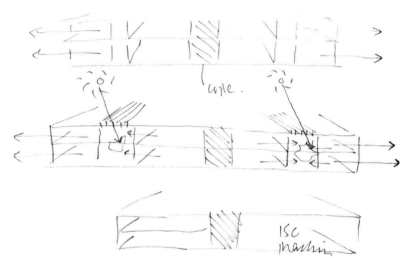

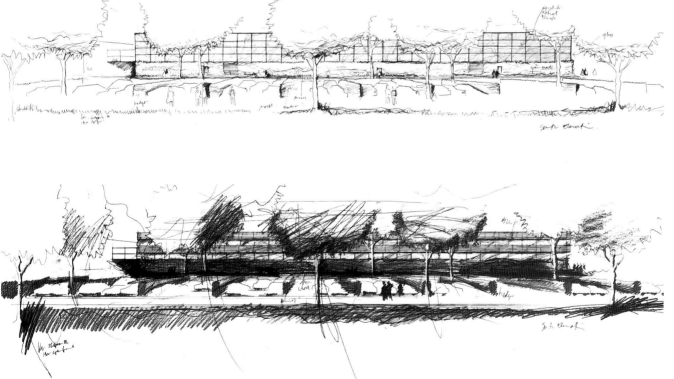

Project architect Ken Shuttleworth's early sketch elevations for the new administrative building. Continuing the eastward thrust deter-mined by the first masterplan, this is the south elevation seen across the tree-lined central mall. A small bridge link to the original ISC is seen on the left. With service cores and atria running east-west parallel to this elevation, the different elevational treatments emphasise the continu-ous horizontal sweep of office space behind the facade.

237

A model of the new administration building in its final form, with service cores now running north-south across a major 'front' building and finger extensions stretching northwards behind.

The 1985 masterplan. As envisaged in 1975, the new buildings stretch eastwards from the original distribution centre and ISC buildings on either side of a (now-extended) central mall. Unexpectedly, small extensions also appear to the west maximising use of an expanded site, made possible if IBM took up an option to buy a small municipal golf-course lying between the original site and the nearby (tree-lined) Greenford Road.

The revised south elevation of the new building, incorporating the north-south service spines clearly expressed and articulating the facade. Vertical service risers with roof-top plant alternate with glass-block fronted stair and lift cores.

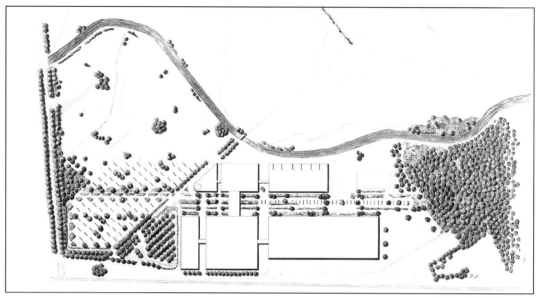

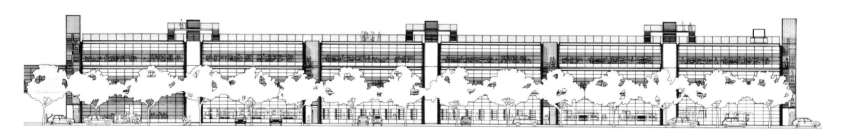

In the final design, two-storey 'fingers' of offices extend north from the main building aligning the mall, with roof-lit atria or landscaped open courtyards between. This is a view down one such atrium, open stairs and balconies promoting a relaxed air suitable for casual meetings and small events.

theme were undertaken. A rectangular building with atria was proposed and so was a building with projecting finger-like wings.

Although this further extension was eventually abandoned for reasons to do with IBM's internal organisation and fast-changing requirements, the exercise remains of interest for two primary reasons. First, it acts as a reminder that the sort of dynamic industry which enabled the practice to express its ideas about industrial buildings continued to be dynamic throughout the 1980s. The sketches of the proposed extension reflect new requirements which the old brief could not have anticipated.

Second, it shows how the practice — post Willis Faber & Dumas and, more importantly, the Hongkong Bank — was now much more committed to the notion of atria and the admission of natural light. The preoccupation with integrating services and structure within deep-plan buildings had not so much subsided — it remains central to Foster Associates' philosophy — as served its purpose.

The computer boom of the early 1970s was over, and IBM Greenford had summarised a line of architectural thought that began with Reliance Controls and the Newport School competition. Future work by Foster Associates would build on that achievement, and it would begin by letting the daylight in.

Graham Vickers

Unlike the earlier offices in the UKDC, with their relaxed interiors, the new building — at IBM's request — incorporated a far higher standard of fit-out, reflecting a corporate shift back to cellular offices for executives. The upper office floors are now fully air-conditioned via a deep ceiling void and, based on experience gained on the Hongkong Bank, the full-height facade of clear glass is backed by adjustable perforated louvres. At ground level major plant is located close to the facade with the possibility of being seen from outside or hidden behind solid panels.

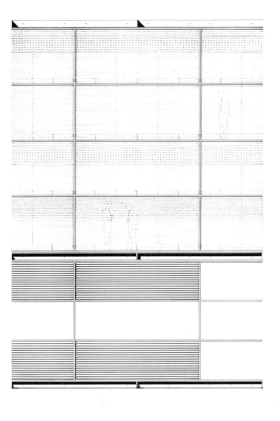

A detail of the building's south elevation, in model form. The revised masterplan was the outcome of a major restructuring of IBM's European operations but, even as design work proceeded, these internal changes continued, leading eventually to the project being abandoned.

A view along the bridge building over the central mall towards the ISC. The perfection of the reflections in the glass reveals the precision with which the aluminium glazing frames were fitted and the high tolerances achieved on the steelwork in general.

"But even a cursory glance at this relatively straightforward structure reveals a feeling for intrinsic quality, an acute preoccupation with the examination of all the minute aspects of a material which make it distinctive and individual. For a technocrat (Foster's) response is very poetic. The way in which he selects, organises and juxtaposes his materials so that the whole outwardly reflects the inner nature of the constituent parts — the glassiness of glass, the steeliness of steel — reveals a very singular imagination."

Lesley Chisholm, *Decor and Contract Furnishing*, February 1979

The vivid green-painted steel structure of the bridge building dominates an otherwise subdued facade. Green landscaping of the mall and the central pedestrian route accentuates the change in level from the lower truck route to the upper access road.

The pedestrian ramp leading from the visitor drop-off point in the mall to the mezzanine-level of the distribution centre. The steel staircase leads directly up into the offices inside the bridge building above. The blue-painted handrails continue inside both main buildings as safety barriers for the glass cladding.

The bridge building seen from the east with, suspended beneath it, the blue-painted ramp sloping up to the UKDC. The glass cladding floats in front of the roof structure to provide the thinnest possible eaves detail. As at IBM Cosham, the line of the false ceiling within is barely perceptible.

A close-up of the bridge building. The glazing on the south side of the ISC and on both sides of the bridge was lined internally with motorised blinds, seen here fully retracted.

The junction of the bridge building and ISC emphasising the finesse of the cladding system, only narrow neoprene fixing beads being visible on the outside. The motorised blinds have been adjusted to obscure the roof zone almost completely.

IBM Greenford was perhaps Foster Associates' greatest achievement in the reconciliation of different functions within a large, precision envelope. Here the tranquil restaurant on the second floor of the distribution centre is illuminated at night. Directly beneath it is the large truck loading dock, its overhead service zone visible above its closed doors with their red warning lights.

"The interesting thing, stylistically speaking, about the buildings of the Foster office is that they have taken the aesthetic of the SOM Chicago office, but removed the magic of structure while retaining its order. The result is a lightness of appearance. This lightness, and the lack of structural ordering, take us some way outside the traditions of architecture that have been handed down to us from the past, and into the realm of industrial design where colours, lettering and finish set the mood."

John Winter, *A&U*, September 1985

The junction of the bridge building with the ISC at night, with motorised blinds down but at different angles. Green structural members and blue door panels with portholes unify the interior treatment of both main buildings and bridge.

"As one surrenders the visitor's plastic 'security' tag on leaving Greenford, it is tempting to dismiss the building as no more than one of the pleasant homes of a wealthy multinational. The 'English mess' of west London, though, quickly reminds one of the rotten conditions in which most of us are still condemned to work, and that what serves IBM so handsomely and economically would do very well for a northern workers' co-operative."

Christopher Woodward, *The Architectural Review*, August 1980

The clear glass cladding at Greenford represents the highest level of development of the original PPG system used on the Fred Olsen amenity centre 10 years before. Here the five-panel-high wall on the north side of the UKDC reflects the bridge building and entrance ramp below.

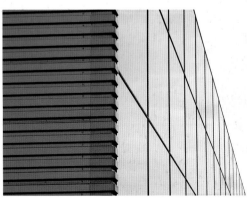

The corner detail of the machine hall showing the crucial role played by the glass-fibre corner pieces that mediate between the heavily profiled aluminium cladding and flat glass surfaces.

The northern glass-clad wall of the machine hall in the ISC, its hard-edge broken only by the outline of the mobile cleaning gantry. The minimal eaves and fixing details at Greenford give the glass walls an almost mechanical perfection.

As with most young practices starting out, there is no exact date that marks the start of Team 4. Richard and Su Rogers had met up with old friends Georgie and Wendy Cheesman on their return from the USA in 1962. Norman Foster joined them in 1963 and Team 4 Architects was created. This photograph was taken in 1966. *Standing:* Tony Hunt, Frank Peacock. *Seated:* Sally Appleby, Wendy Foster, Richard Rogers, Su Rogers, Norman Foster and Maurice Philips.

Partners

Norman Foster
Wendy Foster
Richard Rogers
Georgie Wolton

The Team

Su Rogers

Laurie Abbott
Sally Appleby
Frank Peacock
Maurice Philips
Sophie Read
Mark Sutcliffe
John Young

Dear Mr Cox,

You may remember that we met last December when the factory for our clients, Reliance Controls Ltd, was awarded the Financial Times Industrial Architecture Award. You asked me to let you know if this eventually resulted in any actual jobs. Sadly, the answer is no – absolutely nothing! Apart, that is, from: endless requests from students to visit the factory (Reliance have had to stop this as it is proving too disruptive); continual requests for work opportunities in this office; and continual requests for photos and data from architectural magazines and schools.

If you have any ideas on how we might make use of the award to get work, these would be much appreciated. The present job situation is somewhat desperate!

yours sincerely,
Norman Foster

Written on 24 October 1968 (to Anthony Cox of Architects' Co-Partnership), little could more clearly indicate the job 'situation' a year after the formation of Foster Associates. A few weeks later, Norman Foster met Fred Olsen.

The front room of a flat in Hampstead Hill Gardens, once Wendy Foster's living room but better known as the offices of Team 4 and, later, Foster Associates. The name Foster Associates was more an act of optimism than reality as, initially, there were rarely any full-time staff, let alone associates. That situation changed with the commission from Fred Olsen at the beginning of 1969, but it was not until mid-1970 — with the commission for IBM Cosham — that the office moved, first to Covent Garden and then, in 1972, to Fitzroy Street. A lot of friends and acquaintances passed through the office in those days. Their names have been collated as well as possible but, undoubtedly, some have been missed. This list, therefore, comprises *most* of those who helped Foster Associates on their way in the years 1967-1973.

Partners

Norman Foster
Wendy Foster
Michael Hopkins (1970-1975)

Associates

Reg Bradley
Loren Butt
Birkin Haward
Mickey Kuch
James Meller
Tomm Nyhuus
Norman Partridge
Frank Peacock
Mark Sutcliffe

The Team

Max Aiken	David Nelson
Reg Arney	David Nixon
David Bailey	Truls Ovrum
Prue Bell	Archie Phillips
Paul Berthon	Graham Phillips
Peter Bradford	Louis Pilar
Arthur Branthwaite	Tony Pritchard
Tony Brohn	Ian Ritchie
Lorraine Caunter	Gayle Rose
Chubby Chhabra	Andrew Scott
Barry Copeland	Mark Shapiro
Ray Crandon-Gill	Ken Shuttleworth
Spencer de Grey	Alan Stanton
Justin de Syllas	Christopher Taylor
Giles Downes	Jocelyne v. d. Bossche
Ian Dowsett	Jo van Heyningen
Tim Earnshaw	Ron Walker
Jim Elsdon	Judith Warren
Roy Fleetwood	Jenny Wharton
Robyn Foster	John Wharton
Trish Flood	Stuart Wilkinson
Vivian Fowler	John Willcocks
Martin Francis	John Yates
Muny Ganju	Alison Zinzan
Paul Gibson	
Diana Goddard	
Dave Harriss	**Oslo Office**
Mavis Hudd	
Peter Hufschmid	John Calvert
Jan Kaplicky	Steiner Erikson
John Leach	John Jones
Robin Lorimer	Jørn Narud
Tony Meadows	Helger Saatvedt

  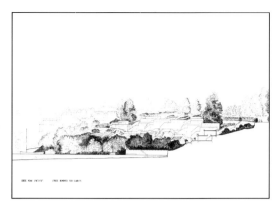

The Retreat
Pill Creek
Feock
Cornwall

Client
Mr & Mrs Marcus Brumwell

Project Team
Norman Foster, Wendy Foster, Frank Peacock,
Richard Rogers, Su Rogers

Consultants
Structural Engineer: Anthony Hunt Associates

Principal Awards
1964 Architectural Design Project Award

Creek Vean House
Pill Creek
Feock
Cornwall

Client
Mr & Mrs Marcus Brumwell

Project Team
Laurie Abbott, Norman Foster, Wendy Foster,
Frank Peacock, Richard Rogers, Su Rogers

Consultants
Structural Engineer: Anthony Hunt Associates
Quantity Surveyor: Hanscomb Partnership

Principal Awards
1969 RIBA Award

Waterfront Housing
in association with Harry Gilbert

Client
Mr & Mrs Marcus Brumwell

Project Team
Laurie Abbott, Norman Foster, Wendy Foster,
Richard Rogers, Su Rogers

Consultants
Structural Engineer: Anthony Hunt Associates
Quantity Surveyor: Hanscomb Partnership
Landscape: M. Branch
Drainage: Tuke & Bell Ltd

Principal Awards
1964 Architectural Design Project Award

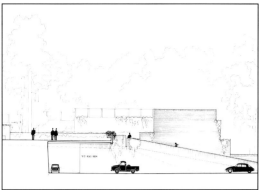

Murray Mews
Camden Town
London

Client
Dr & Mrs Franklin, Mr & Mrs Williams and
Mr D'Marco

Project Team
Laurie Abbott, Norman Foster, Wendy Foster,
Frank Peacock, Maurice Philips, Richard Rogers,
Su Rogers

Consultants
Structural Engineer: Anthony Hunt Associates
Quantity Surveyor: Hanscomb Partnership

Wates Housing

Client
Wates Built Homes Ltd

Project Team
Norman Foster, Wendy Foster, Frank Peacock,
Richard Rogers, Su Rogers

Consultants
Structural Engineer: Anthony Hunt Associates
Quantity Surveyor: Wates Ltd/Hanscomb
    Partnership

Principal Awards
1965 Architectural Design Project Award

Skybreak House
Radlett
Hertfordshire

Client
Mr & Mrs Anthony Jaffé

Project Team
Norman Foster, Wendy Foster, Frank Peacock,
Maurice Philips, Richard Rogers, Su Rogers

Consultants
Structural Engineer: Anthony Hunt Associates
Quantity Surveyor: Hanscomb Partnership

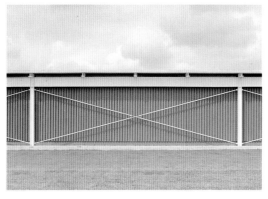

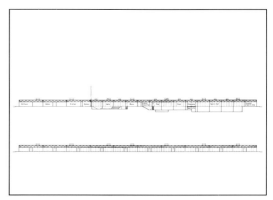

Forest Road Extension
East Horsley
Surrey

Client
Mrs R. G. L. Cheesman

Project Team
Norman Foster, Wendy Foster, Richard Rogers,
Su Rogers

Reliance Controls
Drakes Way
Swindon
Wiltshire

Client
Reliance Controls Ltd

Project Team
Norman Foster, Wendy Foster, Frank Peacock,
Richard Rogers, Su Rogers, Mark Sutcliffe

Consultants
Structural Engineer: Anthony Hunt Associates
Mechanical and Electrical Engineer: G.N. Haden
     & Sons Ltd
Quantity Surveyor: Hanscomb Partnership
Drainage: G.N. Haden & Sons Ltd

Principal Awards
1966 Architectural Design Project Award
1967 Financial Times Industrial Architecture
     Award

Newport School Competition
Short-listed scheme

Project Team
Norman Foster, Wendy Foster, Alan Stanton,
Mickey Kuch

Consultants
Structural Engineer: Anthony Hunt Associates
Mechanical and Electrical Engineers: Peter Jay
     and David Kut & Partners
Quantity Surveyor: Hanscomb Partnership
Acoustics: Arthur Aldersley Williams
Component Consultant: Martin Francis

High-Density Housing

Client
Anthony Jaffé

Project Team
Norman Foster, Wendy Foster, Alan Stanton

Consultants
Structural Engineer: Anthony Hunt Associates
Quantity Surveyor: Hanscomb Partnership

Factory Systems Studies

Project Team
Norman Foster, Wendy Foster

P70 Advanced Factory Unit
Wavendon
Milton Keynes
Buckinghamshire

Client
Milton Keynes Development Corporation

Architects
MKDC Architects Department

Consultants
Systems Analysis: Foster Associates
Structural Engineer: Anthony Hunt Associates
Mechanical and Electrical Engineer: Foster
  Associates
Quantity Surveyor: Milton Keynes Develop-
  ment Corporation

Fred Olsen Amenity Centre
(demolished 1988)

Client
Fred Olsen Ltd

Project Team
Peter Bradford, Barry Copeland, Norman Foster, Wendy Foster, Tomm Nyhuus, Norman Partridge

Consultants
Structural Engineer: Anthony Hunt Associates
Mechanical and Electrical Engineer: G.N. Haden & Sons Ltd
Quantity Surveyor: Hanscomb Partnership
Acoustics: Arthur Aldersley Williams/EDC
Drainage: G. N. Haden & Sons Ltd

Principal Awards
1969 Architectural Design Project Award
1970 Financial Times Industrial Architecture Award Commendation

Fred Olsen Passenger Terminal
(demolished 1980)

Client
Fred Olsen Ltd

Project Team
Peter Bradford, Barry Copeland, Giles Downes, Jim Elsdon, Norman Foster, Birkin Haward, Tomm Nyhuus, Norman Partridge

Consultants
Structural Engineer: Anthony Hunt Associates
Mechanical and Electrical Engineer: ZDB Engineering Ltd
Quantity Surveyor: Hanscomb Partnership
Acoustics: Arthur Aldersley Williams

Air Supported Office
(deflated 1971)

Client
Computer Technology Ltd

Project Team
Loren Butt, Chubby Chhabra, Norman Foster, Wendy Foster, Mickey Kuch

Consultants
Quantity Surveyor: Hanscomb Partnership
Mechanical and Electrical Engineer: Foster Associates

IBM Pilot Head Office
1 Northern Road
Cosham
Hampshire

Client
IBM (UK) Ltd

Project Team
Loren Butt, Chubby Chhabra, Barry Copeland,
Norman Foster, Wendy Foster, Vivian Fowler,
Dave Harriss, Michael Hopkins, Mickey Kuch,
Tomm Nyhuus, Truls Ovrum, Norman Partridge,
Frank Peacock, Andrew Scott, Mark Shapiro,
Mark Sutcliffe, Judith Warren, Stuart
Wilkinson, John Willcocks

Consultants
Structural Engineer: Anthony Hunt Associates
Mechanical and Electrical Engineer: R.S. Willcox
    Associates
Quantity Surveyor: Hanscomb Partnership
Lighting: Derek Phillips & Partners
Acoustics: Arthur Aldersley Williams/
    Engineering Design Consultants
Drainage: Adrian Wilder

Principal Awards
1972 Structural Steel Award
1972 RIBA Award

Computer Technology
Eaton Road
Hemel Hempstead
Hertfordshire

Client
Computer Technology Ltd

Project Team
Loren Butt, Lorraine Caunter, Justin de Syllas,
Norman Foster, Wendy Foster, Martin Francis,
Dave Harriss, Birkin Haward

Consultants
Structural Engineer: Anthony Hunt Associates
Mechanical and Electrical Engineer: G.N. Haden
    & Sons Ltd
Quantity Surveyor: Hanscomb Partnership
Drainage: G.N. Haden & Sons Ltd

Principal Awards
1971 Financial Times Industrial Architecture
    Award Commendation

Office for Foster Associates
16 Fitzroy Street
London W1

Client
Foster Associates

Project Team
Reg Bradley, Loren Butt, Lorraine Caunter, Giles
Downes, Norman Foster, Wendy Foster, Birkin
Haward, Tomm Nyhuus, Norman Partridge,
Archie Phillips, Mark Shapiro, John Wharton

Consultants
Mechanical and Electrical Engineer: Foster
    Associates
Quantity Surveyor: Hanscomb Partnership
Acoustics: Arthur Aldersley Williams
Drainage: Adrian Wilder

Hackney Special School
Ickburgh Road
Hackney
London E5

Client
Spastics Society/Hackney Borough Council/ILEA

Project Team
Reg Bradley, Loren Butt, Justin de Syllas,
Norman Foster, Wendy Foster, Birkin Haward,
Frank Peacock, Jo van Heyningen

Consultants
Structural Engineer: Anthony Hunt Associates
Mechanical and Electrical Engineer: Foster
    Associates
Quantity Surveyor: Hanscomb Partnership
Drainage: Adrian Wilder

Bean Hill Housing
Milton Keynes
Buckinghamshire

Client
Milton Keynes Development Corporation

Project Team
Loren Butt, Tim Earnshaw, Roy Fleetwood,
Norman Foster, Wendy Foster, Birkin Haward,
Michael Hopkins, Frank Peacock, Jo van
Heyningen

Consultants
Structural Engineer: Anthony Hunt Associates
Quantity Surveyor: Davis Belfield & Everest
Landscaping: John Allen

Palmerston Special School
(demolished 1989)

Client
City of Liverpool in association with the
Spastics Society

Project Team
Reg Bradley, Loren Butt, Chubby Chhabra,
Spencer de Grey, Jim Elsdon, Norman Foster,
Wendy Foster, Birkin Haward, Ron Walker

Consultants
Structural Engineer: Anthony Hunt Associates
Mechanical and Electrical Engineer: Foster
    Associates
Quantity Surveyor: Flood & Wilson
Acoustics: Sandy Brown Associates
Drainage: Adrian Wilder

Principal Awards
1976 International Prize for Architecture
1977 RIBA Award Commendation

Factory for SAPA
Tibshelf
Derbyshire

Client
Skandinaviska Aluminium Profiler AB

Project Team
Phase I: Max Aiken, Loren Butt, Chubby Chhabra, Norman Foster, Wendy Foster, Diana Goddard, Michael Hopkins, Tony Meadows, Tomm Nyhuus, Norman Partridge, John Yates
Phase II: Loren Butt, Chubby Chhabra, Mike Elkan, Caroline Lwin, Tomm Nyhuus, John Yates

Consultants
Structural Engineer: Anthony Hunt Associates
Mechanical and Electrical Engineer: Foster
    Associates
Quantity Surveyor: Hanscomb Partnership
Drainage: Adrian Wilder

Modern Art Glass
Eastern Industrial Estate
Thamesmead
Kent

Client
Modern Art Glass Ltd

Project Team
Loren Butt, Lorraine Caunter, Chubby Chhabra, Norman Foster, Wendy Foster, Paul Gibson, Mickey Kuch, David Nixon, Mark Sutcliffe, John Wharton

Consultants
Structural Engineer: Anthony Hunt Associates
Mechanical and Electrical Engineer: Foster
    Associates
Quantity Surveyor: Hanscomb Partnership
Glazing Consultant: Martin Francis
Drainage: Adrian Wilder

Principal Awards
1974 Financial Times Industrial Architecture
    Award

Country Offices

Client
Fred Olsen Group/Aker Gruppe

Project Team
Loren Butt, John Calvert, Jim Elsdon, Steiner Erikson, Norman Foster, Wendy Foster, Birkin Haward, John Jones, Jørn Narud, Tomm Nyhuus, Helger Saatvedt

Consultants
Structural Engineer: Multi-Consult A/S
Mechanical and Electrical Engineer: Erichsen &
    Horgen/Foster Associates
Quantity Surveyor: Hanscomb Partnership
Drainage: Multi-Consult A/S

Son Recreation Centre

Client
Fred Olsen Group

Project Team
Loren Butt, John Calvert, Steiner Erikson, Norman Foster, Wendy Foster, John Jones, Jørn Narud, Tomm Nyhuus, Helger Saatvedt

Consultants
Structural Engineer: Multi-Consult A/S
Mechanical and Electrical Engineers: Erichsen
    & Horgen/Foster Associates
Quantity Surveyor: Hanscomb Partnership
Drainage: Multi-Consult A/S

Pavilion Leisure Centres

Client
MPC Associates Ltd

Project Team
Loren Butt, Chubby Chhabra, Norman Foster, Wendy Foster, Ian Ritchie, Jocelyne van den Bossche

Consultants
Mechanical and Electrical Engineer: Foster Associates
Quantity Surveyor: Hanscomb Partnership
Transport Planning: Freeman Fox & Partners

Orange Hand Shops
(closed 1975)

Client
The Burton Group

Project Team
Loren Butt, Chubby Chhabra, Norman Foster, Wendy Foster, Dave Harriss, Birkin Haward, Mickey Kuch, Jenny Wharton, John Wharton

Consultants
Structural Engineer: Anthony Hunt Associates
Mechanical and Electrical Engineer: Foster Associates
Quantity Surveyor: Davis Belfield & Everest

German Car Centre

Client
Thomas Tilling & Co Ltd

Project Team
Loren Butt, Chubby Chhabra, Norman Foster, Wendy Foster, Birkin Haward, John Wharton

Consultants
Structural Engineer: Anthony Hunt Associates
Mechanical and Electrical Engineer: Foster Associates
Quantity Surveyor: Davis Belfield & Everest
Materials Handling: Demag Systemtechnik AG/ P. E. Consultancy Group

IBM Technical Park
Greenford
Middlesex

Client
IBM (UK) Ltd

Project Team
Loren Butt, Chubby Chhabra, Howard Filbey,
Norman Foster, Wendy Foster, Michael Glass,
Judith Hallam, Alex Lifschutz, Paul Mathews,
David Nelson, Truls Ovrum, Frank Peacock,
Graham Phillips, Michael Rayner, Ken
Shuttleworth, Jamie Troughton

Consultants
Structural Engineer: Anthony Hunt Associates
Mechanical and Electrical Engineer: Foster
    Associates
Quantity Surveyor: Northcroft Neighbour &
    Nicholson
Acoustics: Sound Research Laboratories/
    Wolfson Unit, University of Southampton
Landscaping: Michael Brown Partnership
Transport Planning: Ove Arup & Partners/
    Freeman Fox & Partners
Land Surveying: J.A. Storey & Partners
Drainage: John Taylor & Sons
Materials Handling: Modern Materials
    Management

Bibliography

Banham, Reyner, ed., *Design by Choice,*
Academy Editions 1982
Benedetti, Aldo, *Norman Foster,* Zanichelli
Editore Bologna 1987
Chaslin, François, *Norman Foster,* Electa
Moniteur 1986
Foster Associates, eds., *Foster Associates,* RIBA
Publications 1979
Foster Associates, eds., *Selected Works 1962-
1984,* Whitworth Art Gallery 1984
Foster Associates, eds., *Six Architectural
Projects 1975-1985,* Sainsbury Centre for
Visual Arts 1985
Foster Associates, eds., *Tre Temi Sei Progetti,*
Electa Firenze 1988
Jencks, Charles, *Current Architecture,* Academy
Editions 1982
Lambot, Ian, *The New Headquarters for the
Hongkong and Shanghai Banking
Corporation,* Ian Lambot 1986
Lambot, Ian, ed., *Norman Foster: Buildings and
Projects, volume 2,* Watermark Publica-
tions 1989
Lambot, Ian, ed., *Norman Foster: Buildings and
Projects, volume 3,* Watermark Publica-
tions 1989
Lasdun, Denys, ed., *Architecture in an Age of
Scepticism,* Heinemann 1984
Nakamura, Toshio, ed., *Norman Foster,* A&U
Special Publication 1988
Suckle, Abby, ed., *By Their Own Design,*
Whitney 1980
Sudjic, Deyan, *New Architecture: Foster Rogers
Stirling,* Thames & Hudson 1986
Williams, Stephanie, *Hongkong Bank: The
Building of Norman Foster's Masterpiece,*
Jonathan Cape 1989

General Interest
A A Quarterly, No.1 1973, *Foster Associates* by
Sven Bjork
Architectural Design, May 1970, *Foster
Associates' Recent Work*
Architectural Design, November 1972, *Foster
Associates' Recent Work*
Architectural Design, March 1976, *Hi-Tech to
Appropriate*
Architecture and Urbanism, September 1973,
Works of Foster Associates
Architecture and Urbanism, September 1975,
Special Issue
Architecture and Urbanism, February 1981,
Recent Works of Foster Associates

L'Architecture d'Aujourd'hui,
November/December 1973, *Foster et
Associés*
L'Architecture d'Aujourd'hui, February 1986,
Norman Foster by Marc Emery
BP Shield, March 1969, *Design for Living* by
Norman Foster
Building, 18 March 1983, *Glass by Foster* by
Robert Mathews
Casabella, No.375 1973, *Foster Associates:
Montaggio Senza*
New Society, 9 November 1972, *LL/LF/LE v
Foster* by Reyner Banham
Progressive Architecture, February 1979,
Technical Effects
RIBA Journal, June 1970, *Architect's Approach
to Architecture: Norman Foster*
RIBA Journal, June 1970, *Exploring the Client's
Range of Options* by Norman Foster
RIBA Journal, January 1978, *Designing the
Means to Social Ends* by Barbara Goldstein
Techniques et Architecture, February/March
1974, *Trois Usines en Angleterre*

The Retreat
Daily Telegraph Magazine, 28 March 1969,
Putting the Family Out of the House by
Margaret Duckett

Creek Vean House
Architectural Review, August 1968, *Seaside
House in Cornwall*
Architecture and Urbanism, October 1974,
Brumwell House
Daily Telegraph Magazine, 22 November 1968,
Dream Houses Become Reality by
Margaret Duckett
Die Kunst, June 1979, *Wohnhaus mit
Dachgarten an der Küste von Cornwall*
House and Garden, March 1974, *In Cornwall:
Set Fair High Above Sea, River, Woods and
Valley*

Waterfront Housing
Sunday Times, 14 April 1968, *Planning on the
Septic Tank Pattern* by Nicholas Taylor

Skybreak House
Architectural Review, August 1968, *Hertfordshire Suburban*

Ville Giardini, November 1973, *Struttura a
Gradoni*
Werk, January 1969, *Haus in Radlett*

High-Density Housing
Architectural Review, January 1968, *The
Warren, Radlett*

Wates Housing
Architectural Design, April 1965, *Housing at
Coulsdon, Surrey*

Bean Hill Housing
Architects' Journal, 9 May 1973, *Bean Hill*
Architectural Design, November 1972, *Housing
at Bean Hill*
Architecture and Urbanism, July 1974, *Bean
Hill Housing*

Reliance Controls
Acier Stahl Steel, December 1968, *New Reliance
Controls Factory at Swindon*
Architects' Journal, 19 July 1967, *Factory*
Bauen und Wohnen, No.7 1968, *Fabrik für
Elektronische Geräte Reliance Control Ltd*
Baumeister, No.3 1970, *Tageslicht Gespart?*
Bouwwereld, May 1969, *Gebouw Voor
Wisselende Massafabricage*
Daily Telegraph, 30 December 1968, *Anatomy
of a Factory* by John Chisholm
Design, October 1969, *Reliance Controls,
Swindon*
Domus, February 1967, *Electronic Factory for
Reliance Controls in Swindon*
Financial Times, 30 November 1967, *The
Winning Design*
Industrial Architecture, February 1968, *The
1967 Financial Times Award for Industrial
Architecture*
Observer, 10 December 1967, *Prize For Modesty*
by Ian Nairn

Newport School Competition
Architectural Design, May 1968, *Learning* by
Cedric Price
Bauen und Wohnen, No.2 1970, *Optimale
Flexibilität*
Building, 31 October 1969, *School System —
Sophisticated Package within DES Cost
Limits*

Factory Systems
Architectural Review, November 1969,
Manplan 3: Town Workshop, guest ed.
Norman Foster

IBM Pilot Head Office
Archetype, May 1974, *Anti-Formalism in Contemporary British Architecture* by N. Ross Ramus
Architectural Design, August 1971, *IBM Head Office* by Andrew Rabeneck
Architectural Review, January 1972, *IBM Cosham* by Lance Wright
Architecture Plus, July 1973, *Least is Most*
Design, October 1971, *Two Problems Solved* by Alastair Best
Deutsche Architektenblatt, December 1980, *In Deutschland Nicht Vorstellbar*
Deutsche Bauzeitung, June 1972, *Büroumwelt*
Domus, January 1972, *Scompare*
Glass Age News, 19 March 1973, *Disappearing Buildings*
Glassforum, No.4 1973, *IBM-Versuchsburo in Cosham*
Techniques et Architecture, September/October 1974, *Siège IBM à Cosham*
Werk, June 1972, *IBM-England in Cosham*

Air Supported Office
Bauen und Wohnen, No.1 1971, *730 m² Bürofläche in Acht Wochen Geplant und Gebaut*
Business Management, August 1970, *White, Light and Airy*
Design, March 1970, *Office Beneath the Skin* by Martin Pawley
Queen, April 1970, *Liberty, Mobility, Modernity* by Janet Street-Porter

Computer Technology
Design, October 1969, *Computer Technology*
Design, October 1971, *CT at Hemel Hempstead*
Sunday Times, 5 May 1968, *Wall-to-Wall Carpet on the Factory Floor* by Nicholas Taylor

Fitzroy Street Office
Architectural Design, November 1972, *Fitzroy Street Project*
Architectural Review, September 1972, *Project for Foster Associates*
Crée, September/October 1972, *Aménagements Intérieurs*
Domus, October 1972, *Architectural Office in London*

Special Care Unit
Design, July 1973, *Lessons in Schooling the Handicapped* by Selwyn Goldsmith

Domus, October 1972, *Da Londra: Due Progetti dei Foster Associates*
The Observer Review, 31 March 1974, *Good Design, Happy Children* by Stephen Gardiner

Palmerston Special School
Architectural Review, November 1976, *Low-Profile School* by Jane Hyde and Alastair Best
L'Architecture d'Aujourd'hui, November 1973, *Ecole Spéciale de Palmerston*
L'Architecture d'Aujourd'Hui, April 1981, *Ecole pour Enfants Handicapés*
Bauen und Wohnen, May 1977, *Schule für Behinderte Kinder*
Design, December 1976, *Interiors*

Fred Olsen Amenity Centre
Architects' Journal, 2 December 1970, Dock Buildings
Architectural Design, May 1970, *Foster Associates' Recent Work*
Architectural Review, October 1970, *Operations-Amenity Centre for Fred Olsen*
Bauen und Wohnen, January 1971, *Verwaltungs und Freizeitgebäude Einer Schiffahrtsgesellschaft*
Crée, November/December 1970, *Amenity Centre*
Design, May 1970, *Just Arrived in Port: a New Deal for the Dockers* by Alastair Best
Domus, December 1970, *Carico e Scarico Sul Tamigi*

Fred Olsen Passenger Terminal
Architects' Journal, 2 December 1970, *Dock Buildings*
Architectural Design, February 1971, *Fun, Cover and for Work*
Design, January 1971, *Process Tube for Liner Passengers* by Jose Manser
Guardian, 26 October 1970, *Berth Control* by Richard Carr
Times, 18 February 1970, *The Olsen Line of Success* by Michael Bailey

Factory for SAPA
Architects' Journal, 28 November 1973, *Undecorated Shed*
Architects' Journal, 28 September 1977, *Extrusion Plant's Expansion*
Bauen und Wohnen, May 1974, *Fabrik als Container*

Building Design, 22 March 1974, *Sophisticated Sheds*
Domus, July 1974, *Per Lavorare: Structure-color*

Modern Art Glass
Architectural Review, July 1974, *Glass on the Marsh* by John Winter
Bauen and Wohnen, April 1975, *Lagerbauten*
Building, 14 June 1974, *Modern Art Glass Warehouse*
Design, August 1974, *That Up-stage Blue One* by Jose Manser
Domus, July 1974, *Parc Urbano*
Financial Times, 4 March 1974, *Modern Art's Glass House* by Jose Manser
Guardian, 5 March 1974, *Blue Fit for the Planners* by Judy Hillman

Orange Hand Shops
Baumeister, August 1974, *Orange Hand, London*
Crée, July/August 1973, *A la Main Orange*
Design, May 1973, *Shop Kit For a Roving Chain* by Ilse Gray
Domus, August 1974, *Orange Hand L'Immagine di un Negozio*

IBM Technical Park
Architectural Record, August 1985, *The Metal Skin Technology of Foster Associates*
Architectural Review, August 1980, *IBM Greenford Green* by Christopher Woodward
Baumeister, April 1983, *IBM Technical Park in Greenford*
Building Design, 3 February 1978, *Stretching Glass*
Decor and Contract Furnishing, February 1979, *Inscape* by Lesley Chisholm
Design, August 1980, *Factories as Product Design: Architects Deliver the Goods* by Deyan Sudjic
Designers' Journal, May 1985, *Noel Jordan: Company Man* by Peter Carolin
Techniques et Architecture, June 1982, *Centre IBM à Greenford Green*

Credits

The editor extends his thanks to all those who helped in compiling and preparing the material used in this volume: the clients, consultants and members of Foster Associates, past and present, who gave freely of their time and knowledge; and the commissioned writers who shaped and gave meaning to the considerable amount of information gathered in the process.

Special mention must also be made of those whose contribution to the production of this book has proved equally invaluable. At Foster Associates, Katy Harris for all her help in tracing and sourcing the many hundreds of drawings and photographs selected from the office archives. She was ably assisted by Fiona Millar and Sarah Robson. Jennifer Riedel patiently typed (and retyped) all the text which was then sub-edited and proof-read by Julia Beever and Lesley Chisholm. Liz Chapman, Sarah Conrado, Victoria Reis and Helen Smith prepared all the final layouts and artwork.

My thanks to one and all.

Drawings and Photographs

As far as possible, only contemporary material has been used in the production of this volume. On the rare occasions that original drawings were found to be in too poor a condition for reproduction, they were redrawn in the original style by Russell Clayton.

For the sake of simplicity, the drawings and photographs have not been individually credited; on those pages where the work of more than one draughtsman or photographer is shown, the number in brackets indicates only how many images on that page can be assigned to each contributor. All attempts have been made to credit each image correctly. Where this has proved impossible, credit has been given under the more general name of Foster Associates, from whose extensive library the majority of this material was selected.

Drawings

Reinfriede Bettrich (jacket) 200/201
Russell Clayton 31(3) 55(2) 69(2) 92/93 93 94 98(1) 99 229 251(1)
Wally Conquy 197 199
Barry Copeland 96(1) 108(3)
Spencer de Grey 102(2)
Justin de Syllas 122(1)
Foster Associates 24(1) 26(2) 41(3) 44 61 64 65 77 95 96(1) 97(1) 101 112 113 124(2) 128(1) 129(5) 132 133(1) 136 137(1) 156(3) 163 176 177 187 188(1) 189 191 196 204(1) 207(1) 208(1) 219(1) 233 238(2) 239
Norman Foster 10 11 12 13 16 17 18 19 25(2) 28(1) 30 31(2) 32(1) 33 37 40 41(1) 46 47 48 49 50 51 52 54 55(2) 60 62 63(2) 66 68 69(1) 72 73 76 79(1) 82(1) 83(1) 85 90 91 92 97(1) 98(1) 98/99 100 103(1) 109 120 124(1) 130 133(1) 145(1) 148(1) 184 202 203(1) 206/207(1) 222 223 224(1) 224/225 225 226(1) 227(2) 232 236 237(3) 248 249 250 251(1)
Mike Glass 230 231
Mark Goldstein 230 231
Birkin Haward 29(1) 102(3) 103(2) 108(1) 117 121 122(1) 128(1) 129(1) 130/131 133(2) 137(1) 147(1) 148(1) 149 150 151 156(1) 160 161 166(1) 167(1) 172 173 178 186 203(3) 205 206/207(1) 213(8) 216 219(1) 224(2) 227(1) 228(1)
Tony Hunt 84(2) 144 145(1) 146(1)
Edward Hutchinson 238(1)
Helmut Jacoby 165 204(1) 207(1) 209(1) 210 211(2) 217 218(1) 219(1) 255 256
Ben Johnson 88 89
Jan Kaplicky 32(1) 84(1) 211(1)
Alan Mitchell 27(1) 147(1)
Truls Ovrum 169(1)
Norman Partridge 188(1) 192/193
Frank Peacock 63(2) 166(1) 167(1) 168(1) 169(1)
Pittsburgh Plate Glass 116
Ian Ritchie 208(3) 209(2)
Ken Shuttleworth 237(2)
Mark Sutcliffe 78 79(1) 82(2) 83(1) 146(1) 185
Jamie Troughton 230/231
Jo van Heyningen 164 168(2)
John Wharton 26(1) 103(3) 130/131 195 212 213(1) 218(4) 226(3) 228(1)

Photographs

Aerofilms 110(1)
Architectural Association 184(1)
Architectural Association/B. Cox 185(1)
Architectural Association/M. Handman 21(1)
Architectural Association/E. McCoy 22(1)
Architectural Association/G. Smythe 183(1)
Architectural Press 29(1)
Atelier 5 23(1)
Cameracraft 33(1) 34/35 248(1)
Gus Coral 27(1) 126(1) 252(1)
Daily Telegraph 33(2)
Richard Davies 28(1) 186(1) 187(1) 225 238 239 241(2) 244(1) 245 257
Spencer de Grey 176(1) 181(1)
John Donat 28(1) 32 52/53 54 55 56 57 68 104(1) 105 125(4) 126(2) 127 169 170 171(3) 172 173 174/175 176(1) 177 178 179 180 181(2) 189 190 190/191 191 192 193 205 206 222 223 249(1) 254(2)
Richard Einzig/Arcaid 23(2) 36 38/39 39 42 43 44(2) 45 69 70 71 113(1) 114 115 116(1) 132(1) 136 137 138 140(1) 142(1) 154(1) 184(1) 248(1) 249(1) 253(1)
Foster Associates 17 19 21(2) 22(1) 30 44(1) 50 64 67(1) 78 90 95 96 99 101 104(1) 131 132(1) 147 148 149 167 183(2) 202 210 213 217 246 247 251 255(1)
Norman Foster 18 21(1) 22(2) 24(1) 72 73 74/75 79 80(1) 81 84 85 86 87 128 144 145 147 185(2) 250
Geoffrey Gale 116(1)
Archie Handford 25(1)
Robert Harding 21(1)
Hulton-Deutsch Collection 182(1)
Pat Hunt 150 151 253(1)
Imperial War Museum 182(1)
Ken Kirkwood 133 138/139 140(1) 141(2) 142(2) 143 232 233 234 235 240 241(1) 242 243 244(1) 253(1)
Mickey Kuch 125(1)
Ian Lambot 171(1) 187(1)
Tim Street-Porter 20 26(2) 27(1) 28(1) 29(1) 67(3) 110(6) 111 112 113(1) 117 118 118/119 120 121 122 123 134 135 140(1) 141(1) 152 153 154(7) 155 156 157 160 162 163 194 196 197 198 199 214 215 252(2) 254(1) 255(1) 256
William Toomey 24(2) 77 80(2)
Andy Ward (jacket)